Asian Migrations

D0153495

This textbook describes and explains the complex reality of contemporary internal and international migrations in East Asia. Taking an interdisciplinary approach, Tony Fielding combines theoretical debate and detailed empirical analysis to provide students with an understanding of the causes and consequences of the many types of contemporary migration flows in the region.

Key features of *Asian Migrations*:

- Comprehensive coverage of all forms of migration including labour migration, student migration, marriage migration, displacement and human trafficking.
- Tex tboxes containing key concepts and theories.
- More than 30 maps and diagrams.
- Equal attention devoted to broad structures (e.g. political economy) and individual agency (e.g. migration behaviours).
- Emphasis on the conceptual and empirical connections between internal and international migrations.
- Exploration of the policy implications of the trends and processes discussed.

Written by an experienced scholar and teacher of migration studies, this is an essential text for courses on East Asian migrations and mobility, and important reading for courses on international migration and Asian societies more generally.

Tony Fielding is a Research Professor in Human Geography, Sussex Centre for Migration Research, University of Sussex, UK.

Asian Migrations

Social and geographical mobilities in
Southeast, East, and Northeast Asia

Tony Fielding

Routledge
Taylor & Francis Group

LONDON AND NEW YORK

First published 2016
by Routledge
2 Park Square, Milton Park, Abingdon, Oxon OX14 4RN

and by Routledge
711 Third Avenue, New York, NY 10017

Routledge is an imprint of the Taylor & Francis Group, an informa business

© 2016 Tony Fielding

The right of Tony Fielding to be identified as author of this work has been asserted by him in accordance with sections 77 and 78 of the Copyright, Designs and Patents Act 1988.

All rights reserved. No part of this book may be reprinted or reproduced or utilised in any form or by any electronic, mechanical, or other means, now known or hereafter invented, including photocopying and recording, or in any information storage or retrieval system, without permission in writing from the publishers.

Trademark notice: Product or corporate names may be trademarks or registered trademarks, and are used only for identification and explanation without intent to infringe.

British Library Cataloguing in Publication Data
A catalogue record for this book is available from the British Library

Library of Congress Cataloging in Publication Data
Fielding, Tony (Anthony J.) author.
Asian migrations : social and geographical mobilities in Southeast, East, and Northeast Asia / Tony Fielding.
    pages cm
Includes bibliographical references and index.
1. East Asia–Emigration and immigration. 2. Southeast Asia–Emigration and immigration. I. Title.
    JV8756.5.T54 2016
    304.8095–dc23
                    2015010098

ISBN: 978-0-415-63946-0 (hbk)
ISBN: 978-0-415-63947-7 (pbk)
ISBN: 978-1-315-86356-6 (ebk)

Typeset in Bembo
by Taylor & Francis Books

Printed and bound by CPI Group (UK) Ltd, Croydon, CR0 4YY

To all my East Asian friends over the last 25 years, whose company I have very much enjoyed and from whom I have learnt so much.

Contents

List of figures

List of tables

List of boxes

1 Context

East Asian economy, space and society

1.0 Introduction: migration, time, and place

This book explores the intersection of two bodies of knowledge, each of which is of increasing academic and political importance. The first is migration and mobility. Studies of migration are breaking new ground conceptually and theoretically, and are helping to transform the social sciences through their very strong inter-disciplinarity and their methodological inclusiveness. Migration is also close to the top of the policy agendas of many international organizations, national governments and political parties, and the treatment of immigrant minorities, especially when they are poor and powerless, is one of the best indicators of the social progressiveness and political success of a country in this increasingly multicultural, globally interactive world.

The second is East Asia. Who can now deny the importance of a knowledge and understanding of East Asian societies for the students and decision makers of the 21st century? We have recently witnessed the appalling errors of judgement that follow from a dangerous mixture of arrogance towards, and ignorance of, non-Western cultures and societies on the part of Western leaders who, let's be blunt, 'should have known better'. Can the world afford a repeat of such errors in the forging of new relationships with the increasingly wealthy and powerful countries of East Asia? No, it cannot. So up-to-date descriptions, analyses and interpretations of events and situations in East Asia are essential. That this region remains poorly represented in our school and university courses, in our governmental planning, and in company boardroom discussions represents a significant failure. It is time to change this.

We should establish at the outset, and in the broadest possible terms, where the boundaries of this study are located. As far as migration is concerned, this can be done with the help of Figure 1.1. Our focus in this book is on movements that involve a change of residence and a significant length of stay in a new place (for example, long enough to get a job and earn some money). Those movements that do not imply the crossing of an international boundary are described as 'internal migration'; those that do are described as 'international migration'. It is of the utmost importance, however, to stress that there are internal migrations that, because of the distance moved and of the cultural, social and legal barriers to be overcome, are more typical of international migration (for example, many long-distance migrations within China), while at the same time there are some international migrations that differ little from internal migration (for example, some short-distance migrations between Singapore, Malaysia and Indonesia). Figure 1.1 also helps us to recognize the potential overlaps between migration and other forms of mobility. Visits and 'working holidays', for example, can easily turn into *de facto*, but sometimes undocumented (that is 'illegal'), migration.

The focus of the study is on contemporary migration, and historical material will only be introduced if, and to the degree that, it helps us to understand what is happening now, or has happened in the recent past.

The place we are studying is East Asia, which is defined here as being composed of three groups of countries:

1   Southeast Asia: that is, Indonesia (and Timor Leste), Singapore, Malaysia (and Brunei), Thailand, Myanmar (Burma), Laos, Cambodia, Vietnam, and the Philippines

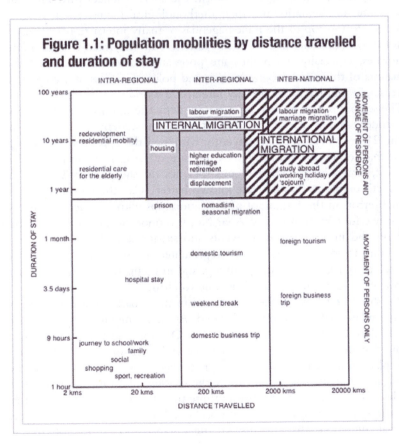

Figure 1.1: Population mobilities by distance travelled and duration of stay

2   China 'plus': that is, the People's Republic of China (PRC, including Hong Kong and Macao), Taiwan, and Mongolia

3   Northeast Asia: that is, Japan, Republic of Korea (South Korea), Democratic People's Republic of Korea (North Korea), and Russia (Russian Far East province)

In practice, little information is available on migrations within some of these countries (for example, Myanmar and North Korea), and the undocumented nature of much of the international migration affecting some of these countries reduces the reliability of that information as well.

1.1 East Asian economy

The purpose of this first section is to provide an overview, necessarily a highly generalized one, of the East Asian economy, selecting those features that are most significant for an understanding of the region's migrations. Let us begin with a few facts.

East Asia is, economically speaking, very large, and is rapidly growing larger. Its share of the global economy in 2011 was 25.3% on a gross national income (GNI) basis (using World Bank data). Since the region's share of the world's population was 31.3%, one can see that despite the extraordinarily high incomes enjoyed by ordinary people in some countries (notably Japan), people were, on average, slightly poorer in East Asia than in the world as a whole. However, this gap between East Asia's share of global wealth and its share of population is shrinking fast.

East Asia is dominated by the national economies of just two states, China and Japan. In GNI terms, the PRC is the world's second largest economy (after the USA, of course), and accounts for 40% of the East Asian economy (Japan is 35%). So these two countries, when put together, represent about three-quarters of the wealth of East Asia.

Per capita incomes in East Asia vary enormously between countries. In GNI per capita per annum, the Japanese and Singaporeans are on average amazingly rich (US$45,000 and $43,000, respectively); Hong Kong/Macao and Brunei residents are rich ($35,000/$45,000 and $32,000); Taiwanese and South Koreans are well off ($22,000 and $21,000); Russians, Malaysians, Thais, and Chinese are poor-ish (though in the last three cases far less poor than they used to be); Filipinos and Indonesians/Timor Leste are poorer still; and those who live in the remaining countries (Mongolia, North Korea, Myanmar, Vietnam, Laos and Cambodia) are extremely poor, with average incomes of the last three countries only around $1,000 per annum. Incomes also vary greatly within countries, and most of the poorest countries have small wealthy elites, which means that the larger parts of their populations are desperately poor. Wealth and poverty are fairly directly reflected in the security of life. The average life expectation at birth for East Asia is 72 years: Japan, Hong Kong and Singapore are exceptionally favoured at 83/82 years; South Korea is the only other country over 80 (81); Taiwan, Brunei, Vietnam, Thailand and Malaysia have figures in the mid-to-high 70s; China is now just above the average at 73; most of the remaining countries cluster at just below the average, but in four cases life expectation is much lower – they are Laos (67), Myanmar (65), Cambodia (63), and Timor Leste (62).

In the years after 1945, communism was adopted by about half of the countries of East Asia, covering (with, of course, different degrees of popular support) about three-quarters of the region's population. At its peak, centrally planned, socialist economies were to be found in the PRC, Vietnam, Burma, North Korea, Cambodia, Laos, and the Soviet Union. However, in the period 1978–90, almost all of these countries experienced a transition, sometimes slowly, sometimes suddenly, away from socialist forms of economic management towards a competitive market economy dominated by capitalist property and employment relations. In one country, North Korea, this transition has, at the time of writing, barely begun, but the changes are well advanced in Vietnam and, above all, in the PRC, where a Communist Party-dominated political system presides over an increasingly capitalist economy, and the transition is virtually complete in the Russian Far East. So, within about 50 years, much of East Asia has experienced two very different forms of economic mobilization, each one being, in terms of its impact on ordinary people's lives, partly very successful, partly disastrous.

Related to these forms of economic management (but not in any simple way, such that all capitalist economies, for example, have increasingly wealthy populations), are the annual rates of growth in gross national product (GNP). In the early post-1945 years, it was Japan that had a booming economy with growth rates from the early 1950s to the early 1970s averaging around 9% per annum. This was followed a few years later by the sudden economic success of the four East Asian 'tiger' economies – South Korea, Taiwan, Hong Kong and Singapore. Soon they were joined by Thailand and Malaysia (and now Vietnam), but, above all, by the PRC, which has had annual GNP growth rates averaging about 10% over the last 25 years. As China has boomed, Japan has stopped still, so that the 1990s came to be seen as Japan's 'lost decade' – a period (now more than two decades) of low or no growth after 40 years of sustained economic expansion.

It is clear that there is a distinctive geography to this pattern of economic growth, so much so that many observers came to adopt a 'flying geese' model of the spatial diffusion of growth. This model sees Japan as pivotal to East Asian development. Led by the early post-1945 boom in Japan, high growth moved to those places that were functionally 'closest' to Japan, that is, South Korea and Taiwan, and the entrepôt city-states of Hong Kong and Singapore. It did so because costs of production in Japan and a rising value of the Japanese currency (yen), were reducing that country's competitiveness in international markets, which, in turn, was leading to a major export of capital from Japan to lower-cost locations in the nearby East Asian region. These 'tiger' economies, as newly industrialized countries (NICs), then became themselves the bases of capital export to nearby regions as they also experienced rising incomes (and stronger currencies). Thus Taiwan and Hong Kong firms were instrumental in the radical capitalist modernization of the Fujian and Guangdong provinces of the PRC. The NICs joined Japan as sources of investment capital in Thailand, Malaysia, Indonesia and the Philippines and as markets for their products, thus boosting these economies as well. The problem, however, with this simple descriptive model is that: (i) it overstates the importance of Japan in the process of East Asian economic growth (at the expense of US and European markets, capital and technology); and (ii) it plays down other sources of endogenous growth in East and Southeast Asia – for example, the important role played by 'developmental state' policies, and by the overseas Chinese.

Together, this rapid growth of the East Asian economies was labelled the 'East Asian miracle'. Why was the word 'miracle' used? It is because it was thought that only in East Asia were 'third world' countries' populations successfully rising out of poverty, and only here were technologically advanced manufacturing companies systematically out-competing firms based in high-income countries. Inevitably, academic, business and political/government observers began to ask why East Asia was experiencing such miraculous rates of economic growth. A sort of answer was provided by the World Bank's report entitled *The East Asian Miracle* (1993). I say a 'sort of answer' because the report conveys more than one message. It claims in its summary statements that the success of the East Asian economies rests on the fact that they were embracing a Western-style liberal market form of economic management with its emphasis on free trade, unregulated capital markets, and competition. In much of the text, however, a different story is being told, one which places the emphasis on the way that 'developmental states' (that is, countries with governments totally committed to the achievement of maximum economic growth) have massively intervened to bolster economic performance. They have done this through 'administrative guidance', the control and/or direction of private investment, the selective protection of domestic production, and the use of public funds for investment in social capital (for example, education) and physical infrastructure (for example, roads, airports, etc.). The debate continues, but whatever the disagreements, all seem to agree that East Asian economic growth has, to a significant degree, been based upon: (i) a remarkable success in exporting to the world's major economies (especially the USA); (ii) a high propensity to save (that is, to sacrifice current consumption for the sake of future production); and (iii) a remarkable success in mobilizing the skills of a well-educated workforce.

While the big story of the East Asian economy is its success (which, despite the economic downturn that began in 2007/08, continues to this day), there was a smaller story which at the time seemed to pose a serious question mark against the inevitability and reliability of economic growth. This was the East Asian economic crisis of 1997. Starting with the forced devaluation of the Thai currency (the baht), domestic and international confidence suddenly evaporated, and several countries (notably Thailand, Indonesia, Malaysia, the

Philippines and South Korea) saw capital flight, and a very sharp downturn in both production and asset values (such as land and property prices, and the value of stock market shares). Many explanations of this frightening event have been offered, but it seems that there is agreement about three things: (i) that land and property speculation had got out of hand; (ii) that institutional capacity and financial regulation had fallen behind the pace of economic growth; and (iii) that such an event could not have happened without the fluidities inherent in the move towards a more globalized world economy.

There is a second qualification to the dominantly positive view of economic success in East Asia. This emphasizes, in a highly critical way, the manner in which these economies are run. It points out that governments (most of them tending to be fairly authoritarian) and business elites (in Southeast Asia these tend to be ethnically Chinese) are often unhealthily close, and that their relationships lack transparency and are not subject to democratic control. Gift giving spills over into bribery, the power of family and friendship networks (*guanxi* in Chinese) surpasses those of professional standards and the rule of law, and rent seeking and nepotism are rife. Money politics and corruption are such a serious problems in the region that some commentators have been inclined to characterize the East Asian capitalist system as 'crony capitalism'.

How does this knowledge of the East Asian economy help us to understand East Asian migrations? We know, of course, that migration decisions are typically complex, and that it is rare for an economic motive to be so dominant that all other considerations (such as family and friendship links, political and religious affiliations, etc.) are rendered irrelevant. Nevertheless, it is also very rare indeed for a migration to be undertaken that is not, to some degree or other, intended to improve the chances of obtaining a job, or achieving a pay rise, or obtaining education and skills, all to advance the material welfare of oneself or one's family. Thus these vast differences in average incomes between the countries of East Asia are crucially important in explaining international migration, and the regional income inequalities within countries are likewise central to explanations of internal migration. Economic growth, other things being equal, will produce new employment opportunities, secure jobs with high pay, and confidence in future prosperity. Economic stagnation will produce unemployment, poverty, powerlessness and a loss of hope for the future. These are immensely powerful incentives for people to migrate.

1.2 East Asian space

Geographically, this East Asian region has one dominant characteristic – its amazing diversity. Rural landscapes that are about as open and empty as any on Earth are to be found in western China and Mongolia, while in other areas, such as parts of eastern China, lowland Japan, Java and the Philippines, there are agricultural landscapes renowned for their density of settlement and intensity of land use. It is the same with urban settlement: in the vast expanse of the Russian Far East (7 million people occupying 1.56 million sq. km) there are just two cities of a little over half a million population each (Vladivostok and Khabarovsk); while in nearby Japan (127 million people on 0.37 million sq. km), 33 million people live in the Tokyo metropolitan area alone, and an area of almost continuous urbanization extends westwards from Tokyo to the Kansai region around Osaka and beyond. Similar zones, consisting of large cities merging together to form vast urban regions, are found in the Pearl River delta area of southern China around Guangzhou, and in the lower Yangtze area around and to the west of Shanghai. If one adds to this the contrasts in climate (extremes of cold and heat, wet and dry), in environmental risk (earthquakes and volcanoes in the Pacific 'ring of fire' and in southern Indonesia, typhoons in the east, droughts in the west), in socio–political systems (military dictatorship, now changing perhaps, in Myanmar and democracy in South Korea), and in wealth and poverty (Japan's GNI per capita is more than 50 times larger than those of Cambodia and Laos), one has a truly remarkable region in which to study human migration.

It is quite difficult to envisage just how vast the East Asian region is. From its western extremity, where it borders the post-Soviet Central Asian republics, to its eastern extremity, where it comes close to touching Alaska, it is almost 120 degrees of longitude, or one third of the distance around the globe. From the southern edge of tropical Indonesia to the northern tip of Arctic Russian Far East it covers almost 90 degrees of latitude, in other words half the distance from Pole to Pole. Being so large, and being located on the eastern side of the world's largest land mass, Eurasia, and on the western side of its largest ocean, the Pacific, it is hardly surprising, perhaps, that it contains such enormously varied places.

These places have been shaped over the centuries by the social organizations and technologies of the peoples who have occupied them. In each historical period the material environments have been transformed by human labour and creativity to produce both (i) the basic needs for immediate consumption (such as food, shelter, clothing, etc.), and (ii) projects to enhance future production, the status of those in power, human safety and security, and cultural and spiritual well-being – especially of the elite – (such as canals and roads, palaces, walls and fortified cities, burial mounds, and places of worship, scholarship and contemplation). These places, bequeathed by their ancestors, are inherited both as physical environments (albeit often much modified by past human practice), land uses and built forms, and as social and cultural milieux, by the peoples of East Asia today.

Despite this diversity and immensity, East Asia has a number of spatial structures that connect people in different places, and supply some order to this complex landscape. First, political and cultural authority: for most of the last 2,000 years the hegemonic power in the region, and therefore its geographical centre, was China. No serious contender existed; you either lived in China, or in a territory that owed allegiance to China, or in an unimportant country located at the periphery of the Chinese world.

This all changed in the eighteenth and nineteenth centuries, as European imperial powers, and then the USA, began to dominate much of the East Asian region. Southeast Asia was split up between the French in Indochina (Vietnam, Laos, and Cambodia), the British in Malaysia/Singapore and Burma, the Dutch in Indonesia (Portuguese in East Timor), and the Spanish (followed by the Americans) in the Philippines. Greater China was partially colonized by these same powers (for example, the British in Hong Kong and the Portuguese in Macao, plus the French and the Germans), while much of the northern part of the region was incorporated into the Russian empire.

By 1900, a modernized and industrialized Japan had joined the European powers as a country with imperial ambitions. It defeated China in 1895 and added Taiwan (Formosa) to its territory. By 1905 it had defeated Russia and added southern Sakhalin to its territory. In 1910 it annexed Korea, and in 1932 added Manchuria (Manchukuo). By 1943, Japanese rule extended to almost the whole of the East Asian region apart from interior and western China. Defeat of Japan in 1945 brought this 'Greater East Asia Co-Prosperity Sphere' to an abrupt end, and the subsequent decolonization of Southeast and Northeast Asia led to the creation of the (semi-)sovereign nation-states that we see in the region today. From 1945 to 1991, the Cold War between the USA and the Soviet Union (the two great 'superpowers') led to two major conflicts – the Korean and Vietnam wars – and created a major geopolitical division in East Asia, with Japan, South Korea, Taiwan, Hong Kong (until 1997), the Philippines, South Vietnam (until 1975), Thailand, Malaysia, Singapore and Indonesia in the US camp, and the rest (North Korea, Mongolia, North Vietnam, Laos, Cambodia, and Myanmar) as mostly (or at times) socialist states aligned (to different degrees) to either Communist China or the Soviet Union.

Second, extending within and across the countries of East Asia is a spatial structure of wealth and social prestige. Its core features are the region's largest cities. These form the pinnacles of urban hierarchies that extend down to the smallest rural villages. Although each national territory has a unique spatial structure, it is possible to see strong common elements. In several countries there are large capital cities (sometimes called 'primate cities') such as Bangkok, Jakarta, Manila and Seoul. These cities massively dominate their respective national territories (Thailand, Indonesia, the Philippines and South Korea). In other cases the urban structure is bi-polar or multi-polar. Vietnam is the stereotypical case of the former, and China of the latter. While Beijing is the dominant centre for Chinese politics and administration, much of the economic and cultural life of this vast country focuses on the coastal cities of Shanghai and Guangzhou (to be joined soon, perhaps, by the interior city of Chongqing). Three East Asian cities, however, stand out from all the others for the importance of their international commercial and financial connections: Tokyo, Hong Kong and Singapore. Through the multiple flows of information, money, goods, reputations and people, these cities serve to bind together the disparate places of East Asia – Tokyo to some degree for the whole region, Hong Kong as a (former) gateway to China, and Singapore for the whole of Southeast Asia.

The main effect of this concentration of wealth and prestige in the main cities is a cruel difference in the living standards and lifetime opportunities faced by urban and rural dwellers. Popular discourse has it, of course, that the cities are modern, efficient, secure, and civilized, and that rural areas are traditional, backward, unsafe and inefficient. The situation is assuredly more complex than this: there are many people living in the city who are very poor and powerless, and some people in the countryside who are significantly rich and powerful, and changes in the spatial divisions of labour (often resulting from new links to global markets) have ensured that many small towns and rural areas are now becoming the sites of modern, high-productivity forms of production in both manufacturing and agriculture. However, the general picture of a rural–urban divide still predominates, and the contrasts in wealth and power are often to be seen at their greatest at the rural-urban interface on the peripheries of rapidly expanding cities. Here great fortunes can be made by entrepreneurs (and sometimes by politicians and bureaucrats as well) through the conversion of land farmed by poor peasants into suburban housing areas and industrial estates.

How does this knowledge of East Asian geography help us to understand East Asian migrations? Well, in some cases the impacts of the geographical environment on human fortunes are fairly direct, as for example, when a natural disaster, such as an earthquake or a volcanic eruption, displaces populations. An exceptional drought or damaging floods can have the same outcome. Generally, though, the effects of geography are more indirect and complex than this. Take, for example, the way that national territories, inherited from the past and therefore reflecting the colonial and post-colonial circumstances of their creation, often fail to match the real functional regions 'on the ground' today (as revealed in the contemporary flows of goods, money, information, and people). Symptomatic of this is the emergence of so-called transnational 'growth triangles' – that is, the development of extended metropolitan regions that cross international borders. Besides encouraging the influx of 'guest workers' from distant Asian countries, these developments imply significant local international migrations. The prime case is the greater Singapore metropolitan region, stretching north into the Johor region of Malaysia, and south into the Riau Islands of Indonesia. Another example is the mismatch between national territories and broad social/cultural regions; this can lead to civil conflict and the periodic migration flows of excluded minorities.

It is not, however, just a case of geography affecting migration. The reverse is also true. The migrations that have accompanied the rapid economic development of East Asian countries have often dramatically, and sometimes extremely detrimentally, affected the fragile geographical environments of those countries. Nowhere is this more the case than in the countries of Southeast Asia where migrants opening up forest lands (for example, for oil palm plantations in Indonesia and Malaysia) have caused deforestation and precipitous declines in biodiversity.

1.3 East Asian society

The events of the last 25 years (i.e. since the end of the Cold War) have demonstrated both (i) the amazing success of Western-style capitalism and liberal democracy (as represented especially by the awesome military strength wielded by the US government, the immense wealth of US corporations, and the dominance of US popular culture in the world's media), and (ii) the strict limitations of that success in countries outside North America and the European Union (EU) – evidence for this is the continuing poverty of 'developing' countries, the current and recent conflicts in Southwest Asia, and the reluctance of many countries in East Asia to embrace the package (hence the debate over 'Asian values') – as well as the striking failures of capitalism and democracy to reduce injustices and inequalities within those Western countries, or to resolve the deep-rooted social conflicts found there.

The vast majority of the world's population, however, and even more so the populations of East Asia, do not communicate in English, or worship under a Christian religion, or relate to their family members in the way that most Americans or Europeans do. Rather, while many would like to benefit from US-style prosperity, technical success and the pursuit of pleasure, they are also critical of Western materialism (for its lack of spirituality), of Western individualism (for its promotion of selfishness), and of the Western tendency to resort to violence (preferring less confrontational forms of problem solving).

As with the false notion that globalization and the ending of the Cold War have brought about the 'end of history', so also, despite their great importance, globalization, US hegemony and the (partial) disappearance of the communist world, have failed to bring about the 'end of geography'. This remains a richly patterned social world that we inhabit. Prominent in that patterning stands the distinctiveness of East Asia *vis-à-vis* the rest of the world, and the striking social and cultural diversity of the countries that make up this vast region.

First, in what ways is East Asia socially and culturally distinctive? We can start by looking at two of the major bases of our 'taken-for-granted worlds': (i) religion/belief system, and (ii) language. East Asia is the home of one of the most powerful and widely held ways of seeing ourselves and the social worlds that we inhabit – Confucianism. With its emphasis on benevolence, duty (including 'filial piety' – the debt of honour that is due to one's parents), respect for others (including towards those [men] in positions of authority), the search for wisdom (hence a strong orientation towards academic study), and the importance of trust and honesty, Confucianism shapes in many ways (albeit often unrecognized) the lives of the vast majority of people living in the East Asian region (but most notably those living in China, Japan and Korea). As for belief systems that are more recognizably religious, Buddhism is dominant in those same countries and in Thailand and Myanmar; Islam in Malaysia and Indonesia (the world's most populous Muslim country), with significant minorities in other countries such as China, the Philippines, and Thailand; Christianity in the Philippines and Russia, with significant minorities in South Korea, China, Vietnam, and Indonesia; and Hinduism in parts of Indonesia and Malaysia. In addition, there are large numbers of people, now typically living in the remoter and/or mountainous areas of East Asia, who adhere to animist/shamanist belief systems (though in this regard it is interesting to note the continuing observance of certain Taoist and Shinto practices in highly developed parts of Northeast Asia).

Even when modes of thought and practice have been imported into East Asia from the West, they have undergone significant transformation. This is true both for communism, which has resulted in forms of government and social philosophies that are highly specific to East Asia (Maoism in China, Khmer Rouge communism in Cambodia, '*Juche*' communism in North Korea), and for democratic liberal capitalism which, despite some recent convergences, still takes very different forms in Japan and South Korea, Taiwan, Thailand, Malaysia and Singapore, from those found in the USA and Western Europe.

Second, the peoples of East Asia communicate with each other in languages that are very distinctly different from the Indo-European languages of Europe and the Western world. Six groups of languages are usually distinguished. Most widely used are Sinitic (Sino-Tibetan) languages, notably the Mandarin Chinese of the cultural 'core' region of northern China, and the many forms of Chinese and Chinese-related languages spoken by people in other parts of China (including Tibet), and in the nearby regions of Southeast Asia (for example, Myanmar). To the north, the main languages (Mongolian, Korean and Japanese) are connected to one another by their Altaic (Central Asian or Turkic) roots, and to the south, many languages are linked through their Austronesian connections to Malay (this includes Javanese Indonesian, and Tagalog spoken in the Philippines). Located geographically between the large Sino-Tibetan language region in the north and the Malay language region in the south are found three smaller groups of languages (all now heavily influenced by Chinese): Hmong-Mien (mostly in mountainous south China, North Vietnam and Laos); Tai-Kadai (now mostly in Thailand, but also in south China, Myanmar, and Laos); and the Austro-Asiatic languages (Vietnamese, Khmer, and Mon). All the major countries of East Asia apart from Japan and Korea have significant linguistic minorities. In many cases these linguistic differences cross-cut other differences such as those of religion, class and 'race', but where they are in alignment with one another, the potential for ethnic conflict (as was seen in parts of Indonesia in the late 1990s) is ever-present, and ordinary people's lives and well-being are at risk.

There is, however, an Indo-European linguistic presence in East Asia: first Russian, of course, dominates the far northern part of the region, English is widely used in the Philippines, and Portuguese is one of the two official languages of newly independent Timor Leste. More significantly, however, as the international language of both business and science (and not surprisingly, therefore, also one of the four official languages of Singapore), English is widely understood and used by East Asian elites, and sometimes also by its non-elites, such as many of those working overseas or people providing services to tourists. English not only allows communication with the outside world, but it helps many people in East Asia (even those from neighbouring countries such as Japan and Korea) to understand each another.

Are the relationships between people the same in East Asia as they are in the West? No, they are not. As capitalist societies, or societies that are transitional from communism to capitalism, class inequality and class relations are, of course, not that different from those with which we are familiar in Western countries. One's power and status depend heavily upon one's class location, with major owners, professionals and managers (plus senior bureaucrats and the top brass in the military) leading privileged lives in comparison with peasant farmers, small owners (who are very numerous in East Asian countries), manual workers, low-level service-sector workers and the un- or underemployed poor. However, social class is cross-cut by other bases of social stratification that matter a lot in East Asia – notably, age/seniority, gender, family/clan, and locality of origin. For example, gender relations are especially salient in Japan where, despite the equal opportunity legislation of 1986 and later years, the career prospects for women remain far worse than those for men. In China, mobilizations around hometown and clan associations are typically easier to achieve than mobilization around common class interests. Above all, throughout the region, family is really important. One's time and effort are very significantly directed towards the fostering of the material interests of one's extended family, and the protection and enhancement of one's family's reputation in the local and wider community.

Has this all changed with increasing prosperity and modernization? No, not completely so. Although ever-higher proportions of East Asia's populations live in cities, and the consumption of mass-produced goods has become the norm, although social values are now being massively influenced by new forms of cultural production and consumption (communicated powerfully through radio, TV, the print media, mobile telephony and the Internet), social relations remain largely focused on the family (where marriage rates remain high), on the village (where the ancestors are buried), and, above all, on the roles played by certain key people. These 'local notables' form the nodes of powerful patron–client networks; they are 'fixers' who get things done and sort things out (while sometimes, of course, operating outside, or at least close to the boundaries of the law, viz. the Triads in China and the Yakuza in Japan).

How does this knowledge of East Asian society and culture help us to understand East Asian migrations? Once again, some of the connections are fairly simple and direct. It is impossible to explain the strange migration events of China during the 1960s (urban-to-rural net migration flows) without reference to the state-sponsored upheavals of Mao's 'Cultural Revolution'. Japan's rather unusual form of capitalism (involving low labour market flexibility – seniority pay, lifetime employment, etc.) explains, in large part, the low spatial mobility of labour in that country.

However, the indirect effects are also important. Take, for example, the frequency with which East Asian governments fall short of international (or are they only Western?) human rights expectations with respect to the treatment of immigrants. Social relations in East Asia have been transformed by new values and new patterns of consumption resulting from the penetration of these spaces by the material and cultural products of advanced capitalist countries (including Japan). This penetration is as yet, however, incomplete, and one of the products of the rather separate histories and geographies of the countries and regions of East Asia is a different conception of human rights, and of what constitutes a good society, from those that dominate discourse in the West. Even today, nearly 70 years after the end of World War II, the descendants of Koreans and Chinese migrating to, or forcibly brought to, Japan in the 1910–45 period, are for the most part non-citizens of their country of birth and upbringing. As recent changes in law and practice in Germany have shown, this is now regarded as intolerable in the West. Nor has Japan, a signatory to the 1951 United Nations (UN) Convention Relating to the Status of Refugees, accepted anywhere near its share of the world's refugees. Is it a coincidence, too, that the politician who is perhaps best known among those supporting the notion of 'Asian values', Prime Minister Mahathir of Malaysia, was the leader of his country at a time when the treatment of 'co-ethnic' immigrant Indonesians was particularly harsh? To state it bluntly, it is very difficult to defend the human rights of an individual immigrant non-national, in a region of the world where collectivism is strong, cultural stereotyping is rife, and ethnic nationalism is the norm.

1.4 East Asian migrations: a typology

The main purpose of this opening chapter was to sketch the East Asian economic and cultural context for an understanding of the region's contemporary migration flows, but what migration flows are we talking about? The rest of the book describes these migrations in considerable detail, and explains their causes and consequences. As a way to see the wider picture (and perhaps also as a 'taster' of what is to come), this final section sets out an overview and typology of East Asian migrations from 1960 to 2010 and presents simplified representations of their geography.

Eight types of migration are judged to be most important:

1   Labour migration – working-class migrations for work – migration of ordinary people trying to get more money, decent jobs and a more secure economic future for themselves and their families. This category is very important at both internal and international levels all over East Asia, and includes, for example, past Chinese migrations to Southeast Asia and recent migrations to the four 'tiger' economies of South Korea, Taiwan, Hong Kong and Singapore, migrations to the Gulf states in the Middle East, and the depopulation of the Russian Far East. More generally, these migrations are often rural-to-urban in character, and are especially strong to major metropolitan cities both inside and outside East Asia (Tokyo, Bangkok, Shanghai, New York, Los Angeles, London). This category also includes frontier settlement, circular and seasonal migration (including nomadism), voluntary contract labour, guest workers, 'trainees', and

migration resulting from landlessness, unemployment, etc. Notice that many of these migrations are, or are intended to be, temporary rather than permanent.

2   Labour migration – migrations of the highly educated and highly skilled. As globalization proceeds this is becoming increasingly important. It often takes the form of intra-organizational transfers both internally (for example, '*tanshinfunin*' – moving away to a job, but leaving the family behind – in Japan), and internationally (for example, managers and technicians accompanying foreign direct investment in China). It also includes Chinese, Taiwanese and Vietnamese returning from the USA, Canada, etc., Indian IT professionals migrating to Japan and Singapore, and, more generally, the migrations of the rich and the famous. Some of these, such as the 'astronauts' (business migrants from Hong Kong who now maintain households in other countries such as Canada and Australia as well as in Hong Kong, and who fly frequently between them – hence the term), and many professional families or members of cultural elites, lead multi-local lives with family members and residences in more than one East Asian country, or, more typically, combining a residence in East Asia with a residence in North America, Europe or Australia/New Zealand. Much of this migration is associated with the development of professional and managerial careers in 'escalator regions' – that is, regions that are rich in opportunities for upward social mobility.

3   Trafficking – migration as a money-making business. Wherever you get extreme differences in wealth combined with weak and/or corrupt governments, you get the vicious exploitation of migrant labour. This occurs in heavy manual work (mostly men – for example, Indonesian construction workers in Malaysia, Chinese agricultural workers in the UK), in lighter manual and care-service work (mostly women – for example, Philippine and Indonesian domestic workers in Hong Kong and in the Gulf), and in the sex industry (mostly women – for example, Thai prostitutes in Japan and Germany). Children are brokered/trafficked within, and from, East Asia for both adoption and exploitation. There are, of course, links between human trafficking and large-scale international criminal organizations, but most trafficking is carried out by small and medium-sized enterprises. This category also includes smuggling, debt bondage, slavery/forced immobility, and overlaps with the contract labour system (see 1, above).

4   Displacements. A threat to one's personal security resulting from violent conflict or 'natural' disaster often leads to migration. There are many examples of such migrations in the past (for example, those provoked by the Mongol invasions of China), but also far too many contemporary cases as well. Examples are the internally displaced persons (IDPs) in Aceh, Timor, West Papua, etc. in Indonesia, and refugees – for example Vietnamese 'boat people', Indo-Chinese and Burmese refugees in Thailand, North Korean escapees in China, etc. Often it is racial and ethnic minorities that are the target for violence which then leads to 'ethnic

cleansing'-type migrations. As for natural disasters, most of the displacements result from severe flooding and prolonged droughts, but recent specific examples of 'environmental refugees' are those produced by the earthquake/tsunamis in Aceh (Indonesia) in 2004 and the one in Tohoku (Japan) in 2011. This category, therefore, includes all types of refugees and IDPs, invasion (by migration), and migrations resulting from the spread of disease, conquest, persecution, social exclusion, expulsion, and ethnic conflict.

5 Place preference migrations. Until now, all the categories of migration discussed have had strong elements of compulsion contained in them (low-income people forced by necessity to migrate for work; professionals and managers transferred by their employers; vulnerable men, women and children trafficked; people displaced by social conflict and natural disaster). However, all decisions to migrate (or not to migrate) involve some element of choice and intention – that is, human agency. This is so even for those who are poor and powerless, but choice becomes increasingly important as average incomes rise and the risks of poverty, violence and ill health decline. Many people migrate to the places where they anticipate that their dreams and ambitions might be realized. Leaving behind those places that they (and their peers) regard as dull and socially restrictive (often as a result of strong 'traditional' family and community values), young adults tend to move to places characterized by modern forms (and levels) of consumption, personal freedom, risk and adventure, fluid social relationships, 'bright lights' and celebrity success. Much of the migration to East Asia's largest and most cosmopolitan cities (Tokyo and Shanghai, Seoul and Beijing, Hong Kong, Singapore, Bangkok, Manila, Jakarta and Ho Chi Minh City) falls into this category. Also included in this category are migrations (of young and old, and sometimes of Westerners) to historic cities such as Kyoto, and to touristic areas such as Bali (Indonesia) and Phuket (Thailand).

6 Life course migrations – students. Most of these are, of course, internal migrations, but one of the most distinctive features of East Asian cross-border student migrations is their orientation towards high-income Western nations (USA and Canada, Australia and New Zealand, and the EU), plus Japan, as the main destination countries. Student migrations are very important because temporary migrations often turn into permanent settlement (for example, the Chinese and Taiwanese in the USA). It follows from this that there are, not surprisingly, large overlaps in the categories that we are using here: students who stay to form a career in the country in which they studied are one example; women who marry 'for love' but also to gain residence in a high-income country to improve the opportunities for themselves, their families back home, and their future families in the destination country, are another. This category also includes adult scholars and teachers, 'rite-of-passage' migrations, and migrations associated with religious teaching and learning such as monks, mullahs and missionaries.

7   Life course migrations – marriages, etc. This is particularly important in East Asia both internally (for example, west–east flows of women in China) and internationally (for example, Vietnamese women migrating to Taiwan, Filipino women to Japan). Sometimes marriage migration is linked to the 'cultural refugee' phenomenon (for example, Japanese women 'escaping' family expectations/obligations and poor promotion prospects in Japan to find, or join, husbands/partners in the USA, Canada, Australia and the UK). Marriage is just one key event in a person's life course; migrations are also associated with the other major social and cultural transitions such as 'coming out' as a homosexual, religious or political conversion, relationship breakdown/divorce, retirement, death of a partner, and loss of independence. This category thus covers all sex, gender and generational aspects of migration, including family reunion. It is probably sensible to include return migration in this category as well. There are many overlaps between this category and that of 'place preferences' (see 5, above).

8   State-sponsored/restrained migration. This takes many different forms, including Maoist rustication (sending urban people to the countryside, as happened during the Cultural Revolution in China and under the Khmer Rouge in Cambodia); subsidized 'internal colonization'-type resettlement (for example, the transmigration programme in Indonesia and the movement westward in China) (but notice that China also has/had migration-restraint policies administered through the '*hukou*' – the household registration system); state-sponsored emigration (for example, Philippines, e.g. nurses and construction workers); displacement due to major infrastructure projects such as the Three Gorges Dam in China; and prison camps (such as those in Xinjiang and the Russian Far East). This category also includes racial exclusion, imperial migrations, colonization, decolonization/return, political exiles/revolutionaries.

Selected references

1.1 East Asian economy

Highly controversial but great fun to read is:
Krugman, P., 1994, The myth of Asia's miracle, *Foreign Affairs* 72(6): 62–93.
See also:
Abegglen, J.C., 1994, *Sea Change: Pacific Asia as the New World Industrial Centre*. New York: Free Press.
Chowdhury, A. and Islam, I., 1993, *The Newly Industrialising Economies of East Asia*. London: Routledge.
Gill, I.S., Huang, Y. and Kharas, H., 2007, *East Asian Visions: Perspectives on Economic Development*. New York: World Bank Publications.
Hobday, M., 1995, *Innovation in East Asia: The Challenge to Japan*. Cheltenham: Edward Elgar.
Kang, D.C., 2002, *Crony Capitalism: Corruption and Development in South Korea and the Philippines*. Cambridge: Cambridge University Press.

Liu, M. and Yin, Y., 2010, *Human Development in East and Southeast Asian Economies: 1990–2010*. UNDP Human Development Research Paper 2010/17.

Regnier, P., 2011, Developmental states and hybrid regimes in South-East Asia: the socio-economic and political challenges of global crises (1998–2008), *Asien* 120: 10–27.

Soderberg, M. and Reader, I. (eds), 2000, *Japanese Influences and Presences in Asia*. Richmond: Curzon.

Specifically, much debate was caused by the publication of the World Bank report, *The East Asian Miracle*. For a powerful critique of the report see:

Wade, R., 1995, The World Bank and the art of paradigm maintenance: The East Asian Miracle as a response to Japan's challenge to the development consensus. University of Sussex, Institute of Development Studies mimeo (published later in *New Left Review*).

World Bank, 1993, *The East Asian Miracle: Economic Growth and Public Policy*. London: Oxford University Press.

On the 1997 economic crisis (which dented confidence in the 'miracle'):

Radelet, S. and Sachs, J., 1998, The onset of the East Asian financial crisis, www.hiid.harvard.edu.

Stiglitz, J.E., 2002, *Globalization and its Discontents*. London: Allen Lane (especially Chapter 4).

Wade, R., 1998, From miracle to cronyism: explaining the great Asian slump, *Cambridge Journal of Economics* (Special Issue on the Asian Economic Crisis) 22: 693–706.

On the relationship between population and economic growth:

Tsen, W.H. and Furuoka, F., 2005, The relationship between population and economic growth in Asian economies, *ASEAN Economic Bulletin* 22(3): 314–330.

1.2 East Asian space

Perhaps the best collections of geographical essays on East Asian development are:

Olds, K., Dicken, P., Kelly, P.F., Kong, L. and Yeung, H.W.-C. (eds), 1999, *Globalisation and the Asia-Pacific: Contested Territories*. London: Routledge (see for example: Friedman, J., *Class formation, hybridity and ethnification in declining global hegemonies*, 183–201).

Watters, R.F. and McGee, T.G. (eds), 1997, *Asia-Pacific: New Geographies of the Pacific Rim*. London: Hurst (see for example the chapter by Edgington on Japan).

Weightman, B., 2008, *Dragons and Tigers: A Geography of South, East, and Southeast Asia*. New York: John Wiley.

Other useful references on the spatial development of East Asia:

Berry, J. (ed.), 1999, *Cities in the Pacific Rim: Planning Systems and Property Markets*. London: Spon.

Blechinger, V. and Legewie, J. (eds), 2000, *Facing Asia: Japan's Role in the Political and Economic Dynamism of Regional Cooperation*. Munich: Iudicium.

Choe, S.-C., 1996, The evolving urban system in North-East Asia, in Lo, F.-C. and Yeung, Y.-M. (eds), *Emerging World Cities in Pacific Asia*. Tokyo: United Nations University Press, 498–519.

Connell, J. and Waddell, E. (eds), 2006, *Environment, Development and Change in Rural Asia-Pacific*. London: Routledge.

Dixon, C. and Drakakis-Smith, D. (eds), 1993, *Economic and Social Development in Pacific Asia*. London: Routledge.

Dutt, A.K., Noble, A.G., Venugopal, G. and Subbiah, S. (eds), 2003, *Challenges to Asian Urbanization in the 21st Century*. Dordrecht: Kluwer, Geoj Libr.

Forbes, D., 1996, *Asian Metropolis: Urbanisation and the Southeast Asian City*. Melbourne: Oxford University Press.

Glassman, J., 2004, *Thailand at the Margins: Internationalization of the State and the Transformation of Labour*. London: Oxford University Press.

Gugler, J. (ed.), 2004, *World Cities Beyond the West: Globalization, Development and Inequality*. Cambridge: Cambridge University Press (chapters on Bangkok, Hong Kong, Jakarta, Seoul, Shanghai and Singapore).

Hart-Landsberg, M. and Burkett, P., 1998, Contradictions of capitalist industrialization in East Asia: a critique of 'flying geese' theories of development, *Economic Geography* 74(2): 87–110.

Heron, R. and Park, S.O. (eds), 1995, *The Asian Pacific Rim and Globalisation*. Basingstoke: Avebury.

Hill, H., 2002, Spatial disparities in developing East Asia: a survey, *Asian-Pacific Economic Literature* 16(1): 10–35.

Huang, Y. and Bocchi, A.M., 2009, *Reshaping Economic Geography in East Asia*. Washington, DC: World Bank.

Kanbur, R., Venables, A.J. and WanG., 2006, *Spatial Disparities in Human Development: Perspectives from Asia*. Tokyo: United Nations University.

Kolb, A., 1963, *East Asia: China, Japan, Korea, Vietnam – Geography of a Cultural Region*. London: Methuen.

Kong, L. and O'Connor, J. (eds), 2009, *Creative Economies, Creative Cities? Asian-European Perspectives*. Berlin: Springer.

Lin, S. (ed.), 2003, *Southeast Asia Transformed: A Geography of Change*. Singapore: Institute of South East Asian Studies.

Lo, F.-C. and Yeung, Y.-M. (eds), *Emerging World Cities in Pacific Asia*. Tokyo: United Nations University Press, 17–47.

Murphy, A.B., 1995, Economic regionalization and Pacific Asia, *Geographical Review* 85(2): 127–140.

Olds, K., 2001, *Globalization and Urban Change: Capital, Culture, and the Pacific Rim Mega-Projects*. London: Oxford University Press (on Shanghai).

Ozawa, T., 2009, *The Rise of Asia: The 'Flying Geese' Theory of Tandem Growth and Regional Agglomeration*. Cheltenham: Edward Elgar.

Pempel, T.J. (ed.), 2005, *Remapping East Asia: The Construction of a Region*. Ithaca, NY: Cornell University Press.

Poon, J.P.H., Thompson, E.R. and Kelly, P.F., 2000, Myth of the triad? The geography of trade and investment blocs, *Transactions of the Institute of British Geographers* 25(4): 427–444.

Rimmer, P.J., 1996, International transport and communications interactions between Pacific Asia's emerging world cities, in Lo, F.-C. and Yeung, Y.-M. (eds), *Emerging World Cities in Pacific Asia*. Tokyo: United Nations University Press, 48–97.

Shaw, D. and Liu, B.J. (eds), 2011, *The Impact of the Economic Crisis on East Asia*. Cheltenham: Edward Elgar.

Smith, D., 2004, Global cities in East Asia: empirical and conceptual analysis, *International Social Science Journal* 181: 397–412.

Yeung, H.W.-C., 2003, Theorizing economic geographies of Asia, *Economic Geography* 79(2): 107–128.

On growth triangles:

Bunnell, T., Muzaini, H. and Sidaway, J.D., 2006, Global city frontiers: Singapore's hinterland and the contested socio-political geographies of Bintan, Indonesia, *International Journal of Urban and Regional Research* 30(1): 3–22.

Chen, X., 2005, *As Borders Bend: Transnational Spaces on the Pacific Rim.* Lanham, MD: Rowman & Littlefield.

Grundy-Warr, C., Peachey, K. and Perry, M., 1999, Fragmented integration in the Singapore-Indonesian border zone: Southeast Asia's 'growth triangle' against the global economy, *International Journal of Urban and Regional Research* 23(2): 304–328.

Jones, G.W., 2004, Urbanization trends in Asia: the conceptual and definitional challenges, in Champion, A.G. and Hugo, G. (eds), *New Forms of Urbanization: Beyond the Urban-Rural Dichotomy.* Aldershot: Ashgate, 113–132.

McGee, T.G. and Robinson, I.M. (eds), 1995, *The Mega-Urban Regions of Southeast Asia.* Vancouver: University of British Columbia Press.

Marton, A., McGee, T. and Paterson, D.G., 1995, Northeast Asian economic cooperation and the Tumen River Area Development Project, *Pacific Affairs* 63(1): 9–33.

Phillips, D.R., Yeh, A.G.O. and Kim, K.-G. (eds), 1987, *New Towns in East and South-East Asia: Planning and Development.* Hong Kong: Hong Kong University Press.

Sparke, M., Sidaway, J.D., Bunnell, T. and Grundy-Warr, C., 2004, Triangulating the borderless world: geographies of power in the Indonesian-Malaysian-Singapore growth triangle, *Transactions of the Institute of British Geographers* 29: 485–498.

Tang, M. and Thant, M., 1997, Recent developments of growth triangles and the implications for labour mobility in Asia, in Campbell, D., Parisotto, A., Verma, A. and Lateef, A. (eds), *Regionalization and Labour Market Interdependence in East and Southeast Asia.* Basingstoke: Macmillan, 174–198.

1.3 East Asian society

On culture and identity:

Kahn, J.S. (ed.), 1998, *Southeast Asian Identities: Culture and the Politics of Representation in Indonesia, Malaysia, Singapore and Thailand.* London: I.B. Tauris.

Keyes, C., 2002, 'The peoples of Asia' – science and politics in the classification of ethnic groups in Thailand, China, and Vietnam, *Journal of Asian Studies* 61(4): 1163–1203.

Social relations in East Asia have been transformed by new values and new patterns of consumption resulting from the penetration of these spaces by the material and cultural products of advanced capitalist countries (including Japan).

Beauchamp, E. (ed.), 2002, *East Asia: History, Politics, Sociology, Culture.* London: Routledge.

Croll, E.J., 2002, Fertility decline, family size and female discrimination: a study of reproductive management in East and South Asia, *Asia-Pacific Population Journal* 17(2): 11–38.

Davis, D.E., 2004, *Discipline and Development: Middle Classes and Prosperity in East Asia and Latin America.* Cambridge: Cambridge University Press.

Katzenstein, P.J. and Shiraishi, T. (eds), 1997, *Network Power: Japan and Asia.* Ithaca, NY: Cornell University Press.

Moeran, B., 2000, Commodities, culture and Japan's corollanization of Asia, in Soderberg, M. and Reader, I. (eds), *Japanese Influences and Presences in Asia.* Richmond: Curzon, 25–50.

Sidorenko, A. and Findlay, C., 2001, The digital divide in East Asia, *Asian-Pacific Economic Literature* 15(2): 18–30.

On ageing, etc., in East Asia:

Caldwell, J.C. and Caldwell, B.K., 2005, The causes of Asian fertility decline: macro and micro approaches, *Asian Population Studies* 1(1): 31–46.

Feeney, G. and Mason, A., 2002, Population in East Asia, in Mason, A., *Population Change and Economic Development in East Asia: Challenges Met, Opportunities Seized.* London: Stanford University Press, 61–95.

Horlacher, D.E. and MacKellar, L., 2003, Population ageing in Japan: policy lessons for South-East Asia, *Asia-Pacific Development Journal* 10(1): 97–122.

McNicoll, G., 2006, Policy lessons of the East Asian demographic transition, *Population and Development Review* 32(1): 1–25.

Phillips, D.R., 1992, *Ageing in East and South-East Asia.* London: Arnold.

Zhao, Z. and Kinfu, Y., 2005, Mortality transition in East Asia, *Asian Population Studies* 1(1): 3–30.

Human rights: this penetration is, as yet, incomplete, and one of the products of the rather separate histories and geographies of the countries and regions of East Asia is a different conception of human rights and of what constitutes a good society, from those that dominate discourse in the West:

Arnason, J.P., 1999, East Asian approaches: region, history and civilization, *Thesis Eleven* 57: 97–112.

Bauer, J.R. and Bell, D.A. (eds), 1999, *The East Asian Challenge for Human Rights.* Cambridge: Cambridge University Press.

Befu, H. (ed.), 1993, *Cultural Nationalism in East Asia: Representation and Identity.* Berkeley: University of California Press.

Chen, K.-H. (ed.), 1998, *Trajectories: Inter-Asian Cultural Studies.* London: Routledge.

Christie, K. and Roy, D., 2001, *The Politics of Human Rights in East Asia.* London: Pluto Press.

Clarke, G., 2001, From ethnocide to ethnodevelopment? Ethnic minorities and indigenous peoples in Southeast Asia, *Third World Quarterly* 22(3): 413–436.

Close, P. and Askew, D., 2004, *Asia Pacific Human Rights: A Global Political Economy Perspective.* Aldershot: Ashgate.

Davidson, A. and Weekley, K. (eds), *Globalization and Citizenship in the Asia Pacific.* London: Macmillan, 221–242.

Eldridge, P.J., 2002, *The Politics of Human Rights in Southeast Asia.* London: Routledge.

Foot, R., 2000, *Rights Beyond Borders: The Global Community and the Struggle over Human Rights in China.* London: Oxford University Press.

Gladney, D.C. (ed.), 1998, *Making Majorities: Constituting the Nation in Japan, Korea, China, Malaysia, Fiji, Turkey and the United States.* Stanford, CA: Stanford University Press.

Goodman, R., White, G. and Kwon, H.-J. (eds), 1998, *The East Asian Welfare Model.* London: Routledge.

Kelly, D. and Reid, A. (eds), 1998, *Asian Freedoms: The Idea of Freedom in East and Southeast Asia.* Cambridge: Cambridge University Press.

Kymlicka, W. and He, B. (eds), *Multiculturalism in Asia.* London: Oxford University Press.

Langlois, A.J., 2001, *The Politics of Justice and Human Rights (Southeast Asia).* Cambridge: Cambridge University Press.

Levinson, D., 1993, *Encyclopedia of World Cultures: East and Southeast Asia.* New York: G.K. Hall.

Winzeler, R.L., 1997, *Indigenous Peoples and the State: Politics, Land, and Ethnicity in the Malayan Peninsula and Borneo*. New Haven, CT: Yale University Press.

Wittfogel, K.A., 1981 (1957), *Oriental Despotism: A Comparative Study of Total Power*. New York: Vintage.

International relations: with the ending of the Cold War, there has been a reassessment of the role of the USA in the region, increasing awareness of Islamic sensitivities, and of the political and military importance of China. See:

Brown, M.E., Lynn-Jones, S.M. and Miller, S.E. (eds), 1996, *East Asian Security*. Cambridge, MA: Massachusetts Institute of Technology Press.

Choi, J., 2003, Ethnic and regional politics after the Asian economic crisis: a comparison of Malaysia and South Korea, *Democratization* 10(1): 121–134.

Rodan, G., Hewison, K. and Robison, R., 2001, *The Political Economy of South-East Asia: Conflicts, Crises and Change*. London: Oxford University Press.

Rumley, D., Chiba, T., Takagi, A. and Fukushima, Y. (eds), 1996, *Global Geopolitical Change and the Asia-Pacific: A Regional Perspective*. Aldershot: Avebury.

Siddique, S., Nakamura, M. and Bajunid, O.F., 2001, *Islam and Civil Society in Southeast Asia*. Singapore: Institute of South East Asian Studies.

The future of the 'East Asian miracle' and of the geography of development in the Asia-Pacific region depends on the containment of certain geopolitical conflicts. For very level-headed treatments of these conflicts, see:

Kim, S.S. (ed.), 2004, *The International Relations of Northeast Asia*. Lanham, MD: Rowman & Littlefield.

Taylor, R., 1996, *Greater China and Japan: Prospects for an Economic Partnership in East Asia*. London: Routledge.

Yahuda, M., 1996, *The International Politics of the Asia-Pacific, 1945–95*. London: Routledge.

See also for general reference:

Hoare, J.E. and Pares, S., 2005, *A Political and Economic Dictionary of East Asia*. London: Routledge.

Tan, A.T.H., 2004, *A Political and Economic Dictionary of South-East Asia*. London: Europa.

2 Context

East Asian migrations – an historical overview

2.0 Introduction

This chapter takes the eight migration categories introduced in Chapter 1 and asks: What were the broad features of these migrations in the East Asian region in the past, and how might these histories influence the characteristics of migration flows in the region today? A cautionary note is appropriate: this chapter engages in a particularly high level of generalization, so it is inevitable that a lot of interesting and important detail has been omitted. It is essential, however, that an historical perspective be provided; without it, much of what is happening today would be difficult or even impossible to understand.

The focus of the chapter is Figure 2.1 (parts a and b). This diagram is a rather ambitious attempt on my part to show the complex histories of East Asian migrations and their socio-political contexts over the last 12,000 years. It is divided horizontally into three macro-regions – the same regions that will be used in the rest of this book: Southeast Asia (at the bottom); 'China plus' (in the middle); and Northeast Asia (at the top). It is divided vertically into three chronological periods: 10,000 BC to AD 0 (on the left of Figure 2.1a); AD 0 to AD 1400 (on the right of Figure 2.1a); and AD 1400 to 1945 (in Figure 2.1b). Migration flows that link the region to the rest of the world are discussed in the text but are not included on the diagram – it is, after all, fairly complicated already!

From their early origins, probably in East Africa, the first 'true humans' (*homo erectus*) spread by migration to Europe and to Asia, including East Asia. Evidence of early human activity in Java (Indonesia) and in northern China (near Beijing, in the middle reaches of the Yellow River, and in the lower Yangtze) suggests that *homo erectus* arrived in East Asia around 1.6 million years ago. Modern humans (*homo sapiens*), however, arrived from Africa much later, probably only about 40,000 years ago and, perhaps because they occupied different ecological niches, they replaced their predecessors rather than interacting and merging with them (the more recent discovery of human remains on the island of Flores, Indonesia, might require us to revise this judgement about replacement).

Human development really began in earnest with the ending of the last ice age around 9,600 BC. Thereafter, under warmer and moister conditions, the domestication of plants and animals led to a transition in most parts of our region from a hunter-gatherer lifestyle to a sedentary agricultural one. The simple distinction between pre-Neolithic nomadic hunter-gatherers and Neolithic sedentary agriculturalists seems, however, to break down in the case of Japan (and maybe also elsewhere) where the *Joumon* hunter-gatherers are thought to have been sedentary. With technological change, social stratification and a more complex division of labour, came agricultural surpluses and the first beginnings of urban economies and cultures. Sometime around 7000 BC, millet and rice cultivation began in the Yellow and Yangtze River basins, from whence they dispersed to other parts of East and Southeast Asia. Pottery, textiles and metalworking followed. By 2000 BC, there was a sophisticated state apparatus in central and northern China, where East Asia's first major cities, peopled largely by traders and bureaucrats, craftsmen, warriors and priests, developed. This same region saw the emergence of writing in the form of Chinese characters at around 1200 BC.

We know little, of course, about the East Asian migrations of the Neolithic millennia from 6000 to 2000 BC, but the signs are that we shall know a lot more in the near future. This is because experts from the three main disciplines handling early human history – archaeology, historical linguistics, and archaeogenetics – are now beginning to collaborate with one another to piece together believable accounts of these early migrations. The migrants conveniently carried with them their mitochondrial DNA, their languages, and their material goods and technologies, leaving behind 'footprints' that we can follow. As a foretaste of what is to come, we know that 'the peoples of north China are more closely related genetically to their northern neighbors outside present-day China than they are to the peoples in south China. These are in turn more closely related to their southern neighbors in Southeast Asia than they are to the northern Chinese' (Wilkinson 2000: 709). This reflects the strong migration links between the northern Chinese and their neighbours in Central and Northern Asia, and those between the southern Chinese and their neighbours in peninsular Southeast Asia. It also adds a new dimension to our awareness that there is a marked linguistic division between the Mandarin-related Chinese dialects of the North and Northwest on the one hand, and those of the Southeast and South on the other.

One thing is obvious, however: a population engaged in the cultivation of grain crops and the rearing of domesticated animals is relatively immobile, and has the potential to display the behaviours, and share the values, of 'earthbound compulsion'.

The evidence seems to show that the Neolithic agricultural revolution arrived much later in southern China (probably around 3000 BC) than in central and northern China (7000 BC), later still in Korea, and in lowland Vietnam and Thailand (2000–2500 BC), and very late indeed in Japan (where the Yayoi agricultural period began about 300 BC). Metal working, however, spread more quickly than millet and rice cultivation, so that by 500 BC virtually the whole of East Asia had entered the Iron Age. The archaeological evidence for the

Figure 2.1(a): East Asian Migrations 10,000BC–1400 AD

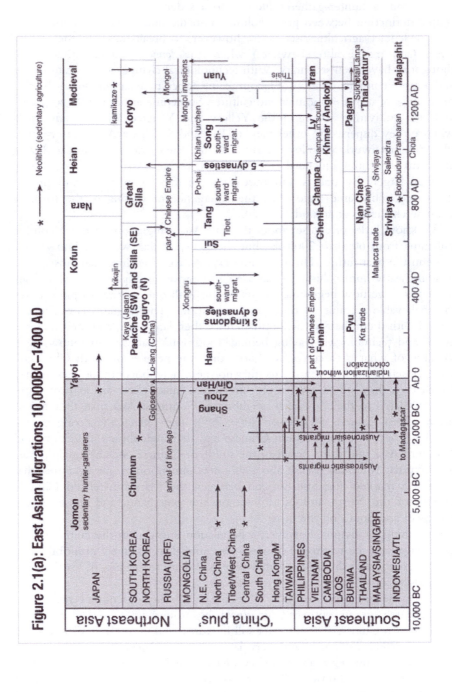

Figure 2.1(b): East Asian Migrations 1400–1950

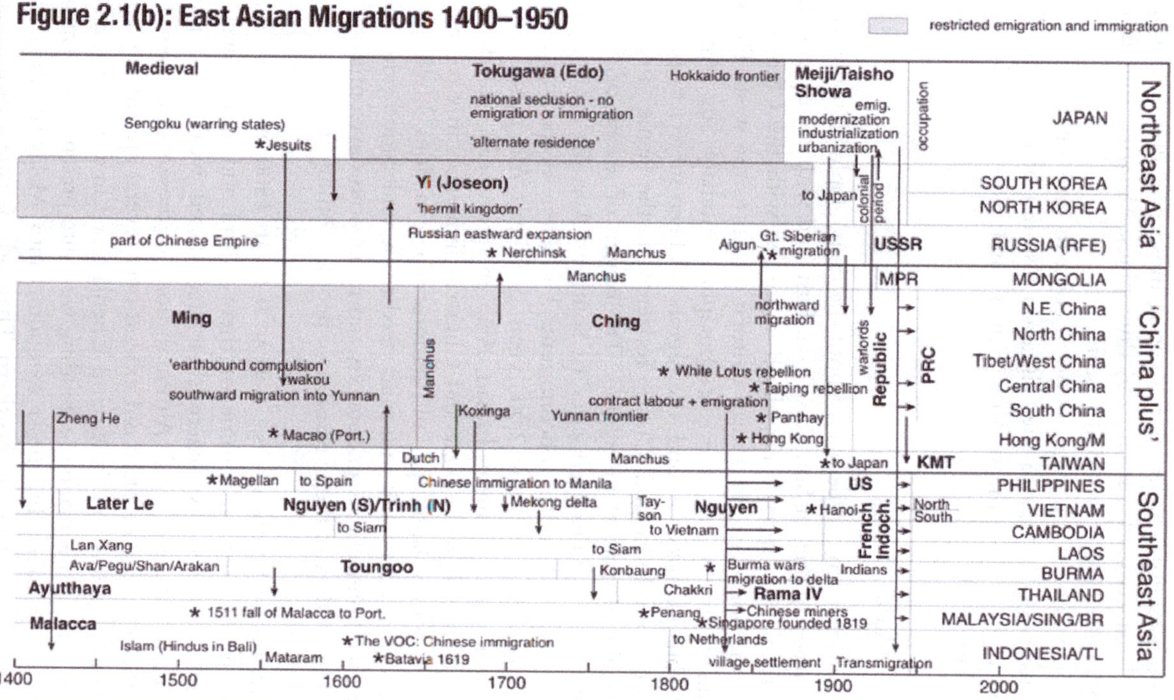

restricted emigration and immigration

Northeast Asia

JAPAN
SOUTH KOREA
NORTH KOREA
RUSSIA (RFE)

Medieval | Tokugawa (Edo) | Hokkaido frontier | Meiji/Taisho Showa

Sengoku (warring states)

★ Jesuits

national seclusion - no emigration or immigration

'alternate residence'

occupation

emig. modernization industrialization urbanization

colonial period

to Japan

Yi (Joseon)

'Hermit kingdom'

part of Chinese Empire

Russian eastward expansion

★ Nerchinsk   Manchus

Aigun, Gt. Siberian ★ migration

Manchus

Manchus

Dutch

northward migration

'China plus'

MONGOLIA
N.E. China
North China
Tibet/West China
Central China
South China
Hong Kong/M
TAIWAN

USSR

MPR

PRC

Republic

warlords

Ming

'earthbound compulsion' ★wakou
southward migration into Yunnan

Ching

Yunnan frontier

contract labour + emigration

★ White Lotus rebellion
★ Taiping rebellion
★ Panthay

★ Hong Kong

Zheng He

Koxinga

KMT

★ to Japan

Southeast Asia

PHILIPPINES
VIETNAM
CAMBODIA
LAOS
BURMA
THAILAND
MALAYSIA/SING/BR
INDONESIA/TL

US

French Indoch.

North
South

★ Hanoi

Nguyen

Chinese immigration to Manila

↓ Mekong delta

Nguyen (S)/Trinh (N)

to Siam

Tay-son

to Vietnam

to Siam

Toungoo

Konbaung

Later Le

Lan Xang

Ava/Pegu/Shan/Arakan

Ayutthaya

Malacca

Islam (Hindus in Bali)

★ 1511 fall of Malacca to Port.

★ Magellan   to Spain

★ Macao (Port.)

Mataram

★ 1619 Batavia

★ The VOC: Chinese immigration

Burma wars

migration to delta

Indians

Chakkri

★ Rama IV

★ Penang   ★ Singapore founded 1819

★ Chinese miners

to Netherlands

village settlement

Transmigration

1400   1500   1600   1700   1800   1900   2000

southward spread of agriculture through migration and settlement, much of it through the 'hub' region of Yunnan in southern China and the southeast coast of China, is backed up by linguistic evidence which suggests that the middle Yangtze valley was the core region for both the Austroasiatic and Austronesian languages of Southeast Asia, the former covering most of peninsular Southeast Asia while the latter covered Taiwan, the Philippines, Malaysia, and most of present-day Indonesia (and on to Madagascar).

To continue the story of the main historical contexts for contemporary East Asian migrations, we now turn to the migration histories of East Asia's three constituent sub-regions – Southeast Asia, 'China', and Northeast Asia – over the period AD 0 to 1950.

2.1 Southeast Asia

Two broad generalizations can be made about the demographic histories of the countries that make up present Southeast Asia. First, and with the exception of Java-Bali, the region was sparsely populated compared with the Chinese cultural region to the north and the Indian cultural region to the west. This surprising emptiness was called the 'demographic anomaly' by American geographer Wilbur Zelinsky. Second, the region has been subject to profound influences from both India and China, reflected in the name 'Indochina' applied to a significant part of the region. The origins of several of the great civilizations were in the 'Indianized states' of Southeast Asia, the result of travel from, and trade with, the Indian subcontinent. The Chinese, too, have settled and traded in the region for some 2,000 years. Southeast Asia is, therefore, a cultural crossroads where Chinese, Indian, Arab and European, and therefore Confucian, Buddhist, Hindu, Islamic and Christian influences mix to create a great range of traditions, landscapes and nations. These nations, however, are separate entities from China and India and need to be understood primarily in terms of their own Southeast Asian contexts and indigenous developments, and not simply as the product of the expansion of peoples coming from outside the region.

The early history of Southeast Asia (see AD 0 to AD 1500 in Figure 2.1) is dominated by major kingdoms, some of them inland and agricultural, but many of them 'thalassocracies' where their trade-based wealth and power depended on their 'rule of the sea'. Although none of these states covered the whole of Southeast Asia, they often did extend over several present-day countries. The major kingdoms are: Funan and Chenla based in the Mekong basin (South Vietnam and Cambodia, but extending west into present-day Thailand); Srivijaya/Sailendra (western Indonesia extending into Malaysia); Nan Chao (Yunnan in China, but including northern Thailand); Champa (south-central Vietnam); Kmer/Ankhor (Cambodia, Thailand and Laos); Pyu followed by Pagan (upper Burma); Majapahit (Indonesia and Malaysia, based on Java); and Ayutthaya (Thailand). These 'Indianized states', are so-called because of their Hindu and Buddhist cultures, legal and administrative practices, architecture (for example, the Borobudur (Buddhist) and Prambanan (Hindu) temples in Java, Indonesia), and their use of Sanskrit. Perhaps rather surprisingly, and despite the success of the Tamil-Indian Chola expedition of the early 11th century, they were not, in general, Indianized through colonial conquest, migration and settlement, but instead through the adoption and adaptation of Indian cultural practices by local rulers.

While much of Southeast Asia during this period was open to the West, other parts, notably Vietnam, were dominated by their relations northwards with China. Indeed, northern Vietnam was arguably part of the Chinese empire until the Dai Viet kingdoms (Ly, Tran and Le dynasties) came into being after the late 10th century. Trade with China was crucial to the region throughout this period. Early on, the southern trade routes linking China with India, Southwest Asia (notably Persia) and Europe, were by sea and across the Kra Peninsula (in what is now southern Thailand). Later, the key ports in this lucrative trade were located in eastern Vietnam, southern Thailand and, above all, in the Straits of Malacca between present-day Indonesia and Malaysia.

So what were the migrations that accompanied the existence, rise and fall of these major Southeast Asian kingdoms in the period before 1500? First, numerically the largest, but not figuring much in the history books, is the extension of agricultural settlement – the long, slow process by which marshy lowlands and the lower slopes of Southeast Asia's many mountain ranges were brought under cultivation for the production of paddy rice, other cereals, fruits and vegetables, and for 'cash crops' (for example, spices) for sale to the traders. Second, the trade routes themselves channelled migration flows, so that the port cities became multicultural enclaves in kingdoms dominated by a single ethnic or linguistic group. Ayutthaya, for example, had separate quarters for its Japanese, Chinese, Viet, Cham, Mon, Portuguese, Dutch, Arab, Indian, Persian and various Malay trading and artisan populations. Third, these were slave societies, and a key resource for the protection or expansion of a kingdom was labour. So the capture of farmers, miners and artisans in war and their enforced relocation to support production in the victor's domain was a fairly normal part of inter-state relations. Finally, of massive significance for the region, was the steady southward overland movement of Thai populations from southern China into peninsular Southeast Asia, resulting in the 'Thai century' and the rise of the Ayutthaya kingdom.

A further stage in the Indianization of much of Southeast Asia occurred in the 13th–16th centuries when most of the rulers and their subjects converted to Islam – predominantly (but not in Aceh) an Indianized, rather mystical, Sufi-influenced Islam. Once again, this change, which affected Malaysia, most of Indonesia, and southern parts of Thailand, the Philippines and Vietnam, was brought about without colonization and settlement.

This all changed in the 16th and 17th centuries as Southeast Asia became subject to the imperial ambitions of major European/Western powers. The Portuguese (Malacca), Spanish (Philippines) and Dutch (Indonesia) led the way, followed in the 18th and 19th centuries by the British (Malaysia, Singapore and

Burma), French (Laos, Cambodia and Vietnam) and Americans (Philippines). The European populations of administrators and soldiers, plantation and mine owners, missionaries and merchants, were typically very small (for example, the population of Batavia (Jakarta) in 1789 was 151,000; the indigenous 'free' population was 79,000, slaves 37,000, Chinese 34,000, and Europeans just 1,000), but their impacts on the economies and societies of Southeast Asia, and, through this, on Southeast Asia's migrations, were huge.

New areas were opened up for agricultural and mining developments, new products introduced (e.g. rubber, tobacco, maize, peanuts and yams), new port cities built (e.g. Singapore), and old cities re-sited and transformed (e.g. Jakarta). All this required labour, disciplined labour, and lots of it. By the end of the colonial era, the region as a whole had sucked in a net 6 million workers from the Indian subcontinent (especially Tamils), and a net 7 million from China (especially Cantonese). The colonial powers used Indian and Chinese labour in manual work, for example as plantation workers and miners, but also as middlemen – as foremen, functionaries, revenue farmers, money lenders and traders. Chinese minority populations, for example, expanded in Manila under the Spanish rule of the Philippines, in Batavia (Jakarta) under the Dutch East India Company's (VOC) rule of what became Netherlands Indies (Indonesia), in Bangkok, capital of independent Siam (Thailand), in the British Malay Peninsula (notably in Penang and Singapore), and in French Indochina (Vietnam, Cambodia and Laos). Facilitated by new forms of transport and communication, these migration flows to Southeast Asia built up during the 19th century, to peak in the 1870s and again in the 1920s.

At the same time, even larger numbers of indigenous workers were mobilized, primarily for rural colonial paddy rice and cash crop production (such as the sugar industry in Java), but also as urban service workers and as domestic servants and employees of the Europeans. The resulting migrations brought many Javanese and Sundanese to Sumatra in Indonesia, Ilocanos to Central Luzon and Manila in the Philippines, and Vietnamese to the Mekong delta in Vietnam. So great was the emphasis on the plantation production of tropical products for export in the early colonial period with its associated de-urbanization, that one author talks about the 'peasantization' of Southeast Asia's population.

The conditions under which this labour was recruited, relocated and put to work varied enormously. Much of the migration was undertaken 'freely'. It is, of course, rather bizarre to think of migration as being freely chosen when the alternative (staying put) was, practically speaking, 'not an option'. To stay often implied a willingness to submit oneself to grinding poverty now and to zero prospects for the future. Such were the conditions faced, for example, by millions of families in southern China during the latter years of the Qing dynasty at a time when lives were made dangerously insecure by crop failure due to drought and widespread civil conflict. However, while this was bad enough, many migrants suffered circumstances that were worse than this. Before the 19th century, the movement of captive peoples and slaves was the primary source of labour mobility (for example, the slave raiding in the late 18th century in the 'Sulu Zone' in Indonesia/Philippines), and until 1820, a sizeable proportion of residents in Southeast Asia's urban centres were captives or slaves. Slavery was slowly eradicated in Southeast Asia during the 19th century, but it came to be partially replaced by 'indenture', that is, a contract labour system that tied migrants (as did, and does, debt bondage), often backed up by the threat of violence, to their employers (many of whom were co-ethnics) who ran the colonial economy. Sometimes tricked, often coerced by their families, but mostly just persuaded by professional recruiters, male migrants went into the service of the plantation owners, public works companies, and mine and factory owners, and female migrants into domestic service and the service of the brothel keepers.

These migration flows into Southeast Asia in the 19th and early 20th centuries were complex in detail (for example, in their geographical origins and occupational destinations, such as Sikhs as policemen), but they tended, especially in the earlier periods, to display two over-riding characteristics: first, they were predominantly male; and second, their stay in Southeast Asia was temporary. These migrants were 'sojourners': they came to make money, lots of it, they hoped, in just a few years, and then return. Many, indeed the vast majority, did eventually return, but many others stayed permanently or at least long enough to become to some degree socially and culturally embedded in the host society. Earlier migrations of Chinese (mostly traders – *huashang* – in the 15th and 16th centuries) had, for example, resulted in the integration of ethnic Chinese into the Thai population, and the emergence elsewhere of indigenized and mixed-race Chinese communities such as the *mestizos* in the Philippines (from Manila many Chinese and *mestizos* went on to Mexico), the *peranakan* in Indonesia, and the *baba-nyonya* in Malaysia. Now the arrival of much larger numbers of mostly manual-worker Indians and Chinese (*huagong*) resulted, due to spatial and occupational segregation, in the establishment of distinctive ethnic enclaves, and more of a 'parallel-lives' relationship to the host population (that is, co-presence but with little social and cultural integration).

Not surprisingly, therefore, when, drawing upon the mobilizing force of ethnic nationalism, freedom from colonial rule was achieved by the peoples of Southeast Asia in the mid-20th century (later in Vietnam), there were violent clashes with ethnic minority Indian and Chinese populations. This resulted in the expulsion of Indians (and others like the Rohingyas) from Burma and the Japanese from the Philippines, and the large losses of Chinese from Indonesia and Vietnam. It also contributed indirectly to the independence of Singapore, and to the rather remarkable ethno-political compromise in Malaysia.

The migration effects of 19th- and early 20th-century European and US colonialisms were not confined, however, to immigration into Southeast Asia or to the redistribution of populations within that region (for example Acehnese to Malacca after 1903). Emigration was also affected. The Dutch contract labour and penal systems, for example, brought 'Indonesians' to South Africa, to French colonies in the Pacific (New Caledonia) and to Surinam in South

America. Other Southeast Asians, many of them ambitious and well educated, found higher education, social promotion, modernity and cultural or political escape in their colonial homelands (Malays and Burmese in Britain, Indonesians in the Netherlands, Indochinese in France, and perhaps especially, Filipinos as US nationals in the USA). It was in their imperial homelands and capitals that the business and political careers of many of Southeast Asia's independence and post-independence leaders were formed.

Before leaving this short overview of the history of migrations in Southeast Asia it is necessary to emphasize one characteristic almost above all others: the long-continuing fluidity and spatially uncontained nature of the region's migrations and other mobilities. This is true for maritime Southeast Asia, where cross-cutting patterns of flows resulted in immensely complex combinations of ethnicities and cultural influences, but also in interior upland peninsular Southeast Asia, where networks of trade, sociability and migration virtually ignored colonial borders, and where populations, despite the powers of the Indianized states before, and of the European colonial administrations that followed, were (and are still today) highly skilled at 'the art of not being governed'.

2.2 'China'

The name for China in Chinese is *zhongguo*, literally 'the middle kingdom'. Within that kingdom, and despite the emphasis in Chinese sociology on the 'earthbound' nature of the population, the Chinese peoples have been highly mobile throughout most of their long history. It is also true, however, that there have been significant and sometimes lengthy periods when movements were strictly controlled. Two general, and partially connected, patterns can be discerned amid all the complexity of movement: a step-wise southern expansion of the Chinese peoples from their heartland in the Yellow River region; and the failure by many Chinese governments to defend their western and northern borders, thus allowing penetration of, and conquest by, non-Han peoples – most importantly, the Mongols and the Manchus.

Despite the prevalence of population movement during the pre-modern period, and not unlike Europe, the widely accepted (and promoted) ideal for China was seen to be a stable, sedentary population; the Chinese were thought to have an 'earthbound compulsion'. Why this idea should have been so strong is still a matter for conjecture, but it is rooted in Confucian culture and attitudes to place. It was, however, a very deceptive ideal. Famines, both local and regional, slavery, but most importantly warfare, caused many disruptions that resulted in displacements of people. Within this matrix of forced movement can be found those associated with peaceful trade, the opening up of new agricultural lands and the growth of towns and industry. China was already a major urban and industrial society, held together by flows of people, goods, money and ideas, when Europe was emerging from its 'Dark Ages'.

During the Qin-Han period (221 BC to AD 220) China became unified within borders that were tighter in the south and west, but were otherwise not very different from those we see today. Great capital cities were built in the Yellow River basin (Chang'an/Sian and L(u)oyang), and the Great Wall was built to keep out the migrant invaders (the Xiongnu or 'huns/barbarians') from the north and west (buttressed by 'peace through kinship' marriages between Han princesses and Xiongnu leaders). To defend this northwestern border further, farmers were encouraged to settle in border regions with the help of land, housing and tax exemptions. This policy was intensified when flooding of the Yellow River in 119 BC led to the migration westwards and northwards of over 700,000 people. At the same time there was a steady drift southwards into the rice cultivation regions of central and southern China. This followed earlier movements of 50,000 Qin people into Sichuan, displacing a similar number of Shu loyalists who migrated south into what is now northern Vietnam.

The Qin-Han period was characterized by a sequence of events that seems to have repeated itself throughout the subsequent history of China. Called 'the dynastic cycle', it looks something like this: following a heroic founding (such as that of the Qin Emperor Shi Huangdi), a period of great power ensues when the territorially extended country is unified, prosperous and at peace; then, following a long decline, total collapse occurs resulting in the breakup of the central state, territorial losses and the rise of regional 'warlords'. Five completed (and one incomplete) dynastic cycles can be identified: (i) Chin/Han (221 BC to AD 220), Three Kingdoms/16 Kingdoms, etc.; (ii) Sui/T'ang (589–907), Ten Kingdoms/Five Dynasties; (iii) Sung/Yuan (979–1368); (iv) Ming (1368–1644); (v) Qing (1644–1911), Republic/civil war; and finally (vi) the People's Republic of China (PRC, 1949–today).

The migrations that accompany this cyclical process are very significant: first, the period of great power is marked by the colonization of new territories and the expansion of ethnic Chinese populations into regions previously inhabited by other groups; then, to maintain control, bureaucrats (not allowed to serve in their province of birth by the 'law of avoidance') are circulated around the territories to administer law and order and to collect tax revenues; later, with the collapse of central authority, comes war, insecurity and poverty leading to the large-scale displacement of populations. The collapse of central authority also leads to incursions from the north, which in turn trigger southward migrations of Chinese towards the Sichuan basin and the regions located to the south of the Yangtze.

Soon after the collapse of the Han dynasty, when Sinicized 'barbarian' invaders controlled much of northern China, elite groups began to turn to Buddhism, seeing it as superior to Taoism and Confucianism, and yet capable of coexistence with both of them. This led to the 'first great student migration of East Asian history', as many scholars travelled to India to collect, study and translate Buddhist teachings at their source.

Through southern conquest, the Chinese empire was reunited under the short-lived Sui dynasty in 589, but it was the succeeding T'ang dynasty (618–907) that came to represent the second golden age for China (the Qin/Han period being the first) – a period in which trade flourished and cities grew (especially so the capital, Chang'an, and port cities such as Guangzhou). The territorial reach of the T'ang dynasty was vast: it included virtually all of the land that is covered by the present country (excluding Tibet), along with much of Central Asia and (as with the Han before them) northern Vietnam. Having helped it to unite the Korean peninsula, the kingdom of Silla became a loyal vassal state. Other states beyond the borders of the empire, such as Japan, accepted a vague Chinese suzerainty at this time. So, from an East Asian perspective, the T'ang ruled the world – a (western) world with which the T'ang rulers and populations were surprisingly connected (for example, via the Silk Road). Central authority in the T'ang world was maintained in a number of ways: by curbing the wealth of the competing centres of power, the large landowners and the rich monasteries; through the 'equal field' landowning system (land owned by the government and allocated to farmers on the basis of ability to use, leading to widespread entitlement); by instituting efficient administrative and tax-collecting systems (with a bureaucracy recruited by examinations on the basis of merit, not connections); by releasing productive potential through major construction projects such as the First Grand Canal linking the Yellow and Yangtze River basins (the latter being now predominant in agricultural production); and by reinforcing the defences (including the Great Wall) against incursion from the northwest. Once again, soldier-farmers were sent to settle lands that protected the northern borders.

During the T'ang dynasty and, especially so, the succeeding Song dynasty (960–1276), further southward migrations occurred (including migrations into the southeastern coastal regions and northern Vietnam). Some of these were provoked by the establishment and expansion of kingdoms to the north (Po-hai, Khitan, and Jurchen) – regions that are now in northeast China, North Korea and the Russian Far East. So strong, in fact, were these northern kingdoms that the Song dynasty was forced to move south, abandoning its northern territories (capital at Kaifeng) to the Jin dynasty, and ruling the remaining 60% of the population from a new capital at Hangzhou (south of the Yangtze). Despite its military weaknesses, the Song dynasty was a period of great cultural, economic and technological development resulting in urban expansion and population growth (in the south, not in the north). However, as the Song regime broke down in the 13th century, it opened the door for the largest incursion of all, this time from the northwest – the Mongol invasion of China. The subsequent Mongol (Yuan) dynasty based in Dadu (Beijing) had major migration effects: it brought Muslim populations to China, redistributed Han populations within China (for example, refugees fleeing south), and put further pressure on non-Han populations living in southern China, which in turn contributed to the Thai migrations into Southeast Asia discussed above.

Han Chinese dominance returned in the 14th century with the establishment of the Ming dynasty (1368–1644). Soon afterwards, China entered a period lasting over 400 years (so covering most of the subsequent Qing dynasty (1644–1911) as well) in which wealth from trade was looked down upon and both immigration and emigration were discouraged. In the early years of the

Ming dynasty, however, engagement with the outside world, and especially with Southeast Asia (including further migration into Vietnam), was strong; this was the time of the famous Zheng He expeditions, when Ming Chinese ships travelled the world's oceans. Then in 1435, the Ming government largely closed the country's borders. This had the effect of cutting off many Chinese living in Southeast Asia, and, reinforced by early Qing policy to move populations inland, also resulted in declining populations in many of the formerly bustling coastal regions of eastern and southeastern China (an outcome that resulted also from the predations of the *wakou* – 'Japanese pirates' – and the general maritime lawlessness of east and northeast Asian seas in the 16th and early 17th centuries). Chinese peoples now lived in a powerful, yet largely inward-looking, agrarian society – mostly prosperous and largely politically stable, primarily sedentary and only locally mobile, yet witnessing significant internal population redistribution as further Han colonization of non-Han southern China and other related migration flows proceeded.

What kinds of internal migration occurred during the Ming period? Much of it was the local and regional movement of poor people going about their normal business – artisans, pedlars, servants, porters, and construction workers (for example, those employed to build defensive walls and irrigation canals). It also included, of course, the planned and enforced circulation of bureaucrats, but also resettlement of lands devastated by conflict (for example, Anhui), further military (soldier-settler) colonization of the northern and southwestern borders, and the relocation of artisans, peasants and gentry consequent upon the decision to move the capital from Nanjing to Beijing in 1421. Finally, unplanned forced migrations arising from both natural and human causes were not unusual – drought, flood, and famine in the former case, regional uprisings and brigandage in the latter.

Following internal dissention (such as factional in-fighting at court), regional peasant revolts, and costly military interventions (such as fighting to oust the Japanese from Korea), the weakened Ming dynasty was overthrown in 1644 by yet another northern invasion accompanied by mass population displacement – this time by the Jurchens/Manchus. The early Manchu emperors of the Qing dynasty (1644–1911), notably Kangxi and Qianlong, were very competent administrators, and the Chinese empire now expanded westward to incorporate the new territories (Xinjiang) of central Asia and northwards into Inner Mongolia and Manchuria. It also presided over the repopulating of Sichuan, consolidated the southern (Yunnan) frontier, and eventually, after defeating in 1683 the Ming loyalists (who, under Zheng Chenggong (Koxinga) had ousted the Dutch), came to dominate the 'uncooked' natives of the Taiwan frontier. It is, however, of the utmost significance that just as the Qing dynasty reached the pinnacle of its power in East Asia in the mid-18th century, so also was emerging the major challenge to that power – the military and commercial might of the Western European colonial empires (Hong Kong, for example, was handed over to Britain in 1842 following the defeat of China in the First Opium War), only to be followed in the late 19th century by the rise of the USA and Japan.

These threats from outside (which were manifested in part by the appearance of significant foreign enclave populations of businessmen, engineers and missionaries in Chinese cities such as Shanghai and Harbin) were bad enough, but much of the long decline of the Qing dynasty was self-inflicted. The central authority became increasingly unsuccessful in controlling its subjects, and a series of violent uprisings – the White Lotus rebellion, the Taiping rebellion, and the Panthay revolt – led to horrific losses of life and to massive displacement of populations. Forced to 'open up' and to concede to the (often outrageous) commercial and territorial demands of Western nations, then defeated in war by Japan, the Qing dynasty came to an ignominious end in 1911.

In a way, however, 1911 represented only the end of a dynasty, not the end of a dynastic cycle. It took another 38 years for an all-(mainland) China stable government to be established. In the meantime, this vast country was racked by conflicts associated with warlord rivalry, revolutionary beginnings (Sun Yat-Sen), the setting up of a republican nationalist government (Kuomintang (KMT)/Chiang Kai-Shek), and the rise of the Chinese Communist Party (Mao Zedong), all of which led to further localized conflict and population displacement. It is not surprising, therefore, that China became a major source country of international migration during the final century of the Qing dynasty and the first half of the 20th century. We have seen that much of this emigration (which was predominantly male), went to Southeast Asia, but the Chinese diaspora touched all the continents of the world (including Latin America, Russia, and even New Zealand), and with the migrants went Chinese languages (especially Cantonese, Hokkien and Hakka) and Chinese social practices (such as the hometown and lineage associations in the early Chinese communities in San Francisco). These overseas Chinese not only participated in economic and political changes in China, but also contributed to key political events in their countries of destination. During the same period China became the refuge for a very much smaller population of escapees from conflicts elsewhere – 'white' Russians after the October Revolution in 1917, and Jewish refugees during World War II.

Alongside this, there was a change in the 'deep structures' of Chinese society, notably the further breakdown of semi-feudal institutions and relationships (the 'tributary mode of production'), and their replacement, accompanied by rapid population growth, by the structures and processes, technologies and values of modern industrial capitalism. This transformation of Chinese society was accompanied by a major redistribution of the population as cities grew at the expense of their rural hinterlands, and as new industrial regions (for example, the cotton textile region around Shanghai/Jiangsu) grew at the expense of backward pre-industrial ones.

These migrations transformed the cities. Some migrants (especially those with location-specific skills and aspirations) were very successful, many others were moderately successful, but others fell on hard times. In the late Qing period, for example, a new working-class ethnic identity emerged as poor migrants from northern Jiangsu (the Subei) came to do the dirtiest, lowest-paid and least-desirable jobs in Shanghai City. To these mostly unrestricted internal migration flows should be added: (i) those brought about by state activity – the forced or subsidised westward frontier migrations of military personnel, farmers and prisoners, associated with the domination and development of Xinjiang, the closing off of Manchuria under the early Qing, and, using the so-called law of avoidance, the forced inter-provincial mobility of state officials (such as magistrates); and (ii) those brought about by the will to survive in an era of poverty, famine and conflict – notably the mass seasonal ('swallow') and permanent migrations (for example, of fur trappers, miners, loggers, and cereal and poppy farmers – plus refugee migrations) to Manchuria from the south, especially from Shandong and Hebei Provinces. Between 1890 and 1942, despite high levels of return migration within a few years, there was a net flow of over 8 million migrants ('reluctant pioneers') into Manchuria. I think many readers would join me in being astonished to learn that this figure is roughly comparable with the far better-known net flow of migrants to the western USA over the same period.

2.3 Northeast Asia

Despite its late start in economic and social development compared with northern China, the history of migration in northeast Asia is just as intriguing. This is partly because of its unique features but perhaps also because it contains some common elements with those of its southern neighbour. Uniquely, for example, a significant part of northeast Asia (i.e. Japan) did not become part of the Mongol empire, but later, in parallel with the partial seclusion of the late Ming and early Qing in China, yet taking it to a much higher level, the Tokugawa Shogunate in Japan and the Yi/Joseon Kingdom in Korea cut themselves off to an extraordinary extent from the outside world.

During most of the first millennium AD, state formation and complex urban societies in northeast Asia were largely confined to the Korean peninsula (only towards the end of that period did such societies emerge in Japan); the rest of northeast Asia was sparsely inhabited by hunter-gatherers and sedentary agriculturalists. Both Korean and Japanese early states were, however, greatly influenced by China (indeed, for about three centuries, part of northern Korea formed the Chinese 'colony' of Lo-lang). They adopted and adapted Chinese forms of art and architecture, literature and religion, administration and technology. Especially during the T'ang dynasty, Korean and Japanese kingdoms were minor, subservient players in the China-centred world. Nor should Korea and Japan be seen as single territorial entities at this time. Korea was divided into three warring kingdoms (plus, for a time, Kaya in the south): Paekche in the southwest, Silla in the southeast, and Koguryo in the north. Only after the 7th century did the peninsula become united, first under Greater Silla and then under the caste-system Buddhist state of Koryo (Korea), based at Kaesong. Similarly, Japan's Yamato kingdom, followed by the Nara and Heian periods, prosperous and cultured as they were, only covered the southern two-thirds of present-day Japan.

Japan's population is thought to be largely composed of the descendants of immigrants from the Asiatic continent, notably the 'Yayoi wave' (400 BC to AD 250), and the three waves referred to as the *kikajin* immigration arriving from Korea between the 4th and 7th centuries. This migration, entering Japan through the gateway island of Kyushu, assisted the process by which many crafts, agricultural practices, Buddhism, Confucianism and Chinese writing came to Japan. It was not a mass migration of hundreds of thousands of people; rather, it was a quiet expansion of settlement into the fertile lowlands of southern Japan.

Korea had already been affected through periodic invasions by the increasing power of the northern peoples, the Khitans and the Jurchens, before the Jin dynasty (1126–1234) came to rule northern China, to which Koryo became a tributary state. However, the real challenge came with the Mongols, who dominated Koryo from the early 13th century until the demise of the dynasty in 1392. Early on they repeatedly ravaged the land, carrying off more than 200,000 captives in 1254 alone. Later they dominated the Koryo court partially through the marriage of Mongol princesses to Koryo kings. Japan, however, was spared both the ravages and the domination. Saved by the *kamikaze* (wind of the gods), the huge Mongol navy failed in 1274 and 1281 to invade Japan, and the country remained free from foreign invasion, though frequently damaged by internal conflict, until the end of World War II.

With the establishment of the Yi dynasty (1392–1910), Korea entered an astonishingly long period of semi-feudal stability (but with continuous factional in-fighting among the privileged *yangban* upper class). It became almost more of a Confucian society than that of the Ming dynasty in China, on which it was largely modelled. Migrations in and out were banned, and internal migration was reduced by the dominance of agrarian relations, the almost total absence of social mobility (despite civil service exams), and the low status of urban trade and manufacturing. There were some trading relations with Japan, but the southern ports were often subject to pirate raids. So weak politically and militarily was the Yi dynasty that, even with Ming support, it failed to repulse the massive invasion of the Japanese under Hideyoshi in 1592. Soon afterwards, the challenge came instead from the northwest as the Manchus came to power first in northern China (invading Korea in 1627), and then in the whole of China.

After the high point of Japanese civilization in the Heian period (9th to 12th centuries; capital Kyoto), the country had broken up into its constituent parts and a long period of 'warring states' (*sengoku*) ensued. It was only at the end of the 16th century that the military successes of Hideyoshi and Nobunaga united the country again. During these years of conflict many displacements of population occurred as regional lords battled it out for ascendancy. Then something very interesting happened. About 200 years after the Yi dynasty began its national seclusion, Japan, under the new Tokugawa Shogunate (1603–1867; capital Edo/Tokyo), perhaps in part reacting against the radical threat to

Japanese tradition represented by the arrival of the Jesuits in the mid-16th century, decided to do exactly the same. For over 200 years (1639–1854), Japan was virtually a fortress, with no immigration or emigration. During this time it experienced very little contact at all with the outside world, except that which resulted from Dutch and Chinese trade links through the port of Nagasaki (plus some relations with Korea through Tsushima and Pusan). Many Japanese authors have seen this 'national seclusion' (*sakoku*) as one element in the creation of a Japanese national character that is uniquely distinct and uniquely uniform (racially pure). The literature that they have produced is called '*nihonjinron*' (literally 'discussion of the Japanese'), and it is sharply criticized in some quarters for its links with Japanese nationalism, and with what some claim to be a general hostility towards foreigners (xenophobia).

Was this lack of migration internationally matched in Japan by low migration rates internally? Yes, in part it was. A semi-feudal social structure characterized by a caste-like hierarchy of six social classes – lords (*daimyou*), warriors (*samurai*), peasants, artisans, merchants, and social outcasts – was not conducive to either social or geographical mobility (apart, that is, from the urbanization, such as the growth of castle towns (*jokamachi*), that was associated with the exercise of political authority or commercial advantage). However, that is not the whole story. Many peasants (especially in northern Japan where the winters were long) worked the land during the growing season but took jobs in the city at other times. Many others (especially craftsmen, such as thatchers and tradesmen) were circular migrants travelling far and wide to find work. Furthermore, towards the end of the Tokugawa/Edo period, Japan had its own nascent capitalist industrialization (for example, silk and cotton textiles) and its own internal fishing and farming frontier – the northern island of Hokkaido, which attracted many settlers from the main island, Honshu, in the late 19th century.

Perhaps the most distinctive form of internal migration during the Tokugawa Shogunate, however, was the 'alternate residence' system (*sankin koutai*). This system forced the 260 regional lords (*daimyou*) to set up residence (with their families and retainers) in the capital city Edo (Tokyo), where they were under the surveillance of (some would say the hostages of) the Shogun. Every second year the lords would process from their home territories to the capital and then back again the following year, leaving much of what mattered to them materially and emotionally in the hands of the Shogun. This 'loyalty card' system led, not surprisingly, to the concentration of great wealth and social prestige in the city of Edo – so much so that for a time it became the largest city in the world.

During the later Yi and Tokugawa periods in Korea and Japan, a new player enters the story of migration in northeast Asia: Russia. From the mid-17th century onwards the Russian state saw Siberia and the Russian Far East as its resource frontier – as a land to be settled and exploited. At first, the commercial interest was in furs, but soon this was extended to minerals, timber, farming and fishing. As with the western frontier in China, the Russian Far East was also to be used for exile and imprisonment. Having obtained the transfer to the

Russian empire of the area north of the Amur River from a weakened China in 1858, the 'Great Siberian migration' began. This brought hundreds of thousands of land-hungry farmers, adventurers and idealists to the sparsely populated eastern half of Russia. Key to the region's development was overcoming the vast distances within Siberia and the Russian Far East and, above all, ensuring rapid and reliable connection to European Russia. Hence the importance, both practically and psychologically, of the project to build the Trans-Siberian railway. Once this had been completed in 1903 and the branch line across Manchuria (through Harbin) to Vladivostok as well, Russia was a serious contender for the territories being shed by the dying Qing dynasty.

In the meantime Japan had 'opened up' to the West following the Meiji Restoration in 1868. It rejected its semi-feudal past, and energetically embraced modern industrial technology, Western institutions, and a fully capitalist economy. Small but very influential groups of Western experts were brought to Japan to assist these changes. Its surprise defeat of Russia in the Russo–Japanese War of 1904–05 ensured that it would be Japan, not Russia, that would step into the power vacuum in northeast China. The Japanese empire was now expanding fast. It had taken over the Ryukyu Kingdom in 1879, annexed Taiwan in 1895, seized Karafuto in 1905, and incorporated Korea by 1910. A good example of the migrations associated with these events is provided by the emigration of farmers and traders from the poorest areas of Yamaguchi Prefecture to Korea in the period 1890–1920. After it took over Manchuria (Manchukuo) in the early 1930s, it embarked on an ambitious programme of settlement of Japanese nationals (farmers, entrepreneurs, engineers, administrators, etc.) to secure its continental possessions. Preceded and accompanied by Korean settlers (who went not only to China but also to the Soviet Far East, from where many were later forcibly relocated to Central Asia), 270,000 young patriotic Japanese men and women, largely unprepared for the social and physical hardships they were to face, migrated into Manchuria. Smaller numbers settled in Taiwan and in Karafuto (the southern half of Sakhalin).

Yet this was not the only emigration from Japan, or for that matter from Korea. The rapid economic development that resulted from the transformation of Japan into a modern industrial nation left many behind. Much of the poverty was rural and was especially serious in those rural districts located furthest away from the busy industrial and commercial Kanto (Tokyo-Yokohama) and Kansai (Osaka-Kyoto-Kobe) regions. Young women from Kyushu, for example, were sold into prostitution in Shanghai, Hong Kong, Singapore and elsewhere (for example, Sandakan in Sabah), and young men from Okinawa went to the Davao region of the Philippines to work in the abaca (hemp) industry. By far the largest flows, however, were to the new world. Following on from the Chinese miners and railway builders before them, workers and their families from Japan, especially from the southwest prefectures of the mainland and from Okinawa, sojourned and emigrated to North and South America. The first destinations (1868–) were Hawai'i and the North American mainland, but after a time these were reduced, and then were blocked in the USA in 1924.

Thereafter Brazil, Peru, Mexico, Bolivia, Dominican Republic and Paraguay became the main destinations (1899–1956). Much of this migration was sponsored and supported by the government in an effort to maintain social order and to combat 'overpopulation'. Migration to Brazil, begun in 1908, was especially important. Recruited mostly as coffee plantation workers in the early years of the 20th century, many Japanese and their descendants achieved upward social mobility into business ownership and the professions, so that they now represent a relatively prosperous ethnic minority within Brazilian society.

Its rapid economic development between 1868 and 1945 also transformed Japan's internal demographic landscape. Massive flows of migrants from rural areas to the burgeoning cities accompanied the almost violent forging of a modern industrial society out of an agrarian semi-feudal one. The outcome was an axis of urban development stretching from the Kanto region around Tokyo west-southwest through Nagoya, to the Kansai region centred on Osaka and Kobe, then continuing along the north shore of the Inland Sea to northern Kyushu. So rapid was this development that migrants from further afield, notably Korea and China, were recruited to fill the labour shortages in coal mining, dock labour, factory work and construction. This immigration of manual workers began before 1910, built up during the boom created by World War I, was increased by voluntary migration in the 1920s and 1930s, before becoming a large state-directed forced migration programme in World War II. Thus came into being a 2 million-strong community of *Zainichi* (living in Japan) Koreans. They were concentrated in the major industrial areas (notably in the Kansai region around Osaka), and in Tokyo where prejudice against them was particularly severe.

2.4 Epilogue: World War II

The rise of Japan in the late 19th and early 20th centuries was quickly translated into military might. Following military successes against China (1895) and Russia (1905), and the full annexation of Korea (1910) and Manchuria (1932), Japan had invaded and occupied almost all of East and Southeast Asia, and the whole of the western Pacific by 1942. The astounding ferocity of this onslaught, especially in China, led to major losses of life and to massive displacements of population. How could people protect themselves and their families from air raids, 'scorched earth' destruction or fierce punishment for resistance, except by fleeing? In addition, workers were commandeered and relocated all over East Asia to support the Japanese war effort. Neither the nationalists (KMT) or the communists in China, nor the European colonial powers in Southeast Asia could hold out against Japan's armed forces (witness the fall of Nanjing and the ignominious surrender of the British in Singapore). However, the USA (following the attack on Pearl Harbor and having interned its Japanese-American population) could, and did resist, and when in the end Japan was itself about to be invaded, and its city populations became the victims of horrific thermo-nuclear attack in 1945, it surrendered.

The ending of the Japanese imperial gamble had a significant migration effect. About 6 million Japanese nationals, members of the armed forces and civilians, returned to Japan in the months following the end of the war, and in the five years before the outbreak of the Korean War, 1.5 million Koreans returned to their home country from Japan. Many Koreans, however, remained stranded in China and the Soviet Union.

2.5 Conclusion: the implications of this history for an understanding of migrations in East Asia today

One can usefully speculate on the multiple influences of this history on the nature and distinctiveness of migration regimes in East Asia today. First, though, I should introduce a word of caution. I am not claiming that these historical legacies produce unique outcomes in our region, but rather that certain migration characteristics, found also in other parts of the world, take on a particular significance in East Asia, or connect together in particular ways in East Asia, and that they do so partly as a result of the 'burden' of this history.

1   Labour migration – working-class migrations for work. There are, it seems to me, three main continuities between the past and the present when it comes to the migration of the relatively poor and powerless. First, the sojourner tradition of temporary migration lives on in many East Asian migration flows today. So strong is the expectation of the early return of working-class migrants that national elites sometimes seem surprised when they discover that those who have stayed, albeit still often a minority, have transformed the ethnic compositions of the towns and neighbourhoods in which they have settled. This becomes most obvious when, typically quite suddenly, a large minority of the primary school children have a 'mother tongue' (or dialect) that is different from that of the host society. Second, and despite the above, the sojourners were in the past largely lone (often married) males. Today the migration is still very often of people migrating alone (that is, without family members), but increasingly they are women, including married women. So family separation, sometimes accompanied by relationship stress or breakdown, continues to be a feature of East Asian migrations. Finally, there is an appalling legacy of treating migrant workers badly. Today, of course, workers are not usually captured and carried off to work in another country (except, I suppose, the curious case of the 16 Japanese nationals captured and taken to North Korea), but modern forms of indenture (for example, being tied to a specific employer), and of debt bondage (having to pay off the debt to the agent sponsoring the migration) mean that exploitation of migrant workers continues both inside the region and in destination areas such as the Middle East. All too often migrant workers suffer the non- or late payment of wages, physical and verbal abuse in the workplace, poor-quality accommodation, and routine negative discrimination in comparison with host-country workers on

matters such as working conditions, security of employment, and levels of pay.

2   Labour migration – migrations of the highly educated and highly skilled. Two continuities seem to stand out: the first is the enduring attraction of the largest East Asian cities as destinations for the ambitious, the rich and the powerful. Examples of this for internal migrations are Jakarta, Manila and Shanghai; examples for international migrations are Tokyo and Singapore. However, another legacy of the past is to be found in the nature of contemporary migrations to East Asia's great cities. To generalize, the great northern capitals, Beijing, Seoul, and Tokyo, continue to attract those who aspire to political advancement or bureaucratic power, while the great southern cities, Singapore, Shanghai, Bangkok and Hong Kong, continue to attract those who aspire to power based on merchant success or money-handling wealth.

3   Trafficking – migration as a money-making business. Making money out of moving people has a long history in East Asia (see earlier references in this chapter to labour captivity through banditry on land and through piracy at sea). Contemporary forms of lawlessness relating to the smuggling and trafficking of men, women and children inherited from the past include the operations of criminal gangs and organizations such as the Snakeheads in China and the Yakuza in Japan. Two continuities seem to be especially significant: first, the trafficking and smuggling of young men for hard manual labour into countries, both inside and outside East Asia, where severe shortages of labour threaten profits in industry and agriculture; and second, the trafficking and smuggling of women for domestic service and sex work. In these cases, deep-rooted values of duty to one's family and of masculinity tend to support both historical and contemporary forms of migrant labour exploitation.

4   Displacements – migrations that are due to a localized threat to one's personal security (for example, arising from war or 'natural' disaster). Past displacements of population due to conflicts and disasters account, to a significant degree, for the immensely complex cultural geographies of many East Asian countries (notably those in Southeast Asia, but also in southern and western China). Those geographies, in turn, through the unresolved conflicts with which they are associated, impact on recent and contemporary migration flows; this is especially so in Indonesia (for example, Muslim vs Christian conflicts in Maluku and Sulawesi), in Myanmar (Buddhist vs Muslim conflicts in Rakhine), and in the Philippines (Christian vs Muslim conflicts in Mindanao).

5   Place preference migrations. The reputations of places, for example, as places of safety in a dangerous world, or conversely as places of pleasure and adventure, have always influenced migration decisions, but with economic development and the release of many people from the choice-restricting necessities of poverty, one would expect that migrants' evaluations of alternative destinations would become more significant. This is

where the choices made by migrants in the past can have a powerful impact on the choices made by migrants now (note, for example, the enduring attraction of multi-ethnic 'gateway' cities such as Shanghai).

6   Life course migrations – students. Despite changes in the space-economies of countries and in global political geography, the continuities in student migration flows are quite striking. While over many centuries it was the civil service exam that took the brightest and the best from all over China to Beijing, now it is those who succeed in the fiercely contested entrance exams to Beijing's top universities (especially Beijing and Tsinghua) who take the same journey. Also, whereas before it was the colonial subjects and political exiles who studied and plotted in the capital cities of Western Europe and the USA, now it is graduate students from all over East Asia who flock to the prestigious and not-so-prestigious universities in these countries (along with those in Australia, Canada and New Zealand) to get their English-language postgraduate qualifications. Would it be too sacrilegious to suggest that there might be some continuity between the life-changing migrations of those who, on journeys of self-discovery, come from Western countries to East Asia (many of them men), plus those who leave East Asia to live in the West (many of them women), and those who in the past sought enlightenment through extended periods of study and prayer at distant holy sites in India, Tibet and eastern China?

7   Life course migrations – marriages, etc. Historically, we have seen that marriage migrations often accompanied the cementing of relations between powerful ruling families; it was one of the strategies employed to protect wealth and power. This instrumental character of much marriage migration continues today. It is often brought about by the need for individuals to secure a future for themselves, for their children, for their family back in the region or country of origin, and is equally instrumental for the family, farm or small business in the country or region of destination. These recent marriage migrations have added a new layer of ethnolinguistic diversity to those inherited from the past (such as those resulting from the migrations of Chinese and Indians to the countries of Southeast Asia). The outcome may not yet be equivalent to the 'superdiversity' of many European, North American and Australasian countries, but the trend is certainly in that direction.

8   State-sponsored/restrained migration. The origins in East Asia of an intervention by the state to restrict the migration of their subjects are complex and ancient. They are to be found, for example, in the need to retain labour in sparsely inhabited Southeast Asia, and in the need to command the farming surpluses in the Confucian tribute economies of China and Northeast Asia. The legacies of such controls can be recognized in the constraints on migration today, notably in the household registration systems of the PRC and Vietnam, and in the ambivalent attitudes in some countries (outright hostility in the case of North Korea) towards those who choose to leave their home country to pursue their lives and livelihoods

elsewhere. Yet, at the same time, East Asia is witnessing some of the world's most pro-migration and pro-displacement interventions. Examples are the transmigration programme in Indonesia, the very proactive sponsoring of emigration in the Philippines, and the planned displacements of populations in the PRC. Capitalist market-based economies they may be, but most East Asian states are 'bureaucratically authoritarian' in attitude and 'managerial' in practice when it comes to the internal and international migrations of their populations. Such, arguably, is in large part the burden of history.

Selected references

2.0 General

Amrith, A.A., 2011, *Migration and Diaspora in Modern Asia*. Cambridge: Cambridge University Press.

Barnes, G.L., 1993, *China, Korea and Japan: The Rise of Civilization in East Asia*. London: Thames and Barnes.

Blench, R., Sagart, L. and Sanchez-Mazas, A., 2004, *The Peopling of East Asia: Putting Together Archaeology, Linguistics and Genetics*. London: RoutledgeCurzon.

Fairbank, J.K., Reischauer, E.O. and Craig, A.M., 1973, *East Asia: Tradition and Transformation*. Boston, MA: Houghton Mifflin.

Hoerder, D., 2002, *Cultures in Contact: World Migrations in the Second Millennium*. Durham, NC: Duke University Press.

Liu, T., Lee, J., Reher, D.S., Saito, S. and Feng, W. (eds), 2001, *Asian Population History*. London: Oxford University Press.

Sanchez-Mazas, A., Blench, R., Ross, M.D., Peiros, I. and Lin, M. (eds), 2007, *Past Human Migrations in East Asia: Matching Archaeology, Linguistics and Genetics*. London: Routledge.

Scarre, C. (ed.), 2005, *The Human Past: World Prehistory and the Development of Human Societies*. London: Thames & Hudson.

2.1 Southeast Asia

Barrett, T.C., 2012, *The Chinese Diaspora in South-East Asia: The Overseas Chinese in IndoChina*. London: I.B. Taurus.

Coedes, G., 1968, *The Indianized States of Southeast Asia*. Honolulu: University of Hawai'i Press.

Cohen, R. (ed.), *The Cambridge Survey of World Migration*. Cambridge: Cambridge University Press.

Doeppers, D.F. and Xenos, P. (eds), 1998, *Population and History: The Demographic Origins of the Modern Philippines*. Madison: University of Wisconsin, Centre for Southeast Asian Studies.

Gooszen, A.J., 1999, *A Demographic History of the Indonesian Archipelago 1880–1942*. Leiden: KITLV Press.

Heidhues, M.F.S., 2000, *Southeast Asia: A Concise History*. London: Thames & Hudson.

Oostindie, G. (ed.), *Dutch Colonialism, Migration and Cultural Heritage*. Honolulu: University of Hawai'i Press/KITLV Press.

Reid, A. (ed.), 1996, *Sojourners and Settlers: Histories of Southeast Asia and the Chinese*. St Leonards, NSW: Allen and Unwin.

Reid, A., 2000, *Charting the Shape of Early Modern Southeast Asia*. Singapore: Institute of South East Asian Studies.

Ricklefs, M.C., Lockhart, B., Lau, A., Reyes, P. and Aung-Thwin, M., 2010, *A New History of Southeast Asia*. London: Palgrave Macmillan.

Sandhu, K.S. and Mani, A. (eds), 1993, *Indian Communities in Southeast Asia*. Singapore: Institute of South East Asian Studies.

Scott, J.C., 2009, *The Art of Not Being Governed: An Anarchist History of Upland Southeast Asia*. New Haven, CT: Yale University Press.

Tarling, N. (ed.), 1992, *The Cambridge History of Southeast Asia: Vol. 1 From Early Times to c. 1800*. Cambridge: Cambridge University Press.

Ward, K., 2009, *Networks of Empire: Forced Migration in the Dutch East India Company*. Cambridge: Cambridge University Press.

Warren, J.F., 1993, *Ah Ku and Karayuki-san: Prostitution in Singapore 1870–1940*. London: Oxford University Press.

Warren, J.F., 2008, *The Sulu Zone, 1768–1898: The Dynamics of External Trade, Slavery, and Ethnicity in the Transformation of a Southeast Asian Maritime State*. Singapore: National University of Singapore Press/University of Hawai'i Press.

Wolters, O.W., 1999, *History, Culture, and Region in Southeast Asian Perspectives*. Ithaca, NY: Cornell University Press/Institute of South East Asian Studies.

Yamazaki, T., 1999 (1975), *Sandakan Brothel No. 8: An Episode in the History of Lower-Class Japanese Women*. New York: M.E. Sharpe.

Yen, C.-H., 2012, *The Chinese in Southeast Asia and Beyond*. Singapore: World Scientific.

Zelinsky, W., 1950, The Indochinese peninsula: a demographic anomaly, *Far Eastern Quarterly* 9: 115–145.

2.2 'China'

Andrade, T., 2008, *How Taiwan Became Chinese: Dutch, Spanish, and Han Colonization in the Seventeenth Century*. New York: Columbia University Press.

Benton, G., 2007, *Chinese Migrants and Internationalism*. London: Routledge.

Bickers, R. and Henriot, C. (eds), 2000, *New Frontiers: Imperialism's New Communities in East Asia 1842–1953*. London: Macmillan.

Crossley, P.K., 2002, *The Manchus*. Hoboken, NJ: Wiley-Blackwell.

Crossley, P.K., Siu, H.F. and Sutton, D.S. (eds), 2006, *Empire at the Margins: Culture, Ethnicity, and Frontier in Early Modern China*. Berkeley: University of California Press.

Ebrey, P.B., 1996, *Cambridge Illustrated History of China*. Cambridge: Cambridge University Press.

Fei, H.-T. and Chang, C.-I., 1945, *Earthbound China (Xiangtu Zhongguo): A Study of Rural Economy in Yunnan*. Chicago, IL: University of Chicago Press.

Gao, B., 2012, *Shanghai Sanctuary: Chinese and Japanese Policy towards European Jewish Refugees during World War II*. London: Oxford University Press.

Ge, J., Cao, S. and Wu, S., 1997, *Zhongguo yi min shi* (History of Migrants in China), 6 vols. Fuzhou: Fuzhou Renmin.

Giersch, C.P., 2006, *Asian Borderlands: The Transformation of Qing China's Yunnan Frontier*. Cambridge, MA: Harvard University Press.

Gottschang, T.R. and Lary, D., 2000, *Swallows and Settlers: The Great Migration from North China to Manchuria*. Ann Arbor: University of Michigan Press.

Hershatter, G., Honig, E., Lipman, J.N. and Stross, R. (eds), 1996, *Remapping China: Fissures in Historical Terrain*. Stanford, CA: Stanford University Press.

Hsu, M.Y-Y., 2001, *Dreaming of Gold, Dreaming of Home: Transnationalism and Migration between the US and South China 1882–1943*. Stanford, CA: Stanford University Press.

Ip, M. (ed.), 2003, *Unfolding History, Evolving Identity: The Chinese in New Zealand*. Auckland: Auckland University Press.

Lary, D., 2012, *Chinese Migrations: The Movement of People, Goods and Ideas over Four Millennia*. Lanham, MD: Rowman & Littlefield.

Lattimore, O., 1932, Chinese colonization in Manchuria, *Geographical Review* 22(2): 177–195.

Lee, J., 1978, Migration and expansion in Chinese history, in McNeill, W.H. and Adams, R.S. (eds), *Human Migration: Patterns and Policies*. Stanford, CA: Stanford University Press, 20–40.

Leong, S.-T., 1997, *Migration and Ethnicity in Chinese History: Hakkas, Pengmin and their Neighbors*. Stanford, CA: Stanford University Press.

Look Lai, W. and Tan, C.-B. (eds), 2010, *The Chinese in Latin America and the Caribbean*. Leiden: Brill.

Millward, J.A., 2007, *Eurasian Crossroads: A History of Xinjiang*. London: Hurst.

Ong, A. and Nonini, D. (eds), 1997, *Ungrounded Empires: The Cultural Politics of Modern Chinese Transnationalism*. New York: Routledge.

Perdue, P.C., 2005, *China Marches West: The Qing Conquest of Central Eurasia*. Cambridge, MA: Harvard University Press.

Reardon-Anderson, J., 2005, *Reluctant Pioneers: China's Expansion Northward 1644–1937*. Stanford, CA: Stanford University Press.

Reid, A. (ed.), 2008, *The Chinese Diaspora in the Pacific*. Aldershot: Ashgate.

Rowe, W.T., 1984, *Hankow*, 2 vols. Stanford, CA: Stanford University Press.

Skinner, G.W., 1976, Mobility strategies in Late Imperial China: a regional systems analysis, in Smith, C.A. (ed.), *Regional Analysis: Vol. 1, Economic Systems*. New York: Academic Press, 327–364.

Tan, C.-B. (ed.), 2013, *Routledge Handbook of the Chinese Diaspora*. London: Routledge.

Wakeman, F. and Yeh, W.-H. (eds), 1992, *Shanghai Sojourners*. Berkeley: University of California Institute of East Asian Studies.

Wiens, H.J., 1967 (1952), *The Han Chinese Expansion in South China*. Boulder, CO: Westview.

Wilkinson, E.P., 2000, *Chinese History: A Manual*, revised and enlarged edn. Cambridge, MA: Harvard University Press.

Yang, B., 2009, *Between Winds and Clouds: The Making of Yunnan (Second Century BCE – Twentieth Century BCE)*. New York: Columbia University Press.

2.3 Northeast Asia

Adachi, N. (ed.), 2006, *Japanese Diasporas: Unsung Pasts, Conflicting Presents, and Uncertain Futures*. London: Routledge.

Befu, H., 1993, Nationalism and *nihonjinron*, in Befu, H. (ed.), *Cultural Nationalism in East Asia*. Berkeley: University of California, Institute of East Asian Studies, 107–138.

Bergsten, C.F. and Choi, I. (eds), 2003, *The Korean Diaspora in the World Economy*. Washington, DC: Institute for International Economics.

Bowring, R. and Kornicki, P. (eds), 1993, *The Cambridge Encyclopedia of Japan*. Cambridge: Cambridge University Press, 40–111.

Buzo, A., 2002, *The Making of Modern Korea*. London: Routledge.

Cobbing, A., 2009, *Kyushu: Gateway to Japan. A Concise History*. Folkestone: Global Oriental.

Dale, P.N., 1986, *The Myth of Japanese Uniqueness*. London: Routledge.

Denoon, D., Hudson, M., McCormack, G. and Morris-Suzuki, T. (eds), 1996, *Multicultural Japan: Paleolithic to Postmodern*. Cambridge: Cambridge University Press.

Dussinberre, M., 2012, *Hard Times in the Hometown: A History of Community Survival in Modern Japan*. Honolulu: University of Hawai'i Press.

Hayami, A., 2001, *The Historical Demography of Pre-Modern Japan*. Tokyo: University of Tokyo Press.

Hirabayashi, L.R., Kikumura-Yano, A. and Hirabayashi, J.A. (eds), 2002, *New Worlds, New Lives: Globalization and People of Japanese Descent in the Americas and from Latin America in Japan*. Stanford, CA: Stanford University Press.

Hirobe, I., 2001, *Japanese Pride, American Prejudice: Modifying the Exclusion Clause of the 1924 Immigration Act*. Stanford, CA: Stanford University Press.

Howell, D.L., 1995, *Capitalism from Within: Economy, Society and the State in a Japanese Fishery*. Berkeley: University of California Press.

Hudson, M.J., 2006, Pots not people: ethnicity, culture and identity in postwar Japanese archaeology, *Critique of Anthropology* 26: 411–434.

Hunter, J., 2003, *Women and the Labour Market in Japan's Industrialising Economy: The Textile Industry before the Pacific War*. London: RoutledgeCurzon.

Itoh, M., 1998, *Globalization of Japan: Japanese Sakoku Mentality and US Efforts to Open Japan*. Basingstoke: Macmillan.

Kaneshiro, E.M., 1999, *'Our Home Will Be the Five Continents': Okinawan Migration to Hawai'i, California, and the Philippines, 1899–1941*. University of California Berkeley PhD thesis.

Kikumura-Yano, A. (ed.), 2002, *Encyclopedia of Japanese Descendants in the Americas*. Lanham, MD: Rowman & Littlefield.

Kitano, H. and Daniels, R., 1988, *Asian-Americans: Emerging Minorities*. New York: Prentice-Hall.

Kodansha, 1993, *Japan: An Illustrated Encyclopedia*, 2 vols. Tokyo: Kodansha.

Kratoska, P.H. (ed.), 2005, *Asian Labor in the Wartime Japanese Empire: Unknown Histories*. Armonk, NY: M.E. Sharpe.

Lesser, J. (ed.), 2003, *Searching for Home Abroad: Japanese Brazilians and Transnationalism*. Durham, NC: Duke University Press.

Lewis, R.A. and Rowland, R.H., 1979, *Population Redistribution in the USSR: Its Impact on Society, 1897–1977*. New York: Praeger.

Lie, J., 2000, The discourse on Japaneseness, in Douglass, M. and Roberts, G.S. (eds), *Japan and Global Migration: Foreign Workers and the Advent of a Multicultural Society*. London: Routledge, 70–90.

Lone, S., 2001, *The Japanese Community in Brazil 1908–1940: Between Samurai and Carnival*. Basingstoke: Palgrave.

Masterson, D.M., 2004, *The Japanese in Latin America*. Champaign: University of Illinois Press.

Park, H.O., 2005, *Two Dreams in One Bed: Empire, Social Life, and the Origins of the North Korean Revolution in Manchuria*. Durham, NC: Duke University Press (Chapter 2: The politics of osmosis: Korean migration and the Japanese empire).

Patterson, W., 2000, *The Ilse: First-Generation Korean Immigrants in Hawai'i, 1903–1973.* Honolulu: University of Hawai'i Press.

Stephan, J.J., 1994, *The Russian Far East: A History.* Stanford, CA: Stanford University Press.

Sugimoto, Y., 1999, Making sense of *nihonjinron, Thesis Eleven* 57: 81–96.

Suzuki, T., 2010, *Embodying Belonging: Racializing Okinawan Diaspora in Bolivia and Japan.* Honolulu: University of Hawai'i Press.

Tamanoi, M.A., 2009, *Memory Maps: The State and Manchuria in Postwar Japan.* Honolulu: University of Hawai'i Press.

Treadgold, D.W., 1957, *The Great Siberian Migration.* Princeton, NJ: Princeton University Press.

Tsuchida, M., 1998, The history of Japanese emigration from the 1860s to the 1990s, in Weiner, M. and Hanami, T. (eds), *Temporary Workers or Future Citizens? Japanese and US Migration Policies.* Basingstoke: Macmillan, 77–119.

Vaporis, C.N., 1997, To Edo and back: alternate attendance and Japanese culture in the early modern period, *Journal of Japanese Studies* 23(1): 25–67.

Walker, B.L., 2001, *The Conquest of Ainu Lands: Ecology and Culture in Japanese Expansion 1590–1800.* Berkeley: University of California Press.

Waswo, A. and Nishida, Y. (eds), 2003, *Farmers and Village Life in Twentieth Century Japan.* London: RoutledgeCurzon.

Weiner, M., 1994, *Race and Migration in Imperial Japan.* London: Routledge.

Wender, M.L., 2005, *Lamentations as History: Narratives by Koreans in Japan 1965–2000.* Stanford, CA: Stanford University Press.

Wigen, K., 1995, *The Making of a Japanese Periphery, 1750–1920.* Berkeley: University of California Press.

Yamazaki, T., 1999 (1975), *Sandakan Brothel No. 8: An Episode in the History of Lower-Class Japanese Women.* New York: M.E. Sharpe.

Yoon, I.-J., 2000, Forced relocation, language use, and ethnic identity of Koreans in central Asia, *Asian and Pacific Migration Journal* 9(1): 35–64.

Young, L., 1998, *Japan's Total Empire: Manchuria and the Culture of Wartime Imperialism.* Berkeley: University of California Press.

3 Heaven's door

Southeast Asia's international migration flows

3.0 Introduction

At, or soon after, the end of World War II, most of the remaining countries of Southeast Asia joined Thailand as independent nation-states. Good news perhaps, except that their populations were predominantly rural and poor, were often socially divided – specifically by language, ethnic origin, political ideology and religion – and were largely powerless, both with respect to their new political masters and as 'third world' inhabitants in a bi-polar world dominated by the USA and the Soviet Union. In the 60–70 years between then and now much has changed. Yes, of course, to the shame of global corporate leaders, national economic planners and local political elites alike, poverty and powerlessness are still there in abundance, as are social conflict, ignorance and poor health, but living standards have risen enormously (along with inequality), social modernization and urbanization have proceeded apace, and, for very different reasons (such as growth in the size of the economy, the importance of commercial and financial services, major new resource developments, and the success of the manufacturing sector) several of the countries of Southeast Asia (notably Indonesia, Singapore, Thailand, Vietnam and Malaysia) now really matter in the global order of things.

So what has brought about these changes and why should they affect international migration flows? The short answer is, of course, 'globalization'. This is not a well-defined concept, but in its economic form it means the transformation of what were formally distant and isolated economic activities into close and connected ones. This happens at both the aggregate and individual levels: at the aggregate level, Southeast Asian low-wage economies, rich in agricultural and mineral resources and straddling key global trading routes, become beneficially connected to high-income economies in North America, Europe, Northeast Asia and Australasia. Mobile international corporate capital cooperates with local entrepreneurial resources and expertise to initiate new 'circuits of capital'. They do this by (i) spending money investing in land/built form, machinery, etc., and recruiting labour (most of it locally); (ii) creating a production platform in the Southeast Asian country by bringing these means of production together in the production process often located in, or near, the capital city-region or in a major port; and then (iii) making money by selling their goods and services locally, regionally and, above all, in the rich consumer markets of the high-income countries, thereby earning much more than they spent on (i) and (ii) together, and thus making a profit on their investment. These new circuits of capital enrich the giant (mostly foreign) corporations and their local 'comprador' friends (many of whom in Southeast Asia are ethnically Chinese), generate jobs for middle-class functionaries (technical, professional and managerial employees), and employ the poor. Unfortunately, there are so many poor people looking for work that the wages that the employer is forced to pay are very low. This means that while globalization can bring great wealth to some people, such as landowners, company owners and middlemen (rent seekers), it tends, up until the point at which the supply of poor people dries up, to ensure that the mass of poor people remain poor.

At the individual level, globalization and its associated changes in the technologies of transport and communication (especially cheap air travel, new roads and bridges, radio, TV, internet computing and mobile phones) have the effect of much reducing the 'friction of distance'. In practice, this means that people looking to earn money to support themselves and their families need no longer confine their search to the local area, to the wider region within which they live, or even to their country of birth and current residence. They can, albeit usually with practical and emotional difficulty (due especially to the obligations they feel towards their co-resident older or elderly parents), work abroad in male manual (for example, construction) jobs in the Persian Gulf, become global seafarers, or work as female domestic servants in Hong Kong. By extension, they can study in the UK, marry in South Korea, or be resettled in the USA.

Evidence of this trend is provided by the growing number of people born in Southeast Asia living in Australia: just 3,000 in 1947, it was 38,000 in 1971, and 487,000 in 2001 (of whom 155,000 were from Vietnam, 104,000 from the Philippines, and 79,000 from Malaysia). All told, it is estimated that around 20 million Southeast Asians worked outside their home countries in the late 2000s with around half of these in the Middle East. The net effect of these millions of individual decisions (each one typically the outcome of negotiations with the 'left-behind' at the household or family level) has been (i) to bring very significant remittance income into Southeast Asia, and (ii) to open up spatially Southeast Asian countries and their populations to the wider world. Much of what follows in this chapter represents the many varied ways in which international migration is both cause and consequence of this spatial opening-up process (that is, to globalization).

Before that, however, there is one migration story that needs to be told that affects almost the whole of Southeast Asia, although once again in different ways and to different degrees. It is the legacy of those older, and late 19th- and early 20th-century migrations from south China into Southeast Asia (the region known to the Chinese as the *Nanyang*) discussed in the previous chapter. Over the generations, embeddedness ('localization'), creolization, and assimilation have occurred. The early migrants were 'overseas Chinese' (*huaqiao*), they then became 'ethnic Chinese' (*huaren*), and finally became people of 'Chinese descent' (*huayi*). Every country in Southeast Asia has a part of its population whose origins can be traced back to the region of southern China now largely occupied by the provinces of Guangdong, Hainan, Fujian and Zhejiang. In almost all cases, the ethnic Chinese, although occupying varied class locations (including manual labourers, especially in Malaysia) and reflecting contrasting sub-ethnic origins (Hokkien, Teochiu, Cantonese, Hakka and Hainanese), tend to be particularly strongly represented in occupations associated with trade, manufacturing and finance (for example, wholesale and retail commerce, shipping and road transport, the hospitality sector, personal services, finance, insurance and real estate) – although the role of culture in this occupational concentration is hotly contested.

As a result, with many of the most successful companies owned and managed by ethnic Chinese, the members of the Chinese community have had a significant influence on the performance of individual Southeast Asian national economies, have been instrumental in realizing globalization through their diaspora linkages, and have thereby sometimes been a target for nationalist resentment. However, that is where the similarities end. Yes, for some, it may be 'chic' to be Chinese in Southeast Asia today, with many members of the elite expressing pride in their Chinese ancestry (for example, Cory Aquino, former president of the Philippines), and popular culture is also turning towards a celebration of Chineseness as pluralist policies have replaced assimilationist ones (for example, the renewed attractiveness of Hakka identity).

The truth, though, is that the nature of the relationship between ethnic Chinese and their host communities varies greatly: in Singapore, the Chinese are the host community (at about 75% of the population in 2000). In Malaysia (26% of the population), despite the institutionalized advantages awarded to ethnic Malays (for example, in formal politics, business, religion, public-sector employment and university entrance) and despite living rather separate 'parallel lives', there is a largely peaceful 'compromise' relationship between the Chinese and the majority Malay population and with the other large minority, the South Asian population – something that did not seem likely in the conflict-stricken early post-war period. In Indonesia, Vietnam, Cambodia, Laos and Myanmar (Burma), the relations between the majority population and the minority Chinese community (all less than 4%) tend to be more fraught (an example is the anti-Chinese violence in Myanmar/Burma in 1967). This is especially so in Indonesia where widespread racial violence directed at the Chinese has stained inter-community relations on several occasions, especially in 1965, but most recently in 1997–98. Finally, in the Philippines (1%), and above all, in Thailand (9%), the high levels of assimilation, reflected, for example, in high rates of intermarriage, have resulted in a much lower salience of Chinese minority-host country majority ethnic difference. Here other ethnic differences, such as those between ethnic Thais and Thailand's 'hill tribes', and social class differences, such as those between the 'red' and 'yellow' factions in

Thailand, become centre stage. Furthermore, the representation of the Chinese in Southeast Asia has reflected major historical changes in China itself: in the late 19th and early 20th centuries they were seen as involuntary migrants with their main loyalty not to their country of immigration, but to their home towns and villages; in the mid-20th century they were seen by many as the potential carriers of socialist revolution (this view was soon to be undermined by the brutal treatment of families with overseas links during the Cultural Revolution); and all along, but perhaps especially today, they were, and are, seen as successful capitalist entrepreneurs. This final representation is being reinforced by recent migration: there are many new Chinese immigrants in Southeast Asia (*xin yimin*), mostly entrepreneurs, professionals and students, and, unlike their predecessors, they are increasingly not from the rural, poverty-stricken parts of China, but from its prosperous middle-class cities.

Much of what has been written here about the Chinese communities in Southeast Asia, especially relating to integration and assimilation, applies also to the Indian communities (including those from Tamil Nadu), and to the much smaller Arab minorities (such as the Hadramis from Yemen).

3.1 Indonesia (and Timor Leste)

Vast in both area and population (240 million at the time of the 2010 Census), Indonesia is better known, perhaps, for its internal migrations than for its international migrations. Nevertheless, six main post-World War II international migration flows can be identified (see Figure 3.1), two of which are massive (to the Middle East and to Malaysia), while the rest involve far smaller numbers but are nevertheless significant and interesting. First, as often happens during the decolonization process, those among the colonized who worked closest to the colonial power usually face a bleak future through a loss of status and influence, and can face discrimination. On Indonesia achieving its independence, not only did 100,000 Dutch nationals return to the Netherlands, but many Moluccans, having initially chosen separatism, decided, when that failed, to migrate to their 'mother country' (that is, the Netherlands) rather than remain in a country that was now dominated economically, culturally and politically by people resident in Java. In the mid-2000s the Moluccans in the Netherlands numbered about 120,000. Others were displaced within Indonesia by the civil conflict (for example, there were 10,000 Bugis refugees in Sumatra in 1956).

Then, after the 'oil crisis' in the early 1970s, vast wealth was diverted to Saudi Arabia and the Persian Gulf states. This 'Gulf' region lacked the reserves of both manual and low-level non-manual labour to support rapid economic growth, which resulted in a massive recruitment of workers from South and Southeast Asia. Over the next 35 years emigration from Indonesia to the Middle East (Saudi Arabia, United Arab Emirates (UAE), Kuwait and Bahrain), most of it legal, built up to become of great economic and socio-cultural significance (in the 1975–90 period about 70,000 were leaving Indonesia each

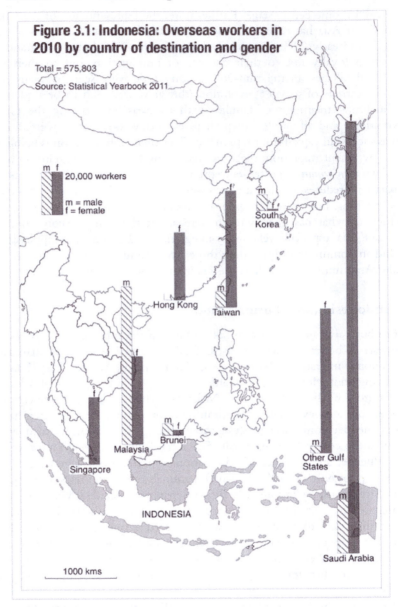

Figure 3.1: Indonesia: Overseas workers in 2010 by country of destination and gender

Total = 575,803

Source: Statistical Yearbook 2011

year). This migration of Muslims, most of them to Saudi Arabia (where, of course, the pilgrimage city of Mecca is located) has remained significant. Millions of migrants, many using social networks and middlemen, have been involved, and millions of families in Indonesia have benefited from the remittance income sent home by these migrants. The early migrants were mostly male construction workers and drivers, followed and vastly outnumbered later by female domestic workers, who typically work for long hours under highly restrictive conditions; but Indonesians now perform many roles, and form a vital part of the very large, lower-status, disenfranchised (foreign worker) strata of Middle East society upon which the individual economies and their wealthy elite households have become dependent.

A third, and again very large flow of migrants, many of them young adult males lacking authorization, is the emigration of Indonesians to the nearby countries of Malaysia and Singapore. This migration is strongly facilitated by close family and friendship connections and by the migration 'industry' (brokers, recruiters, agents, middlemen, etc.) – these facilitators often being more reliable and better trusted than the official government-run system. In 2009, it was estimated that there were 2.1 million migrant workers in Malaysia, 50% of whom were from Indonesia. Construction workers also figure in this flow, but the majority of male workers are employed as manual workers in agriculture and forestry, the service sectors, and manufacturing. Female workers are domestic servants, factory and plantation workers, service-sector employees and care workers.

Geographically, this is not one flow, but three: the first consists of migrants, both legal and illegal, to peninsular Malaysia, often from Java but via northern Sumatra; the second, again legal and illegal, consists of migrants from, or through, Kalimantan to the Malaysian provinces of Sarawak and Sabah; and the third is migration to Singapore – much of this in the early post-war period from the island of Bawean, north of Java. Temporally, these migrations can be short term or long term, but either way they often involve repeat migrations – so much so, that it is said that people come to lead pluri-local lives. Indonesian migrants in Malaysia, largely male and many of them irregular, have, however, borne the brunt of the Malaysian government's policies (i) to reduce radically the number of migrant workers during the economic crises of 1997 and 2008; and (ii) to legitimize a 'voluntary civilian paramilitary body' (that is, in effect, a vigilante group – RELA) in its efforts to expose and deport those who have no legal right to live and work in Malaysia (foreigners are often targeted for their alleged criminality or for being suspected of being HIV positive). They are also at the mercy of corrupt officials and predatory agents in Indonesia. So serious has this latter problem become, that the Indonesian government has established special measures to ensure a safe return for migrant workers to their home villages. Indonesians working in Singapore are largely employed in construction, manufacturing and as domestic workers. Of the 200,000 foreign domestic workers in Singapore, about one half come from Indonesia. Some working-class labour migration is, however, to destinations other than those located close by in Southeast Asia. Indonesian manual workers in manufacturing and the services are found in Taiwan, South Korea and Japan, and further away still in Australasia and North America.

Fourth, there is Chinese emigration. Initially, this was largely consequent upon the insistence after independence that Chinese with dual nationality choose between Indonesia and China. Over 100,000 Chinese left Indonesia in

1960 as a result of this. Subsequently, despite high levels of assimilation of Chinese Indonesians (*Peranakan*) into the wider Indonesian population, inter-ethnic conflicts have on occasions caused the sudden uprooting of Chinese Indonesians and, in the early period, their resettlement in Taiwan and the People's Republic of China (PRC). This so-called 'return migration' is no such thing (for a start it was typically their (great-)grandparents who migrated to Indonesia). The problem is that the 'welcome home' is often accompanied by hostility and suspicion. In Indonesia these men and women are regarded as Chinese; in the PRC and Taiwan they are seen as Indonesian – the Indonesian Chinese are 'trapped in ambivalence'. We shall find many more instances of this inter-ethnic identity limbo in later chapters of the book.

Relations between ethnic Chinese and 'indigenous' (that is, non-Chinese) Indonesians reached a low point in 1998. The violence against them led to the departure of 110,000 ethnic Chinese and their temporary or permanent settlement in Singapore, Hong Kong, Canada, and Australia. Since that time, under the 'liberalization, democratization, and decentralization' that followed, there has, it is claimed, been something of a revival of Chinese culture in Indonesia and a shift towards the acceptance of multiculturalism and of creolization (at least in Jakarta). So the risk attached to returning to Indonesia or to staying there has been somewhat reduced, as has the need for ethnic Chinese to emigrate.

In recent years, a growing number of Indonesian women have left the country to become care workers, domestic servants and wives in the countries of Southeast, East and Northeast Asia, and many moving accounts of their experiences have been written. A very small number settle as nurses in Japan (though many make the attempt), but much larger numbers become domestic 'helpers' (servants) and care workers in South Korea, Hong Kong, Singapore, and in Taiwan where Indonesians form the largest group of foreign nationals other than those who come from mainland China. East and Northeast Asian countries host a number of Indonesian men as factory workers, but also as seafarers in their fishing industries and as workers in the related fish products processing plants. Many men and women (but women especially so) suffer exploitation and abuse at their places of employment. The Indonesian government has taken some steps to protect the interests of their nationals working abroad, but it is the migrant labour non-governmental organizations (NGOs) and migrant labour associations that have often offered the crucial lifeline to those whose situations have become intolerable (for example due to the non-payment of wages, excessive hours, confiscation of documents, etc.).

Not all of the migration from Indonesia results from decisions taken free from constraint or in circumstances of the migrants' choosing. First, there is the trafficking of Indonesian men and women to other countries in Southeast Asia, especially for plantation work in East Malaysia. As is the case elsewhere, the boundaries between trafficking and commercially facilitating migration are not easy to draw. Indeed, the unintended outcomes of a heightened regulation of labour migration can result, some would claim, in the state itself becoming almost complicit in trafficking-like practices. Second, while the vast majority of the displacements resulting from inter-ethnic and other civil conflicts in Indonesia remained internal to the borders of the country, that in Aceh spilled over into Malaysia, where many political exiles had settled over the years. Others who were fleeing the effects of the tsunami in 2004/05 joined them. Malaysia having refused to accept them as permanent refugees, a small number were, to their surprise, accepted by Canada (where their language, downward social mobility and other adjustment problems, but also their resilience and successes, were recorded). When the Helsinki Memorandum of Understanding was signed in 2005, thereby much reducing the conflict over Aceh's separation from Indonesia, the Acehnese in Malaysia faced the decision whether or not to return to their homeland. Similarly, and facing the same dilemma, the conflict in Irian Jaya/Papua has resulted in cross-border refugees, this time as 'permissive residents' in Papua New Guinea.

Very different from these migrations of low-income men and women seeking work or security abroad, Indonesia is the source of many student migrations, and of some 'brain-drain' migrations of professional and technical workers.

Finally, although Indonesia is primarily a country of emigration, it does have new immigrants (as well, of course, as very many return migrants). It was also the destination for about 30,000 refugees ('boat people') from Vietnam, most of them arriving in 1979. Though small in number and often staying only a few years, recent immigrants fall into two main groups. First are those (notably from Northeast Asia, North America, Australasia, and Western Europe) who are transferred to Indonesia as part of the operations of large multinational corporations (usually to Jakarta, which had 50% of Indonesia's 31,000 foreign workers in 2006). The second group are those, many from countries like Japan and Germany, who, typically following a tourist trip to Bali, decide to settle there. They do so to escape from their own 'rat-race' societies, sometimes in search of sunshine, sea and sexual partners, sometimes to seek a supposedly less stressful and more culturally rewarding way of life. In addition, some intermediate-level jobs in Indonesia are taken by migrants from India and the Philippines.

As a footnote, it is necessary to record that Indonesia is often in the news not because of its own migrations, but because it is a country of passage for other migrants, many of them from the war-torn countries of Iraq, Syria and Afghanistan, who are seeking refuge and a new life in Australia.

Conflict accounts for the 123,000 East Timorese refugees living in Indonesia in 2002 after 240,000 had crossed the border in 1999. This migration, both voluntary (of people on the losing side) and involuntary, resulted from the violence that broke out following the vote for independence in 1999 in East Timor (Timor Leste, population now 1.2 million). Most have since returned, leaving only about 28,000 in West Timor. However, the lengthy conflict (civil war, then invasion, then fight for independence) also produced long-distance migration, notably to Australia, sometimes via Portugal. Many East Timorese joined earlier migrants to Australia from the 1975 civil war, most of whom were ethnic Chinese. Rather like the Acehnese in Vancouver, they had many difficulties in settling: they had physical and mental health problems, housing and employment problems, and perhaps above all, language problems, since few spoke English and most spoke only Tetum or Hakka. Although dreaming of return, and, since 2002, being able to return, many have chosen to stay in Australia.

3.2 Singapore

Singapore is almost everything that Indonesia is not. It is rich, minute in area, ostentatiously urban, spotlessly neat and tidy, and almost frighteningly efficient. It is, in a manner of speaking, the commercial, managerial and financial capital of Southeast Asia, and also a strong contender for 'global city' status. Its post-war migrations have contributed enormously to its economic success, which, in turn, now largely explains the nature of its current international migration flows. Like other global cities it is an 'escalator region' (see Box 4.1 at the end of the next chapter), in that (i) it attracts young, able and ambitious men and women, (ii) occupationally and socially promotes them at rates that are far higher than alternative locations in the Southeast Asian region, and (iii) then loses a proportion of them as they move on to 'pastures new'. Like other global cities, it recruits from outside both into its higher echelons and into its menial jobs – at the top and at the bottom. Singapore truly is an immigrant society. For example, with its excellent reputation, the National University of Singapore can hope to attract staff from among the best teachers and researchers in the world. The same applies to Singapore's top financial and business services institutions. At the same time, however, a veritable army of manual and low-level service workers are required to keep the city-state moving. Cleaners, domestic servants, factory, transport, workshop and warehouse workers, building labourers ... all are essential for the functioning of the modern city.

This was not how things looked in the 1950s. Following large inflows after World War II, Singapore restricted the in-migration of manual workers in the early 1950s. Population growth at this time was rapid, but largely the consequence of a high birth rate, not in-migration. Indeed, during the 1950s there was much poverty in the city with about 100,000 people (10% of the population) living in squatter settlements in 1957. Poverty and under-employment were rife. As with Hong Kong, this 'surplus labour' was a major factor in promoting import substitution (producing domestically many products and services that had previously been imported), then, after independence in 1965, in promoting the export-oriented manufacturing investments that followed. However, unlike Hong Kong, the state was centre-stage in the process. It intervened a great deal to achieve this foreign direct investment (FDI) export-led industrialization and the capital deepening that followed. So successful was this strategy that manufacturing employment came to account for about one-third of total employment by the mid-1990s, since when, of course, producer services (especially financial services) have been the main engine of economic growth. During the high-growth period after 1965 unemployment came down and labour shortages were increasingly met by the recruitment of (temporary) foreign migrant workers. In 1968 foreign workers constituted only 0.8% of the workforce; by the end of the 1980s this had increased to 12–13%, and by 1997 to about 25%. In 2000, the 1.1 million foreign workers accounted for 34.7% of the total labour force. Unlike the situation elsewhere in Southeast Asia, the 1997/08 financial crisis did not have a major impact on foreign workers in Singapore, nor was the 2008 crash as severe in its effects on resident or migrant workers as might have been expected.

It is important to stress that this is a highly managed migration process. It is highly managed so that the two very different flows of migrants to Singapore experience very different conditions: those who are highly educated/skilled or rich can stay, bring in their families, and live in luxury; the unskilled or manually skilled must work for specific employers on short-term contracts, live in dormitories or in residencies near to those for whom they work, and avoid doing anything that would assist their settlement or embedding in Singaporean society. The new migrants are entering a city-state that already has a complex multiethnic character with four official languages (Mandarin, English, Malay and Tamil) and great diversity both within and beyond the official CMIO (Chinese, Malay, Indian and other) race-based system (a system that fits uncomfortably with the growing reality of mixed-race households and identities). Among the ethnic immigrant minorities, some are socially and spatially excluded (for example, Bangladeshis); others (such as the Malays) are assimilated, but in ways that seem to ensure lower income and poorer prospects for them – the so-called 'Malay plight'. With the help of the state-sponsored discourses of 'meritocracy' and 'multiracialism', migrants and minorities are being assimilated into what some regard as a Chinese elite-dominated society. Racial categories in Singaporean politics tend to be homogenized and essentialized, and the links between immigrant minorities and Singapore's multiracialism are complex.

As part of this managed migration process, and in response to claims that immigration implies costs as well as benefits (lower productivity growth, pressure on housing, health risks, social cost of crime, and damaged diplomatic relations with sending countries), the Singapore government sets quotas that (i) place upper limits on the proportion of the workforce in each sector that is foreign, and (ii) reflect the degree of difficulty in recruiting Singaporean nationals. Furthermore, like Malaysia and Thailand, it charges a levy that varies over time and by sector on the employment of foreign workers. It also implements harsh rules about the punishment for those employing irregular migrants, and, to prevent settlement, about the marriage and childbirth behaviours of immigrant women employed as domestic servants.

The 2010 Census results for Singapore are very revealing. Of the resident population of 3.77 million people, 2.91 million were born in Singapore, meaning that 860,000 or 22.8% of the population (56% of them female) were born elsewhere. Of these, 44.9% (mostly ethnically Chinese) were born in

Malaysia, 20.4% were born in the PRC (including Hong Kong and Macao), 14.4% were born in South Asia, 6.4% (mostly female) were born in Indonesia (again many of them ethnic Chinese), 10.5% (mostly female) were born in other Asian countries (these include some of the female domestic workers from the Philippines, Indonesia, Thailand and Vietnam), and 2.9% (mostly male) were born in Europe, North America and Australasia. Although many of the migrants from Malaysia and Indonesia were ethnic Chinese (very few of whom are Muslims), Singapore does have a Muslim population; it is made up of long-standing groups such as the Malays, South Asians and Arabs plus new Muslim migrants from Malaysia, Indonesia and Bangladesh. Since the terrorist attacks on the USA on 11 September 2001, and in response to the activities of Jemaah Islamiyah, Muslim identity and the nature of Singaporean multiculturalism have become more salient as policy issues.

Combined with other data from the Census, a clear pattern of the role of migrant labour in the Singaporean economy emerges. This role should be seen against the backdrop of current very low fertility rates. In 2010 the total fertility rate was at about 50% of replacement level. From the countries of South and Southeast Asia where incomes are lower (often far lower) than those in Singapore, young men (particularly from South Asia) and women (particularly from Southeast Asia) are migrating to Singapore, usually on two-year contracts, to do the working-class jobs that Singaporeans cannot, or will not, do themselves. Figures for the late 2000s suggest that there were 200,000 Malaysian nationals, 150,000 Indonesians, 136,000 Filipinos, 90–100,000 Indians, 80–90,000 Bangladeshis, 50–60,000 Burmese and 45,000 Thais living in Singapore. This same source gives a figure of 200,000 for Chinese nationals. With the help of the 'migration industry', many foreign workers come from the PRC – the so-called 'new' Chinese immigration. This migration includes women from the PRC who come to Singapore to marry Singaporean men, or as 'study mothers' to obtain a Singaporean education for their children, or to work in the sex industry. The sex industry in the form of 'jungle brothels' is also the destination for some trafficked women from Thailand.

Other examples of foreign worker migrants are the 'good, docile and other-ed' Bangladeshi and Thai construction workers, who live almost their whole lives at the construction site cut off from the rest of the population, and domestic servants or 'foreign maids', numbering 140–150,000, who mostly come from Indonesia, the Philippines and Sri Lanka, and who are crucially linked to their families and friends back home through their mobile phones. This relationship between sending and receiving societies has recently been the theme of popular films, which depict, in the Philippines case for example, the contrast between their high status as 'breadwinners' in their country of origin with their subservience as 'maids' in Singapore (albeit cosmopolitan and emancipated). Initially most of these domestic workers did come from the Philippines (often preferred because of their ability to speak English), but cases of violence and abuse led the Philippine government to set stricter criteria for the employment of their nationals, which, after 1996, encouraged the switch to lower-waged and more compliant Indonesians. A relatively new phenomenon is the arrival of Vietnamese women as the commercially arranged 'foreign brides' of Singaporean men.

From some of these same countries come professional, technical and managerial workers such as nurses from the Philippines and many university students: 18% of Singapore's undergraduates are foreign students – they see the city-state as the 'premier destination within the region for high-quality education' (Cheng 2014: 390). Note, for example, that ethnic Indians, who make up only 8.6% of the resident workforce, nevertheless comprise 14.3% of the employment in information and communication services. These South and Southeast Asian immigrants form part of the much sought-after 'foreign talent' – mostly highly educated Westerners (predominantly male), but also Japanese (predominantly female), and PRC/Hong Kong immigrants (some of whom are 'trailing spouses' and downwardly mobile labour migrants). These professional, technical and managerial workers (26,000 Japanese, 20,000 British, 15,000 American and Australian, and 13,500 South Korean) may form a smaller proportion of the immigrant population than those from other backgrounds, but their work impacts enormously on the Singaporean economy. As they open up Singapore to global forces (for example, through their global financial and trading connections), they lead privileged but largely closed lives locally as expatriates. So high has been the immigration of managers and professionals in Singapore's 'knowledge-based economy' that some have argued that the opportunities for the country's own educated middle classes have been curtailed.

Singapore is also, of course, a country of emigration. An estimated 192,000 Singaporeans lived abroad in 2011: 50,000 in Australia, 40,000 in the UK, and 20,000 each in the USA and China. Many of its entrepreneurs and its managerial and professional middle-class employees, along with students mainly from the same social class backgrounds, seek out 'overseas experience' and new opportunities in other countries in East Asia, North America and Western Europe, and, above all, in Australia. Singaporean expatriates are predominantly male (70%); many of them belong to 'global households' in which parents, wives and children are left behind, sometimes causing stress in family relationships (though some, of course, emigrate partly to escape family pressures). The Singaporean government, while encouraging overseas employment, is aware of the problem of 'brain drain', and places importance on 'Asian family values' and 'transnational inclusion' to bind emigrants to the country (which it wants to be viewed as a 'home, not a hotel') and to ensure their return. However, affection for, and strong obligations towards, family members would, in any case, encourage many migrants to return.

As the Singapore economy has grown and diversified, and as the city has physically expanded, so also has the trend towards a spillover of investment and employment into the neighbouring regions of Malaysia (the Iskandar Development Region) and Indonesia (Riau and Riau Island Provinces). Often this decentralization takes the form of branch plants and back offices, but tourism is also involved. New local (but international) migration flows are resulting from this process. Occasionally, however, Singaporean investment takes Singaporeans further afield. This is especially true for Singapore-based businesses operating in the PRC.

3.3 Malaysia (and Brunei)

For much of the post-war period Malaysia was a country of net emigration. Along with most of the other countries of East and Southeast Asia, it suffered a significant loss of its brightest and best through 'brain-drain' migration (many of them as students) to countries such as Australia and New Zealand, Canada and the USA, and the countries of Northwest Europe, especially the UK. Some 250,000 Malaysians were working overseas in 2003, 785,000 in 2010, many of them highly skilled, and the total size of the Malaysian diaspora could now be as large as 1.5 million. During the 1980s, at a time of a widening ethnic divide between Malaysian Chinese and Malays under the New Economic Policy, there was a significant emigration of middle-class ethnic Chinese. About 130,000 Malaysians went to Australia, which was the second largest destination after Singapore, and many of these migrants were highly educated professionals and managers. In 2005 there were also about 20,000 Malaysian students in Australia, many of whom would stay on to develop their careers there.

A fascinating snapshot of this loss of talent is provided by a journalist, Mary Chin, who, in an article in the *East Malaysia Daily Express* (26 August 2012), tried to trace the current whereabouts of all of the 'star-quality' ethnic Chinese women in Sabah. She found that none had stayed, but the interesting thing is where they went: Australia topped the list, Singapore came second, and the UK and USA came joint third, but (and this may be a sign for the future) one finished up as an architect based in Shanghai, designing shopping malls being built all over China. Their reasons for leaving were primarily for study and career development, but they stayed away also for marriage and family reasons and because they preferred the social and political lifestyles of their adopted countries over that of Malaysia.

Migration of skilled and unskilled construction, factory and service-sector workers to Singapore (with large-scale daily commuting as well), Taiwan, Hong Kong and Japan, has also been very significant, as has migration to other South and Southeast Asian states, notably the Philippines, Indonesia, India and Pakistan (though very much smaller, of course, than the migrations in the other direction).

However, before discussing Malaysia's main migration experience, that of immigration, it is necessary to recount the strange story of a migration that happened, and then did not happen. Approximately 255,000 Vietnamese 'boat people' were given temporary asylum in Malaysia in eight camps. Of these, 246,000 were resettled in Western countries while 9,000 were returned to Vietnam. As one commentator put it, 'Malaysia was perhaps the most resolute of the Southeast Asian first-asylum countries in pursuing the repatriation of Vietnamese boat people' (US Committee for Refugees and Immigrants 1997).

What changed Malaysia's migration story was the success of Malaysia as a modern industrial economy. It became a country of net immigration, with a vast majority of the migrants being employed on short-term contracts for manual work. This, it was argued, benefited the economy by boosting growth through relieving labour shortages, and by acting as a buffer to business cycle effects on the labour market. First, drawing upon their close family and friendship networks, they came for plantation work and other agricultural work, mostly Indonesians in Johor and Pahang, plus some Thais in the north (there were 500,000 foreign workers in Malaysia in 1984). Second, they came to feed the labour demands of the construction industry especially in the Kuala Lumpur capital city-region (by 1995, 80% of construction workers were immigrants), with most of the migrant workers coming either from Indonesia (Indonesian workers were praised for their hard work and ability to understand Malay), or from Bangladesh – many of whom in the early years were smuggled into Malaysia through Thailand. Finally, they came for jobs in the many new mostly foreign or ethnic Chinese-owned factories being built to produce all kinds of consumer goods, but especially wood and rubber products, clothing, and electrical/electronic goods, for the global market. Once again, the migrant workers were mostly Indonesians, but also Nepalese, Bangladeshis, Vietnamese, Burmese and Indians (there were 1.75 million foreign workers in Malaysia in 1996, and 2–2.5 million foreign workers in 2004; 2.8 million by 2006). By the time of the East Asian financial crisis in 1997/98, the Malaysian economy had become so structurally dependent on foreign workers that attempts by the government to stop the in-flow of new migrants had to be quickly reversed. This is highly significant because it indicates how little substitution there was between domestic labour and foreign labour – they largely occupy different parts (sectors, levels, niches) of the labour market.

The foreign workers are located both in peninsular Malaysia and in East Malaysia. About one-third are living in the Kuala Lumpur capital city-region (Kuala Lumpur plus Selangor), another third in Sabah, and most of the rest in Sarawak and Johor. Sabah has witnessed in the 1990s and 2000s an influx of Filipino economic migrants on a similar scale to the earlier immigration of refugees (many of whose children are stateless). They consist of men seeking work on the plantations, and in the logging, fishing and mining industries, and women in raw material processing industries and also in the service industries (including the sex industry). There is a slight element of a security aspect to this migration because of the historical claim, recently revived, to the territory of Sabah by the Sultanate of Sulu (which is now a province of the Philippines). About 65% of migrants in Sabah, however, come from Indonesia. As a result of all these Indonesian and Filipino migrations into Sabah, the proportion of foreigners there (23.6%, or 615,000 people, according to the 2000 Census) is far larger than in any other province of Malaysia (except Labuan), and is four times higher than the national average of 5.9%. On a much smaller scale, an increasingly permanent flow of female factory workers, joins a mostly seasonal and temporary flow of migrants who come to peninsular Malaysia to work in agriculture or the services from the Muslim provinces of southern Thailand.

The picture provided by the 2010 Census is, of course, incomplete because it fails to measure many of those foreigners whose stays in Malaysia are temporary or are undocumented. Nevertheless, the Census does record 2.25 million foreign residents, and it allows us to see where they are living (see Figure 3.2). The highest concentrations are (i) in Sabah, especially in the eastern half of the state; (ii) in Kuala Lumpur, and in the districts surrounding the capital in Selangor State; and (iii) in southern Johor (across from Singapore). Secondary concentrations are to be found in the plantation interiors of Johor and Sarawak, and in touristic areas such as Penang, the Cameron Highlands and Langkawi. Much of western Sarawak and the northern and eastern parts of peninsular Malaysia have proportions of foreign residents less than half the national average of 8.2% (i.e. location quotients of less than 0.50 – see Box 3.1).

Box 3.1 Location quotients

A 'location quotient' (LQ) is a means of measuring and depicting the importance of a particular variable locally/regionally relative to the national/global average. In Malaysia, for example, foreign residents account for 27.82% of Sabah's population. The national proportion is just 8.20%. So the location quotient is 27.82 divided by 8.20, which equals 3.39. A location quotient of 1.00 means that the local importance of that variable is the same as the national average. A value of 0.50 would mean that the local importance was just half the national. The LQs, when mapped, provide a quick and easy way of showing the spatial patterns of key migration-related variables.

The treatment of these foreign workers in Malaysia is, with of course some exceptions, typically poor. Often being unfairly blamed for a host of social ills, notably the spread of disease and the increase in crime, the discrimination against them is often severe and widespread, with a special antagonism, it seems, directed at foreign worker-Malaysian marriages. Their working environments have frequently been hazardous (with many deaths and injuries at building sites, for example) and their low-quality housing and neighbourhood environments likewise contribute to low morale and poor health (some construction workers are accommodated on site by the employers in unventilated container vans, others live in squatter settlements outside the main cities and in Malay Reserve Areas).

As the Malaysian economy has matured, the proportion of the workforce employed in manufacturing has gone down slightly. This did not reduce, however, the potential for immigration. Migrants not only took over a larger share of manufacturing employment, but became increasingly important in the service sector (where about half of them were women), and many immigrant Southeast Asian women entered domestic service. It is not just the mostly

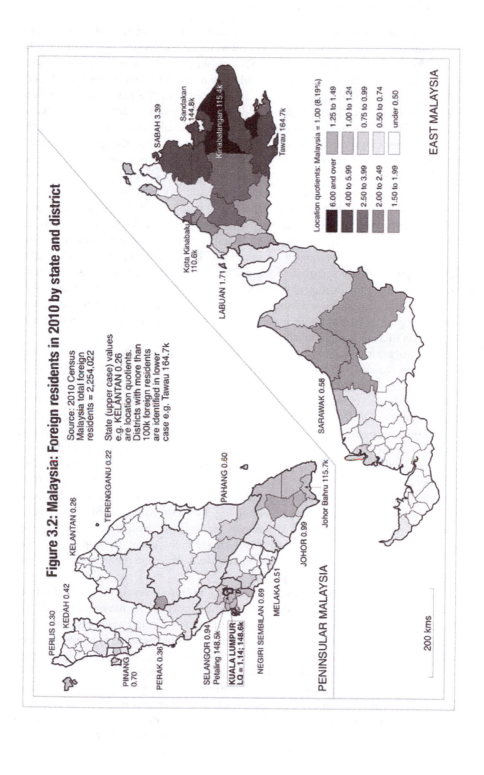

Figure 3.2: Malaysia: Foreign residents in 2010 by state and district

Source: 2010 Census
Malaysia total foreign
residents = 2,254,022

State (upper case) values
e.g. KELANTAN 0.26
are location quotients.
Districts with more than
100k foreign residents
are identified in lower
case e.g. Tawau 164.7k

PERLIS 0.30

KEDAH 0.42

KELANTAN 0.26

TERENGGANU 0.22

PINANG 0.70

PERAK 0.36

SELANGOR 0.94
Petaling 148.5k

KUALA LUMPUR
LQ = 1.14; 148.6k

NEGIRI SEMBILAN 0.69

MELAKA 0.51

PAHANG 0.60

JOHOR 0.99

Johor Bahru 115.7k

PENINSULAR MALAYSIA

SARAWAK 0.58

LABUAN 1.71

SABAH 3.39

Sandakan
144.8k

Kinabatangan 115.4k

Tawau 164.7k

Kota Kinabalu
110.6k

Location quotients: Malaysia = 1.00 (8.19%)

6.00 and over	1.25 to 1.49
4.00 to 5.99	1.00 to 1.24
2.50 to 3.99	0.75 to 0.99
2.00 to 2.49	0.50 to 0.74
1.50 to 1.99	under 0.50

EAST MALAYSIA

200 kms

male migrants working in agriculture, construction, and manufacturing who lack effective labour protection and suffer social exclusion; the women who come from the Philippines and Indonesia to work as domestic servants do so as well, arguably even more so, despite Malaysian NGO activism on their behalf. They are, claims one author, 'caught in the nexus of the capitalist-patriarchal-racialized ideologies' that underpin Malaysian economic development (Chin 1997: 355). As low-wage indigenous Malay female labour was recruited for the new factories to produce export goods for global markets, the growing middle classes faced a problem: who would do the 'women's work' around the house? So, having met the rules set by the government (an employer must be rich enough, be in a nuclear family household, and, initially at least, could only employ a Muslim – that is, an Indonesian – if the family were also Muslim), the employer could then add to the family's social status by selecting from the private employment agency the most suitable and productive foreign servant, and by so doing, allow herself to enter the labour market at a much higher level of pay and job security. To the Philippines and Indonesia as the major source countries for domestic workers, have been added Sri Lanka, Cambodia, and Thailand. Cambodian domestic worker immigration, in circumstances that are often just as bad as those experienced by the Indonesians migrants before them, has increased dramatically in recent years.

So who are these new immigrants? Overwhelmingly (about 64%), in both peninsular Malaysia and in Borneo, they are Indonesians. This should not be surprising, as *Bahasa Malaysia* and *Bahasa Indonesia* belong to the same language family, with each being 80% comprehensible to the native speakers of the other. This, together with a partially shared history, strong Muslim identities, a common and permeable border in Borneo, and close geographical proximity overall, means that practical and cultural barriers to the settlement of Indonesians in Malaysia are relatively low. Add to this the wealth of the average Malaysian compared with the average Indonesian (3:1), the tradition of 'rite of passage' migration in Indonesia (*merantau*), and perhaps the question becomes instead why so few Indonesians are living in Malaysia. One of the answers, perhaps, is that, for much of the recent period, the treatment of Indonesian nationals in Malaysia has varied from moderately good to appallingly bad (examples of the latter are the mass repatriations of Indonesian foreign workers and the 'hire Indonesians last' policy).

With few rights and minimal means to redress grievances (and often no means to prove their legal status because their documents have been withheld by the employer), many working-class Indonesian foreign workers have been exploited in their workplaces, and harassed both there and elsewhere (for example, unfairly suspected of criminal behaviour, preyed upon by corrupt officials, or beaten up by RELA vigilantes). They are rendered immobile by the fact that their permit is conditional on working for the specified employer; they are taxed – a levy is imposed on each type of worker and is often taken out of that worker's wages by the employer; and their contracts are short term to ensure that their stay in Malaysia is temporary, and that they do not settle down. Regularization was used on several occasions to turn illegal migrants into guest workers, and when this failed the authorities resorted to detention and deportation. A 1995 report by NGO Tenaganita on human rights abuses at detention centres led (and to many this is almost unbelievable) to the arrest of its author, Irene Fernandez, who was convicted in 2003 (!) and then acquitted in 2008. Steps taken to clamp down on irregular migration in the early 2000s led the prisons to overflow with migrant workers. Most of them were from Indonesia, but they also came from other countries in Southeast Asia, China and South Asia. The heavy-handed deportation of foreign workers back to Indonesia at Nunukan on the border between Sabah and East Kalimantan during 2002, for example, came close to resulting in a major humanitarian disaster.

The problem of irregular or undocumented migrants is common to all of the countries of East Asia, but it is thought to be particularly serious in the case of Malaysia. For the most part, actions taken by the Malaysian government to control and regularize the migration to the country have not been successful. A recent registration process in 2011 revealed the scale of the problem. In peninsular Malaysia, of the 1.7 million foreign workers, 51% were there illegally; in Sabah, of the 1.9 million foreign workers, 53% were there illegally. This illegality adds enormously to the vulnerability of migrants. One example is the danger that children born to irregular migrants will not only have no or restricted access to education and health services but may also become stateless. Moreover, to the many bases for discriminating against foreign workers (class, gender, ethnicity, and nationality) is added the bonus to the employer of knowing that the worker cannot complain at his or her treatment, however awful it may be, because of the well-based fear of detection, detention, caning and deportation (according to Amnesty International, this caning or 'judicial whipping' is a form of torture and violates international law).

This low and vulnerable status of immigrants as well as the high cost of migration (a discouragement to return) is part of the story of the migration flows of Indonesians, Bangladeshis, Nepalese, Burmese, Cambodians, Filipinos and Vietnamese to Malaysia, but the problems are particularly severe for refugees. Perhaps most poignant is the case of the 80,000 refugees from Myanmar who are 'living in limbo' in Malaysia. As Muslim co-religionists suffering violence and expulsion in their own country, one might expect Malaysia at least to open its doors to the Rohingyan 'boat people' who comprise about a quarter of these Myanmar refugees. However, like several countries in Southeast Asia, Malaysia is not a signatory to the raft of UN conventions on refugee protection and support, so refugees just become 'illegal immigrants' to whom ID cards and work permits cannot be granted. The 15,000 or so Rohingyans who arrived in the early 1990s, following mass expulsions from Myanmar, initially merged into the informal economy, but thereafter they suffered crackdowns, detentions, beatings, and deportations (many were forced over the border into Thailand), along with many other *sans papiers* immigrants. By 2012, with further arrivals, the number of Rohingyans in Malaysia had risen to about 20,000 and yet little alleviation of their vulnerability in the face of legal and social exclusion was in sight (though 10,000 early-arrival Rohingyans were 'accepted' as refugees). In a similar vulnerable position are the refugees from conflict in the Mindanao region of the Philippines who migrated in large numbers (200,000) into Malaysian Sabah in the 1970s and 1980s, many of whom were repatriated. One author estimates that there were 152,000 refugees and asylum seekers in Malaysia in 2006; about 67,000 of these were from the Philippines, 53,000 were from Myanmar (including Chins and Rohingyans), and 30,000 were from Indonesia (mostly Acehnese). Only about half of the Acehnese diaspora returned to Aceh after the conflict.

The 'indigenous' population of Malaysia (*Bumiputera* or 'sons of the soil'), who are mostly ethnic Malay but include also the 18 tribes of the 'original people' (*orang asli*), comprise 62.0% of the total population of 28.6 million (figures taken from the 2010 Population Census). Ethnic Chinese, very few of whom are new migrants, account for 22.5% of the population (but for urban areas the proportion is higher – ethnic Chinese comprise, for example, almost exactly half the population in the capital city, Kuala Lumpur). Ethnic Indians account for 6.7%, and other Malaysian citizens for 0.8%. This leaves recorded non-Malaysian citizens, at about 2.3 million, comprising 8.1% of the total population (this figure sits uncomfortably with claims that, if undocumented migrants are included, 4–6 million foreigners live in Malaysia). This proportion of foreign residents, though lower, of course, than that for Singapore, is far higher than that for most East Asian countries, including wealthier countries such as Japan and South Korea. This fact may not fit well with either government policy or with its popular self-image, but Malaysia is indeed a 'country of immigration'. What all this new immigration has done, it is claimed, is slightly reduce wage levels for unskilled labour (seen by some as a benefit), block technological and skill upgrading, for example in the electronics industry, add greatly to remittance outflows, but perhaps most significantly of all, add a new layer of diversity to a society that was already one of the most ethnically diverse in the world, consequent upon earlier migrations including the Arabs, and the Chinese and South Asian migrations of the late 19th and early 20th centuries.

Not all of the immigrants, however, are labour migrants or trainees/students. Malaysia has recently joined Singapore, Taiwan, South Korea and Japan as a destination country for marriage migrants. Specifically, Malaysian men are marrying, with the help of brokers, foreign brides from Vietnam and the Philippines. It is, of course, often futile to try to distinguish between economic and other motives for this migration. The Filipino and Indonesian women in Sabah, for example, are looking for love and motherhood as well as for a better life.

Finally, in stark contrast to all this, Malaysia, like Singapore, welcomes 'talent' – that is, well-educated professional, technical and managerial staff (and their partners! – typically Asian professional women migrating to Malaysia with their husbands), associated with international business, higher education, etc. This 'global talent' is expected to enhance Malaysia's economic growth. One of the largest groups is composed of 20,000 Indian IT professionals, but there are also Japanese managers, and 'expatriates' from South Korea, Taiwan, Singapore, the PRC and a number of Western countries, plus students. The government is particularly keen to attract back to Malaysia the former emigrants who now possess the special scientific and technical skills needed to foster a knowledge-based economy. One-fifth as many Malaysian migrants to Australia, for example, migrate from Australia to Malaysia, many of them as managers, while many others move back and forth between the two countries. In practice, this invitation to migrate to Malaysia is extended to the wealthy in general; older wealthy foreigners, for example, can join the 'silver hair programme', which encourages retirement migration to Malaysia, or the 'Malaysia My Second Home' (MM2H) programme (for reference to Japanese retirement migrants see Chapter 7).

Brunei, as a country of immigration, has many of the migration characteristics of an oil- and gas-rich Persian Gulf state – that is, a local Muslim royal family-dominated elite employing foreign experts in an economy dependent on the imported labour of working-class migrant workers and middlemen. Many of these workers are Chinese (who make up 15% of the total population of 413,000) and some of these are stateless, the other main immigrant ethnic minorities being Malay and Filipino.

3.4 Thailand

Thailand's international migration flows are surprisingly complex. One of the reasons for this is that in addition to the uprootings associated with social modernization and economic globalization shared with other countries in Southeast Asia, Thailand borders four countries that, during the post-war period, have experienced the horrors of civil war (China, Myanmar, Laos and Cambodia). For this reason, migrants entering Thailand (population 69.9 million) have typically been seeking refuge as well as economic opportunity. At the same time, despite rapid economic growth and the fact that Thailand has the highest per capita income levels in the Greater Mekong Subregion and therefore attracts migrants, the poverty of the vast majority of its own citizens, especially those living in rural areas, has led to major emigration flows to high-income countries in Asia and elsewhere.

As far as immigration is concerned, the first post-war influx of people displaced by civil war was the arrival of part of the population that finished up on the losing side of the civil war in China. Of course, most of the pro-capitalist, pro-Western republicans (the Kuomintang) crossed the Straits of Taiwan to establish the Republic of China in Taiwan, in fierce opposition to the communist People's Republic of China on the mainland. However, Kuomintang (KMT) forces and followers also crossed into Thailand, sometimes having first settled in Myanmar, but then being ousted by pro-PRC militias. Since that time a Yunnanese migrant community has emerged in northern Thailand.

However, this was a very small influx compared with those that followed from (i) the fallout from the war in Vietnam, and (ii) the ethnic/separatist conflicts in Myanmar. The US–Vietnam war in Indochina (1955–75) was brutal and prolonged; the human cost was horrific, over 2 million dead and many more than this wounded, and massive displacements of population. The aftermath of the conflict in Vietnam was civil war and regime change in both Laos and Cambodia, resulting in refugee flows into the poor, but relatively safe, northeast region of Thailand. Some 700,000 refugees entered Thailand during the period 1975–86: about 280,000 came from Cambodia, 310,000 from Laos and 110,000 from Vietnam. Most of these were resettled outside Southeast Asia, with 380,000 going to the USA, 87,000 to Western Europe, and 35,000 each going to Canada and to Australia/New Zealand, leaving 125,000 (many of them 'hill tribe' Lao) in the camps in Thailand in 1986 (these figures are for people who were classified as refugees by the UN High Commissioner for Refugees (UNHCR); an additional 240,000 Cambodians lived in encampments along the Thai–Cambodia border). Following a successful repatriation programme in 1992–93, the last of the camps was closed in 1999.

On the other side of the country, ethnic conflict in Myanmar has likewise had a depressingly long and violent history. It has displaced hundreds of thousands of ethnic minority people, many of whom, mostly Karen, Karenni and Shan, have crossed the border and set up 'home' in western Thailand. It is this population (118,000 in 2004), many of them illiterate and lacking identification documents, that, with the addition of economic migrants, now constitutes the largest immigrant group in Thailand (estimated to be about 2 million in total). Thailand is not a signatory of the Geneva Convention and has no policies for granting refugee status or for providing permanent residency for refugees. Nevertheless, some 68,000 refugees living in camps along the border with Thailand were resettled in third countries (mostly the USA) in the period 2005–10.

Thailand has not been completely free from civil conflict itself. In addition to the ongoing pro- and anti-Thaksin social class-based conflict which, at the time of writing, threatens to tear the country apart, there is a significant displacement of population resulting from the insurgency in the south of the country, and some of this migration involves members of the ethnic Malay Muslim population crossing the border into Malaysia, joining the seasonal and circular migrations of women across the same border.

Finally, immigration (most of it irregular, much of it brokered) into Thailand for economic reasons has become the norm for many hundreds of thousands of Burmese, Cambodians, Chinese (Yunnanese) and Laotians. Though primarily economic, this large flow of migrants is also stimulated by 'pirated' images of Thailand available on televisions in Myanmar. By the time of the registration programme in 1996, the official figure was of 734,000 migrants, of whom 294,000 were registered, but according to one estimate, the official figures for this date undercounted irregular migrants by about 400,000.

As in Malaysia, government attempts to clamp down on irregular migration led to conflict with employers and sudden reversals of policy. In 2000 there were 790,000 registered migrant workers in the country – 350,000 working in agriculture and fisheries, 320,000 in manufacturing and 90,000 in construction. They were distributed very unevenly across the country, with most of them living in coastal areas, and most of the rest living along the Thai–Myanmar border. Attempts were made to substitute Thais for foreign migrant workers at the time of the 1997–98 crisis and again in 2008/09, but because of the 'gap-filler' nature of their employment, little transpired and the structural dependence on foreign labour continued. By the late 2000s there were over 1 million Burmese registered as migrants in Thailand; some were Burmese in ethnicity but there were also many Shan, Mon and Karen as well. A high proportion of these migrants, especially women, work in factories (for example, clothing factories) located close to the western border, such as at Mae Sot in Tak Province, from whence some move on in an attempt to realize the 'Bangkok dream', or to achieve resettlement abroad. These factories are often owned by, or are joint ventures with, companies based in Taiwan, Hong Kong, Singapore or Japan. Other immigrants work as agricultural workers (vegetables, fruit), or in construction, but especially in the aquaculture/fishing (mostly men) and shrimp/fish processing industries (mostly women), some of whom were trafficked to Samut Sakhon, while many women are employed as domestic servants in Bangkok and other Thai cities.

Immigration makes a major contribution to Thailand's economic growth. At almost no cost to social services (housing, health, education, etc.) the migrants work long hours for very low wages. However, there are also costs such as remittance flows and low investment in technological upgrading. One of the fears arising from political changes in Myanmar is that this will lead to large-scale return migration of Burmese foreign workers and to a lack of new migrants, resulting in labour shortages in Thailand.

Typically, the working and living conditions of Burmese migrant workers are extremely poor (which, incidentally, contributed to their high death toll from the 2004 tsunami). The wages paid to female immigrants are especially low in domestic service and for males who work on the fishing boats. As one commentator put it, 'the abusive practices against migrants are systematically rooted in the lack of a rights-based approach to formally manage the flows of migration … irregular migrants … are often exposed to discrimination, exploitative conditions and abuse' (Archavanitkul and Hall 2011: 68). While the migrants' wages are far higher than in Myanmar (ten times higher), they generally do the dirtiest and most dangerous jobs, they live in fear of violence, arrest and detention, they cannot protest their circumstances (indeed they are very politically passive), and they are vulnerable to being cheated by all and sundry, including the local police and criminal gangs. Especially before the mid-2000s when a stronger migrant registration scheme came into operation, and in the context of a poor implementation of laws and policies protecting migrants' rights, the situation of these immigrants was very precarious, they suffered a high risk of deportation, were accused of committing crime and carrying diseases such as HIV/AIDS, had poor or no access to health care, and lacked decent childcare and schooling for their children. Since then, concerted efforts have been made to turn semi-permanent irregular migrants into registered four-year guest workers. There are many obstacles to this process, one of them being the near impossibility of policing the borders both physically (borders run through mountainous, forested terrain or along rivers) and socially (the same ethnic groups on both sides of the border). A commonly expressed judgement about immigration control and regulation seems to be that 'Thailand's past migration policies have been short-term, reactive and not consistent with realities' (Rukumnuaykit 2009: 15).

On the occasion of the 2004 attempt to register migrants, many Cambodians (184,000) and Laotians (180,000), facing similar conditions to the Burmese (921,000), registered as migrants in Thailand. Migration to Thailand is very significant for the Cambodian economy. Some of this migration from Cambodia and Laos is circular or seasonal; when work is short in low-income Cambodia, for example, villagers cross into Thailand for work at wage rates that are lower than those of Thais but higher than those back home. Village studies show that up to 30% of the able-bodied workers in the border villages had moved to Thailand for the short or medium term. Migrants from Laos were overwhelmingly from farm backgrounds, and predominantly female, working in domestic service or as general labourers; if male, then they worked in agriculture and fishing, as general labourers, or as factory workers. The trafficking of men, women and children across the western, northern and eastern borders of Thailand, much of it for low-status manual work, some of it for the entertainment industry (in many instances this means prostitution), is common. By 2012, the estimated number of migrants in Thailand had reached 3.5 million, of whom around 1 million remained unregistered.

An incomplete, but nevertheless very useful, picture of Thailand's immigrant populations is provided by Figure 3.3 and the accompanying Table 3.1. It is incomplete because based upon the national population and housing census, it omits, perhaps inevitably, most of the short-stay migrant workers in Thailand, many of whom are 'undocumented'. It is useful because it depicts not just the regional distribution of the 2.46 million foreign nationals living in Thailand in 2010 who were recorded (provided by the regional LQs), not just the relative presence in each region of these foreign residents (shown by the heights of the columns), but also the absolute number of foreign residents (shown by the areas of the columns).

Four main features stand out from this map: (i) the high concentration of foreign residents in Bangkok, the central region and, to a lesser extent, in the south; (ii) the massive dominance of Burmese nationals especially in the western regions and, more generally, the tendency for nationals of countries that border Thailand to dominate in those regions within the country that are closest to their borders (notice, for example, the high values for China in the north, Cambodia in the central region, Laos in the northeast and Malaysia in the south); (iii) the incredible diversity of Bangkok – nationals from countries located all over the world are strongly represented in the capital city, including the USA, Japan, India, Russia and China; and (iv) the high LQs for German

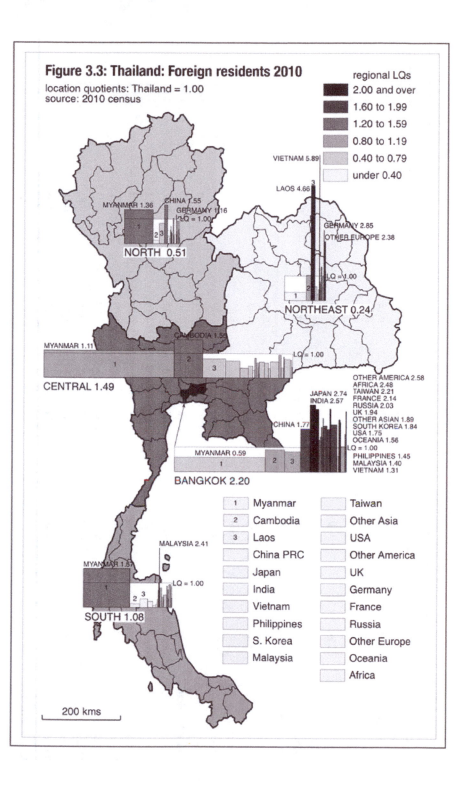

Figure 3.3: Thailand: Foreign residents 2010

location quotients: Thailand = 1.00
source: 2010 census

regional LQs
- 2.00 and over
- 1.60 to 1.99
- 1.20 to 1.59
- 0.80 to 1.19
- 0.40 to 0.79
- under 0.40

VIETNAM 5.89

LAOS 4.66

MYANMAR 1.36
CHINA 1.55
GERMANY 1.16
LQ = 1.00

NORTH 0.51

GERMANY 2.85
OTHER EUROPE 2.38

LQ = 1.00

NORTHEAST 0.24

CAMBODIA 1.55

MYANMAR 1.11

LQ = 1.00

CENTRAL 1.49

OTHER AMERICA 2.58
AFRICA 2.48
JAPAN 2.74   TAIWAN 2.21
INDIA 2.57   FRANCE 2.14
RUSSIA 2.03
UK 1.94
OTHER ASIAN 1.89
SOUTH KOREA 1.84
CHINA 1.77   USA 1.75
OCEANIA 1.56
LQ = 1.00
PHILIPPINES 1.45
MALAYSIA 1.40
VIETNAM 1.31

MYANMAR 0.59

BANGKOK 2.20

MALAYSIA 2.41

MYANMAR 1.57
LQ = 1.00

SOUTH 1.08

1	Myanmar		Taiwan
2	Cambodia		Other Asia
3	Laos		USA
	China PRC		Other America
	Japan		UK
	India		Germany
	Vietnam		France
	Philippines		Russia
	S. Korea		Other Europe
	Malaysia		Oceania
			Africa

200 kms

Table 3.1 Foreign residents in Thailand in 2010 (LQs)

Country of origin	Bangkok	Central	Northeast	North	South	Total
Myanmar	0.59	1.11	0.34	1.36	1.57	1.00
Cambodia	0.91	1.55	1.02	0.12	0.15	1.00
Laos	0.83	0.78	4.66	0.81	0.35	1.00
PRC	1.77	0.69	0.57	1.55	0.25	1.00
Japan	2.74	0.40	0.26	0.30	0.09	1.00
India	2.57	0.49	0.45	0.19	0.13	1.00
Vietnam	1.31	0.31	5.89	0.54	0.32	1.00
Philippines	1.45	0.81	1.31	0.70	0.70	1.00
South Korea	1.84	0.62	0.43	0.48	1.01	1.00
Malaysia	1.40	0.43	0.53	0.43	2.41	1.00
Taiwan	2.21	0.63	0.76	0.43	0.17	1.00
Other Asian	1.89	0.66	0.63	0.35	0.80	1.00
USA	1.75	0.62	1.36	1.02	0.42	1.00
Other American	2.58	0.39	0.58	0.28	0.27	1.00
UK	1.94	0.67	0.95	0.37	0.51	1.00
Germany	0.64	0.95	2.85	1.16	0.87	1.00
France	2.14	0.42	0.99	0.48	0.72	1.00
Russia	2.03	0.86	0.14	0.09	0.37	1.00
Other European	1.06	0.77	2.38	0.92	0.93	1.00
Oceania	1.56	0.73	1.19	0.56	0.85	1.00
Africa	2.48	0.44	0.51	0.25	0.38	1.00
Total	2.20	1.49	0.24	0.51	1.08	1.00

Source: 2010 Census.

nationals (and, in the case of the northeast region, 'other' Europeans) in the rural regions of north and northeast Thailand. This reflects the marriage, cohabitation, and sex-work relations built up over many decades between Thai women and German men, both in Germany and in Thailand. It is relevant in this respect that the foreign resident community in Thailand with the highest male-to-female sex ratio (at 497 when equality = 100) is the German community (UK 334, USA 301, but Laos just 70, i.e. many more women than men).

Emigration from Thailand has been on a large scale. It built up during the 1990s, and has lasted until the present, but is now much lower than immigration. A small minority have been highly educated 'brain-drain' migrants, but the vast majority have been working-class migrants (mostly using agents) seeking good wages to support themselves and their families back home. As a result, significant Thai male migrant worker minorities have emerged: (i) in the Gulf states/North Africa, early on in Saudi Arabia and Libya (where in the 1980s, 65,000 were leaving Thailand each year to work as overseas contract workers), then in Israel (12,000 in 1999), later UAE and Qatar; (ii) in the wealthier countries of East and Northeast Asia, above all Taiwan (50–60% of these are contract workers, employed mostly in construction and textiles), but also Singapore, Malaysia, Brunei, Hong Kong, South Korea and Japan; (iii) in Western countries (mostly North America and Australasia); and (iv) as crewmen on international shipping lines. Often spending just a few years away in one country, returning for a while, and then going off to a new country, these migrants tend to lead transnational lives. They do not always succeed, but when they do, their remittances transform their family's social status in the village and their standard of living and quality of life.

Over time, the proportion of the migrants who were female has increased. Thai women are also to be found in the same East and Southeast Asian countries and in Western Europe, both as employees (for example, factory workers in Taiwan, domestic servants in Hong Kong, and low-level service-sector workers in many places) and as marriage migrants (notably in Germany, Scandinavia, and the UK). Marriage migration, with its flow of benefits to the family and the community through 'daughter duty', has become commonplace, even welcomed, in northeast Thailand. A number of the female migrants from Thailand have become sex workers in countries such as Germany and Japan. Sometimes it was sex work in Thailand that led to marriage to a foreigner and emigration; there can be complex overlaps between marriage migration and prostitution.

The trafficking of Thai female sex workers to Japan has received particular political and academic attention. It is argued that the post-war sex industry in Thailand, already well developed through high domestic demand and increasingly based upon the recruitment of young women migrants from the villages of central, northern and northeastern Thailand, was greatly boosted by the use of Bangkok as a 'rest and recuperation' posting by the US military during the Vietnam War. For about 20 years after that ended in 1975, the sex industry in

Thailand became the main target for (mostly) Japanese individual and corporate sex tourism. Japanese companies and the men who worked in them had enormous wealth internationally due to their rapidly rising profits and incomes and due also to the newly gained strength of the Japanese currency (the yen). Thai sex workers were also migrating to Japan where, while some were treated atrociously, others flourished despite debt bondage. Partly due to political pressure on Japan by the US government during the mid-2000s, steps were taken to reduce the exploitation of Southeast Asian women in the Japanese sex industry. This had the effect of sharply reducing the flows of sex workers from Thailand and the Philippines to Japan.

This is not quite the end of the story, however. On a larger scale than that of Bali, both Bangkok and major tourist destinations in Thailand such as Pattaya and Phuket have become sought after by Westerners (mostly men, and many of them 'over-stayers') who, for all sorts of personal reasons, such as business or personal relationship failure, want to lead a different way of life in new surroundings. Many of the resulting relationships with locals end badly. Retirement migration has also become significant (22,000 in 2008; some of them are Japanese living in Chiang Mai and in resort towns like Hua Hin). In the broader picture of Thailand's international migration flows, the numbers of Western, Australasian and Northeast Asian residents (mostly employees of large corporations or international organizations located in Bangkok) are very small, but the local economic and social effects of their migration can be quite significant. The largest group of such professionals and managers are Japanese. There were 23,000 Japanese with work permits living in Thailand in 2006, more than double the figure for 1996. Particularly poignant are the feelings and experiences of educated Burmese living in Thailand. This is because they are the co-nationals of the country's stigmatized 'other'. Also very significant, economically and socially, is the return migration of highly educated Thai nationals. Finally, there are around 20,000 people in Thailand on student visas.

3.5 Myanmar/Burma

Myanmar (population 48.7 million) is probably the Southeast Asian country whose migrations are most difficult to discern. This is partly because northern areas of the country such as the Kokang area close to the Yunnan border, through which many migrants have passed, are inhabited by groups of diverse ethnicity (and with an economy dependent over much of the recent period on smuggling and opium farming), who are skilled at 'the art of not being governed' – governed, that is, by the Burmese authorities located in Yangon, or now in the new capital city, Naypyidaw.

In the early post-war period, by far the largest immigrant and immigrant-descended group in Myanmar was the Indian population, but following the 1962 military coup and the switch to the 'Burmese way to socialism', 300,000 Indians and 100,000 Chinese left the country. There is, however, still a significant population of Burmese of Indian descent (estimated at 2.5–3.0 million), especially concentrated in Yangon and Mandalay. They have Burmese names and speak *Bamar*, and have to a great extent been 'Burmanized'. Specifically, the proportion of Hindus has declined sharply. People of Indian descent form part of the country's lower-middle class – a largely urban-based 'petite bourgeoisie'.

The literature suggests that there have been four principal international migration flows since that time. The first two relate to the migrations across the Myanmar–PRC border. A small, but long-standing Chinese community, mostly located in Yangon and Mandalay, which traces its origins to the migrations of the late 19th and early 20th centuries, survived the political changes of the 1960s. Since the early 1990s, however, according to several sources, there has been a large influx of Chinese farmers and traders migrating illegally into northern Myanmar. Very little seems to be known about this migration, but it is thought possible that it might amount to hundreds of thousands of people. One author wrote:

> In Burma's new market economy [that is, since the SLORC takeover in 1988], the Sino-Burmese minority have been transformed almost overnight into a garishly prosperous business community. In addition, tens of thousands of poor but entrepreneurial immigrants from China, sweeping down from nearby Yunnan, have bought up the identity papers of dead Burmans for as little as three hundred dollars, becoming Burmese nationals overnight … Nor is Chinese dominance only an urban phenomenon. After two years of severe flooding in southern China, large numbers of Chinese farmers – over a million, some estimate – poured into northern Burma. These new Burmese 'citizens' now grow rice on the cleared hill country they have taken over. Entire Chinese villages have sprung up in this way.
>
> (Chua 2003: 24–25)

Much of the literature emphasizes how 'porous' the Myanmar–PRC border is, and with co-ethnic populations such as the Kachin on both sides of the border, 'marriage migration' is not uncommon.

Second, and more recently, we need to add the migration of construction workers, technicians, etc., associated with Chinese infrastructure investments (mining and dam construction) in central and northern Myanmar (40,000 according to one estimate). It is claimed that northern Myanmar–Thailand has also acted as one of the main corridors along which irregular Chinese migration, mostly from Fujian Province, to Western countries has taken place.

Third, well-researched and massively important in both numerical and humanitarian terms have been the migrations associated with ethnic conflict in Myanmar, a country that has an unusually high level of ethnic diversity. These sporadic conflicts throughout the post-war period have displaced hundreds of thousands of people, many of whom, mostly of Shan, Karenni, Karen and Mon ethnicity, have finished up as political refugees/economic migrants in the western border provinces of Thailand (see the previous section on Thailand). A small number of the most vulnerable refugees are resettled in Western countries, but most remain in Thailand. The living conditions of these Burmese emigrants in Thailand have been judged by human rights groups to be particularly shocking. They have no legal protection, no political rights or representation, are cruelly exploited as cheap labour by farm, workshop and factory employers, suffer poor housing conditions in settlements that lack basic amenities, and are often discriminated against by members of the host population. Nevertheless, the remittances sent back to families and villages in Myanmar have had significant developmental effects. Also resulting from ethnic conflict, in the early 1990s around 250,000 Muslim Rohingyans migrated from northwest Myanmar to Bangladesh (about 325,000 still live as stateless persons in Bangladesh, about a quarter of them in the refugee camps set up close to the Myanmar border), from where some have moved on to the Gulf states and Afghanistan. More recently, Rohingyans have taken extreme risks to escape ethnic cleansing by migrating to Malaysia (along with Christian Chins). In addition, due to the suppression of its separatist movement by the Burmese army, Kachin refugees have crossed into Yunnan Province in China, as did 10–30,000 Kokang (ethnic Chinese) in August 2009.

Finally, although the majority of Myanmar's economic migrants go to Thailand, Burmese foreign workers are becoming significant minorities in a number of Southeast and East Asian countries, including Malaysia, South Korea and Japan. In addition, students leave Myanmar for Singapore, Australia and the UK. Immigration of Myanmar nationals consists very largely of return migrants from Thailand, Malaysia, etc., and of children born to migrant workers outside the country being brought back to Myanmar to be cared for by their grandparents. Recent political changes in Myanmar are not expected to have immediate effects on the country's international migration flows, but should significant return migration occur, it has been argued that it could influence political change in a progressive way.

3.6 Laos

There are interesting parallels between the migration situations in the Lao People's Democratic Republic (PDR – population 6.4 million) and Myanmar. As in Myanmar, most of the emigration derives from two causes: poverty and conflict (gross domestic product (GDP) per capita is about three times higher in Thailand than in Laos). In the case of economic migrants, the Mekong River, which forms much of the political frontier between Laos and Thailand, links rather than separates the Lao ethnic region, resulting in daily cross-border commuting from Laos into Thailand for better wages as agricultural workers, as well as seasonal and more permanent migration into and through northeast Thailand. Improvements in transport infrastructure (such as bridges) and communications technologies have facilitated this migration. Many migrants go further and work semi-permanently as 'overstayers' in the central southern provinces or in Bangkok. They work as agricultural and fisheries labourers, factory and building workers, and as domestic servants. Indeed, a majority of the migrants from Laos into Thailand are women; they have the reputation for being hard working and cheap to employ. Some are trafficked for sex work in Thailand. Anti-trafficking programmes exist but are considered by some commentators to be ineffective. Ethnic conflict and land use changes such as rubber plantations in Laos can increase the likelihood of emigration and trafficking. Ethnic minority Laotians living close to the borders with other states will often cross that border to take advantage of opportunities on the other side, or to avoid disadvantages on their side – an example of this being the Brao, who cross back and forth between Laos and Cambodia.

The US–Vietnam War, and its violent political aftermath in Laos, caused many deaths and injuries as well as large displacements of population. For example, 360,000 fled the country as refugees after the Lao PDR was established in 1975. Very large refugee camps became established across the border in northeast Thailand to cope with these refugees. Eventually, most of their inhabitants returned to Laos, but between 1975 and 1991, the USA accepted 121,000 Laotians for resettlement (while others went to Australia). Many were members of the Hmong minority, the majority of whom now live in the US mid-western state of Minnesota, where their psycho-cultural adjustment has been difficult. Lowland Lao were initially dispersed throughout the USA. They then voluntarily relocated to places like Rhode Island, where suitable jobs were available and co-ethnic populations lived.

As with other low-income countries, brain-drain migration is a problem. It is estimated that 37% of educated Laotians currently live outside the country.

There are small communities of (i) ethnic Chinese (both descendants of migrants from before World War II and new migrants, some of whom are brought to Laos by Chinese construction projects and by Hong Kong investments in Las Vegas-style gambling cities located close to the Chinese border), and (ii) Vietnamese migrants living in Laos, consisting of both urban skilled and semi-skilled workers and rural farm workers.

3.7 Cambodia

Given the significance of the Chinese community in Cambodia today and its powerful, and partly clandestine, political influence, boosted by the arrival of several hundred thousand new 'mainlander' migrants from the PRC (*xin yimin*), it is surprising, perhaps, to learn that this immigrant community along with a separate Chinese identity was suppressed and all but eradicated in the early post-colonial period, and only began to re-establish itself after the end of the Vietnamese occupation in 1989 (reflected in the U-shaped fortunes of Chinese schools, for example). The worst years were during the Khmer Rouge regime of 1975–79 when, despite the presence of 10–15,000 PRC advisers and of young ethnic Chinese supporters of the revolution, it is thought that 215,000 ethnic Chinese were killed. In the context of the class war of that regime, to be seen as an urban, educated, capitalist entrepreneur was quite likely to result in your death.

Five international migrations can be identified for Cambodia (population 14.5 million) during the post-1950 period. The first of these are the migrations affecting the Vietnamese minority. Emigration was caused initially by Khmer chauvinism under Lon Nol directed against the Vietnamese. This was followed by the many cross-border displacements of the war in Vietnam, then the subsequent civil war in Cambodia (when 420,000 Vietnamese were expelled or fled to Vietnam), and finally by the invasion by Vietnamese forces, accompanied by economic and return migration, that ended that war (bringing the Vietnamese community back to about 300–450,000 in the mid-1980s). The Vietnamese are mostly labourers, craftsmen and small business owners. Between 1992 and 2000 there were many outbreaks of violence towards this minority and discrimination against them was widespread. A majority of Vietnamese are not Cambodian citizens and face legal and social exclusion. The reason for this is a central myth of the nationalist ideology that Cambodia's existence is threatened by Vietnam. This also helps, it is said, to explain the contrast with the recent favourable treatment of the Chinese community and the acceptance of new Chinese immigration.

As with Laotians, most Cambodians fleeing conflict finished up in refugee camps in the eastern parts of Thailand. A majority of these displaced people returned to Cambodia in the early 1990s through the UNHCR repatriation process, when it was judged to be politically expedient and relatively safe to do so, but some found their way to distant countries in North America, Australasia and Western Europe where they came to form locally segregated minority communities.

The second category is emigration for economic reasons. Most of the migrants go through the very porous border to Thailand and are (or become) irregular/illegal, and many others go to Malaysia and Singapore (see references in sections above). Cambodia has one of the lowest per capita income levels in the whole of East Asia, and has recently suffered many floods and droughts, so it is not surprising that many Cambodians seek employment in neighbouring Southeast Asian countries, even sometimes in Vietnam, in the richer countries of Northeast Asia, and elsewhere. They work as farm and fishery labourers, construction and factory workers, and maids in Thailand, as maids in Singapore, as factory workers in Malaysia, South Korea and Taiwan, and as construction workers in the Middle East. Cambodia became, temporarily, a major source of domestic workers for Malaysia. The time and money costs of legal migration are high (too high for most Cambodians), but the risks attached to illegal migration (imprisonment, debt, non-payment of wages, etc.) are also very high. As is usually the case, Cambodian migrant workers overwhelmingly complement rather than compete with indigenous workers – they are 'gap fillers' doing the jobs that the locals cannot, or will not, do.

The third migration is the trafficking of Cambodian men, women and children to other parts of Asia, especially to Thailand. An International Labour

Organization (ILO) report emphasizes: (i) the very large number of children and very young adults amongst the migrants; (ii) the dependence on brokers; (iii) the many kinds of abuse endured; and (iv), the risks of arrest and physical violence. So desperate is the poverty that sex trafficking of Cambodian women to Thailand (especially to the main tourist sites), other countries in Southeast Asia, Hong Kong and Hainan Island in the PRC is a lucrative trade. Vietnamese women (some of them Khmer Krom) also migrate to Cambodia to engage in sex work. Some commentators, however, see these Cambodian and Vietnamese migrants not as victims, but as independent agents, and make a forceful case against equating sex work with trafficking.

Fourth, another route to economic survival and the economic support of the family back home is the migration of Cambodian women to become wives through brokered marriages to men (many of them poor farmers) in Taiwan, South Korea and elsewhere (see later chapters).

Finally, small in number, but enormously important in terms of economy and society, is the return migration of foreign-educated Cambodians, often immediately into positions of power and influence in their 'home' country, and hence sometimes at odds with the domestic non-migratory elite (who tended to doubt the returnees' commitment to Cambodia because of their dual citizenship). To quote one researcher:

> The most controversial dual citizens were those returning to high-level government posts ... The majority of Cambodian exiles returned from the US, Canada, Australia, and France, which recognized some form of dual citizenship. For the first five years of the new government, more than half of the National Assembly and the top officers of key ministries were dual citizens.
>
> (Poethig 2006: 73–74)

Having lived in the West offers a Cambodian a taste of positional superiority when returning 'home', but it is also a painful reminder that 'to be Cambodian ranks one as third class in the global hierarchy of nations' (Poethig 2006: 84).

Cambodia is also, but to a much smaller degree, a country of foreign immigration. Vietnamese migrants of many backgrounds, including some ethnic minority Montagnard farmers displaced by the Kinh settlement of the Central Highlands, and Khmer Krom similarly displaced in the Mekong Delta region, live and work in the country. These 150,000 new immigrants from Vietnam join the 1.1 million who relocated from Vietnam to Cambodia between 1985 and 1998. As in the cases of Myanmar and Laos, ethnic Chinese migrant workers (for example, construction staff and technicians) accompany inward Taiwanese, Hong Kong, PRC and Singaporean business investment in the garment industry, and managers and technicians also accompany other investments in Cambodia by companies based in Northeast Asia (notably South Korea) and elsewhere.

3.8 Vietnam

The tumultuous post-World War II history of Vietnam (population 89.7 million) has resulted in many international migrations. First, decolonization from France, and the legacy of close relationships with the French, brought a significant number of Vietnamese to France in the early post-war period. That same decolonization brought ethnic Vietnamese back from the newly formed nation-states of Laos and Cambodia where, during the colonial period, they had performed the roles of merchants, skilled craftsmen and clerical staffs. It also resulted in a forced assimilation of ethnic Chinese.

Second, the long and appallingly violent US–Vietnam War displaced hundreds of thousands of people, and some of that displacement took place across international borders (but also included the importation by the USA of labour from the Philippines, South Korea and Thailand for infrastructure investments in South Vietnam). What, however, became well known outside the Southeast Asian region was not so much the migrations caused by the war itself, or by the first wave of emigration to the USA (130,000) coinciding with the end of the war in 1975, but the migration of the 804,000 Vietnamese 'boat people' in the years following the military victory of the communist north over the capitalist south. This migration resulted in large part from the anti-capitalist steps taken by the new government, and by the new vulnerability of those who had previously worked (or had come under suspicion of having worked) with members of the losing side – that is, with the US armed forces and the US-backed South Vietnamese administration.

Where did the 'boat people' go? Many emigrants were not, in fact, 'boat people' at all – about 260,000 (230,000 of them ethnic Chinese) crossed the land border to the PRC (many of these 'out of place' migrants did not settle well in their new village homes and subsequently emigrated). Those who took to sea and who survived the sea journey (10–20% did not) were accepted as refugees, not so much in Southeast Asia, where (as has been said before) refugee acceptance is low and where temporary residence was provided only on the understanding that resettlement would take place – not there, but in other parts of the world. Many other escapees from Vietnam languished in refugee camps in Hong Kong, and in Malaysia, Indonesia and Thailand, some later arrivals being repatriated under the 'Comprehensive Plan of Action' 1989–97 back to Vietnam (and Cambodia), sometimes at considerable psychological cost. Most early arrivals and about a quarter of later ones moved on to Western countries such as the USA (64% of total, where half of them live in California), Canada and Australia (12% each) and France (3.4% of the total, where half live in the Paris region). About 75% of the 'boat people' and other emigrants in the period 1975–79 were Vietnamese of Chinese descent (*Hoa*), who suffered a double prejudice – for being potential fifth columnists during the conflict with China, and for being bourgeois. This means that the economic losses to the newly reunited country consequent upon their leaving were highly significant. Together with migrations before and since the 'boat people' exodus, the total number of people of Vietnamese descent (overseas Vietnamese or *Viet kieu*) living outside the country amounts to about 3.6 million with, according to the 2010 Census, 1.8 million of these living in the USA.

The US presence in South Vietnam had another migration effect. The links between the two countries produced a very specific migration flow of Vietnamese to the USA: those who came as 'GI brides' – that is, as the wives of US servicemen. Indeed, 79% of all Vietnamese women in the USA in 1980 who married outside the Vietnamese community were married to a serving or former member of the armed forces. However, these bi-cultural relationships also left a problematic legacy in Vietnam: Amerasian children, fathered by Americans and born to Vietnamese mothers who remained in Vietnam were often bullied and mistreated by their peers. Many subsequently achieved immigrant status in the USA.

When Vietnam was reunited under the communist government in 1975, a new stage in its international migration began. By the time that the Soviet system collapsed in 1989–90, and reflecting the strong political and economic ties between Moscow and Hanoi, around 244,000 (42% of them female) had migrated to the Soviet Union and other countries in Eastern Europe, mostly Czechoslovakia, but also East Germany, Poland and Bulgaria. By then (that is, after 1986), however, the *Doi Moi* (renovation) policy of opening up the economy to market mechanisms was in operation and a transition to a state–run capitalist economy was under way. By the end of 1991, about 170,000 workers had returned from Russia and Eastern Europe, though some have since joined others in migrating to a reunited Germany.

This *Doi Moi* transition was eventually successful in GDP terms. Recently the Vietnamese economy has been growing quickly with a sizeable mobilization of the labour force and significant inward investment, especially from Singapore, Taiwan, Hong Kong, Japan and South Korea. This growth started slowly and from a very low base, however – a war-torn country plagued by poverty, a male labour force reduced by war losses and injuries, and a countryside extensively damaged by poisons, abandoned munitions and mines. With future prospects so poor it is hardly surprising that economic migration from Vietnam has been a major feature for most of the period since 1986. This 'export of labour' is encouraged by the government as a meaans to increase employment, generate more income for workers and to meet poverty alleviation and socio-economic development strategic targets. Remittances grew to reach US$7.2 billion by 2010, and were spent on both investment savings and current expenditure. The government has also influenced to some degree the gender balance of emigration by restricting the migration of domestic workers.

Some of this migration, often of a circular nature, was, and still is, to neighbouring countries such as Malaysia (with over 100,000 Vietnamese migrants – mostly factory workers) and the PRC, but notably to Cambodia, where the lack of skilled entrepreneurial labour following the disastrous Khmer Rouge regime led to many opportunities for Vietnamese immigrants. Further afield, Vietnamese communities now exist in many countries: (i) the high-growth/high-income countries of East Asia, notably Taiwan (80,000), South Korea (45,000) and Japan (20,000) (where they are either government-supported contract factory workers on 'guest worker'-type visas, or 'trainees', and the economic returns to migration are high); in addition, 10,000 Vietnamese (mostly construction workers) have migrated to the UAE since 2004; and (ii) Western countries such as the USA and Canada, Australia and New Zealand, the UK and France, and several other countries in Europe including in Eastern Europe.

That same poverty of prospects has also been instrumental in sex trafficking, and adoption. It also contributes to the significant flows of largely brokered Vietnamese marriage migrants, especially to Taiwan (80,000 by 2010) and South Korea (40,000 by 2010). It follows from all of this that remittance income is important for many households, especially in those rural areas from which many of the marriage migrants come (such as the Mekong Delta region). The benefits to families with daughters married to foreigners have also changed gender relations in the villages of origin, raising the bargaining power of women and reducing the marriage prospects of single men. In some cases, highly educated Vietnamese women are marrying low-wage US citizens (including overseas Vietnamese) – men who were 'bottom among men, top among nations'.

Whether for work or marriage (and in some cases, such as the trafficking/migration of Vietnamese women into southern China, it is difficult to differentiate between the two), these migrations imply disruptions to family relationships. Sustaining families across transnational spaces and especially caring for children left behind is a major challenge for many Vietnamese emigrants. In addition, about 35% of the elderly in Vietnam benefit directly or indirectly from migrants' remittances – about 40% of this by value is from international migration, and two-thirds from North America. Sometimes the returnees – *Viet kieu* – find the demands put upon them by their relatives, and the uses/vices on which their generosity is spent, distinctly upsetting.

In addition to emigration for work and marriage reasons, there were in 2010 about 80,000 Vietnamese students studying abroad, 25,000 in Australia, 13,000 each in China and the USA, and 7,000 in Singapore. Many stay on and enter the labour market for a period of time after they have graduated. Some commentators see this sizeable migration as evidence of a brain drain.

Finally, recent economic success has encouraged many Vietnamese to return home after a period studying, working or developing a career abroad. Sometimes, of course, return is not completely voluntary, as when asylum seekers are turned away or the irregular status of a migrant is revealed. Then, the process of re-embedding in Vietnamese society can be an extremely difficult one. This return of overseas Vietnamese, many of whom are of Chinese ethnic descent, is very important in the development of the Vietnamese economy (although they frequently experience petty discrimination). Typically, they have acquired language skills and other forms of 'social capital', experience of capitalist economies and corporations, and an orientation towards innovation, risk taking, and wealth accumulation. As one writer put it, 'although their "Chinese" identity (as *Hoa*) had once made them risk their lives by sailing out on the roaring sea, their "Vietnamese" identity (as welcomed returnee *Viet kieu*) brought them back to Vietnam' (Chan 2013: 525). Even without return, the economic impacts of the *Viet kieu* on Vietnam can be highly significant, through tourism and investment, for example, and not just through remittances.

Up until now, the settlement of Western and Northeast Asian professional, technical and managerial staffs in Vietnam has been relatively small: 34,000 foreigners were thought to be working in Vietnam in 2007, mostly from Japan, South Korea and China (including Hong Kong and Taiwan).

3.9 Philippines

The Philippines is the big story of Southeast Asian international migration. This is not just because the numbers of migrants are enormous (8.6 million Filipinos were working overseas in 2009 – for the 2.3 million of those in 2013 who went through official channels see Figure 3.4) and the proportion of those of Filipino descent living abroad is extraordinarily high (thought to be about 20% of the current resident population of the Philippines of 96.5 million), or even because the Philippines government is uniquely active in promoting emigration, but because the Philippines case raises very important theoretical issues about the economic, social and political effects of migration.

In particular, this case sits uncomfortably with the current fashion to see international migration as a 'win, win, win' process. According to this view, migration produces: (i) gains for the receiving country through the supply of cheap labour in the form of hard-working young adults to solve difficult and costly recruitment problems; (ii) gains for the migrants themselves through improvements in their living standards and future prospects; and (iii) gains for the sending country in reducing unrest and unemployment, in the form of remittance income, and in investment by returnees who are seen as 'heroic' agents of modernization.

At the start of the post-World War II period the prospects for prosperity and development were higher in the Philippines than they were for any other Southeast Asian country, but now the country is not far from being the poorest, most unequal, most conflict-ridden society in the region. This is despite the vast wealth that has entered the Philippines through migrants' remittances. In 2010, remittance income, which had continued to rise through the economic crisis after 2008, came to a staggering US$21.4 billion – equal to 41.6% of the value of Philippines exports in that year! It might seem impossible that this enormous monetary gain could be outweighed by the effects of the loss of the country's 'brightest and best', and yet, while migration is, of course, only part of the picture of national development, it is the judgement of this author that you cannot lose to emigration a high proportion of your most ambitious and hard-working non-graduates, and one out of every three graduates, over several generations without putting at risk social development and economic

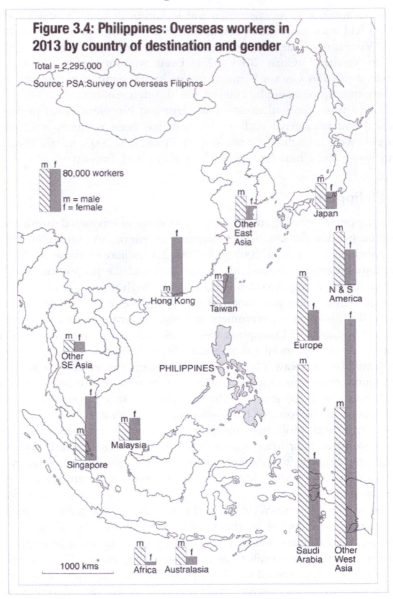

Figure 3.4: Philippines: Overseas workers in 2013 by country of destination and gender

Total = 2,295,000

Source: PSA:Survey on Overseas Filipinos

80,000 workers

m = male
f = female

Other East Asia

Japan

Hong Kong

Taiwan

N & S America

Other SE Asia

PHILIPPINES

Europe

Malaysia

Singapore

Saudi Arabia

Other West Asia

1000 kms

Africa   Australasia

performance. I am not alone in thinking this way: the ILO's Manolo Abella writes 'There are not a few (including this author) who wonder if the sluggish growth of the Philippine economy is attributable not only to political uncertainties but also to the massive scale of migration, which has undoubtedly robbed the country of some of its most critical human resource and, often also with them, considerable capital flight' (Abella 2007: 164).

While it is rightly seen as overwhelmingly a country of emigration, the Philippines achieved independence in 1946 with a large immigrant minority, albeit one that was already fairly well integrated – the Chinese. In the 1950s, a Filipino First policy reflected the nationalism of the time, and barriers were erected to make it difficult and costly for the Chinese to obtain Filipino citizenship. During the Marcos years of 1965–86, however, the 'crony capitalism' sponsored by the state resulted in a liberalization of naturalization laws affecting the Chinese and a major expansion of Filipino-Chinese businesses followed. However, so much wealth, some of it corruptly gained, meant that Chinese elite families were often the targets for the many kidnappings of the mid-1990s.

The Philippines was also a transit country for Indochinese refugees on their way from camps in Thailand, Malaysia, Palawan (Philippines) and Hong Kong to resettlement in the USA. Between 1980 and 1987, 208,000 refugees passed through the refugee transit camps: 109,000 were Vietnamese, 67,000 were Cambodian and 33,000 were Laotian – all but a handful (who went to Western Europe) went on to the USA.

The culture (or 'taken-for-granted world') of migrating away from the Philippines to find work and a better life (especially in the USA) was well established before 1946, but has flourished since then (a 2010 study found that over 50% of people aged over 14 wanted to work abroad on a temporary basis and nearly 20% wanted to migrate permanently from the Philippines). Over the last 50 years, Filipinos have migrated to almost every country in the world, partly in response to the context of their lives – poverty and poor job prospects, and to the fatalism generated by the country's class structure and its politics – but also, as Aguilar argues, because they decide to go on a journey:

> International labour migration is an analogue of the ancient religious journey, a modern, secularized variant of the ritual pilgrimage ... overseas employment entails hardships, sacrifices, and social dislocation for the migrant worker who must demonstrate fortitude and determination to persevere through the trials of a journey which culminates in the rite of a successful homecoming.
>
> (Aguilar 1999: 102–103)

You migrate to see the world, to grow up, to avoid the people who bore you (pun intended), and to have fun – you possess agency in the migration decision.

Emigration built up during the 1970s and 1980s, and, realizing the potential for remittance income (but also the threat to good international relations when things go wrong for overseas Filipino workers – for example, the deaths of Contemplacion in Singapore and Sioson in Japan), the 'labour brokerage' state, with NGO backing, became centrally involved in the creation and support of the overseas employment programme and the protection of overseas contract workers. Most of the migrants come from central and northern Luzon, especially from the Ilocos region, and from Metro Manila, which tends to gather

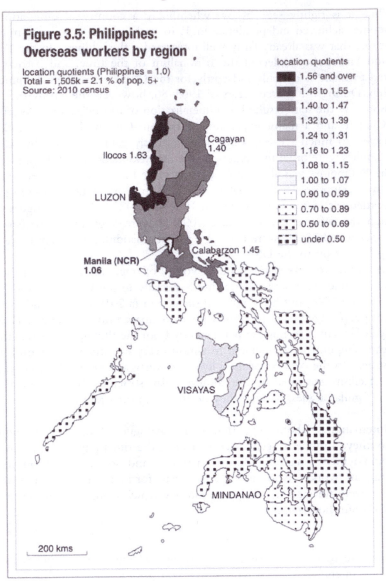

Figure 3.5: Philippines: Overseas workers by region

location quotients (Philippines = 1.0)
Total = 1,505k = 2.1 % of pop. 5+
Source: 2010 census

location quotients
- 1.56 and over
- 1.48 to 1.55
- 1.40 to 1.47
- 1.32 to 1.39
- 1.24 to 1.31
- 1.16 to 1.23
- 1.08 to 1.15
- 1.00 to 1.07
- 0.90 to 0.99
- 0.70 to 0.89
- 0.50 to 0.69
- under 0.50

future emigrants by internal migration from other areas such as Southern Tagalog. Results from the 2010 Census (Figures 3.5 and 3.6) show: (i) that many of the source regions of overseas workers are parts of the country that have above-average per capita incomes – such higher incomes facilitate new emigration due to higher levels of education and more resources to finance the migration, but they also reflect the economic benefits derived from the remittance incomes from past emigration; (ii) that the gender composition of

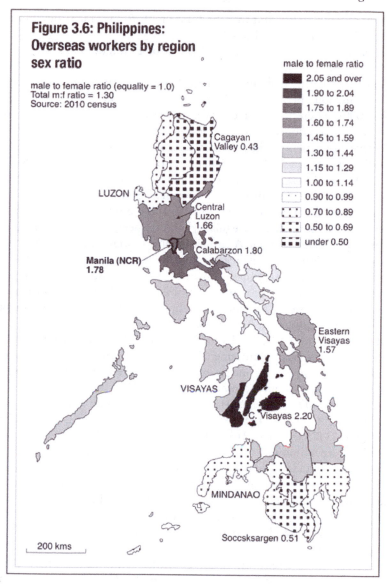

Figure 3.6: Philippines: Overseas workers by region sex ratio

male to female ratio (equality = 1.0)
Total m:f ratio = 1.30
Source: 2010 census

male to female ratio
- 2.05 and over
- 1.90 to 2.04
- 1.75 to 1.89
- 1.60 to 1.74
- 1.45 to 1.59
- 1.30 to 1.44
- 1.15 to 1.29
- 1.00 to 1.14
- 0.90 to 0.99
- 0.70 to 0.89
- 0.50 to 0.69
- under 0.50

Cagayan Valley 0.43
LUZON
Central Luzon 1.66
Manila (NCR) 1.78
Calabarzon 1.80
Eastern Visayas 1.57
VISAYAS
C. Visayas 2.20
MINDANAO
Soccsksargen 0.51

200 kms

emigration flows is very regionally distinctive – the high rates of male emigration tend to be in the central regions of the country (central Luzon and the Visayas), while the high rates of female migration are found in the far north (where young women leave to work as domestic workers in Hong Kong and Singapore), and in the far south (where young women leave to work as domestic workers in Muslim countries such as Malaysia, Saudi Arabia and the Gulf states). The 2000 Census had already shown that there were 992,000

Filipino overseas workers and that the households from which they came were better off than non-migrant households.

Five main economic migration streams can be distinguished:

1   Continued permanent migration to North America – to both the USA (3.43 million people of Philippines descent in 2011), and Canada (843,000), where many have arrived under the Live-in Caregiver Program and are sometimes seen as 'ideal immigrants'. A steady stream of Filipinos achieve permanent residency in the USA (that is, they obtain a 'green card' – 57,000 in 2011), and many also go on to become US citizens (42,000 in 2011). Populations of Filipino descent are especially highly concentrated in California and Hawai'i. Some of the recent female migrants to the USA are caregivers and domestic workers who live in a situation of 'normalized irregularity'. It has been argued that Filipinos in Los Angeles, due to their Asian geographical origin and their Spanish and American colonial inheritances, have developed a hybrid 'pan-ethnic consciousness'. This sometimes, however, has the effect of locating them socially not alongside the upwardly mobile Asians, but closer to their Latino neighbours. Some of the child migrants to the USA from the Philippines are adoptees, others are Amerasians.

2   Migration to the Middle East (during the 1980s and early 1990s this migration flow was an amazing 250–300,000 per annum). These are predominantly temporary contract workers deployed through the Philippine Overseas Employment Administration (POEA), which estimates the stock of migrants in December 2004 to be 994,000 in Saudi Arabia (1.55 million in 2011), 206,000 in UAE (680,000), 92,000 in Kuwait (187,000), 58,000 in Qatar (342,000), and 215,000 in the rest of West Asia. These migrant workers are employed in all kinds of jobs, including professional and managerial middle-class ones, but numerically dominant were male construction workers in the early days, followed more recently by female domestic workers and nurses, notably to Saudi Arabia, the UAE (194,000 in 2008), Kuwait, Qatar, Jordan, but also to Israel.

3   Migration to Australasia: permanent migration to Australia is also very important (385,000).

4   Migration to Western European countries, especially to Italy (185,000 mostly as domestic workers), but also to the UK (220,000), Germany, France and Spain, where many are nurses and care workers (au pairs in Denmark), but some are professionals.

5   (Increasing) migration to East Asian countries (43% of it illegal/irregular), notably to Singapore, Malaysia and Hong Kong, but also Taiwan, South Korea and Japan (where many of the early migrants were female 'entertainers' – hostesses, sex workers and dancers). Most of these migrants are employed as domestic workers (but not in Japan), factory workers (especially in Malaysia, Taiwan, and South Korea, but also Saipan in the Marianas), and construction workers. Once again, many of the migrants are

contract workers deployed through POEA. In December 2004 POEA estimated that the stock figures for migrants were 353,000 for both Japan and Malaysia, 197,000 in Hong Kong, 161,000 in Taiwan, 136,000 in Singapore and 341,000 in the rest of East and Southeast Asia (the equivalent figures for 2011 were Malaysia 569,000, Japan 221,000 – notice the sharp drop – Singapore 180,000, and Hong Kong 175,000).

6   Not so much a migration as a long-term absence, the Filipino seamen who crew many of the world's cruise and cargo ships (they were 20% of all seafarers in 2000). It has been argued that through the daily experience of hard physical labour and risk, many Filipino seafarers have acquired the 'package deal' of successful masculinity – something that is difficult to achieve in the low-opportunity environments of Philippine urban and rural areas. Some Filipino seamen, however, leave the Philippines altogether and become based in foreign countries (such as the Netherlands). In this way, the boundaries between transnational employment and migration become blurred.

Philippines emigration was, as might be expected, significantly influenced by the Asian financial crisis in 1997/98: it halted the growth of emigration; differentially affected land-based and sea-based workers (favouring the latter), and particularly hit new hires rather than re-hires; flows to Malaysia and South Korea were most severely reduced (by more than 50%); men were more affected than women; and, for a time, remittances were lower (especially from land-based workers). Broadly speaking, the recent economic recession has not, however, slowed down international labour migration from the Philippines, which is about 1 million persons per annum, but it has, at least temporarily, slowed its increase. Conflict in the Middle East and North Africa has necessitated the return of Filipino workers, notably from Kuwait, Iraq, Libya and Syria.

Earlier migrations were biased towards male manual workers in construction and factory work (as well as seamen). After 1992, however, migrations were biased towards Filipino women working as nurses, care workers and domestic servants. Most of the reasons given for this high level of emigration relate in one way or another to the poor prospects at home, notably high unemployment, low incomes, and few opportunities for upward social mobility, but some commentators emphasize, in addition, population pressure and uneven spatial development. All migrants were influenced (but often in complex ways) by the social networks in which they were embedded, and the social capital that they possessed. Many find that connections forged through worship at a Catholic Church help them to settle in the host country. There are, in addition to the skilled and unskilled working-class migrants, many Filipino professionals, managers and entrepreneurs living abroad, but one of the defining characteristics of Philippines migration has been its 'brain waste' character – that is, the tendency for employers to recruit Filipino workers for jobs that are below their level of qualification and experience, in other words, labour market de-skilling.

Female migrants in particular, despite being the active agents of change at home (see, for example the agricultural changes in a part of northern Luzon brought about by remittances from emigrant domestic workers) are forced to 'perform subordination' overseas: 'this includes compliance with gender scripts, minimizing assertiveness, downplaying aspects of identity that might suggest class advantages, constraint of body language, and the depiction of a "subordinated self" that draws on cultural perspectives of Filipinos as subservient' (Barber and Bryan, in Barber and Lem 2012: 233). This subordination and de-skilling in the labour market sometimes pushes Filipino women (and even some men) towards marriage. Certain writers, of course, reject this victim discourse along with its opposite (the migrant as a hero of national development), arguing instead for a view of the migrant Filipino female domestic worker as being upwardly socially mobile, and belonging to a social class (in practice this means petite bourgeoisie – a small-scale business (co-)owner and/or landlord) that is in the 'process of becoming'.

In this debate, Filipino female nurses and domestic workers have attracted a particularly high level of political and academic attention. So strong has been the tendency for doctors and nurses to seek employment outside the Philippines that the efficiency of the country's own health-care sector has been put at risk. Despite the efforts of the Philippines government, NGOs and labour unions to protect the interests of Philippines overseas workers, women in the health and social care professions often face poor working conditions, discrimination, long working hours and low wages. On top of this, there is concern that while caring for the wealthy or relatively well off in the countries of immigration, and saving their often meagre wages to send home to support their families, Filipino women (and often their left-behind children) are missing out on their own family life. They are, in short, part of a 'care chain', in which it is their labour, looking after the children and the elderly of the rich elsewhere, that releases those privileged women (and men) in the countries of destination from their 'duty of care' for their own relatives, thereby allowing them either to lead a life of leisure or to develop their own professional and managerial careers (at incomes much higher, of course, than those of the carers upon whose labour they have come to depend). Meanwhile, the migrants' mothers, sisters and husbands/partners care for their children in the Philippines, albeit with the benefit of the remittances sent back home by the migrant which may be used in ways that improve the education of the children (for example, enrolment in private school – thereby enhancing the likelihood of their emigration), or the health and well-being of the migrants' elderly parents. As gender roles back home can be reversed with the men left behind becoming carers, so also left-behind women sometimes take on male roles in farming. However, even without gender role reversal, the power relations between men and women can be drastically altered by the earning capacity of female migrants.

While some migrant domestic workers adjust well in the destination country – especially those who were adventurous, had relatively high status, who had good social networks (for example, made friendships through church going) and were earning good wages – others suffer psychological stress, due to three main causes: the abusive behaviour of their employers, their burden of debt, and the threat of failure of their family relationships. Despite the advantages that it brings to some, this care-chain complex of social and economic relationships is clearly full of social injustices, both great and small. One is tempted to come to the judgement that it, alongside other abuses of migrant labour (notably bullying related to debt and the bonded labour contract), tends to reproduce in the post-colonial world of today the very same exploitative power relations, in which class, gender and ethnicity intersect to produce multiple disadvantage, that characterized the colonial period prior to World War II.

While the vast majority of female migrants from the Philippines are seeking advantages through employment in mainstream jobs in the receiving country, there are two migration streams that form exceptions: first are the marriage migrations arranged by matchmaking agencies now using websites, which take Filipino women to Japan, the USA, Australia and elsewhere. These marriage migrations all too often draw upon Western eroticized images of deferential Filipino women. Second are migrations associated with sex work. These are sometimes disguised as 'entertainment' (though originally, and perhaps paradoxically, many of the early Filipino migrants in Japan were, indeed, jazz musicians). This latter migration was, at one time, a major feature of migration from the Philippines to Japan and South Korea (with major income and status effects back in the Philippines). However, largely as a result of changes in policy and procedures mostly around 2005 (brought about by pressure from a lobby group-influenced US government), this migration flow has greatly decreased.

Finally, while the Philippines is overwhelmingly a country of emigration, it has attracted, and does still attract, some international migrants, many of them senior or middle-level managers and professionals working for Japanese, Korean or other countries' multinational companies. Their number tends to reflect the degree of confidence in the political stability of the country: when confidence is high, FDI flows in and with it come the managers and technicians, but when political turmoil returns (as in 2000), the investments disappear and immigration is stemmed. The 2010 Census results show that 120,000 people living in the Philippines at that time had been living outside the country five years earlier. Many of these (especially those living outside the capital region) were, however, returnees. The Philippines, of course, attracts many returnees – what one author has called the 'big unknown' of Philippines international migration. Having experienced living in a different country and culture (which sometimes, even against the odds, facilitates independence, empowerment (breadwinner status) and a better quality of life), attitudes towards returnees are typically ambivalent. This is despite the strong pull of home and family, and the governmental welcome extended to returnees – indeed some return migrations, notably those of scientists and businessmen, receive state support and subsidy.

As with other Southeast Asian countries, there were some early post-war immigrants of Chinese descent (who were affected by the Taiwanese dominance of the Philippines Chinese school system), and some immigrants of Indian and Syro-Lebanese descent. However, there are also many new migrants from the PRC. Most of the earlier ones coming in the 1970s and 1980s were from Fujian and were family reunion migrants, but more recent migrations from China are from all over the country, and their reasons for living in the Philippines are varied – some are professionals and technicians, others are students or student/traders; some are the children of wealthy officials, others are avoiding Chinese regulations such as the one-child policy; and still others are illegal/irregular migrants (perhaps as many as 90,000, many of whom have fake documents, and a minority of whom are members of transnational criminal gangs). In addition, some Chinese also use the Philippines as a transit country for migration to the USA. Recent immigrants to the Philippines also include Filipino-US and -Canadian citizens, a small number of white Westerners who settle in the Philippines, sometimes marrying Filipino women, and also some South Korean and Japanese retirement migrants, plus many English-language students (again mostly Koreans – about 100,000!).

3.10 Conclusion

Much has changed in Southeast Asian international migration. Formerly a region of low exchanges intra-regionally, and of large net immigration from China and South Asia, it now has major migration flows between its constituent nations and large net emigration to the rest of the world (according to the Association of Southeast Asian Nations (ASEAN) and ILO there are 13.5 million Southeast Asian migrants working outside their country of origin, 39% of them in other Southeast Asian countries). Many Southeast Asians have migrated to high-income countries (roughly 5 million to the USA, 1 million to the EU/Japan, and 500,000 each to Canada and Australasia). Those of Chinese descent have migrated to Western countries such as the USA, Canada and Australia, where they form a large part of the Vietnamese, Malaysian, Indonesian and Singaporean communities.

The line-up of Southeast Asian countries in terms of their dominant international migration characteristics is as follows: (i) mainly emigration: Philippines, Indonesia, Cambodia, Myanmar, Laos, and Vietnam; (ii) mainly immigration: Singapore, Brunei; (iii) both significant immigration and emigration: Malaysia and Thailand. Some commentators place great emphasis on the demographic characteristics of these countries as an explanation of their migration situations (for example, higher fertility rates leading to oversupply of labour, resulting in high unemployment and greater emigration), but it is at least possible that the direction of causality is the reverse – that is, that emigration leads to poverty and unemployment, which in turn lead to high fertility. In the complex real world of Southeast Asia, it is likely, of course, to be both.

It is not, however, only the numbers of migrants and the geography of their migration flows that have changed. It is what kinds of people the migrants are. Far more of them are women; some of these are marriage migrants who, while retaining the 'cultural citizenship' of their countries of origin, become the 'mother-citizens' of their adopted countries. Indeed, in a majority of cases the official figures show that women now outnumber men amongst the out-migration and in-migration flows. In particular, there has been a significant increase in the number of women migrating to enter domestic service and care-worker employment. Frequently, these women are married and leave behind young children and elderly parents when they migrate, raising issues about their welfare and development. Many migrants (especially those from Myanmar to Thailand) are children. While some women are 'family members' migrating with their wage-earning husbands, an increasing proportion of them are independent migrant workers. While sojourning is still common (notably in migrations to the Middle East), an increasing number of families are migrating together on a permanent or semi-permanent basis, too. This has partly come about through the replacement of one set of barriers to immigration to high-income countries – those related to racial and ethnic origins which dominated previously – by another set of barriers – those related to occupational class and educational qualifications. This has facilitated privileged access of Southeast Asians to the labour markets of high-income Western countries for professional, technical and managerial workers (and their families), and for those whose skills and experience match the gaps in the supply of labour onto those countries' labour markets.

For those with professional or technical qualifications, the link with the destination country was in many cases established through migration for study. Student migrations linking Southeast Asian countries with the educational institutions of high-income countries have increased enormously. Some stay on and settle in the country where they studied, others return straight away, but many stay for a few years and then return to their 'home' country. This latter group constitutes the 'reverse brain drain' so sought after by Southeast Asian governments and corporations.

It is also not just a question of who migrates, but how they migrate. One of the big changes has been the growth of migration as a business. It will be said, quite correctly, that Chinese and Indian workers migrating to Southeast Asia in the late 19th and early 20th centuries were also actively recruited through intermediaries, but with globalization, the scale and sophistication of the migration business has reached new heights for both legal and illegal (irregular or undocumented) forms of migration. Trafficking, despite the 2001 UN Convention, is a problem in every country in the region, but especially so, perhaps, for migrations into and out of Thailand. One estimate puts irregular migration in East and Southeast Asia at about 40% of total migration (2.4 million out of 6.1 million). Smuggling is widespread and, in certain border areas, a significant source of income. Services providing advice on travel arrangements, documentation, visa applications, jobs and housing at destination, remittance payment security, etc., have mushroomed, and the brokerage of international marriages is big business. Rich and poor, highly educated/skilled and unskilled alike have come to depend on a multitude of private-sector firms or organizations that promote or facilitate international migration.

So important has migration become to the economic well-being of the populations of Southeast Asia (especially through remittance income), so dependent on immigrant workers have certain sectors in Southeast Asian countries become, and so economically integrated have the countries become both amongst themselves and with the rest of the world, that some are now asking if Southeast Asian borders should not be completely opened. Such an opening, it is argued, would allow imbalances resulting from differential economic growth rates and differential demographic change to be eliminated through labour migration. Progress towards any such opening, however, has been pitifully small. There have been some bilateral non-legally binding 'memoranda of understanding' on migration issues, the Bali Concords in the early 2000s tried to push forward 'mutual recognition arrangements' for professionals to facilitate free movement of professional staffs, and the ASEAN Declaration on the Protection and Promotion of the Rights of Migrant Workers in 2007 addressed some of the issues surrounding the exploitation and mistreatment of migrant workers, but successful action has been limited. The ILO and the International Organization for Migration (IOM) have also been active in promoting migration policy reform in the region, but again with limited effect (for example, only two of the main Southeast Asian countries, the Philippines and Indonesia, have ratified the ILO's Migrant Workers Convention). This lack of progress reminds us that migration is, of course, a sensitive issue on which states in Southeast Asia, as elsewhere, are reluctant to agree to anything that limits their national sovereignty.

In the meantime, however, millions of migrants in Southeast Asia have benefited from the relative economic prosperity and political stability of Thailand and Malaysia, and while most migrants to Singapore do the jobs that Singaporeans do not want to do themselves, the lucky few, through business success or professional achievement, enter George Borjas's 'heaven's door' to share a quality of life comparable to that found in the finest cities in the world.

Box 3.2 The gains and losses from international migration

Gains

1   To the sending countries: *Gain of lowered unemployment due to the departure of actually or potentially unemployed young adults* – the problem with this argument, of course, is that if the 'brightest and best' had chosen to stay, they would not only be unlikely to be unemployed themselves, but they would probably, through their energy and initiative, have contributed to the employment of others. Furthermore, there is no evidence that the departure of many workers raises the wages of those who remain (Jalilian and Reyes, in Jalilian 2012: 35). *Gain through the departure of political malcontents* – yes, but if those able young people had 'voiced' their frustrations rather than 'exited', they might have brought about the often much-needed political reform. *Gain of foreign-country acquired skills and experience* – this can be significant, but is probably overstated in the literature. The reason for such scepticism is that, insofar as skills and experience are gained (and in very many cases due to the nature of the work, they are not), there is only a fairly small chance that these skills will be appropriate to the economy of the sending country. However, gains to the sending country do occur when new productive investments are made, as sometimes happens, when migrants return. *Gains through remittances* – this is, as can be seen from the case of the Philippines given above, a major gain in monetary terms and a boost to the sending country's economy, even if, as is usually the case, they are primarily spent on housing and consumption goods rather than on investment goods or education, and only rarely help the poorest of the poor. *In summary, the gains to the sending country are typically modest, except, that is, for remittance income.*

2   To the migrants: *Gains to migrants through higher wages and better job prospects* – in general, as with internal migration, migrants gain through international migration (they are climbing a 'stairway to heaven' see Box 7.1). These gains are, however, different for different groups of workers. For the well qualified, emigration may be the start of significant upward social mobility into prestigious jobs in high-income countries, while for the less-well qualified (and those many whose qualifications are not recognized or not rewarded), migration might mean no more than a temporary, but significant, improvement in pay, sometimes at the expense of poor working conditions, and having to deal with dishonest brokers and abusive employers. *Gains to migrants through freedom* to act independently of cultural and familial constraints – migration as escape from boredom and obligation. *Gains to migrants through greater personal security* – this applies specifically to those fleeing civil conflict and oppression. *Gains to migrants through travel and adventure* – often the standing of a migrant on his or her return is higher than that of a

non-migrant, partly because of the courage and independence they have demonstrated, and the exciting knowledge of the outside world that they have gained. *In general, the gains to the migrants themselves are life changing and considerable.*

3   To the receiving countries: *Gain to employers* – they can now employ obedient, hard-working young adults at rates of pay that are extremely favourable to the employer (Gibson and Graham 2002). *Gain arising from the filling of posts by immigrants that might otherwise have remained unfilled* – it is difficult to overstate the importance of this gain. Whole sectors of the economy, whole levels in employment hierarchies, vast numbers of difficult, dangerous and extremely unpleasant jobs are done by immigrant workers. Without them, the efficiency of private-sector companies (such as palm oil plantations), public-sector services (such as transport services), individual households (where domestic servants work), and growing cities (dependent on immigrant construction workers) would be put at risk. This argument applies equally to certain jobs requiring specialized professional skills (such as those needed for hospitals, universities and major civil engineering projects). *Gain to receiving countries of young adults who are often the 'brightest and the best' of the countries from which they come* – this is often portrayed as a subsidy from the poor to the rich. The arrival of healthy young adults onto the labour markets of high-income countries who bear none of the costs of their upbringing represents a massive economic gift. Are all of them grateful for this gift? Not to judge by the hostility towards immigrants expressed by many xenophobic citizens and politicians in the receiving countries. At the level of wider society, *gain of cultural diversity through immigration* – in an increasingly interconnected world, to live in an ethnically homogenous, mono-cultural society is judged by many, especially well-educated young adults, to be deeply dissatisfying (see Chapter 7 on cultural refugees from Japan). *Overall, the gains to the receiving countries through international migration are enormous.*

Losses

1   To the sending country: *Loss of young adults* – whose financial and emotional costs since birth have been borne by the sending country through food and shelter (parents/family), education and health (parents/state), care and support (family, neighbourhood). The sending country might also bear further costs of elderly or sick returnees. *Loss of the 'brightest and the best'* (mostly – sometimes, of course, the least intelligent and the worst) – the selectivity of migration ensures that those who leave are, typically, more ambitious, intelligent, cunning, qualified, self-confident, adventurous, and determined to succeed, than those who stay. These are precisely the qualities desperately needed by people living in poverty and powerlessness to (i) confront and solve their

problems, and then (ii) enrich and empower themselves and those around them. *Loss to the upper- and middle-class rich of a servile working class* – it is difficult to control those whom you want to employ for next to nothing, when they can get 'rich' by doing the same jobs for foreign others. *Loss to the working-class poor of the physical labour, security and protection, care and support provided by their young adult children plus, quite often, the extra burden of responsibility for the raising of their children's children.* At the level of the wider society, *loss of competitiveness through higher wage costs, and through the so-called 'Dutch Disease'* – remittance income, it is argued, raises the value of the currency and thereby lowers export performance. *Loss of practical and symbolic cultures* – replacement of local/national cultures ('taken-for-granted worlds') by the goods, and associated values and lifestyles, of the ('superior' or 'modern' or 'advanced') country from which the remittance wealth has been derived. *Altogether, the losses to the sending country are generally significant.*

2   To the migrants themselves: *Loss of control over their work, residence and relationship environment* – leads to vulnerability and powerlessness at the hands of people whose behaviour they cannot predict and whose motives might well be dishonest, in the context of a society whose language and customs they do not understand and whose laws they may be breaking. *Cost of paying for the migration* – this can be significant, so much so that many migrants are in debt and must pay back, sometimes in highly exploitative situations, what they have borrowed to effect the migration. *Loss of contentment* (the feeling of being 'crippled inside' – see Box 7.1) – separation from the family and the familiar, often leading to relationship failure (for example, divorce). In many cases, migrants draw upon their contacts (family and friends) and other social networks to reduce their vulnerability to harm and build up 'social capital' helpful to them in adjusting to their new country. Nevertheless, sometimes the losses to the migrant are significant; it depends very largely on their *social class location* – *those who are highly qualified, well resourced and welcomed usually lose little and gain much, while those who are 'unqualified', poor, lacking documents and stigmatized can suffer greatly.*

3   To the receiving country: *Loss of jobs by, and lower wages for, indigenous workers as a result of an influx of foreign migrant workers* – this is an argument that is usually grossly exaggerated by those who have an interest in fomenting xenophobia (such as those seeking to gain political power). In reality, the high degree of labour market segmentation, and the reluctance of indigenous workers to do low-status jobs (for example, those called '3D' or 3K jobs), usually ensures that there is very little competition between immigrant workers and domestic labour. *Higher social welfare costs* – generally not an issue due to the youth, strong work orientation and vitality of immigrant workers. *Loss of ethnic*

homogeneity leading to threat to social order – once again, a largely spurious argument: the efforts made by immigrants to adjust to the host society's norms are typically significant and the bases for conflict are thereby much reduced. *In general, the losses to receiving countries are not significant.*

Many of the more economic arguments presented here (though with a rather different emphasis) are covered in Jalilian and Reyes, in Jalilian 2012: 1–117.

Selected references

3.0 General

Ananta, A. and Arifin, E.N. (eds), 2004, *International Migration in Southeast Asia*. Singapore: Institute of South East Asian Studies.

Arnold, F. and Shah, N.M. (eds), 1986, *Asian Labor Migration: Pipeline to the Middle East*. Boulder, CO: Westview.

Asian Development Bank, 2006, *Workers Remittance Flows in Southeast Asia*. Manila: ADB.

Asian Migrant Centre, 2005, *Resource Book: Migration in the Greater Mekong Subregion*. Hong Kong: AMC.

Athukorala, P., Manning, C. and Wickramasekara, P., 2000, *Growth, Employment and Migration in Southeast Asia: Structural Change in the Greater Mekong Countries*. Cheltenham: Elgar.

Battistella, G. and Asis, M.M.B. (eds), 2003, *Unauthorized Migration in Southeast Asia*. Quezon City: Scalabrini Migration Center.

Caouette, T., Sciortino, R., Guest, P. and Feinstein, A., 2007, *Labor Migration in the Greater Mekong Sub-Region*. Bangkok: Rockefeller Foundation, Southeast Asia Regional Program: Learning Across Boundaries.

Dang, N.A. and Chantavanich, S. (eds), 2004, *Uprooting People for their own Good? Human Displacement, Resettlement and Trafficking in the Greater Mekong Sub-Region*. Hanoi: Social Sciences Publishing House.

Elmhirst, B. and Saptari, R. (eds), 2004, *Labour in Southeast Asia: Local Processes in a Globalizing World*. London: Routledge.

Ford, M., Lyons, L. and Van Schendel, W. (eds), 2012, *Labour Migration and Human Trafficking in Southeast Asia: Critical Perspectives*. London: Routledge.

Hugo, G. and Young, S. (eds), 2008, *Labour Mobility in the Asia-Pacific Region*. Singapore: Institute of South East Asian Studies.

Iredale, R., Hawksley, C. and Castles, S. (eds), 2003, *Migration in the Asia Pacific: Population, Settlement and Citizenship Issues*. Cheltenham: Edward Elgar.

Jalilian, H. (ed.), 2012, *Costs and Benefits of Cross-Country Labour Migration in the GMS*. Singapore: ISEAS.

Kaur, A. and Metcalfe, I. (eds), 2006, *Mobility, Labour Migration and Border Controls in Asia*. Basingstoke: Palgrave

Kneebone, S., 2010, The governance of labor migration in Southeast Asia, *Global Governance* 16: 383–396.

Lorente, B.P., Yeoh, B., Shen, H.H. and Piper, N. (eds), 2005, *Asian Migrations: Sojourning, Displacement, Homecoming and Other Travels*. Singapore: Asia Research Institute.

McKay, D., 2012, *Global Filipinos: Migrants' Lives in the Virtual Village*. Bloomington: Indiana University Press.

Naik, A., Stigter, E. and Laczko, F., 2007, *Migration, Development and Natural Disasters: Insights from the Indian Ocean Tsunami*. Geneva: International Organization for Migration.

Robinson, W.C., 1998, *Terms of Refuge: The Indochinese Exodus and the International Response*. London: Zed Books.

Sandhu, K.S. and Mani, A. (eds), 1993, *Indian Communities in Southeast Asia*. Singapore: Institute of South East Asian Studies.

Suryadinata, L. (ed.), 2011, *Migration, Indigenization and Interaction: Chinese Overseas and Globalization*. Singapore: World Scientific.

Wille, C. and Passl, B. (eds), 2001, *Female Labour Migration in South-East Asia: Change and Continuity*. Bangkok: Chulalongkorn University, Asian Research Centre for Migration.

Yeoh, B. and Willis, B. (eds), 2004, *State/Nation/Transnation: Perspectives on Transnationalism in the Asia-Pacific*. London: Routledge.

3.1 Indonesia (and Timor Leste)

Anggraeni, D., 2006, *Dreamseekers: Indonesian Women as Domestic Workers in Asia*. Sheffield: Equinox Publishing.

Fechter, A.-M., 2007, *Transnational Lives: Expatriates in Indonesia*. Aldershot: Ashgate.

International Organization for Migration, 2010, *Labour Migration from Indonesia: An Overview of Indonesian Migration to Selected Destinations in Asia and the Middle East*. Jakarta: IOM Mission Indonesia.

Silvey, R., 2004, Transnational migration and the gender politics of scale: Indonesian domestic workers in Saudi Arabia, *Singapore Journal of Tropical Geography* 25(2): 141–155.

Suryadinata, L. (ed.), 2008, *Ethnic Chinese in Contemporary Indonesia*. Singapore: Institute of South East Asian Studies.

Wise, A., 2006, *Exile and Return Among the East Timorese*. Philadelphia: University of Pennsylvania Press.

Wong, T.-C. and Rigg, J. (eds), 2011, *Asian Cities, Migrant Labour and Contested Spaces*. London: Routledge.

3.2 Singapore

Barr, M.D. and Skrbis, Z., 2009, *Constructing Singapore: Elitism, Ethnicity and the Nation-Building Project*. Honolulu: University of Hawai'i Press.

Beaverstock, J.V., 2002, Transnational elites in global cities: British expatriates in Singapore's financial district, *Geoforum* 33: 525–538.

Cheng, Y., 2014, Time protagonists: student migrants, practices of time and cultural construction of the Singapore-educated person, *Social & Cultural Geography* 15(4): 385–405.

Chua, B.H., 2009, Being Chinese under official multiculturalism in Singapore, *Asian Ethnicity* 10(3): 239–250.

Ho, E.L.-E., 2011, Migration trajectories of 'highly-skilled' middling transnationals: Singaporean transmigrants in London, *Population, Space and Place* 17: 116–129.

Huang, S. and Yeoh, B.S.A., 2005, Transnational families and their children's education: China's 'study mothers' in Singapore, *Global Networks* 5(3): 379–400.

Hussin, M., 2012, *Singapore Malays: Being Ethnic Minority and Muslim in a Global City-State.* London: Routledge.

Saw, S.-H., 2007, *The Population of Singapore.* Singapore: Institute of South East Asian Studies.

Yeoh, B.S.A. and Yap, N., 2008, Gateway Singapore: immigration policies, differential (non)incorporation, and identity politics, in Price, M. and Benton-Short, L. (eds), *Migrants to the Metropolis: The Rise of Immigrant Gateway Cities.* Syracuse, NY: Syracuse University Press, 177–202.

3.3 Malaysia (and Brunei)

Asis, M.M.B., 2005, The Filipinos in Sabah: unauthorized, unwanted and unprotected, in Jatrana, S., Toyota, M. and Yeoh, B.S.A. (eds), *Migration and Health in Asia.* London: Routledge, 116–140.

Chin, C.B.N., 1997, Walls of silence and late 20th century representations of the foreign female domestic worker: the case of Filipina and Indonesian female servants in Malaysia, *International Migration Review* 31(2): 353–385.

Chin, C.B.N., 1998, *In Service and in Servitude: Foreign Female Domestic Workers and the Malaysian Modernity Project.* New York: Columbia University Press.

Garces-Mascareas, B., 2011, *Labour Migration in Malaysia and Spain: Markets, Citizenship and Rights.* Amsterdam: University of Amsterdam Press.

Hilsdon, A. and Giridharan, B., 2008, Racialised sexualities: the case of Filipina migrant workers in East Malaysia, *Gender, Place and Culture* 15(6): 611–628.

Human Rights Watch, 2004, Help wanted: abuses against female migrant domestic workers in Indonesia and Malaysia, *Human Rights Watch* 16(9B): 1–91.

Jones, S., 2000, *Making Money off Migrants: The Indonesian Exodus to Malaysia.* Amsterdam: International Institute of Social History.

Missbach, A., 2011, *Separatist Conflict in Indonesia: The Long-Distance Politics of the Acehnese Diaspora.* London: Routledge.

Nah, A.M. and Bunnell, T., 2005, Ripples of hope: Acehnese refugees in post-tsunami Malaysia, *Singapore Journal of Tropical Geography* 26(2): 249–256.

Pillai, P., 1999, The Malaysian state's response to migration, *Sojourn* 14(1): 178–197.

Ullah, A.A., 2010, *Rationalizing Migration Decisions: Labour Migrants in East and South-East Asia.* Farnham: Ashgate.

US Committee for Refugees and Immigrants, 1997, US Committee for Refugees World Refugee Survey 1997 – Malaysia, 1 January, www.refworld.org/docid/3ae6a 8b960.html (accessed 19 April 2015).

3.4 Thailand

Amnesty International, 2005, *Thailand – The Plight of Burmese Migrant Workers.* London: AI.

Angeles, L.C. and Sunanta, S., 2009, Demanding daughter duty: gender, community, village transformation, and transnational marriages in Northeast Thailand, *Critical Asian Studies* 41(4): 549–574.

Aoyama, K., 2009, *Thai Migrant Sex Workers: From Modernization to Globalization*. Basingstoke: Palgrave Macmillan.

Archavanitkul, K. and Hall, A., 2011, Migration and human rights in a Thai context, in Huguet, J.W. and Chamratrithirong, A. (eds), *Thailand Migration Report 2011: Migration for Development in Thailand: Overview and Tools for Policymakers*. Bangkok: IOM, 63–74.

Chantavanich, S., 2007, *Thailand Policies Towards Migrant Workers from Myanmar*. Bangkok: Asian Research Centre for Migration.

Derks, A., 2010, Migrant labour and the politics of immobilization: Cambodian fishermen in Thailand, *Asian Journal of Social Science* 38(6): 915–932.

Grundy-Warr, C. and Wong, E., 2002, Geographies of displacement: the Karenni and the Shan across the Myanmar-Thailand border, *Singapore Journal of Tropical Geography* 23(1): 93–122.

Hewison, K. and Young, K. (eds), 2006, *Transnational Migration and Work in Asia*. London: Routledge.

Howard, R.W., 2008, Western retirees in Thailand: motives, experiences, wellbeing, assimilation and future needs, *Ageing and Society* 28: 145–163.

Huguet, J.W. and Chamratrithirong, A. (eds), 2011, *Thailand Migration Report 2011: Migration for Development in Thailand: Overview and Tools for Policymakers*. Bangkok: International Organization for Migration.

Huijsmans, R. and Phouxay, K. (eds), 2008, *'Whether you go Legally or Illegally in the End it's the Same, you're Cheated': A Study of Formal and Informal Recruitment Practices of Lao Workers Migrating to Thailand*. Vientiane: International Labour Organization.

Human Rights Watch, 2010, *From the Tiger to the Crocodile: Abuse of Migrant Workers in Thailand*. New York: HRW.

Kusakabe, K. and Pearson, R., 2010, Transborder migration, social reproduction and economic development: a case study of Burmese women workers in Thailand, *International Migration* 48(6): 13–43.

Martin, P., Abella, M. and Kuptsch, C., 2006, *Managing Labor Migration in the Twenty-first Century*. New Haven, CT: Yale University Press (Chapter 6 on Thailand).

Molland, S., 2010, 'The perfect business': human trafficking and Lao-Thai cross-border migration, *Development and Change* 41(5): 831–855.

Pearson, E. et al., 2006, *The Mekong Challenge: Underpaid, Overworked and Overlooked: The Realities of Young Migrant Workers in Thailand*. Bangkok: International Labour Organization.

Pearson, R. and Kusakabe, K., 2012, *Thailand's Hidden Workforce: Burmese Migrant Women Factory Workers*. London: Zed Books.

Rukumnuaykit, P., 2009, *A Synthesis Report on Labour Migration Policies, Management and Immigration Pressure in Thailand*. Bangkok: International Labour Organization.

Sciortino, R. and Punpuing, S., 2009, *International Migration in Thailand 2009*. Bangkok: International Organization for Migration.

3.5 Myanmar/Burma

Chua, A., 2003, *World on Fire: How Exporting Free Market Democracy Breeds Ethnic Hatred and Global Instability*. London: Arrow Books.

Egreteau, R., 2011, Burmese Indians in contemporary Burma: heritage, influence, and perceptions since 1988, *Asian Ethnicity* 12(1): 33–54.

Grundy-Warr, C. and Wong, E., 2002, Geographies of displacement: the Karenni and the Shan across the Myanmar-Thailand border, *Singapore Journal of Tropical Geography* 23(1): 93–122.

Human Rights Watch, 2004, *Out of Sight, Out of Mind: Thai Policy Toward Burmese Refugees and Migrants*. London: HRW.

Lintner, B., 2002, Illegal aliens smuggling to and through Southeast Asia's Golden Triangle, in Nyiri, P. and Saveliev, I. (eds), *Globalizing Chinese Migration: Trends in Europe and Asia*. Aldershot: Ashgate, 108–119.

3.6 Laos

Asian Development Bank (Chamberlain, J.), 2009, *Broken Lives: Trafficking in Human Beings in the Lao People's Democratic Republic*. Manila: ADB.

3.7 Cambodia

Amer, R., 2006, Cambodia's ethnic Vietnamese: minority rights and domestic politics, *Asian Journal of Social Sciences* 34: 388–409.

Ehrentraut, S., 2011, Perpetually temporary: citizenship and ethnic Vietnamese in Cambodia, *Ethnic and Racial Studies* 34(5): 779–798.

Maltoni, B., 2006, *Review of Labour Migration Dynamics in Cambodia*. Phnom Penh: International Organization for Migration.

Ong, A., 2003, *Buddha is Hiding: Refugees, Citizenship, the New America*. Berkeley: University of California Press.

Poethig, K., 2006, Sitting between two chairs: Cambodia's dual citizenship debate, in Ollier, L.C-P. and Winter, T. (eds), *Expressions of Cambodia: The Politics of Tradition, Identity, and Change*. London: Routledge, 73–85.

3.8 Vietnam

Barbieri, M., 2000, Les Vietnamiens à l'étranger, in Gubry, P. (ed.), *Population et Développement au Viet-Nam*. Paris: Karthala, 285–311.

Belanger, D., Tran, G.L. and Le, B.D., 2011, Marriage migrants as emigrants: remittances of marriage migrant women from Vietnam to their natal families, *Asian Population Studies* 7(22): 89–105.

Chan, Y.W., 2013, Hybrid diaspora and identity-laundering: a study of the return overseas Chinese Vietnamese in Vietnam, *Asian Ethnicity* 14(4): 525–541.

Chantavanich, S. and Reynolds, E.B. (eds), 1988, *Indochinese Refugees: Asylum and Resettlement*. Bangkok: Chulalongkorn University, Institute of Asian Studies.

Dang, N.A., 2007, Labour export from Vietnam: issues of policy and practice, *Vietnam's Socio-Economic Development* 51: 19–32.

Dorais, L.-J., 2010, Politics, kinship, and ancestors: some diasporic dimensions of the Vietnamese experience in North America, *Journal of Vietnamese Studies* 5(2): 91–132.

Hillman, F., 2005, Riders on the storm: Vietnamese in Germany's two migration systems, in Spaan, E., Hillmann, F. and Van Naerssen, T. (eds), *Asian Migrants and European Labour Markets: Patterns and Processes of Immigrant Labour Market Insertion in Europe*. London: Routledge, 80–100.

Hoang, L.A. and Yeoh, B.S.A., 2012, Sustaining families across transnational spaces: Vietnamese migrant parents and their left-behind children, *Asian Studies Review* 36(3): 307–325.

Long, L.D. and Oxfield, E. (eds), 2004, *Coming Home? Refugees, Migrants, and Those Who Stayed Behind*. Philadelphia: University of Pennsylvania Press.

Ministry of Foreign Affairs (Vietnam), 2012, *Review of Vietnamese Migration Abroad*. Hanoi: Consular Department, Ministry of Foreign Affairs.

Pfau, W.D. and Giang, T.L., 2010, The growing role of international remittances in the Vietnamese economy: evidence from the Vietnam (Household) Living Standards Surveys, in Kee, P. and Yoshimatsu, H. (eds), *Global Movements in the Asia Pacific*. Singapore: World Scientific, 225–248.

Viviani, N., 1984, *The Long Journey: Vietnamese Migration and Settlement in Australia*. Melbourne: Melbourne University Press.

Yarborough, T., 2005, *Surviving Twice: Amerasian Children of the Vietnam War*. Washington, DC: Potomac Books.

3.9 Philippines

Abella, M. et al., 2007, Should governments encourage migration? *Kasarinlan* 22(1): 161–191.

Aguilar, F.V., 1999, Ritual passage and the reconstruction of selfhood in international labour migration, *Sojourn* 14(1): 98–139.

Aguilar, F.V. (ed.), 2002, *Filipinos in Global Migrations: At Home in the World?* Paris: UNESCO.

Ang See, T., 2007, Influx of new Chinese immigrants to the Philippines: problems and challenges, in Thuno, M. (ed.), *Beyond Chinatown: New Chinese Migration and the Global Expansion of China*. Copenhagen: Nordic Institute for Asian Studies Press, 137–163.

Asis, M.M.B., 2002, From the life stories of Filipino women: personal and family agendas of migration, *Asian and Pacific Migration Journal* 11(1): 67–94.

Asis, M.M.B., Huang, S. and Yeoh, B.S.A., 2004, When the light of the home is abroad: unskilled female migration and the Filipino family, *Singapore Journal of Tropical Geography* 25(2): 198–215.

Ball, R., 2004, Divergent development, racialised rights: globalised labour markets and the trade in nurses – the case of the Philippines, *Women's Studies International Forum* 27(2): 119–133.

Barber, P.G. and Lem, W. (eds), 2012, *Migration in the 21st Century: Political Economy and Ethnography*. London: Routledge.

Battistella, G., 2012, Multi-level policy approach in the governance of labour migration: considerations from the Philippine experience, *Asian Journal of Social Science* 40(4): 419–446.

Carino, B.V., 1992, Migrant workers from the Philippines, in Battistella, G. and Paganoni, A. (eds), *Philippine Labor Migration: Impact and Policy*. Quezon City: Scalabrini Migration Center, 4–21.

Carino, B.V. (ed.), 1998, *Filipino Workers on the Move*. Paris: UNESCO, MOST, Philippine Migration Research Network.

Choy, C.C., 2003, *Empire of Care: Nursing and Empire in Filipino American History*. Durham, NC: Duke University Press.

Constable, N., 2006, Brides, maids and prostitutes: reflections on the study of 'trafficked' women, *PORTAL Journal of Multidisciplinary International Studies* 3(2) (online).

Espiritu, Y.L., 2002, Filipino navy stewards and Filipina health care professionals: immigration, work and family relations, *Asian and Pacific Migration Journal* 11(1): 47–66.

Fresnoza-Flot, A., 2009, Migration status and transnational mothering: the case of Filipino migrants in France, *Global Networks* 9(2): 252–270.

Gibson, K. and Graham, J., 2002, Situating migrants in theory: the case of Filipino migrant contract construction workers, in Aguilar, F.V. (ed.), *Filipinos in Global Migrations: At Home in the World?* Paris: UNESCO, MOST, Philippine Migration Research Network, 39–59.

Gibson, K., Law, L. and McKay, D., 2001, Beyond heroes and victims: Filipina contract migrants, economic activism and class transformations, *International Feminist Journal of Politics* 3(3): 365–386.

Go, S.P., 1994, Of barangays, institutional mechanisms and international migration: the Philippine experience, in Iyotani, T. and Tanaka, Y. (eds), *Cross-National Labour Migration in Asia and Regional Development Planning: Implications for Local-Level Management*. Nagoya: UN Centre for Regional Development, 41–62.

Go, S.P., 2005, Filipino diaspora, in Gibney, M.J. and Hansen, R. (eds), *Immigration and Asylum: From 1900 to the Present*. Santa Barbara: ABC/CLIO, 241–246.

Go, S.P. and Postrado, L.T., 1986, Filipino overseas contract workers: their families and communities, in Arnold, F. and Shah, N.M. (eds), *Asian Labor Migration: Pipeline to the Middle East*. Boulder, CO: Westview, 125–144.

Gonzalez, J.L., 1998, *Philippine Labour Migration: Critical Dimensions of Public Policy*. Singapore: Institute of Southeast Asian Studies.

Guevarra, A.M., 2010, *Marketing Dreams, Manufacturing Heroes: The Transnational Labor Brokering of Filipino Workers*. New Brunswick, NJ: Rutgers University Press.

Hilsdon, A.-M., 1997, The good life: cultures of migration and transformation of overseas workers in the Philippines, *Pilipinas* 29: 49–62.

International Labour Organization, 2006, *Migration of Health Workers: Country Case Study Philippines*. Geneva: ILO.

International Organization for Migration, 2005, *Labour Migration in Asia: Protection of Migrant Workers, Support Services and Enhancing Development Benefits* (mostly South Asia, but also the Philippines). Geneva: IOM.

International Organization for Migration, 2013, *Country Migration Report: The Philippines 2013*. Makati City, Manila: IOM.

Johnson, M., 2010, Diasporic dreams, middle-class moralities and migrant domestic workers among Muslim Filipinos in Saudi Arabia, *Asia Pacific Journal of Anthropology* 11(3–4): 428–448.

Liebelt, C., 2008, On sentimental Orientalists, Christian Zionists, and working class cosmopolitans: Filipina domestic workers' journeys to Israel and beyond, *Critical Asian Studies* 40(4): 567–585.

Lindio-McGovern, L., 2004, Alienation and labour export in the context of globalization: Filipino migrant domestic workers in Taiwan and Hong Kong, *Critical Asian Studies* 36(2): 217–238.

Parrenas, R.S., 2001, *Servants of Globalization: Women, Migration and Domestic Work*. Stanford, CA: Stanford University Press.

Parrenas, R.S., 2005, *Children of Global Migration: Transnational Families and Gendered Woes*. Stanford, CA: Stanford University Press.

Paul, A.M., 2013, Good help is hard to find: the differential mobilization of migrant social capital among Filipino domestic workers, *Journal of Ethnic and Migration Studies* 39(5): 719–739.

Rodriguez, R.M., 2010, *Migrants for Export: How the Philippine State Brokers Labor to the World*. Minneapolis: University of Minnesota Press.

Tyner, J.A., 2004, *Made in the Philippines: Gendered Discourses and the Making of Migrants*. London: RoutledgeCurzon.

Tyner, J.A., 2009, *The Philippines: Mobilities, Identities, Globalization*. London: Routledge.

3.10 Conclusion

Dauvergne, P., 1997, *Shadows in the Forest: Japan and the Politics of Timber in Southeast Asia*. Cambridge, MA: Massachusetts Institute of Technology Press.

Dean, J., Lovely, M. and Wang, H., 2005, *Are Foreign Investors Attracted to Weak Environmental Regulations? Evaluating the Evidence for China*. Washington, DC: World Bank, Policy Research Working Paper.

Hurst, P., 1990, *Rainforest Politics: Ecological Destruction in South-East Asia*. London: Zed Books.

King, V.T. (ed.), 1998, *Environmental Challenges in South-East Asia*. London: RoutledgeCurzon.

Marcotullio, P.J., 2003, Globalisation, urban form and environmental conditions in Asia-Pacific cities, *Urban Studies* 40(2): 219–247.

Parnwell, M., 1996, *Environmental Change in South-East Asia: People, Politics and Sustainable Development*. London: Routledge.

Rambo, A.T. and Aoyagi-Usui, M., 2003, Environmental consciousness in Southeast and East Asia, *Southeast Asian Studies* 41(1): 5–100.

You, J.-I., 1995, The Korean model of development and its environmental implications, in Bhaskar, V. and Glynn, A. (eds), *The North, the South and the Environment*. London: Earthscan and UNU Press.

4 Shadows in the forest
Southeast Asia's internal migration flows

4.0 Introduction

What migration flows result from the rapid capitalist modernization of a 'demographic anomaly'? It will be remembered that Southeast Asia was described as anomalous because the richness of its physical environment (fertile plains, forested ridges, alluvial deltas; vast mineral and hydrocarbon resources; volcanic soils and marine abundance; complex intersection of land and sea), plus its strategic location between the advanced civilizations of East Asia and South Asia, contrasted sharply with the surprising sparseness of its population. The answer is that Southeast Asia has become, over the last 70 years, far less anomalous due to rapid population growth, and that the geography of this growth has reflected the importance of two main redistributions of population: (i) the migration of rural populations to already existing and newly built cities – the growth of the region's largest cities (Jakarta, Bangkok, Manila, Ho Chi Minh City, Kuala Lumpur, and Singapore) has been truly extraordinary, while typically, the migration of the rural poor is to slum districts within or on the outer edges of the metropolitan area which then, in many cases, suffer enforced clearance; and (ii) migration to previously relatively empty areas now being developed for new wealth-generating purposes – for agricultural crops (such as coffee in Vietnam), fish products (such as shrimps in Thailand), mineral resources (such as copper and gold in West Papua), tourism (both domestic and foreign, especially in Bali and southern Thailand), manufacturing (such as clothes and footwear in Cambodia), and forest products (notably palm oil in Sumatra and Borneo). The lives of very few Southeast Asians have been left untouched by the direct experience, or indirect influence, of these internal migrations during this period.

Internal migration should not, however, be seen as only the passive outcome of forces in the political economy of these countries. It was, itself, a major agent in the capitalist modernization project. People moved both because they wanted to make money and because they wanted the modern goods and life-styles that that money could help them buy. As they moved, they undermined the social practices and certainties of long-established village life, and helped to forge the more fluid, ephemeral and self-referential lives of the city dweller.

The product of their migrations were new settlements, some of them slums in and around the city. Elsewhere, these new settlements were often built at the expense of the former inhabitants, frequently leading to resentment – witness, to take just one example, the continuing conflict between the Penan forest-dweller (Dyak) people of interior Sarawak and the Samling Group timber company, whose operations are backed by laws implemented by the Sarawak government. Internal migration has, in recent decades, been a highly contentious phenomenon in Southeast Asia.

Protest might be thought, on reflection, to be a fully justifiable response to what is going on. Population redistribution consequent upon capitalist modernization has transformed the landscapes of the region. There is now very little primary tropical forest left; logging and cash crop planting have largely seen to that. Much of this forest clearance has been illegal; where the clearances are (ostensibly) legal, they are typically the product of 'crony capitalism' – specifically, the granting of permits to develop land (for example, for palm oil estates, mining projects, or major infrastructure investments) to those individuals and organizations that are already part of, or can demonstrate their loyal support for, the ruling elite. With the clearance of forest comes smoke pollution and upland gully erosion, and the destruction of downstream fluvial environments; with tourist resort development often comes the destruction of coastal areas (for example, mangrove swamps), and of their contiguous and off-shore marine environments; and with the rapid expansion of urban areas (residential, industrial, utilities, and commercial land uses) comes the loss of agricultural land and a rise in environmental pollution.

4.1 Indonesia (and Timor Leste)

The first thing to say about internal migration in Indonesia is that it is well known for its indigenous population mobility systems. Bugis and Makassarese trader migrants from Sulawesi are found in coastal regions all round the country, while the Minangkabau are renowned for their traditions of 'rite-of-passage' migrations (*merantau*) when young adult males set out to make their fortunes elsewhere before returning to marry and settle down in their home region in West Sumatra. These traditional movements have not disappeared, but they have become altered and overlain by four major new patterns of internal migration in the post-1950 period.

The first is the most tragic and the most episodic. Indonesia, as a newly independent state, inherited a very complex ethnic geography. Some of that complexity has already been touched upon, specifically the close association between Malukans and the Dutch colonial administration through service in the military and so on, but this association was also strengthened by the fact that many inhabitants in the eastern islands of Indonesia (but also the Batak in Sumatra) were Christian, not Muslim, and Islam was, and remains, central to the Indonesian national project. Episodes of violent inter-ethnic conflict in the Malukas (especially Ambon), northern Sulawesi, and elsewhere have led to the displacement of large numbers of people (as internally displaced persons – IDPs). The separatist conflict in Aceh province, reflecting cultural and religious differences between this province and the rest of Indonesia, also led to displacement and loss of life. These refugee migrations (sometimes, as in the cases of the Bugis from Sumatra and the Madurese from Kalimantan, 'return' migrations) often start out as the temporary migrations of those seeking safety by escaping the violence, but they can then morph (for example, through recognition of customary law) into permanent migrations and a further step towards an ethnically cleansed socio-cultural geography. A particularly severe outbreak of inter-ethnic violence occurred in the 1998–2002 period, when many Christians and Muslims were killed and injured, settlements were razed to the ground, and a new layer of fear, distrust and animosity added to that which had existed before. At the height of the post-Suharto conflict (2001) there were an estimated 1.4 million IDPs in Indonesia, and in Ambon about one-third of the population was displaced. In many of the inter-ethnic conflicts, religious differences were of little or no importance. Competition for land and for trade, for example, were at the root of Dyak–Madurese violence in West Kalimantan and Madurese–Bugis violence in East Kalimantan. Another cause of internal displacement is the simmering conflict between indigenous Papuans and the agencies of the Indonesian state over the status of West Papua.

Arising not from political conflict but from a natural disaster, about 500,000 IDPs resulted from the terrifying tsunami that struck Aceh and northwest Sumatra in December 2004, killing 150,000 people. Volcanic eruptions also often cause significant displacement.

The second pattern of migration flows is the opposite to episodic. It is the usually slow (but sometimes quite rapid), relentless shift of rural populations towards the major urban areas and main industrial development zones, and of people leaving the poorer provinces of eastern Indonesia for the wealthier provinces of western Indonesia. The overall rate of urbanization has slowed somewhat in the recent period, but the direction of net flow remains up the urban hierarchy – from village to town, from town to city, and from city to metropolis (Jakarta). Recorded gross flows, of course, show that many migrants move from the village to the city or metropolis, missing out the intermediate stages. Some of this migration involves the movement of indigenous peoples from upland sparely inhabited interior regions to fast-growing lowland urbanized regions – a good example being the migration of the Kayan and the Kenyah to the areas of growth and opportunity in East Kalimantan. Are the gains and losses from these internal migration flows similar to those for international migration discussed in the last chapter? With some allowance for the legal and citizen status of the internal migrant in contrast with the often illegal and non-citizen status of the international migrant, the answer is 'yes'. Despite the importance of the informal sector as the first employment destination for migrants to Indonesian cities, the core regions for internal migration tend to benefit as if they were destination countries in international migration (as do the long-term migrants themselves who, on average, earn more than the non-migrants in the destination city), and the peripheral regions in Indonesia tend to lose rather in the same way as sending countries do in international migration. This is hardly surprising. Indonesia is, after all, a vast and geographically diverse country, and processes of circular and cumulative causation are at work (see Box 6.2).

The third pattern of migration flows is the movement of people towards new lands – areas that are being opened up for agricultural (and aquaculture) development, mining, forestry, etc. Much of this migration is spontaneous, resulting from individuals and families deciding that their prospects are better if they move away from where they live now towards the 'frontier' provinces, where land is plentiful and a good living, or maybe even a fortune, can be made.

An example of this is the migration of ethnic Bugis from southern Sulawesi to plant cocoa in other parts of the island during the 'cocoa boom' of the 1990s. However, the literature on this kind of migration is dominated by studies of the state-sponsored *transmigrasi* or 'transmigration' programme established to reduce the enormous contrasts in population density between 'inner Indonesia' (Java-Madura-Bali) and 'outer Indonesia' (the rest of the country). This was begun under the Dutch in the 1930s, expanded enormously during the nation-building period after independence (assisted by prestigious international organizations like the World Bank), continued during the Suharto period, but recently became no longer central to Indonesian government planning and development efforts.

The stated logic of the transmigration programme was to relieve the overpopulation of Java, where shortage of land and underemployment kept people poor, by moving such 'surplus populations' to places such as Lampung, South Sumatra, Riau and Jambi in Sumatra, Kalimantan, Sulawesi and West Papua, where the problem was that there was thought to be too much land and too few people to develop it. The unstated (or at least less-stated) logic was one of binding the disparate parts of Indonesia together into one nation, or, viewed from the perspective of the original inhabitants of these supposedly empty areas, the 'Javanization' of the territorial space of Indonesia. Reflecting this perception, some have likened it to a policy of 'internal colonialism'. That the numbers of migrants moving away from Java to settle successfully in these new areas was remarkably large, cannot be denied (in the period 1952 to 1999 the number of officially backed transmigrants from Java-Madura-Bali alone came to about 4 million – many of whom went to southern Sumatra in the early period, but elsewhere in outer Indonesia in the later period). However, neither can it be said that the process was always progressive or just. Relationships between the newcomer populations and the original (often indigenous) inhabitants were frequently fraught, and the power relations were unequal and generally favoured the newcomers (especially when they had government administrative and financial backing). In addition, the transmigration households were largely nuclear family households leading to the loss of multigenerational co-residence, and, related to this, the roles ascribed to male and female transmigrants were reinforcingly patriarchal (men hold the land title and credit is issued in their names). Furthermore, the outcome of the process was (with the benefit of hindsight) predictable. In many cases, but perhaps especially so in Papua, the in-migrants were seen largely as newcomers, or even as invaders – as ethnic outsiders who understood little, and cared even less, about local people, their cultures and traditions, human rights, economic interests, values and beliefs. It is significant culturally and politically, perhaps particularly so in the post-2001 era of political decentralization, that, as is the case in Papua, the indigenous populations of many of the peripheral provinces have already been outnumbered, or are in the process of being outnumbered, by the 'settler' populations and their descendants (thought by now to be about 20 million people), many of them having arrived since the peak transmigration policy period.

Finally, the recent period has witnessed a new pattern of internal migration – one that reflects the dynamism and wealth-generating potential of the Singapore economy (see Figure 4.1). Those parts of northern Sumatra closest to Singapore, specifically Riau Islands province, have experienced high rates of net internal migration gain over the last two inter-Census periods (1990–2010). The spillover of manufacturing employment and the growth of tourism have combined with more illicit forms of making a living (sex work and smuggling) to turn this corner of Indonesia into a prosperous frontier region. A kind of 'gold-rush' migration has been the result.

The results from the 2010 Census confirm much of what has been written above. Altogether, about 12% of Indonesia's 238 million population in 2010 lived outside their province of birth. The figures for Jakarta and the Riau Islands provinces, however, were three to four times higher than this (42% and 48%, respectively). Comparing the Census results over time shows that it was the capital city-region, hydrocarbon-rich Aceh, and the main agricultural transmigration areas located in southern and eastern Sumatra and East Kalimantan that were the main destination areas in the early-mid post-independence period (late 1970s and late 1980s), but that it was the new mining and agribusiness areas in Kalimantan, Papua and Bangka Belitung, along with the manufacturing provinces close to Singapore and in the outer parts of the capital city-region, that were the main destination areas in the recent period (late 1990s and late 2000s). Finally, Jakarta has continued to dominate internal migration flows in Indonesia. This is hardly surprising. In 1975, incomes per capita there were 2.6 times the national average, while by 2000 this ratio had increased to 4.0 times the average, where it has remained since. For all its 'mega-urban' social and environmental problems, the capital city-region remains a magnet for internal migration.

The outcomes of some of these patterns and processes are shown in Figure 4.1. Based on 2010 Census data, it shows net internal migration rates by province for the five-year period 2005–10. The West Java area, containing Jakarta, West Java itself, and Banten, has high absolute net migration gain (+485,000) but no longer the highest rate of net migration gain. Instead the highest rates of gain are found in the agribusiness and mining areas such as Central and East

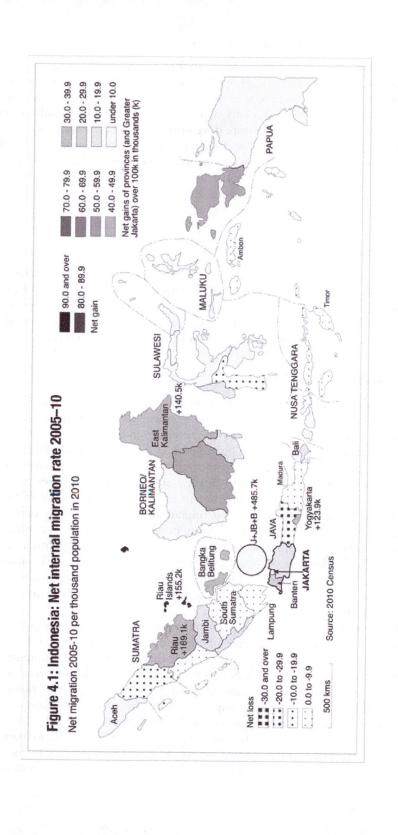

Figure 4.1: Indonesia: Net internal migration rate 2005–10

Net migration 2005-10 per thousand population in 2010

Net gain

90.0 and over
80.0 - 89.9

70.0 - 79.9
60.0 - 69.9
50.0 - 59.9
40.0 - 49.9

30.0 - 39.9
20.0 - 29.9
10.0 - 19.9
under 10.0

Net gains of provinces (and Greater Jakarta) over 100k in thousands (k)

Net loss

-30.0 and over
-20.0 to -29.9
-10.0 to -19.9
0.0 to -9.9

500 kms

Source: 2010 Census

SUMATRA

Aceh

Riau
+169.1k

Riau Islands
+155.2k

Jambi

South Sumatra

Bangka Belitung

Lampung

Banten

JAKARTA

BORNEO/ KALIMANTAN

East Kalimantan
+140.5k

J+JB+B +485.7k

JAVA

Madura

Yogyakarta
+123.9k

Bali

NUSA TENGGARA

SULAWESI

MALUKU

Ambon

Timor

PAPUA

Kalimantan, Bangka Belitung, and West Papua, and in the now much more extensive region around Singapore (Riau Islands, Riau and Jambi provinces).

Timor Leste's hydrocarbon resources (notably a natural-gas field in the Timor Sea being developed jointly with Australian companies) might provide a boost for the new country's future development, but in the meantime political unrest rooted in poverty and poor governance remains a problem. On three occasions since 1975 over 100,000 people have been uprooted by conflict: 300,000 in 1975–79, 400,000 in 1999 at the time of the struggle over independence, and 150,000 people were displaced internally by the outbreak of violence in 2006.

4.2 Singapore

So small in area is the island city-state of Singapore that its internal migrations consist very largely of moves associated with new suburban (mostly high-rise) mass housing developments, and those that result from inner-area regeneration and land reclamation. Some significant recent redistribution also resulted from luxury housing developments (often also located on reclaimed land).

4.3 Malaysia (and Brunei)

In one respect the internal migrations in Malaysia are unique. Instead of being one national migration space, Malaysia is several. To move from one part to another, one often needs an 'internal travel document' (essentially a passport), and for entry into East Malaysia (Sabah and Sarawak), permission from the state (i.e. not the federal) immigration authorities. These arrangements arise from the '20-point agreement' with North Borneo and the '18-point agreement' with Sarawak in 1962 before the establishment of the independent state of Malaysia in 1963. These internal barriers to migration were designed to prevent the negative effects of 'transmigration' from peninsular Malaysia, but some claim that they have been misused to control the movements of political activists. This is the first instance of something that we shall find is not at all uncommon in East Asia: controls on the migration of people within national territories, which, in certain respects, make such migrations take on some of the characteristics of international migration.

In the early post-war period population redistribution was only partly spontaneous in response to economic opportunities. Much was brought about by attempts to resolve the security situation in the context of a communist insurgency. Hundreds of 'new villages' were built, for example, and rural populations in many parts of peninsular Malaysia were concentrated in them. After 1960, the security situation improved but the rural populations largely remained in the new settlements to which they had been forcefully moved. By 1970 two main streams of internal migration were dominant in peninsular Malaysia: the first was the massive migration gains of Selangor state due to the urban growth of the capital region, and the second was the net migration gains of Pahang state as agricultural settlement proceeded. From 1970 to 2000 agricultural resettlement continued but at a much lower level – rural–rural migration fell from 1.1 million in 1986–91 to 250,000 in 1995–2000; urban development associated with employment growth in manufacturing and the services took over as the strongly dominant force in population redistribution. Thus, during the period 1995–2000 the Kuala Lumpur (KL) capital city-region (KL, Selangor and Negeri Sembilan) gained a remarkable 160,000 migrants from the rest of Malaysia. The only other states to show net migration gains were Johor, Penang and Melaka, while Kelantan lost nearly 60,000 and East Malaysia 45,000.

Figure 4.2 provides an overview of population change in the 2000–10 period at the administrative district level. Much, but by no means all, of this population change is due to internal migration. The two other sources of population growth are: (i) natural increase (births minus deaths), which is particularly significant in the high fertility states of northeast peninsular Malaysia – Kelantan and Terengganu; and (ii) net international migration, which is particularly important in Sabah and in the more urban parts of southeastern peninsular Malaysia.

Three pattern elements of rapid population growth remain unexplained, however, by these other sources of population growth and are therefore primarily the product of internal migration. First is urbanization – the rapid population growth of the KL capital city-region in particular, but also the growth of several of the major cities of peninsular Malaysia along the axis that runs from Penang in the north, through Ipoh and KL, to Johor Bahru opposite Singapore in the south, plus the other state capitals, both in peninsular Malaysia and in East Malaysia. The converse of this is the population declines and low population growths of many rural districts – especially so in northeast peninsular Malaysia and in the low population density regions of interior Sarawak. Second is the spread of urban manufacturing and service-sector development (and hence population) from some of these major cities to their surrounding districts. This is especially noticeable in the case of the capital city-region, where KL has expanded into Selangor state southwestwards down the Klang Valley, and southwards with the building of the new administrative city of Putrajaya, but also southeastwards into Seremban in the state of Negeri Sembilan. Another interesting instance of this urban population spread is the spilling over of Kuching in Sarawak into Samarahan where a new university city has been built. Finally, third is the in-migration associated with the opening up of new lands for agricultural, forestry, and mineral resource development, and for major infrastructure projects. Initially state sponsored in peninsular Malaysia (notably to Pahang) by the Federal Land Development Authority, these redistributions are now predominantly small in scale, local in their effects, and are only sometimes illegal (as in the case of agricultural encroachment on the Cameron Highlands). However, in Sarawak and Sabah, vast tracts of land are being cleared of tropical forest, both for their valuable timber, and for the crop monocultures that take their place (notably palm oil plantations). The high rates of population growth in the Daro, Matu, Tongod and Kinabatangan districts are due to these expansions of large-scale plantation agriculture. In the case of

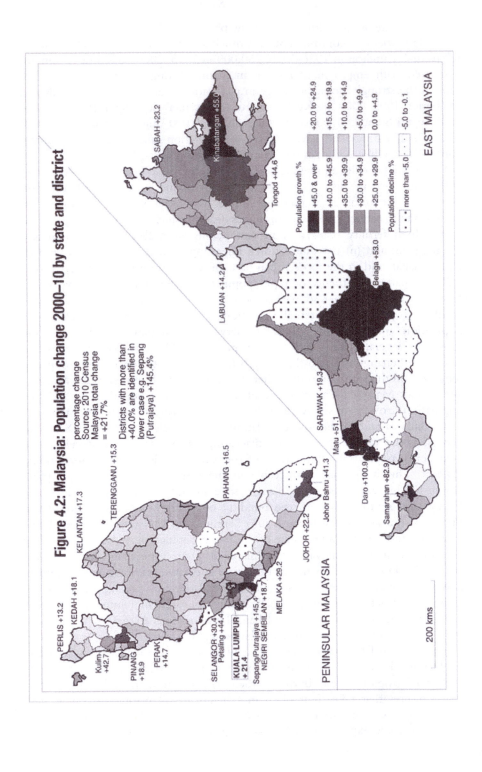

Figure 4.2: Malaysia: Population change 2000–10 by state and district

percentage change
Source : 2010 Census
Malaysia total change
= +21.7%

Districts with more than
+40.0% are identified in
lower case e.g. Sepang
(Putrajaya) +145.4%

PERLIS +13.2
KEDAH +18.1
Kulim +42.7
PINANG +18.9
PERAK +14.7
KELANTAN +17.3
TERENGGANU +15.3
PAHANG +16.5
SELANGOR +30.4
Petaling +44.4
KUALA LUMPUR +21.4
Sepang/Putrajaya +145.4
NEGIRI SEMBILAN +18.7
MELAKA +29.2
JOHOR +22.2
Johor Bahru +41.3

PENINSULAR MALAYSIA

SABAH +23.2
Kinabatangan +55.0
Tongod +44.6
LABUAN +14.2
SARAWAK +19.3
Belaga +53.0
Matu +51.1
Daro +100.9
Samarahan +82.9

EAST MALAYSIA

Population growth %

+45.0 & over   +20.0 to +24.9
+40.0 to +45.9   +15.0 to +19.9
+35.0 to +39.9   +10.0 to +14.9
+30.0 to +34.9   +5.0 to +9.9
+25.0 to +29.9   0.0 to +4.9

Population decline %

· · · more than −5.0   · · · −5.0 to −0.1

200 kms

Belaga district, located in interior Sarawak, the boost to population growth is not so much related to forest clearance as to the construction of the massive Bakun Dam (completed in 2011), built to supply electricity to peninsular Malaysia.

Despite these many investments, the opportunities for advancement in East Malaysia (Sabah and Sarawak) are fairly narrowly circumscribed. Palm oil is big business, as are oil and gas, forest products and tourism. However, East Malaysia is lacking the diversity of employment that comes with large cities, good communications, and broad-based manufacturing industry, so at the same time that it needs to import foreign workers from Indonesia and the Philippines for its plantations and timber product factories, it has exported many of its own workers to peninsular Malaysia.

In terms of numbers, however, and despite the peaking of this flow in around 2000, the main internal migration story in both peninsular Malaysia and in East Malaysia remains rural–urban migration. Malaysia's economy in the late 19th and early 20th centuries was dominated by mining and forest products (especially tin and rubber); this, along with the importance of subsistence agriculture, encouraged job and population dispersal, except, that is, for some employment concentration in port locations. The now much more diversified economy and its wealthier population is urban based. This is where the manufacturing jobs are to be found and where the service sector has dramatically expanded. The villages (*kampung*) remain, but it is Kuala Lumpur and its capital city-region (including the new city of Putrajaya), and the other main cities of peninsular Malaysia, which now dominate Malaysian space and society. Generally speaking, as can be seen in Figure 4.2, the more rural or peripheral a state, or an area within a state, the more likely it is that it has lost population through internal migration; the more urban, the more likely that it has gained.

This is not, however, the whole story. As with Indonesia, though on a much smaller scale, there has been some planned settlement and resettlement of Malaysian populations: (i) in rural areas, associated with the opening up of new areas for agricultural development and timber resources; (ii) in rural areas, associated with major infrastructure investments (for example, the building of dams) which have often caused the displacement of residents including original people (*orang asli*); and (iii) the building of new towns, the most notable example of which is the administrative city of Putrajaya, located within the 'multimedia super-corridor' south of KL.

Finally, as with Indonesia, the rapid growth in the economic significance of Singapore is impacting on internal migration in a neighbouring country. The Johor region in the southern section of peninsular Malaysia has attracted many migrants from other regions as job opportunities there have resulted from major investments in both manufacturing and services.

4.4 Thailand

For much of the post-war period internal migration in Thailand has also been dominated by rural–urban migration. Economic growth, rising living standards, and new transport infrastructures have focused production, exchange and consumption in the major regional cities and, above all, in Bangkok. Indeed, it is the growth of Bangkok, both in population and in physical extent, that is the main physical and social expression of Thailand's remarkable modernization.

This is very clearly demonstrated by the patterns of population change depicted in Figure 4.3. Apart from the regional capital and a couple of frontier provinces, northeast Thailand is completely a region of population decline in the 2000–10 period. With the notable exception of Chiang Mai province, population decline also characterizes much of the Northern Region. The Southern Region has a population growth rate that is slightly higher than the national one, but spectacular growth occurred in Phuket Province where the ethnically diverse population grew by 276,000 in ten years (meaning that it more than doubled in size during that period). It is, however, the Central Region that shows the largest absolute and relative rates of growth – six of its provinces added more than 200,000 to their populations in ten years, and at its centre, the national capital Bangkok grew by nearly 30% and added 1.894 million to its population. This is spectacular growth in a country that now has low fertility rates. It has largely been brought about directly, and indirectly (through the effects of age-selective migration on age structure), by internal migration.

The nature of economic development has shaped internal migration affecting, for example, whether the migration took the form of one-way permanent migration, away and return flows (perhaps several times), seasonal migration (often reflecting the level of demand for agricultural labour), or circulation (which is common in all Southeast Asian countries). Much of Thailand's social modernization and economic development took the form of a strong growth in manufacturing employment that often gave rise to more permanent forms of internal migration. Industrial estates, large factories and small workshops have sprung up all over the country, but especially so in the Central Region located close to the capital, and in Bangkok itself.

The other main stimulus to that economic development was the success of Thailand as a tourist destination that generated both permanent and temporary forms of migration. Tourist locations in four areas (Bangkok itself, the northwest, around the Gulf of Thailand, and on the Indian Ocean coast in the far southwest) have seen major hotel, resort, transport and new shopping investments, rapid urban development and net in-migration from other regions of the country. It follows from this that much of the migration was of young men and women from relatively poor backgrounds moving to Bangkok and the Central Region for working-class jobs as construction workers (men), factory workers (textiles, leather goods, etc. – men and women), domestic servants (women) and other service workers (men and women – some men for example becoming taxi drivers, but especially women, some becoming sex workers).

In addition, much rural–rural migration (including squatting) has resulted from market forces that have undermined rural livelihoods in specific areas – a problem facing in particular those living in the Northeastern Region, many of whom in the past migrated to the Northern Region. With the opening up of

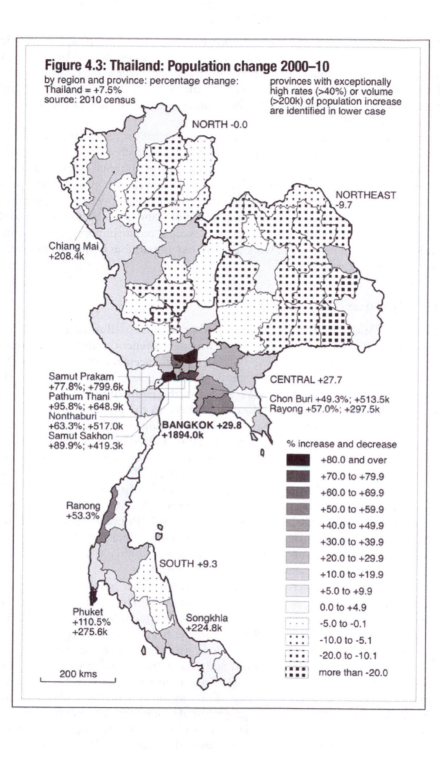

Figure 4.3: Thailand: Population change 2000–10

by region and province: percentage change:
Thailand = +7.5%
source: 2010 census

provinces with exceptionally
high rates (>40%) or volume
(>200k) of population increase
are identified in lower case

NORTH -0.0

NORTHEAST
-9.7

Chiang Mai
+208.4k

Samut Prakam
+77.8%; +799.6k
Pathum Thani
+95.8%; +648.9k
Nonthaburi
+63.3%; +517.0k
Samut Sakhon
+89.9%; +419.3k

CENTRAL +27.7

Chon Buri +49.3%; +513.5k
Rayong +57.0%; +297.5k

**BANGKOK +29.8
+1894.0k**

% increase and decrease

	+80.0 and over
	+70.0 to +79.9
	+60.0 to +69.9
	+50.0 to +59.9
	+40.0 to +49.9
	+30.0 to +39.9
	+20.0 to +29.9
	+10.0 to +19.9
	+5.0 to +9.9
	0.0 to +4.9
	-5.0 to -0.1
	-10.0 to -5.1
	-20.0 to -10.1
	more than -20.0

Ranong
+53.3%

SOUTH +9.3

Phuket
+110.5%
+275.6k

Songkhla
+224.8k

200 kms

formerly undeveloped land through road building, new farm products (mostly for export) have developed in new locations (an example would be the sugar cane industry in the Chonburi district in the 1970s). These have created local labour shortages which are then met by the recruitment of agricultural and fishery workers from elsewhere in the country (and, as we saw in the previous chapter, from abroad).

It is of great importance politically that Bangkok has for a very long time been almost the only destination choice for Thailand's upwardly mobile professional-technical and managerial-bureaucratic middle classes. Internal migration flows have thereby contributed to the cultural chasm between the pro-stability, pro-monarchy, pro-establishment right-of-centre middle class 'yellow' populations of most of the metropolitan capital city region (and parts of the South and West), and the populist, pro-income and wealth redistribution, pro-Thaksin, anti-establishment peasant and working-class 'red' populations of the Northeastern and Northern regions.

4.5 Myanmar

The largest movements of population within Myanmar (Burma) over the last 60 years have been caused not by economic development, which for the most part has been depressingly slow, but by the displacement of people due to conflict. The nature of this conflict is complex in detail, but it has one dominant characteristic: it involves the resistance of the ethnic minority populations, Kachin, Shan, Karen, Karenni, Mon, and others, to the political and economic demands of the Burmans, and especially to the authority of their military rulers. This resistance takes the form of refusal to be mobilized by the junta for natural resource projects, and a strong predilection to seek secession from the Burmese state as a solution to all development and identity problems. To escape the conflict (which has involved the burning of hundreds of villages), many people cross the international border, especially to Thailand, but even larger numbers (thought to be around 500,000 in 2006) remain as IDPs inside Myanmar, living for periods of time in mountainous terrain where thick forest cover, steep slopes, heavy rain, and poor communications make it difficult, if not impossible, for the authorities to establish and maintain control.

As if the ethnic conflicts were not enough, Myanmar has also suffered from natural disasters such as the Nargis typhoon in 2008. This violent storm caused 146,000 deaths and resulted in 800,000 people being displaced due to land and property damage and extensive flooding in the Irrawaddy Delta region.

Nevertheless, there has been some rural–urban migration, and the two main cities – Yangon (formerly Rangoon) and Mandalay – have grown in population. The military junta has also decided, as often happens with autocratic regimes, to build a new capital city. The city, begun in the mid-2000s, has been built nearer to the population-geographical centre of the country (so between Yangon and Mandalay), at Naypyidaw. It is claimed that the population of this new capital is now around 1 million – a figure that is doubted by some observers.

Finally, away from the more populated sections of the central valley, migrant labour has been recruited, or in some cases commandeered, for major mining and power-generation projects.

4.6 Laos

The turmoil of the second Indochina War 1954–75, with its massive displacements of population (700,000 or about 25% of the population) many of them members of the Hmong and Mien minorities, may be over, but the population of Laos is still on the move. Poverty and hopelessness drive people away from the interior, more mountainous regions towards the lowland areas with towns and modern communications, and especially to Vientiane. This results in a highly complex ethnic geography, as 'upland' and 'midland' Laotians join the numerically dominant 'lowland' Laotians in the destination regions. Some of this migration has been policy driven. Attempts to develop focal sites as growth poles (along with village consolidation) have entailed the resettlement of shifting cultivator ethnic minority populations away from the forests and into lowland wet rice locations to the detriment, according to many commentators, of both their economic independence and their indigenous cultures. This policy was met largely by 'sullen resistance' on the part of those who were resettled, but others moved on, or returned to the hills. Some ethnic minority populations have also had their livelihoods threatened or been displaced by the building of hydro-electric dams (for example, the controversial Xayaburi Dam currently under construction on the Mekong in northern Laos).

The results from the 2005 Census show the main patterns of net interprovincial migration during the period 1995–2005. The capital, Vientiane, and its surrounding area with its many (clothing) industrial and service-sector jobs, was far and away the main net gainer by migration (at +58,000), recruiting most of its migrants (many of them female) from the northern provinces, which were the main ones to lose by migration, along with two of the most southern provinces. More recent speculative investments by China-Hong Kong companies in tourism/gambling projects located in special economic zones might be contributing to a tendency already there in the 2005 Census results for frontier provinces in the far northwest of the country to also be net gainers by internal migration.

The recent growth of tourism in Laos, though some of it takes the form of low-spending backpacker tourism, has meant new opportunities in Luang Prabang, which has become a secondary pole of net in-migration in the north, while the towns of southern Laos have attracted migrants from their agricultural hinterlands.

4.7 Cambodia

Cambodia joins China as one of the very few countries in East Asia (or elsewhere for that matter) that has experienced a period of mass urban–rural migration in its recent history. When the war in Vietnam came to an end, the

Khmer Rouge regime in Cambodia, armed with its Maoist cultural revolutionary zeal, acted against the country's bourgeoisie and its vested interests. This meant the emptying of the city for the re-education of what were now 'class enemies' in the countryside. The small indigenous educated elite was destroyed. They, and entrepreneurs (many of them ethnically Chinese and Vietnamese), were rounded up, and if they survived the 'killing fields' (around 3 million people did not), were dispersed into the countryside and put to work on the farms. Phnom Penh became a ghost town. It was, perhaps, the most violent instance of enforced rustication in human history. Whatever its high ideological objectives might have been, it was a disaster for the economy, and a personal nightmare for most urban households in Cambodia.

Following the Khmer Rouge and the short-lived Republic of Kampuchea established by the Vietnamese, Cambodia returned to a kind of normality. Unfortunately, it was and remains a normality dominated by poverty and underemployment in the countryside, and unemployment and low wages in manufacturing and services in the city. Rural–rural and rural–urban migration accompanies the desperate search for employment. Many of the migrants finish up in Phnom Penh where average living standards are very low but where a great diversity of opportunities for making a living, often in the black economy, exists. Two major boosts to the urban economy have been: (i) the development of Cambodia as a major international tourist destination, mostly attracted by the remains at Angkor Wat; and (ii) the growth of the garment industry employing mostly female workers, many of them recruited from the countryside.

This picture is largely confirmed by the results of the 2008 Census and the 2013 Inter-Censal Population Survey. From both we can see that the highest rates of recent population growth occur in two different kinds of places: (i) the largest cities (Phnom Penh, Siem Reap, Kampong Cham, Sihanoukville, and Poipet), but especially in Phnom Penh; and (ii) mostly peripheral upland rural provinces undergoing agricultural settlement. Internal migration to Phnom Penh between 1997 and 2008 accounted for a remarkable 47.8% of the population of 1.5 million at the latter date. These migrants largely came from neighbouring provinces and from secondary urban centres. They were young, disproportionately female (41% of whom went into the garment sector), and when they were male they were often students (25%). The other net migration gain areas are very different. They are the largely peripheral provinces where forested land is being opened up for agricultural settlement. These areas are located mostly to the northeast and northwest of the country away from the high-rural density central Tonle Sap basin and the Mekong Delta, where land is scarce. Overall, therefore, there is a rural–rural migration flow that is transferring population from the lowland rice-based regions to upland cash-crop regions. A good example of this migration is the movement of farmers to Pailin province located close to the Thailand border (78% of this province's population in 2008 were recent migrants). They came from southern and southeastern

Cambodia, settled on land near to existing roads, and were largely responsible for a massive 52% drop in forest land over a 16-year period.

4.8 Vietnam

Decolonization came late to Vietnam and it came at a terrible price. War between the communist North and the capitalist South, and its aftermath – the disruption of village economies and of their environments, the disruption of family life through death, injury and prolonged separation, and general poverty, displacement and vulnerability – were suffered at length by populations in both parts of the country. However, on top of that were the specific migration effects of a generation at war. The mobilization of people for the war effort resulted in the uprooting of millions, with many being sent to work or to fight in other parts of the country. As part of the effort to defeat the Viet Cong (the communist forces fighting the Americans in South Vietnam), rural dwellers were forced out of their villages and corralled into camps set up by the American and South Vietnamese forces. This, it was thought, would make it possible, through the chemical defoliation of the vegetation cover and massive superiority of arms, to flush out the enemy from their rural underground hideouts. In the end it was all for nothing, it did not work, and the victory of the communists resulted in the collapse of the South Vietnamese regime, and the ignominious departure of the US forces, in 1975.

Internal migrations associated with the post-conflict reconstruction and later rapid economic development of Vietnam have taken four main forms: (i) initially, a de-urbanization of the cities of the South as those associated with the former capitalist economy were sent back to their home villages (many subsequently moving on to become urban 'floating populations'); (ii) a regional shift of populations towards the south and especially towards Ho Chi Minh City (formerly Saigon); (iii) a significant opening up of new lands for agricultural development in the Central Highlands (much of it for coffee plantations); and (iv) a massive overall shift of populations towards the major cities from the countryside, starting before 1986, but accelerating thereafter. Much of this rural–urban migration is temporary, and until fairly recently has been affected by the residence rules connected to the household registration system.

The growth of Ho Chi Minh City in particular has been spectacular. Its population in 1975 was about 2.4 million; in 2010 it reached 7.4 million. Much of this growth has resulted from local migrations from the Mekong Delta region, but commercial and industrial prosperity has also, despite significant ethnic differences, brought people from central and northern regions of the country.

The opening up of the interior Central Highlands region of Vietnam represents a major shift in the country's space-economy. Migrants have poured into the 'red hills' to take advantage of the opportunities to produce cash-crop products for export, especially during the 'coffee boom' period in the 1990s. Steep slopes covered in scrub and forest in a largely inaccessible region, have been replaced by a landscape of plantations and a dense network of roads and settlements.

The rapid growth of the economy, especially since the *doi moi* reforms of the mid-1980s, has led to massive rural–urban migration. This can be seen all over Vietnam but perhaps especially in its two largest city-regions – Ho Chi Minh in the south and Hanoi, the administrative capital of the country, in the north. The drivers of this migration (an increasing proportion of whom are young women) are the usual ones: rural poverty, growth of manufacturing employment in urban areas and in export-industry development zones, and above all, growth in urban service employment, much of it in the informal sector. Few become seriously rich in Vietnam's cities, but there are many who do well enough to enjoy moderately good living standards, either through the massive small and medium-sized business sector or though middle-class (professional, technical and managerial) employment. As the urban economies grow and diversify, so multiple niches arise for the incoming rural migrant to fill (domestic servants, construction workers – many of them day labourers, employees in small businesses, street hawkers and other casual labourers). Furthermore, some temporary displacements brought about by natural disasters (flooding/drought) can morph into permanent rural–urban migration.

These migrations are shown effectively through the mapping of the net internal migration and population change data from the 2009 Census, in Figure 4.4. The pattern of net migration gains and losses shows the enormous gains to Ho Chi Minh City and its surroundings in the five-year period 2004–09 – together amounting to more than 1.7 million people. The gains by the Hanoi/ Hai Phong capital city-region pale by comparison – around 300,000. The only other urban province to show significant net gains is Da Nang, located roughly half way between these two metropolitan regions. As for the rural areas, they fall into two groups: the larger consists of provinces experiencing net migration loss (often on a very large scale as in the Mekong Delta in the south and in mountainous areas in the north-central and northern parts of the country); and the smaller consists of four provinces in the Central Uplands, and two that border the People's Republic of China (PRC) in the north.

The relationship between net internal migration and population growth is explored in Figures 4.5 and 4.6. It can be seen that natural increase (births minus deaths) is sufficient to turn many rural areas from net migration loss provinces into provinces with modest rates of population growth; this is especially so for the Mekong delta area and many areas in the Red River Basin in the north. When the relationship is plotted on a scatter diagram, two features stand out: (i) the strength of the positive relationship overall, assisted by the joint net migration gains and population increases of the three main urban growth zones (Ho Chi Minh City, Hanoi and Da Nang); and (ii) the importance of the provinces opened up for agricultural settlement in the Central Uplands where the youthfulness of the in-migrants (and perhaps also the lack of certain constraints on family size found in urban areas) results in high population growth rates relative to net migration gains.

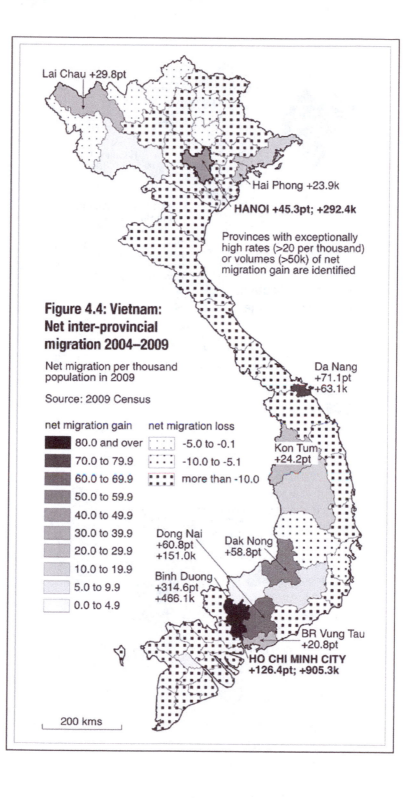

Lai Chau +29.8pt

Hai Phong +23.9k

HANOI +45.3pt; +292.4k

Provinces with exceptionally
high rates (>20 per thousand)
or volumes (>50k) of net
migration gain are identified

**Figure 4.4: Vietnam:
Net inter-provincial
migration 2004–2009**

Net migration per thousand
population in 2009

Source: 2009 Census

Da Nang
+71.1pt
+63.1k

Kon Tum
+24.2pt

net migration gain		net migration loss	
	80.0 and over		-5.0 to -0.1
	70.0 to 79.9		-10.0 to -5.1
	60.0 to 69.9		more than -10.0
	50.0 to 59.9		
	40.0 to 49.9		
	30.0 to 39.9		
	20.0 to 29.9		
	10.0 to 19.9		
	5.0 to 9.9		
	0.0 to 4.9		

Dong Nai
+60.8pt
+151.0k

Dak Nong
+58.8pt

Binh Duong
+314.6pt
+466.1k

BR Vung Tau
+20.8pt

**HO CHI MINH CITY
+126.4pt; +905.3k**

200 kms

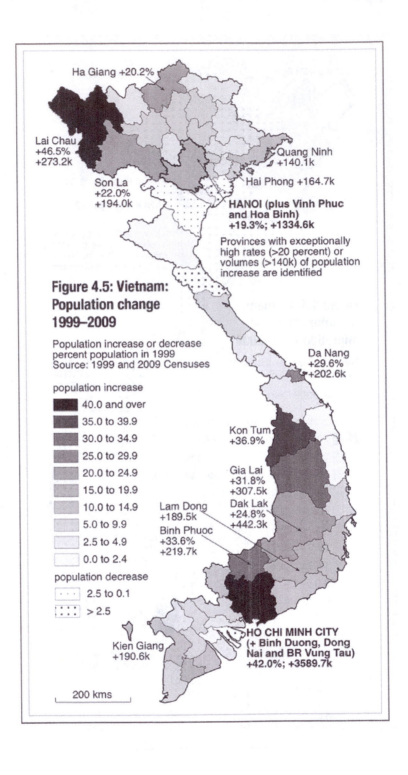

Figure 4.5: Vietnam: Population change 1999–2009

Ha Giang +20.2%

Lai Chau
+46.5%
+273.2k

Son La
+22.0%
+194.0k

Quang Ninh
+140.1k

Hai Phong +164.7k

**HANOI (plus Vinh Phuc
and Hoa Binh)
+19.3%; +1334.6k**

Provinces with exceptionally
high rates (>20 percent) or
volumes (>140k) of population
increase are identified

Population increase or decrease
percent population in 1999
Source: 1999 and 2009 Censuses

Da Nang
+29.6%
+202.6k

population increase

	40.0 and over
	35.0 to 39.9
	30.0 to 34.9
	25.0 to 29.9
	20.0 to 24.9
	15.0 to 19.9
	10.0 to 14.9
	5.0 to 9.9
	2.5 to 4.9
	0.0 to 2.4

population decrease

	2.5 to 0.1
	> 2.5

Kon Tum
+36.9%

Gia Lai
+31.8%
+307.5k

Lam Dong
+189.5k

Dak Lak
+24.8%
+442.3k

Binh Phuoc
+33.6%
+219.7k

Kien Giang
+190.6k

**HO CHI MINH CITY
(+ Binh Duong, Dong
Nai and BR Vung Tau)
+42.0%; +3589.7k**

200 kms

Figure 4.6: Vietnam:
The relationship between population change and net migration

By Province. Population growth 1999-2009 (percent) (Y axis); net migration 2004-2009 (per thousand population) (X axis)
Sources: 1999 and 2009 Censuses

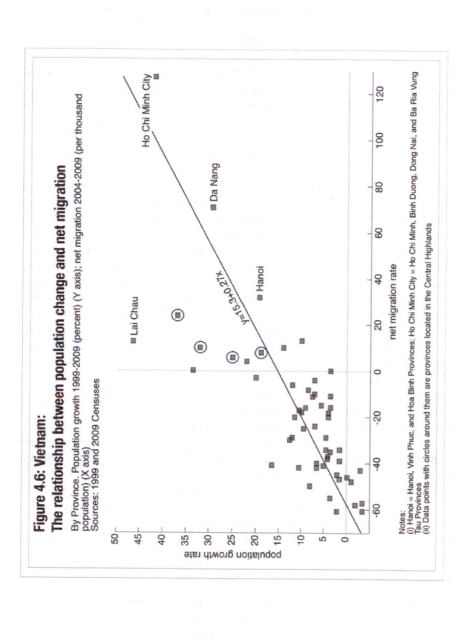

Notes:
(i) Hanoi = Hanoi, Vinh Phuc, and Hoa Binh Provinces; Ho Chi Minh City = Ho Chi Minh, Binh Duong, Dong Nai, and Ba Ria Vung Tau Provinces
(ii) Data points with circles around them are provinces located in the Central Highlands

4.9 Philippines

The Philippines is almost as noteworthy for its internal migrations as it is for its international migrations. While predominantly the result of economic inequalities between countryside and city, and above all, between the capital city-region (Metro Manila) and the rest of the country, internal migrations have also resulted: (i) from the opening up of 'empty' lands (especially in the 1950s and 1960s from the Visayas in the central Philippines southwards towards Mindanao); (ii) from the long-running ethnic conflict in the south (also especially in Mindanao, where 2 million people have suffered displacement); and (iii) temporary migrations resulting from natural disasters such as volcanic eruptions, typhoons and earthquakes – the IOM, for example, estimated that 2 million people were still displaced six months after the 'super-typhoon' Haiyan hit the Philippines in 2013.

Unlike most of the countries of Southeast Asia, the Philippines has yet to complete its 'demographic transition' – that is, its movement from being a country of high birth rates and high death rates to one of low birth rates and low death rates. As a result, with life expectancy relatively high and completed family size also high, population growth is rapid and the population is young. This, in turn, results in the arrival each year of many more young people onto the labour market than there are older people departing. Many of these young people then migrate, of course, to the major cities and especially to the capital city-region. Unfortunately, the performance of the Philippines economy in the last 60 years has rarely, if ever, been sufficient to witness the effective absorption of this influx of young adults into these urban labour markets. The outcome has been inevitable – poverty and underemployment in rural areas and a large 'lumpenproletariat' or 'precariat' population in the cities. So Philippines cities are typically highly segregated: elite quarters house the wealthy and the highly educated (much of this wealth derives from either land ownership or from business interests closely connected to political power), while poor quarters and 'informal' slum settlements cover much of the rest of the city, especially those areas most liable to flooding and pollution. One of the outcomes of this inequality is the vulnerability of urban neighbourhoods to large-scale redevelopment by increasingly 'privatized' forms of urban planning. In Metro Manila, for example, it was anticipated in 2008 that major redevelopment projects (typically combining transport infrastructure, shopping malls and residential land development) would cause the displacement of 206,000 people.

4.10 Conclusion

Of course, each Southeast Asian country has its own unique internal migration patterns and processes, and yet clear common themes emerge. The first is the volume, persistence and spatial scale of rural–urban migration. Southeast Asia is urbanizing quickly as its economies grow through both export success and growth of domestic consumption, and as its populations seek out modern urban lifestyles. These lifestyles require the things that come to the city first – electricity for lighting and modern convenience goods (cookers, washing machines, air conditioners and refrigerators), clean running water for drinking, washing and flushing toilets, and the means for modern communication (mobile phones, computers, radio and TV).

Second, and very sadly, internal displacement of people through ideological and/or ethnic conflict is common to many of the countries of Southeast Asia.

Finally, the demographic anomaly – a resource-rich and productive environment occupied by very few people is disappearing. Not only has population growth in the post-war period been rapid, but internal migration flows have ensured that most of the 'empty' terrain has been brought into productive use, often through the setting up of smallholdings producing cash crops such as cocoa, coffee, oil palm, rubber and shrimp. Much has been lost in the process. In addition to small-scale farming, large-scale capitalist development of Southeast Asia's less populated regions has destroyed forest environments for palm oil production, mountain landscapes for mining, and coastal and marine environments for fishing, tourism and urban built form. In particular, a combination of predatory capitalism, political corruption, and weak regulation have resulted in appalling decreases in terrestrial and marine biodiversity – this is Peter Dauvergne's 'shadow in the forest'.

Box 4.1 Migration, social class and social mobility

Social class and migration

Three assertions set the context for a discussion of the relationships between migration and social class (the following passages draw heavily upon Fielding 2005). The first is that class is central to an understanding of the causes, character and consequences of migration. Without social class analysis, 'migration' risks becoming a 'chaotic concept'. Second, class location (or position in the class structure of a country, city or region) determines the choices that individuals have when engaging in migration. Location in a higher class gives the person more choice about leaving, more choice about destination, and more choice about the manner of insertion into the destination society. Finally, class position before migration is typically different from that after migration. Indeed, often the purpose of migration is to change one's own or one's family's class location (for example, 'to better oneself'). The shift from class before to class after migration is often mediated by a change in institutional status – for example, enrolling as a university student in a foreign country, or entering into an international marriage. As with these examples, my comments in this first section will refer to international migration, but with often only fairly minor adjustments, these arguments can also be applied to long-distance internal migrations.

1 Class before migration: the class specificity of emigration

Four broad generalizations can be made about class locations before emigration. First, it is generally not the poorest members of the working class who emigrate. This is partly due, of course, to their inability to pay for a successful migration. The exceptions to this generalization are, however, important. They include forced migrations due to civil war, ethnic cleansing or environmental disaster, and migrations conducted under 'semi-feudal' social relations – such as debt bondage. Second, other members of the working classes may have good reason to emigrate and also the means to do so (for example, through the pooling of family resources to pay the people-smugglers), but their migration is likely to be constrained by immigration policies favouring the highly qualified and the rich over the unskilled and the poor. Third, members of the professional, technical and managerial middle classes generally have a strong incentive to emigrate – they can gain higher wages for the same work (assuming their qualifications are recognized) and better prospects for their children. However, their migration often implies an initial downward social mobility and a significant loss of status and power (for example, no servants). Finally, for the very wealthy, emigration is generally not a problem – most countries of immigration have special schemes to facilitate their arrival, settlement and investment in the receiving country.

2 Class after migration: the social class locations of immigrant minorities

Seven broad generalizations can be made. First, there is a big difference between intra-generational and intergenerational social class locations. First-generation immigrants are often confined to the working-class jobs they took on arrival or they achieve modest upward mobility through the small business sector. Second- and subsequent-generation immigrants often enter professional occupations through the acquisition of formal qualifications. Second, however, members of immigrant minorities show a high vulnerability to downward mobility into unskilled (and unwanted) working-class jobs and unemployment. Third, in comparison with the social structure of the host population, immigrant minorities tend to be very strongly represented in the petite bourgeoisie, and the small-business sector can play a major role in their upward social mobility. Fourth, a key role in the achievement of professional and managerial jobs is played by cultural capital (especially language skills). Those lacking such cultural assets tend to be confined to working-class jobs or to an 'ethnic enclave' in the small-business sector. Fifth, gender relations inherited from the country of origin are often important in determining whether immigrant minorities enter the white-collar or blue-collar working classes. In cases where a very strong family system is linked with patriarchal gender relations, for example, women tend to work in blue-collar and low-level white-collar jobs in family-owned businesses. Sixth, ethnicity is extremely important in determining rates of social promotion (in ways that are sometimes difficult to explain). Thus immigrant groups arriving at the same time and sharing similar class backgrounds can nevertheless experience very different social class trajectories in the country of destination. Finally, class location in the destination country is greatly affected by the migrant's legal status: the range of categories includes the invited 'key worker' or 'global talent' (middle class), the 'permanent resident' and 'co-ethnic returnee' (often stable working class), and the over-stayer, refused asylum seeker and illegal entrant (underclass).

3 Class structures of countries of emigration and immigration

Many of the social class effects of emigration and immigration are partially covered in Box 3.2 because they represent important gains and losses from migration, but three further points about the effects of migration on the class structures of destination countries need to be made. First, immigration typically implies additions to both the top and the bottom of the social class structure, so that the net effect of migration is social class polarization (this is equally true, incidentally, for internal migration). This is generally the case even if the majority of the migrants are 'gap fillers', since the gaps that need to be filled are both those at the bottom of the social hierarchy (those involving danger, dirt and drudgery) and those at higher levels for which there is a shortfall in domestic recruitment (such as medical professionals and high-technology specialists). Second, the intersection of social class and race/ethnicity results in widespread, but often partially hidden, social exclusion on grounds of nationality or country of origin. This in turn leads to the formation of an underclass of migrant workers and their families. The opposite applies in migration from rich to poor countries, where the immigrant often enjoys elite status regardless of his or her class location in the country of origin. Third, the intersection of class and gender means that in patriarchal destination societies the underclass is often predominantly female. The exception to this is migration from high-gender role segregation societies to low-gender role segregation societies, which can sometimes lead to a significant improvement in the class location of women.

Migration and social mobility

The vast majority of people in the world, and even more so in East Asia, are not born and brought up in places where it is easy to get secure, well-paid employment, or live in good housing in healthy and safe neighbourhoods, where one can be confident that one's children will enjoy prosperity and social well-being. If you want to 'get on', and the possibility of doing so locally is low or even zero – as it so often is – then you have to 'get out'. Migration, in these circumstances, is a prerequisite for upward social/ occupational mobility.

Rather strangely, this link between migration and intra-generational social mobility has not received a lot of attention by researchers in the social sciences. Indeed, one foremost British sociologist went so far as to call it the 'missing link' in social research! Perhaps one of the reasons for this was that until fairly recently, large data sets were cross-sectional rather than longitudinal, which meant that you could discover a great deal about a group of people at a point in time, but could not follow their situations as they unfolded over time.

As the use of longitudinal data became increasingly routine and consequently the results of empirical analyses of both social mobility and spatial mobility accumulated, the evidence seems to point to a number of broad generalizations about the links between them (the following passages draw heavily upon Fielding 2007): (i) that there is, without doubt, a link – those who migrate are more likely to change their social class/occupational class locations than those who do not migrate; (ii) that the effect of spatial mobility is generally favourable to upward social mobility – on balance, more people improve their class locations through migration than suffer downward social mobility; (iii) that migration roughly doubles the likelihood of upward social mobility from working-class jobs into the professional, technical and managerial middle classes; (iv) that gender differences are significant – both men and women benefit from migration up the urban hierarchy towards a major metropolitan region, but women relatively more so than men, while in contrast, men gain or move sideways from migration down the urban hierarchy away from a major metropolitan region, but women, on average, lose out badly; and finally (v) immigrant minorities vary greatly in their social mobility experiences, but where they succeed in achieving upward social mobility it is often through the small business sector (petite bourgeoisie) in the case of the first and second generations, and through educational qualifications leading to professional careers in the case of second and later generations.

I now want to show that several of these empirical generalizations can be brought together through the notion of the 'escalator region'. By escalator region, I mean a region dominated by a large city – typically a 'global city' or a very large metropolitan area that connects with the biographies of able and ambitious men and women in a very specific manner: (i) it attracts these people at the school or university leaving and job and university entering stages in their life course from far and wide (akin to stepping on the escalator); (ii) it provides the rich opportunity environment for their upward social mobility at rates that are distinctly higher than elsewhere (akin to being taken up by the escalator); and (iii) it then loses through out-migration a significant proportion of them to other places as their careers progress, or at, or close to, retirement when assets accumulated in the city are often cashed in to provide for a high standard of living in an amenable environment (sometimes in the region from which they originally came) (akin to stepping off the escalator).

This rather simple idea that there is a kind of circulatory system that links social and geographical mobility during an individual's life course has proven attractive to many researchers. A word of caution, however, is appropriate. Simple models of human behaviour tend to mask as well as enlighten. It is important, therefore, to list some of the important things that the escalator region concept does not claim to be true, or about which it has little or nothing to contribute. It most assuredly does not claim that the likelihood of upward social mobility is a simple function of city size or position in the urban hierarchy, nor does it claim that all migrants to major cities benefit economically from their migration. Indeed, empirical research on the social mobility of migrants informs us again and again that a fairly typical trajectory is one of initial downward mobility (when migrants do work that is below their level of qualifications, skills, potential and experience) followed by upward mobility as they 'learn the ropes' – as they come to realize how they can manoeuvre to their advantage in the urban labour market.

Similarly, it definitely does not claim that it is only educated and ambitious young men and women who migrate to the major cities. In low-income developing countries, the vast majority of the migrants to the major cities are likely to be (agricultural and craft-industry) skilled, but lacking in formal qualifications; ambitious, but resource poor and lacking in 'social capital'. In high-income developed countries, the proportion of educated and well-connected young men and women among the migrants is likely to be much higher. Nor does the concept imply either that there is no migration of young adults away from the major cities or that it is only young adults who migrate to such cities. Finally, it is important to stress that the escalator region is a concept for use only with intra-generational social mobility. It contributes little or nothing to discussions about inter-generational social mobility.

The big question then becomes (despite these qualifications listed above): Can the 'escalator region' idea be used for cases other than the one for which it was first formulated (UK internal migration)? Judging by the many occasions on which other researchers have found the concept to be helpful, the answer is a resounding 'yes'. A subsidiary question is: Can the 'escalator region' concept be used to help us understand international migration as well as internal migration? Again, the answer is, in this author's opinion, a resounding 'yes'. Yet, up until now, the concept has not been used to help explain migration processes and patterns in East Asia at either the internal level or the international level (see Fielding 2015 for an attempt to fill this gap).

Although the patterns of social and geographical mobility and the links between them are, of course, immensely complex in detail, the evidence seems to show that many of the generalizations listed above do indeed apply to migration and social mobility in East Asia. The major cities of Southeast Asia – Jakarta, Kuala Lumpur, Bangkok, Ho Chi Minh City and Manila – do act as 'escalator regions' within their national space-economies, with Singapore towering over the whole region as a major site of social promotion. Provincial cities within the PRC perform a similar role to those Southeast Asian national capitals, but with Beijing as the preferred site for rapid political, cultural and bureaucratic advancement, while Hong Kong and Shanghai have become international 'escalator regions' for careers in business and finance. Finally, Seoul and Tokyo perform key roles in middle- and upper middle-class formation in South Korea and Japan, with upwardly mobile young adults siphoned to them through provincial university cities. However, with Japan yet to embrace fully the 'global search for talent' (despite policy rhetoric to the contrary), Tokyo acts rather less than might perhaps be expected as a magnet for, or even a stepping stone in, international professional and managerial careers.

References

Fielding, A.J., 2005, Class, in Gibney, M.J. and Hansen, R. (eds), *Immigration and Asylum: From 1900 to the Present*, Vol. 1. Los Angeles, CA: ABC Clio Press, 97–100.
Fielding, A.J., 2007, Migration and social mobility in urban systems: national and international trends, in Geyer, H.S. (ed.), *International Handbook of Urban Policy Volume 1: Contentious Global Issues*. Cheltenham: Edward Elgar, 107–137.
Fielding, T., 2015 (forthcoming), *Migration: The Economic Drivers of Contemporary Labour Mobility in East Asia*. Singapore: World Scientific (Globalization in Eurasia and the Pacific Rim, Vol. 4, 157–174).

Selected references

4.0 General

Bell, M. and Muhudin, S., 2009, Cross-national comparisons of internal migration, UNDP, Human Development Research Paper 2009/30.

Chia, L.S. (ed.), 2003, *Southeast Asia Transformed: A Geography of Change.* Singapore: Institute of South East Asian Studies.

Dang, N.A., 2003, Internal migration policies in the ESCAP region, *Asia Pacific Population Journal* 18(3): 27–40.

Dauvergne, P., 1997, *Shadows in the Forest: Japan and the Politics of Timber in Southeast Asia.* Cambridge, MA: MIT Press.

Dun, O., 2011, Migration and displacement triggered by floods in the Mekong Delta, *International Migration* 49: 200–224.

Guest, P., 2009, Urbanization and migration in Southeast Asia, in Luong, H.V. (ed.), *Urbanization, Migration, and Poverty in a Vietnamese Metropolis: Ho Chi Min City in Comparative Perspective.* Singapore: National University of Singapore Press, 359–380.

Hall, D., 2011, Where the streets are paved with prawns: crop booms and migration in Southeast Asia, *Critical Asian Studies* 43(4): 507–530.

Hauser, P.M., Suits, D.B., Ogawa, N. (eds), 1985, *Urbanization and Migration in ASEAN Development.* Tokyo: National Institute for Research Advancement.

Leinbach, T. and Ulack, R., 2000, *Southeast Asia: Diversity and Development.* Upper Saddle River, NJ: Prentice Hall.

McGee, T.G., 1967, *The Southeast Asian City.* London: Bell.

Pryor, R.J. (ed.), 1979, *Migration and Development in Southeast Asia.* Kuala Lumpur: Oxford University Press.

4.1 Indonesia (and Timor Leste)

Adam, J., 2010, Post-conflict Ambon: forced migration and the ethno-territorial effects of customary tenure, *Development and Change* 41(3): 401–419.

Alisjahbana, A. and Manning, C., 2010, Making it in the city: recent and long-term migrants in the urban labour markets in Indonesia, in Meng, X., Manning, C., Li, S. and Effendi, T.N. (eds), *The Great Migration: Rural-Urban Migration in China and Indonesia.* Cheltenham: Edward Elgar, 194–221.

Duncan, C.R., 2005, Unwelcome guests: relations between internally displaced persons and their hosts in North Sulawesi, Indonesia, *Journal of Refugee Studies* 18(1): 25–46.

Elmhirst, R., 2000, A Javanese diaspora? Gender and identity politics in Indonesia's transmigration programme, *Women's Studies International Forum* 23(4): 487–500.

Elmhirst, R., 2012, Displacement, resettlement, and multi-local livelihoods: positioning migrant legitimacy in Lampung, Indonesia, *Critical Asian Studies* 44(1): 131–152.

Firman, T., 2004, Demographic and spatial patterns of Indonesia's recent urbanization, *Population, Space and Place* 10: 421–434.

Hardjono, J., 1977, *Transmigration in Indonesia.* Kuala Lumpur: Oxford University Press.

Hedman, E-L.E. (ed.), 2008, *Conflict, Violence, and Displacement in Indonesia.* Ithaca, NY: Southeast Asia Program, Cornell University.

Hill, H., Resosudarmo, B.P. and Vidyattama, Y., 2009, Economic geography of Indonesia: location, connectivity, and resources, in *Reshaping Economic Geography of East Asia.* Washington, DC: World Bank, 115–134.

Hugo, G., 1977, Circular migration, *Bulletin of Indonesian Economic Studies* 13(3): 57–66.

Hugo, G., 2002, Pengungsi – Indonesia's internally displaced persons, *Asian and Pacific Migration Journal* 11(3): 297–332.

Hugo, G., Hull, T.H., Hull, V.J. and Jones, G.W., 1987, *The Demographic Dimension in Indonesian Development*. London: Oxford University Press.

Jones, G.W., 1996, The changing employment structure of the extended Jakarta metropolitan region, *Bulletin of Indonesian Economic Studies* 32(1): 51–70.

Kong, S.T. and Effendi, T.N., 2011, Occupational choice and mobility among migrants to four cities, in Manning, C. and Sumarto, S. (eds), *Employment, Living Standards and Poverty in Contemporary Indonesia*. Singapore: Institute of South East Asian Studies, 134–158.

Leinbach, T.R., 2004, *The Indonesian Rural Economy: Mobility, Work and Enterprise*. Singapore: Institute of South East Asian Studies.

Lindquist, J.A., 2008, *The Anxieties of Mobility: Migration and Tourism in the Indonesian Borderlands*. Honolulu: University of Hawai'i Press.

Manning, C. and Sumarto, S. (eds), 2011, *Employment, Living Standards and Poverty in Contemporary Indonesia*. Singapore: Institute of South East Asian Studies.

McNicoll, G., 1982, Recent demographic trends in Indonesia, *Population and Development Review* 8(4): 811–819.

Meng, X., Manning, C., Li, S. and Effendi, T.N., 2010, *The Great Migration: Rural-Urban Migration in China and Indonesia*. Cheltenham: Edward Elgar.

Muhidin, S., 2002, *The Population of Indonesia: Regional Demographic Scenarios Using a Multiregional Method and Multiple Data Sources*. Amsterdam: Rozenberg.

Muhidin, S., 2014, Migration patterns: people on the move, in Hill, H. (ed.), *Regional Dynamics in a Decentralized Indonesia*. Singapore: Institute of South East Asian Studies, 317–341.

Naik, A., Stigter, E. and Laczko, F., 2007, *Migration, Development and Natural Disasters: Insights from the Ocean Tsunami*. Geneva: International Organization for Migration.

Oey, M., 1982, The transmigration program in Indonesia, in Jones, G.W. and Richter, H.V. (eds), *Population Resettlement Programs in Southeast Asia*. Australian National University, Development Studies Centre, Monograph 30: 27–51.

Silvey, R., 2000, Diasporic subjects: gendered migration in Indonesia, *Women's Studies International Forum* 23(4): 501–515.

Silvey, R. and Elmhirst, R., 2003, Engendering social capital: women workers and rural-urban networks in Indonesia's crisis, *World Development* 31(5): 865–881.

Spaan, E., 1999, *Labour Circulation and Socioeconomic Transformation: The Case of East Java, Indonesia*. The Hague: Netherlands Interdisciplinary Demographic Institute.

Speare, A. and Harris, J., 1986, Education, earnings, and migration in Indonesia, *Economic Development and Cultural Change* 34(2): 223–244.

Sukamdi, Haris, A. and Brownlee, P. (eds), 2000, *Labour Migration in Indonesia: Policies and Practice*. Yogyakarta: Gadja Mada University, Population Studies Center.

Tirtosudarmo, R., 1995, The political demography of national integration and its policy implications for a sustainable development in Indonesia, *The Indonesian Quarterly* 23 (4): 369–383.

Van der Eng, P., 2002, Bridging a gap: a reconstruction of population patterns in Indonesia, 1930–1961, *Asian Studies Review* 26(4): 487–509.

Williams, C.P., 2007, *Maiden Voyages: Eastern Indonesian Women on the Move*. Singapore: Institute of South East Asian Studies.

4.2 Singapore

Loh, K.S., 2009, Conflict and change at the margins: emergency kampong clearance and the making of modern Singapore, *Asian Studies Review* 33: 139–159.

4.3 Malaysia (and Brunei)

Bunnell, T., 2004, *Malaysia, Modernity and the Multimedia Super Corridor*. London: RoutledgeCurzon.

Chattopadhyay, A., 1997, Family migration and the economic status of women in Malaysia, *International Migration Review* 31(2): 338–352.

Chitose, Y., 2003, Effects of government policy on internal migration in peninsular Malaysia: a comparison between Malays and non-Malays, *International Migration Review* 37(4): 1191–1219.

Hew, C.S., 2002, *Women Workers, Migration and Family in Sarawak*. London: RoutledgeCurzon.

Hew, C.S. (ed.), 2007, *Village Mothers, City Daughters: Women and Urbanization in Sarawak*. Singapore: ISEAS.

Jali, M.R.M., 2009, *Internal Migration in Malaysia: Spatial and Temporal Analysis*. University of Leeds PhD thesis.

Lin, C.Y.O., 2008, Indigenous peoples, displacement through 'development' and rights violations: the case of the Orang Asli of peninsular Malaysia, in Grabska, K. and Mehta, L. (eds), *Forced Displacement: Why Rights Matter*. Basingstoke: Palgrave, 178–200.

Saw, S.-H., 1988 (2007), *The Population of Peninsular Malaysia*. Singapore: Singapore University Press.

Soda, R., 2007, *People on the Move: Rural-Urban Interactions in Sarawak*. Kyoto: Kyoto University Press/Trans Pacific Press.

Thompson, E.C., 2007, *Unsettling Absences: Urbanism in Rural Malaysia*. Singapore: Singapore University Press.

4.4 Thailand

Askew, M., 2002, *Bangkok: Space, Place and Representation*. London: Routledge.

Chamratrithirong, A., 2007, Research on internal migration in Thailand: the state of knowledge, *Journal of Population and Social Studies* 16(1): 1–20.

Clausen, A., 2002, Female labour migration to Bangkok: transforming rural-urban interactions and social networks through globalization, *Asia-Pacific Population Journal* 17(3): 53–78.

De Jong, G.F., Johnson, A.G. and Richter, K., 1996, Determinants of migration values and expectations in rural Thailand, *Asian and Pacific Migration Journal* 5(4): 399–416.

Douglass, M., 1995, Global interdependence and urbanization: planning for the Bangkok mega-urban region, in McGee, T.G. and Robinson, I.M. (eds), *The Mega-Urban Regions of Southeast Asia*. Vancouver: University of British Columbia Press, 45–77.

Esara, P., 2004, 'Women will keep the household': the mediation of work and family by female labor migrants in Bangkok, *Critical Asian Studies* 36(2), 119–216.

Fawcett, J.T., Khoo, S.-E. and Smith, P.C. (eds), 1984, *Women in the Cities of Asia: Migration and Urban Adaptation*. Boulder, CO: Westview Press.

Garip, F. and Curran, S., 2010, Increasing migration, diverging communities: changing character of migrant streams in rural Thailand, *Population Research Policy Review* 29: 659–685.

Goldstein, S. and Goldstein, A., 1986, *Migration in Thailand: A 25 Year Review*. Honolulu: Papers of the East-West Population Institute 100.

Guest, P. and Punpuing, S., 2003, *Report of Round 2 Survey (2001)*. Mahidol University: Institute for Population and Social Research Pub. 275.

Guest, P. et al., 1994, Internal migration in Thailand, *Asian and Pacific Migration Journal* 3(4): 531–545.

Hauser, P.M., Suits, D.B. and Ogawa, N. (eds), 1985, *Urbanization and Migration in ASEAN Development*. Tokyo: National Institute for Research Advancement.

Jampaklay, A., Korinek, K. and Entwistle, B., 2007, Residential clustering among Nang Rong migrants in urban settings in Thailand, *Asian and Pacific Migration Journal* 16(4): 485–510.

Knodel, J. and Saengtienchai, C., 2007, Rural parents with urban children: social and economic implications of migration for the rural elderly in Thailand, *Population, Space and Place* 13(3): 193–210.

Mills, M.B., 2012, Thai mobilities and cultural citizenship, *Critical Asian Studies* 44(1): 85–112.

Ogena, N.B. and De Jong, G.F., 1999, Internal migration and occupational mobility in Thailand, *Asian and Pacific Migration Journal* 8(4): 419–446.

Rigg, J. and Salamanca, A., 2011, Connecting lives, living and location: mobility and spatial signatures in Northeast Thailand, 1982–2009, *Critical Asian Studies* 43(4): 551–575.

Vanwey, L.K., 2004, Altruistic and contractual remittances between male and female migrants and households in rural Thailand, *Demography* 41(4): 739–756.

4.5 Myanmar

Bosson, A., 2007, *Forced Migration/Internal Displacement in Burma*. Oslo: IDMC (Internal Displacement Monitoring Centre).

Oo, Z.M. and Kusakabe, K., 2010, Motherhood and social network: response strategies of internally displaced Karen women in Taungoo district, *Women's Studies International Forum* 33: 482–491.

4.6 Laos

Baird, I.G., 2009, Internal resettlement in Laos, *Critical Asian Studies* 41(4): 605–620.

High, H., 2009, The road to nowhere? Poverty and policy in the south of Laos, *Focaal – Journal of Global and Historical Anthropology* 53: 75–88.

Phouxay, K. and Tollefsen, A., 2010, Rural-urban migration, economic transition, and status of female industrial workers in Lao PDR, *Population, Space and Place* 17(5): 421–434.

Rigg, J., 2007, Moving lives: migration and livelihoods in the Lao PDR, *Population, Space and Place* 13(3): 163–178.

4.7 Cambodia

Derks, A., 2008, *Kmer Women on the Move: Exploring Work and Life in Urban Cambodia*. Honolulu: University of Hawai'i Press.

Haapala, U., 2003, *Where Do You Go? Migration and Urbanization in Cambodia*. Phnom Penh: Mekonginfo.

National Committee for Population and Development (Cambodia), 2009, *A Review of Migration in Cambodia*. Phnom Penh: NCPD.

4.8 Vietnam

Agergaard, J. and Thao, V.T., 2010, Mobile, flexible, and adaptable: female migrants in Hanoi's informal sector, *Population, Space and Place* 17(5): 407–420.

Barbieri, M. and Belanger, D. (eds), 2009, *Reconfiguring Families and Gender in Contemporary Vietnam*. Stanford, CA: Stanford University Press.

Dang, A.N., 1999, Market reforms and internal migration in Vietnam, *Asian and Pacific Migration Journal* 8(3): 381–410.

Dang, N.A., 2009, Household registration system and the well-beings of rural-to-urban migrants, *Vietnam's Socio-Economic Development* 59: 75–80.

De Brauw, A., 2010, Seasonal migration and agricultural production in Vietnam, *Journal of Development Studies* 46(1): 114–139.

Djamba, Y.K., Goldstein, S. and Goldstein, A., 2000, Migration and occupational change during periods of economic transition: women and men in Vietnam, *Asian and Pacific Migration Journal* 9(1): 65–92.

Gubry, P. (ed.), 2000, *Population et Developpement au Viet-Nam*. Paris: Karthala-CEDES.

Gubry, P. and Huong, T.H., 2005, Are the 'left-behind' really left? Shared advantages in rural-urban migration from the Mekong Delta to Ho Chi Min City, *Vietnam's Socio-Economic Development* 44: 54–70.

Hardy, A., 2003, *Red Hills: Migration and the State in the Highlands of Vietnam*. London: Routledge.

Hoang, L.A., 2011, Gendered networks and migration decision-making in Northern Vietnam, *Social and Cultural Geography* 12(5): 419–433.

Luong, H.V. (ed.), 2009, *Urbanization, Migration, and Poverty in a Vietnamese Metropolis: Ho Chi Min City in Comparative Perspective*. Singapore: National University of Singapore Press.

Marx, V. and Fleischer, K., 2010, *Internal Migration: Opportunities and Challenges for Socio-Economic Development in Viet Nam (+ Call to Action)*. Hanoi: UN Viet Nam.

McElwee, P., 2008, 'Blood relatives' or uneasy neighbors? Kinh migrant and ethnic minority interactions in the Truong Son mountains, *Journal of Vietnamese Studies* 3(3): 81–116.

Nguyen-Hoang, P. and McPeak, J., 2010, Leaving or staying: inter-provincial migration in Vietnam, *Asian and Pacific Migration Journal* 19(4): 473–500.

Phan, D. and Coxhead, I., 2010, Inter-provincial migration and inequality during Vietnam's transition, *Journal of Development Economics* 91: 100–112.

Rushing, R., 2006, Migration and sexual exploitation in Vietnam, *Asian and Pacific Migration Journal* 15(4): 471–494.

Zhang, H.X., Kelly, P.M., Lockec, C., Winkels, A. and Adger, W.N., 2006, Migration in a transitional economy: beyond the planned and spontaneous dichotomy in Vietnam, *Geoforum* 3(7): 1066–1081.

4.9 Philippines

Chant, S. and McIlwaine, C., 1995, *Women of a Lesser Cost*. London: Pluto Press.

Findley, S.E., 1987, An interactive contextual model of migration in Ilocos Norte, the Philippines, *Demography* 24(2): 163–190.

Kelly, P.F., 2000, *Landscapes of Globalisation: Human Geographies of Economic Change in the Philippines*. London: Routledge.

Ulack, R., 1977, Migration to Mindanao: population growth in the final stage of a pioneer frontier, *Tijdschrift voor Economische en Sociale Geografie* 68(3): 133–144.

Wernstedt, F.L. and Spencer, J.E., 1967, *The Philippine Island World: A Physical, Cultural and Regional Geography*. Berkeley: University of California Press.

5 Asia's global diaspora

China plus's international migration flows

5.0 Introduction

The post-war development of China's international migrations, oscillating wildly as it does in numbers, and shifting in the origins of its immigrants and destinations of its emigrants, almost beggars belief. Following the tumultuous years of the civil war ending in 1949 with the mass migration of about 2 million Kuomintang (KMT) troops, families and supporters to Taiwan, the communist People's Republic of China (henceforth the PRC, or just China) 'locked down' as it were. That meant very few people came in (just a handful of foreigners who were trusted by the new regime), and almost nobody went out (just a few workers on China-sponsored infrastructure projects in developing countries). Over the next 30 years, the PRC became what it had been through earlier periods of its history – a country without international migration flows. The very minor exceptions to this rule were some students in Eastern Europe and the courageous people who managed to escape to Hong Kong, sometimes by swimming along the shore.

However, once the Deng Xiaoping reforms began to take effect after 1978, the situation changed dramatically. The PRC became the source of two very important but very different kinds of international migration: (i) the mostly illegal migration of relatively poor people from Fujian, Zhejiang and other southeastern provinces to North America, Western Europe and elsewhere (now much reduced); and (ii) the legal but circumscribed migration of Chinese students and researchers to Western (mostly North American) universities (still increasing).

As the opening-up process continued, coastal southeast regions of the PRC became the destination for foreign migrant businessmen and technicians (typically not accompanied by their families), associated with foreign direct investment (FDI) in the Pearl River Delta area by successful capitalist corporations, many of them based in Hong Kong or Taiwan. The reversion of Hong Kong to China in 1997, however, had much less effect on migration flows than had been expected.

Finally, in the recent period, after the PRC has enjoyed over 30 years of rapid economic growth, three signs of maturity in China's international migration flows can be identified. First, there is the completion of the global Chinese diaspora by the arrival of significant numbers of migrant workers, plus a small number of settlers, in the one part of the world – tropical sub-Saharan Africa – that had previously figured very little in Chinese emigration. Second is the emergence of truly multicultural cities in China – Beijing, of course, because of its administrative, diplomatic and cultural importance, but above all, Shanghai. Because of Shanghai's commercial, industrial and financial predominance in the whole China 'plus' region, a large population of foreign permanent and semi-permanent residents now live there, contributing enormously to the city's dynamism and diversity. The third sign is the recent emergence of China as a country of new immigration flows – an example being the small, but until recently rapidly growing, West African community in Guangzhou.

5.1 Chinese diaspora: North America

North America (especially the USA) had figured prominently in the 19th-century exodus from late Qing China, and this meant that a significant population of Chinese descent persisted through the period of the policy of Asian exclusion, which built up in the late 19th century, became total in 1924, and lasted until well after World War II. Subsequently, the doors began to open again. Partly this was ideological. In the context of the Cold War between the forces of 'freedom' (that is, the capitalist democratic West) and those of 'tyranny' (i.e. the communist authoritarian East), it was judged essential to demonstrate how welcoming the West was to those who rejected the ideology of the communist bloc. So dissidents from the Soviet Union and 'Red China' were treated as guests in the USA. A similar, albeit guarded, welcome was also extended to students and researchers from the PRC who wanted to study in North America.

However, the vast majority of migrants from China to the USA and Canada, in flows that built up rapidly in the 1980s and 1990s, were neither political dissidents nor researchers; they were very ordinary people mostly from southeastern China (Guangdong, Fujian, and Zhejiang) who wanted to make good money doing low-level jobs in the high-wage West. Having paid for the passage, many thousands of such migrants disappeared into the 'Chinatowns' of North American cities, both those located on the west coast and those in the east, especially New York. Close networks of mutual obligation based on family connection and hometown loyalty provided the 'social capital' needed to survive, and then possibly prosper, in such a different economic and cultural environment.

The 2010 Census shows that there are approximately 3.8 million people of Chinese descent in the USA (with, of course, an increasing proportion of these being of mixed descent). They are concentrated in urban areas and have some of the characteristics of a 'model minority' in that they do not for the most part represent a threat to law and order, they are predominantly employed in secure, well-paid jobs, and they demonstrate, especially through educational success, the 'get-up-and-go' spirit of American individualism – in short, they tend to live, and thereby lend legitimacy to, the 'American dream'. Those who are less educationally successful and have not joined the ranks of professionals or managers, usually work in the small business sector, especially in the personal services, catering and convenience stores, and clothing industries. A similar picture emerges for Canada, where the Chinese 'community', added to by large numbers of students who have stayed on after completing their studies, have, broadly speaking, been financially and socially successful, albeit with many challenges to overcome, including discrimination. The Canadian policy environment has been particularly favourable to Chinese immigrants due to the 'path to citizenship' that it offers. So, integration within a society that is, or at least has been up until fairly recently, multicultural both in spirit and practice, has been relatively straightforward.

5.2 Chinese diaspora: Western Europe

As elsewhere, the recent migrations of Chinese people to Western Europe were not the first. There already existed in most countries a small but relatively successful community of Chinese people working in family businesses in retailing, catering and personal services. The new arrivals fall into three main groups: (i) students, both undergraduate and postgraduate, some of whom stay on after graduation; (ii) industrial and service-sector workers who are well connected within supportive networks that provide the jobs, shelter, advice and know-how (for example, about regularization of immigration status) needed to allow successful insertion into the host society; and (ii) very vulnerable young adult migrants arriving illegally and put to work in high-risk situations. Far too many of these young people have suffered death or injury either during the migration journey itself (witness the deaths of 58 Fujian migrants in a cold store truck at Dover in the UK in 2000), or while working in dangerous conditions under the weak or non-existent supervision and care of gang masters (for example, the deaths of 21 Fujianese while collecting mussels in Morecombe Bay in the UK in 2004).

Most Western European countries have new Chinese migrants: in most countries they are students (typically enrolled on courses taught in English or designed to improve their English), but in some countries they join sizeable existing communities in the urban service-sector economy. In others, however, their role has been rather different. For example, in Italy, the new Chinese have played a significant role in the 'third Italy' high-fashion textile, clothing, accessories (for example, handbags) and footwear industries, located mostly around Prato in the central-northern region of the country.

5.3 Chinese diaspora: other countries

While North American and Western European destinations have been sought after by most Chinese emigrants in the recent period, other places have also attracted new migrants from the PRC. Some of these have already been mentioned in the chapter on Southeast Asia, but Chinese migrants have also figured prominently in the recent immigrations to Australia and New Zealand, South Korea and Japan, and to certain Latin American countries.

One particular migration attracts a great deal of attention – indeed perhaps more attention than it really deserves considering the small numbers of people involved: the migration of Tibetans to India. This is where truth and myth become easily entangled; so much national pride, ethnic identity, and human rights activism is involved. If one tries to pick one's way through the rhetoric, the facts seem to be: (i) that the 'liberation' of Tibet from 'feudalism' by the communist Chinese forces in the 1950s was not experienced as such by a number of Tibetans who felt that their Tibetan ethnicity and Buddhist religion were being trampled upon; (ii) with their spiritual leader, the Dalai Lama, they escaped to India, where, at Dharamsala, they set up a Tibetan 'government in exile', represented themselves to the world as the authentic voice of the oppressed Tibetan people, and acted as a gathering place for new refugees; (iii) meanwhile, the practical integration of Tibet as a region, an economy and a people, and of Buddhism as a religious identity, within the wider Chinese development process, continued and continues. This does not mean that dissenting voices have disappeared – they have not (witness the recent tragic self-immolations in Sichuan and Qinghai); however, nor does it mean that the narratives of the 'splittists' (the term used by the Chinese government to describe those who seek Tibetan independence) should be accepted without due caution.

Finally, the Chinese have a significant presence in the countries of Eastern Europe, and above all, in Russia, where they form an important part of the Eurasian migration system (see Chapter 7).

5.4 Contemporary emigration from the PRC

The rapid growth of the Chinese economy since 1978 has led to two distinctively new features of Chinese emigration. The first is the presence in all the major world centres of trade and finance, of company offices and government agencies manned by Chinese nationals set up to protect and enhance Chinese economic and political interests in those parts of the world. Chinese private-sector, state-owned enterprise, and sovereign-fund investments in both Western advanced capitalist countries and in developing countries have increased rapidly in the recent period – so much so that the country is expected to become a net exporter of FDI in a few years' time. Political, professional and technical staffs are required to manage such investments in the receiving countries.

The second distinctive feature of recent emigration from the PRC is the sudden appearance of many Chinese (maybe as many as 1 million 'Chinese') in sub-Saharan Africa. Journalistic misrepresentations of this process emphasize the 'land-grab' aspect of this new presence, the idea being that the rapid growth in the need for food in China, and the lack of confidence in global food markets, is encouraging the Chinese government and business interests to invest in land in countries like Tanzania and Mozambique to secure future food supplies. However, the arrival of the Chinese in Africa is both more complex and more interesting than this. Most of the Chinese are there for purposes of trade and investment. Africa supplies all sorts of products for the Chinese market, but the key ones are oil and gas, the many minerals such as copper and rare earths needed for Chinese manufacturing industry, and certain food and other products not available in China. Other Chinese are the temporary migrant employees (both professional-technical and manual) of major companies engaged in infrastructure projects in Africa, while yet others, though still very small in number, are trying to make a living as farmers. Most, though, are there as the proprietors of small family businesses (as has so often been the case in earlier Chinese migrations). They own shops, run bars and brothels, provide personal services (as barbers, etc.), and generally insert themselves into that part of the local economy which involves exchange and distribution.

5.5 Illegal migration from China: trafficking

In the 1980s and 1990s China became a major source country for illegal migration. While some of this was sex trafficking, most was for labour exploitation. Organized crime syndicates were involved in the process. It was said that the 'Snakehead' gangs were in charge, and that they linked up with criminal organizations in the destination countries, notably the Yakuza in Japan and Mafia in the USA. Closer inspection of the trafficking process, however, showed that it was more typically the case that migrants were being channelled by small-scale loosely connected networks of agents, many of them linked to one another by family and/or hometown origin. The 'granny' human-smuggling entrepreneur of a small town in Fujian Province seemed to be the norm rather than the exception.

5.6 Chinese immigration: return migration

There are six main types of post-1950 immigration to the PRC. The first to appear was the migration of business people (almost entirely ethnic Chinese men) in the early years following the opening up of China after 1978. One of the largest groups of such migrants was those from Taiwan (the *taishang*). They were particularly involved in the investments made by Taiwanese companies in the Pearl River Delta region, for example in Shenzen and Dongguan, using low-cost, locally recruited labour (much of it female) to produce cheap consumer goods such as toys, clothing and footwear, electrical goods, etc. Hong Kong-based companies also figured prominently in these early ventures. Over time the business immigrants came to form close-knit communities, often relating strongly with their origin countries but rather little, despite their *guanxi* advantages, with their host populations, while the products made went up the value chain from toys and clothes in the early days to electronic components for, and finished goods such as TVs, computers, cameras and mobile phones more latterly. Soon companies from other East Asian countries, notably Japan, South Korea and Singapore, and other parts of the world, notably the USA and Germany, joined in the rapid development of this southeast coastal region of China. The numbers of migrants were small, and their stay in China was often for only a few years, but nevertheless this represented the first significant presence of civilian, non-colonial foreigners in China since the 'decadent days' of Republican Shanghai in the 1930s.

Return migrants from the USA and elsewhere comprise the second group of immigrants. These are mostly former university students who went abroad to North America, Western Europe or Australasia to study, who often stayed on for a time and began to develop careers as professional or technical employees in large companies, or as teachers and researchers, but who then decided that they wanted to return to China. This decision was typically for a combination of reasons – to be a participant in national renewal and capitalist development, to take advantage of new employment prospects and the rapid promotion that was often offered to returnees, and, of course, to reconnect with family and community.

The third group of immigrants are the many young adults almost entirely from English-speaking countries who are attracted to China to teach English to the Chinese at all levels from the junior high school to university and beyond. Although English-language teaching is, in line with public-sector education, scattered around the country, there is a particular concentration of private-sector language schools and their foreign staffs in the main centres of administrative and commercial activity, namely Beijing and Shanghai. As yet, however, the number of English-language schools in China (1,600) does not match those in South Korea (2,000) or Japan (4,600). In turn, China also attracts Western (and other Asian) students and researchers, though not yet on as large a scale as Japan.

Fourth, the opening up of the PRC has resulted in the arrival of major companies wanting to sell into the Chinese domestic market, and forming joint ventures with Chinese organizations (both private sector and state owned) for production in China to supply goods for export and for domestic consumption. These second-wave business migrants (Taiwanese and Hong Kong entrepreneurs located in the Pearl River Delta being the first wave) are to be found in Shanghai rather than in Dongguan or Shenzen. They started the process whereby China's largest cities began to have semi-permanent foreign populations. The kinds of jobs they are doing and their reasons for being there have diversified enormously over time, so that these foreigners are no longer just 'salarymen' and their families, but include students, young professionals, ambitious career women, artists and performers, adventurers and charlatans. It is reported, for example, that there are now about 100,000 Japanese nationals living in mainland China, many of them in Shanghai (with a further 20,000 living in Hong Kong/Macao). Indeed, the Shanghai city-region has become a kind of 'escalator region' for much of East Asia – that is, a place to which young, able and ambitious men and women migrate (akin to stepping on the escalator), where careers are advanced far faster than elsewhere (being taken up by the escalator), and from which one can move on while benefiting from the privileged experience and contacts that one has amassed (akin to stepping off the escalator). Add to this the mutual advantage to the English-speaking foreigner (often male) and to the aspiring local (often female) of inter-ethnic socialization (sometimes including sexual relations), and the recipe for excitement, celebration and success (as well as for deceit and disappointment) is complete.

Fifth, northeast China is the destination for most of the migrants (escapees) from North Korea. One authority estimated that there were about 200,000 North Koreans illegally residing in China in 1999. This number has probably fallen somewhat since then (partly through regularization), but 30,000 refugees were thought to be hiding in China in 2012.

Finally, so successful has China become economically, so competitive are its goods on world markets, so many opportunities exist to make money through imports and exports, that surprising new immigration flows have suddenly appeared. The most notable of these, perhaps, is the arrival of migrants from sub-Saharan Africa manifested in the rapid growth of communities of West African traders in Guangzhou (Guangdong Province) and Yiwu (Zhejiang Province). In particular, the presence of a community of about 16,000 black-skinned African people from Nigeria, Ghana, francophone West Africa and Angola resident in Guangzhou has received much public attention and media coverage. A source of great curiosity, these Africans are sometimes treated well – almost as celebrities – but more often, it seems, receive only suspicion and contempt from the host population. It was estimated that China had an immigrant population (that is, excluding returnees) of about 700,000 in 2010, with this figure increasing rapidly in the late 2000s. China has become a country of immigration – albeit as yet on a very small scale relative to its population.

5.7 Hong Kong/Macao: immigration and emigration

Hong Kong's post-World War II migration history has been very complex in detail, but four stages, each involving very different migration streams can be identified: (i) the pre-1978 period dominated by restrictions on both emigration from and immigration to the PRC, when most of Hong Kong's migration related to its administrative and commercial role as a British colonial outpost; (ii) the period from then until 1997 when Hong Kong became the major gateway port to the southern PRC, when that country was opening up rapidly to foreign manufacturing investment and to international trade; (iii) the return of Hong Kong to China in 1997, which resulted in some very specific migration flows; and (iv) the post-1997 period in which Hong Kong has experienced the types of migration usually associated with a major global commercial and financial services centre.

Due to the loss of its port functions, deportations by the Japanese, and food shortages, the population of Hong Kong had declined during World War II from 1.64 million in 1941 to just 5–600,000 in 1945. Many returned from China in 1945/46, but then the civil war and its aftermath brought large new inflows to Hong Kong from the mainland in the late 1940s and early 1950s, many of them middle-class families from Shanghai. By 1956 the population had jumped to 2.6 million. A high proportion were unemployed so the basis for a rapid capital accumulation founded on a low-wage, export-oriented manufacturing economy, based mainly on textiles and clothing, was established. Subsequently, the colonial government adopted a rather laissez-faire approach both to the economy as a whole and to labour migration. This helped to produce significant flows of migrants into Hong Kong both from the PRC and from elsewhere in East Asia.

In the period from the mid-1950s to the opening up of the PRC after 1978, the wealth difference between Hong Kong and the nearby areas of Guangdong Province, and the rest of southern China was enormous. This alone would have encouraged migration from the PRC to Hong Kong. In addition, however, southern China had suffered some of the worse effects of the great famine, and with the rest of the country had experienced the upheavals of the Cultural Revolution. So, although the risks accompanying migration were high, about 600,000 desperate people escaped the PRC (sometimes by swimming across the border) to 'reach base' in Hong Kong and join the ranks of its manufacturing working class or its sizeable petite bourgeoisie. At the same time, Hong Kong was the centre for the UK's expatriate business operations in the 'Far East'. This meant that many companies ran their East Asian affairs out of Hong Kong – banking, financial services, sales and marketing, and export and import operations. This called for an immigration of mostly 'public' (that is, private) school-educated young adult male expatriates from Britain, who also filled key roles in administration and security (for example, as senior police officers).

(This laissez-faire approach to the economy did not extend to refugees from Vietnam – the Vietnamese 'boat people' – who were detained for many years in large camps, detached and disconnected from Hong Kong society and economy.)

This migration situation changed dramatically after 1978. Hong Kong businesses were at the forefront of the investment boom that transformed the Pearl River Delta in the nearby PRC into the 'workshop of the world' (by the early 1990s 3 million workers in the Pearl River Delta were employed by Hong Kong firms or firms partly financed out of Hong Kong). Drawing upon vast reserves of cheap labour in the hinterlands of the major cities, Hong Kong businessmen, often in joint ventures with local interests, built new factories (in truth, whole new cities of factories) to meet the demands for consumer goods in advanced capitalist economies, notably the USA. This boom brought Hong Kong managers, professionals, engineers and technicians into southern China, and southern Chinese migrants into Hong Kong. The social relations of these migrants were sometimes complicated. Many Hong Kong men had 'second families' in southern China, and the difficult issue of the rights of those family members to enter Hong Kong remains to this day.

The return of Hong Kong to China in 1997 produced its own rather peculiar migration flows. The settlement included agreements that certain people, typically those close to the colonial administration, would be allowed to settle in the UK. In the event, however, the numbers taking up this opportunity were very small. Instead, what happened was that many upper- and middle-class families decided to 'hedge their bets' on the future of Hong Kong within 'one country, two systems' by seeking immigrant status in one of the 'new commonwealth' countries (Canada, Australia, New Zealand). This would be fully taken up if things went seriously wrong in Hong Kong, but in the meantime the wives and children would settle abroad while the husband/father would continue to work and look after family interests in Hong Kong. The frequent airline movements of such men between Hong Kong and the countries of immigration attracted the description 'astronauts', and, to distinguish them from the poor and often destitute migrants from Vietnam, they were sometimes, perhaps a little unkindly, referred to as the 'yacht people'.

In the post-1997 period Hong Kong has continued to play its gateway role to southern China, but has also become a major centre for commercial and financial services. As incomes have risen, many Hong Kong residents have set their sights above the menial jobs in manufacturing and services that were previously sought after (in 2011, manufacturing industry accounted for less than 5% of total employment). This has created opportunities for migrants from poorer countries in Southeast Asia to fill the gap. So, starting in the 1970s, but especially after 1989, Filipinos, Indonesians and Vietnamese did the low-level manual jobs if they were men (typically on two-year renewable contracts), and these plus domestic servant and care sector jobs if they were women.

Over the last 40 years Hong Kong has become a significant destination for international migration. This can be seen from the results of the 2011 Census: in that year the population of Hong Kong stood at 7.072 million: 93.6% of these people were ethnic Chinese, with Indonesians and Filipinos dominating the rest (1.9% each and almost entirely female); whites (largely consisting of the 34,000 British) and South Asians comprised just under 1% each, and the remainder were largely made up of other East Asians (including Japanese). Almost 100,000 of those who had Chinese nationality actually lived outside Hong Kong, and about 25,000 of the migrants to Hong Kong were students. Perhaps the most striking figure to come from this Census, though, is that relating to place of birth: 32.1% of Hong Kong's population in 2011 were born in mainland China, Macao or Taiwan (a very high proportion of them, one must assume, in mainland China).

On the matter of place of birth, it is worth mentioning one strange but interesting feature of contemporary migration to Hong Kong. Because of (an albeit very restrictive) *jus soli*, which ensures that someone born in Hong Kong has the right to live there, many mainland women (that is, women who are not permanent residents in Hong Kong) who are pregnant by husbands who are also not permanent residents in Hong Kong (and who are therefore defined as 'doubly non-permanent resident pregnant women') nevertheless give birth to their babies in Hong Kong. They accounted for about 40,000 of the total of 95,000 births in Hong Kong in 2011.

Macao tends to show many of the same features as Hong Kong but on a much smaller scale. It too attracted escapees in the pre-reform period, and has since the hand-over in 1999 become a tourist attraction and casino city with migrants from all over East and Southeast Asia. A small but not trivial indication of the diversity of backgrounds and origins of foreign migrants to Macao is provided by the presence there of a community of students from Nigeria.

5.8 Taiwan: emigration and immigration

Taiwan's post-World War II migration history has been very closely linked to events across the Taiwan Strait in the PRC. In the first years the story is of the emigration of the Japanese and the much larger (2 million people) arrival of the KMT. The relations between the KMT (the 'mainlanders' or *waishengren*) and the indigenous Taiwanese were at best cool and were often marked by violent hostility. It was essentially a political coup in which the mainlanders took control of Taiwan and, backed by their Cold War supporters, the Americans, ran it forcefully in their interests. This tension between newcomer immigrant and host populations is still, even after 65 years and the democratization of the country, a major feature of Taiwanese politics with the now pro-cooperation with the PRC KMT 'blues' competing over Taiwanese identity with pro-independence 'greens'.

Many young educated Taiwanese in the 1970s and 1980s turned their backs on both low incomes and the political project of the KMT and its methods of running the country. They left in their thousands to study in the USA and to develop their careers there rather than back home. However, this coincided with the rapid industrialization of Taiwan. Its success as a low labour-cost location for the assembly of electrical and electronic consumer goods and the production of IT components (especially printed circuit boards) for world markets ensured rapid modernization and big improvements in living standards. By the 1990s and 2000s not only were many skilled workers returning to Taiwan, but so great was the need for industrial workers that state-regulated recruitment of migrant workers from Southeast Asian countries began. Vietnamese, Thai, and Filipino male workers were attracted by the job opportunities in the 'silicon belt' south and west of Taipei, while Filipino women, and, above all, Indonesian women worked also as domestic servants and social care personnel. Vietnamese women joined many mainlander women as immigrant brides for Taiwanese men.

The foreign residents living in Taiwan in 2010 are shown in Figure 5.1 and Table 5.1. The highest concentration of foreigners live in the 'silicon belt' consisting of Hsinchu City, and the counties of Taoyuan, Hsinchu and Miaoli. Especially strongly represented here are migrants working in manufacturing

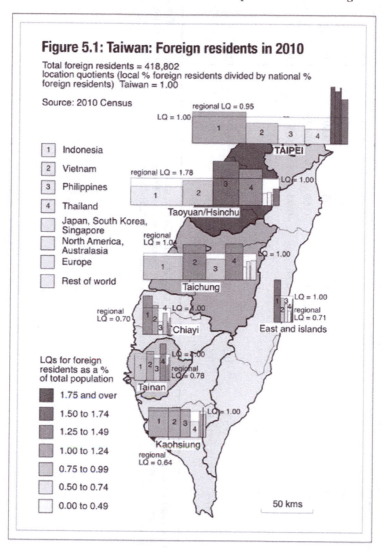

Figure 5.1: Taiwan: Foreign residents in 2010

Total foreign residents = 418,802
location quotients (local % foreign residents divided by national %
foreign residents) Taiwan = 1.00

Source: 2010 Census

1 Indonesia
2 Vietnam
3 Philippines
4 Thailand
Japan, South Korea, Singapore
North America, Australasia
Europe
Rest of world

LQs for foreign residents as a % of total population

1.75 and over
1.50 to 1.74
1.25 to 1.49
1.00 to 1.24
0.75 to 0.99
0.50 to 0.74
0.00 to 0.49

regional LQ = 0.95
LQ = 1.00
TAIPEI
regional LQ = 1.78
LQ = 1.00
Taoyuan/Hsinchu
regional LQ = 1.00
LQ = 1.00
Taichung
regional LQ = 0.70
LQ = 1.00
Chiayi
LQ = 1.00
regional LQ = 0.71
East and islands
LQ = 1.00
regional LQ = 0.78
Tainan
LQ = 1.00
Kaohsiung
regional LQ = 0.64

50 kms

industry coming from the Philippines and Thailand. South of this zone, the area around Taichung also has many foreign workers, and once again they come from the poorer countries of Southeast Asia. Vietnamese are present in the industrial areas, but are consistently over-represented in the more rural regions of southern Taiwan where many Vietnamese women are married to Taiwanese farmers and owners of small businesses. A small but interesting feature is the importance of Indonesians in the east and islands region, where they

Table 5.1 Foreign residents in Taiwan in 2010 (LQs)

	Taipei	TaoHs	Taich	Chia	Tain	Kaoh	E&I	Total
Indonesia	1.19	0.70	0.88	1.45	0.94	1.12	1.59	1.00
Vietnam	0.77	0.93	1.31	1.10	1.10	1.12	0.91	1.00
Philippines	0.68	1.65	0.79	0.49	0.85	1.05	0.69	1.00
Thailand	0.56	1.37	1.35	0.81	1.39	0.60	0.43	1.00
Japan, South Korea and Singapore	2.16	0.45	0.49	0.49	0.56	0.98	0.34	1.00
North America and Australasia	1.99	0.49	0.70	0.42	0.59	0.87	0.61	1.00
Europe	2.11	0.40	0.53	0.23	0.64	1.13	0.69	1.00
Rest of world	1.69	0.63	0.74	0.62	0.87	0.88	0.88	1.00
Total Taiwan	0.95	1.78	1.04	0.70	0.78	0.64	0.71	1.00

Notes: Taipei = Taipei City, Taipei County, and Chilung City; TaoHs = Taoyuan, Hsinchu City, Hsinchu County, and Miaoli; Taich = Taichung City, Taichung County, Changhua, and Nantou; Chia = Chiayi City, Chiayi County, and Yunlin; Tain = Tainan City, and Tainan County; Kaoh = Kaohsiung City, Kaohsiung County, and Pingtung; E&I (Eastern and Islands) = Ilan, Hualien, Taitung, Penghu Islands, Kinmen, and Lienchiang.
Source: 2010 Census.

are employed in the fishing and fish processing industries. However, the big contrast with all this is Greater Taipei. Here it is the migrants from high-income countries in Asia and elsewhere that dominate the picture. The location quotients for Japan, South Korea and Singapore (2.16), North America and Australasia (1.99), and Europe (2.11) show how heavily concentrated these immigrants are in the capital city and its surrounding region. The location quotient for Indonesians is also slightly above 1.00, which reflects the importance in the Taipei region of Indonesian women in domestic service and as workers in care-sector jobs. It is noticeable that other Southeast Asians are distinctly under-represented in Greater Taipei (though in absolute terms, their numbers are large – the areas of the columns on this map are proportional to the absolute numbers involved).

Immigration is only part of the picture, however. Two types of emigration have had a major effect on Taiwan's recent development. First, as the country became industrially successful as an East Asian newly industrialized country, its labour costs went up and a 'hollowing-out' process began. Hollowing out occurs when domestic firms shift their investments abroad to escape high production costs at home. Where did Taiwanese firms look to invest? Just at the right moment – that is, after 1978 – the PRC changed policy and opened up its economy to foreign investment. Taiwanese companies stepped in and invested heavily in the coastal provinces of Guangdong, Fujian and Zhejiang – all of them, of course, located close to Taiwan. This brought a significant migration flow of company employees (managers, professionals and technicians) into China. As growth in the PRC continued during the 1990s and 2000s, their need for corporate deals bringing in foreign technology and investment lessened, but at the same time their interest in recruiting the 'brightest and the best' individuals grew, so as the *Taishang* migration of corporate employees especially to the Pearl River Delta has gone down relatively speaking, a second emigration resulting from the recruitment of Taiwanese skilled migrants to fill the many opportunities being created, especially in Shanghai, has gone up.

5.9 Mongolia: emigration and immigration

During most of the post-war period Mongolia has been a slight net loser by international migration, with Mongolian nationals forming a very small section of the immigrant communities in Japan and South Korea. However, with the discovery and development of vast mineral resources, Mongolia is taking on some of the characteristics of a Persian Gulf state. A country with very few inhabitants looks set to become very wealthy, and a likely migration result will be the attraction of two groups of people: skilled foreign managers, engineers and technicians needed to command the infrastructure, mining and construction operations; and foreign manual workers to do the hard graft. If the wealth is significantly distributed amongst the Mongolian nationals, then there may also be demand for immigrant service workers (for example, domestic servants and care-sector staff).

5.10 Conclusion

Migration processes tend to build slowly and decline slowly. This is because of the way in which social networks tend to operate. Pioneer migrants send back information to their friends and relatives, and, if the message is positive (which, perhaps to justify their own decision, it often is), this encourages others to follow in their footsteps. Word gets round, support networks are established, and a self-reinforcing migration stream comes into being. The international migration flows of China 'plus' show several examples of such processes. For example, the smuggling of young Chinese men and women into Europe and North America lasted long after the coastal provinces of China began their rapid industrialization and urbanization. Another example is the migration of *Joseonjok* (ethnic Korean) migrants from northeastern China to South Korea. Or take the migration to the PRC of businessmen from Taiwan and Hong Kong, which built up after 1978 but is still significant today.

Nevertheless the dominant characteristic of this region's recent migration history is the superiority of the political over the economic, and of the great importance of the sudden policy shifts that accompany changes in the balance of political forces. The PRC's turbulent history since 1949 has shaped the region's migrations: first, once the KMT were settled in Taiwan, it brought international migration in the region almost to a halt; then it generated flight from the effects of Maoist excess; then new emigration of both the skilled and the unskilled, accompanied by immigration of foreign businessmen following the policy shift in 1978; then the peculiar migrations associated with the return of Hong Kong to China in 1997; and finally now the sudden appearance of a multicultural diversity (albeit as yet a highly localized one) consequent upon migration flows from all over the world (including Africa, Northeast, Southeast and South Asia, and the West) to the world's rapidly growing second-largest economy. It is possible that we are witnessing the start of a curious reversal of China's international migration history. Whereas in the 19th and 20th centuries, as described in Wang Gungwu's *The Chinese Overseas*, people left China to sojourn or to settle in almost every country in the world – East Asia's global diaspora – perhaps in the 21st century people from almost every country in the world will come to sojourn or to settle in China.

Box 5.1 The 'new immigration model' applied to East Asia

Description and application of the model

At several points in this book, the similarities and interdependencies between internal migration and international migration have been explored. I want now to draw attention to the relationship between economic development and international migration flows to show: (i) that this relationship has some rather puzzling characteristics (which can be expressed as a paradox); and (ii) that this paradox can be resolved by examining the connections between internal and international migration.

First, here is the paradox. In the early post-1950 period, first Japan, then South Korea, and then Taiwan experienced rapid economic development. They did so without attracting large-scale international labour migration. In fact, rather the opposite – they continued to lose by international migration to the high-income countries of North America and elsewhere, to new settlement countries such as those in South America, and, in the case of South Korea, to the emerging oil revenue-rich countries of the Persian Gulf states. However, just at that moment when their economies began to turn down towards stagnation or low growth, they suddenly became countries of net international migration gain – 'new immigration countries'. For Japan, this turning point was around 1990, coinciding with the shift from the high-growth 'bubble economy' of the 1980s to the 'lost decade' of the 1990s (now the lost two decades 1990–2010) (Fielding 2010). How could a country that is now suffering poor economic performance, laying off or not recruiting its own workers, leading to higher unemployment, be recruiting at the same time foreign workers in such numbers that it was turning itself into a net immigration country?

The solution to this puzzle lies in Figure 5.2. It sets out a three-stage representation (a schematic model) of a dual labour market economy (with high-productivity and low-productivity sectors) undergoing rapid economic development (this section draws heavily on Fielding 2014). During stage 1 there are effectively unlimited supplies of (unskilled) labour (Lewis 1954) onto urban labour markets due to rapid rural–urban migration of young adults whose prospects for making a living from agriculture and from traditional rural industries are very poor. This keeps wages down to a low level both for the indigenous urban low-productivity sector, and for the modern mass-production high-productivity sector. This latter is especially profitable as the distance between the high productivity of its workers and what it has to pay them in wages is great. Rapid capital accumulation leads to high rates of investment in the high-productivity sector. Low wages in the cities means that some people from rural areas will continue to emigrate.

Eventually, the momentum of growth will be such, despite improvements in labour productivity, as to result in labour shortages on urban labour markets – we enter stage 2 of the model. Now, emboldened by their scarcity

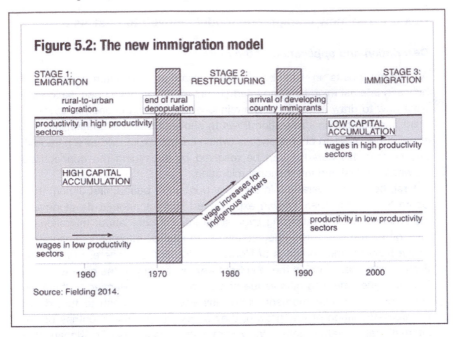

Figure 5.2: The new immigration model

STAGE 1:
EMIGRATION

STAGE 2:
RESTRUCTURING

STAGE 3:
IMMIGRATION

rural-to-urban migration

end of rural depopulation

arrival of developing country immigrants

productivity in high productivity sectors

LOW CAPITAL ACCUMULATION

wages in high productivity sectors

HIGH CAPITAL ACCUMULATION

wage increases for indigenous workers

productivity in low productivity sectors

wages in low productivity sectors

1960   1970   1980   1990   2000

Source: Fielding 2014.

(resulting also from slower growth in the labour force due to demographic changes), the workers in the high-productivity sector are successfully bargaining up their wages to levels commensurate with other high-income economies. This has two effects: (i) it undermines production in the low-productivity sector of the economy, where producers simply cannot afford to pay the higher wages and must make do with older workers and with the least qualified of the new labour market entrants; and (ii) it severely reduces the profitability of the high-productivity sector, because the margins now between labour productivity and wages paid to workers are so small. The outcome of these effects (following the Lewisian 'turning point') is shown in stage 3.

Facing tighter margins due to high labour costs, producers in the high-productivity sector will invest abroad to find new sources of low-cost labour and so remain competitive in global markets. Their disinvestment in the home country will result in the closure of production sites and the laying off of indigenous workers. At the same time, producers in the low-productivity sector, unable, due to their small size and limited financial clout, to internationalize, will recruit low-cost labour from abroad (see Athukorala and Manning 1999: chapter 3). In this way the paradox set out at the beginning of this section is resolved: the country turns from being a net loser by international migration to being a net gainer at precisely the same time as its growth rate goes down and its unemployment rate goes up.

Conformable with this view of the relationships over time between internal and international migration (notably that, for the smaller companies which often act as the suppliers to the large multinationals, there is a substitution of foreign immigrant workers for internal rural–urban migrant workers), is the tendency for the immigrant workers to go to the same places and into the same branches of production as were previously occupied by internal migrant workers (Fielding 2010: 117). This is indeed broadly the case in Japan, South Korea and Taiwan.

Clearly, the immigration-dominated city-states of Hong Kong and Singapore do not fit this model. They did not have supplies of surplus rural labour sufficient to meet the labour needs of rapid industrial growth in the 1970s to 1990s. They did, however, have very large unemployed and underemployed urban populations, which acted, to some extent, as an alternative source of labour in the early years of industrialization. When this supply had been exhausted, foreign migrant workers were drawn in as a 'reserve army of labour'.

The implications of the 'new immigration model' for demographic change in East Asia

The demographic implications of stage 1 of the model are:

1   That rural–urban migration breaks links to traditional values favouring large families, multigenerational households, mutuality in social relations, etc., and so tends to result in lower fertility. It also brings young adults into urban environments (usually cramped and expensive dwellings) that do not favour family formation, or favour only small nuclear families, which also results in low fertility.
2   That low wages in overcrowded cities make it difficult to buy extra domestic space for raising a family – so further constraining fertility rates.

The demographic implications of stage 2 of the model are:

1   That higher wages bring better health and less child mortality, leading to a reduced need for large families and a preference for smaller ones. This lowers fertility. At the same time, however, the higher wages facilitate suburban house or apartment purchase and more space to raise children, which raises fertility.
2   By this stage, however, the rural family model (*ie* in Japan) has been largely left behind (along with the mother-in-law), to be largely replaced by 'modern' urban styles of living which include: more material consumption (the 'three treasures' – the television, the refrigerator and the washing machine), more formal-sector employment for women, and more individualism – all of which tend to depress fertility.

The demographic implications of stage 3 of the model are:

1   Low investment in the high-labour productivity sector leads to high youth and young adult un- and underemployment ('freeters' in Japan), and also a lack of security in employment (for example, far less 'lifetime employment'). This can result in a reluctance to commit to marriage on the part of men, and avoidance of the 'burden' of marriage and child-rearing on the part of women. It can also lead to an inability to set up an independent 'home', hence 'parasite singles' (men and women in their twenties and thirties living with their parents). All this leads to later or no marriage, fewer or no children.

2   This is significantly counteracted by 'mother-citizens' (formerly foreign brides who become naturalized), and the arrival of immigrants in marriage and family-formation age groups.

It can be clearly seen from the above that the balance of effects of these processes is low fertility leading to an ageing population and a slowdown of, or reverse in, population growth. Japan, South Korea and Taiwan have amongst the lowest fertility rates in the world. Immigration, especially that from Southeast Asia, is having some effect in raising these rates, and the arrival of many young adults is slightly slowing the increase in the median age of the population, but immigration would have to be a whole order of magnitude greater to make a real difference to either of these demographic variables.

Migration is correctly seen as one of the fundamental links between economy and population. As economic processes work themselves out over national and international spaces, they set in motion flows of people, mostly from those places where opportunities are low or declining towards those where they are high or expanding. However, in the case of the new immigration model, it has been possible not only to trace the impacts of post-World War II economic restructuring on the internal and international flows of labour migrants, but also to consider how the conditions under which those migrants lived and worked influenced their family-formation behaviours at each stage of the model. For analytical purposes, fertility and mortality (natural increase or decrease) on the one hand, are separated from in-migration or immigration and out-migration or emigration (net migration gain or loss) on the other. However, this discussion box has demonstrated how very closely interrelated these socio-demographic processes are.

References

Athukorala, P. and Manning, C., 1999, *Structural Change and International Labour Migration in East Asia: Adjusting to Labour Scarcity*. London: Oxford University Press.

Fielding, T., 2010, The occupational and geographical locations of transnational immigrant minorities in Japan, in Kee, P. and Yoshimatsu, H. (eds), *Global Movements in the Asia Pacific*. Singapore: World Scientific, 93–122.

Fielding, T., 2014, Taiwan's (extra)ordinary migrations, in Chiu, K.-F., Fell, D. and Lin, P. (eds), *Migration to and from Taiwan*. London: Routledge, 227–243.

Lewis, W.A., 1954, Economic development with unlimited supplies of labour, *Manchester School of Economic and Social Studies* 22: 139–191.

Selected references

5.0 General

Chen, T., 2012, *Chinese Migrations, with Special Reference to Labour Conditions*. Singapore: National University of Singapore Press/University of Hawai'i Press.

Djao, W., 2003, *Being Chinese: Voices from the Diaspora*. Tucson: University of Arizona Press.

Hsu, F.L.K. and Serrie, H., 1998, *The Overseas Chinese: Ethnicity in National Context*. Lanham, MD: University Press of America.

Kuah-Pearce, K.-E. and Davidson, A.P. (eds), 2008, *At Home in the Chinese Diaspora: Memories, Identities, and Belongings*. Richmond: Palgrave Macmillan.

Ma, L.J.C. and Cartier, C. (eds), 2003, *The Chinese Diaspora: Space, Place, Mobility and Identity*. Lanham, MD: Rowman & Littlefield.

Ma Mung, E., 2000, *La Diaspora Chinoise: Géographie d'une Migration*. Gap: Ophrys.

Nyíri, P. and Saveliev, I. (eds), 2002, *Globalizing Chinese Migration: Trends in Europe and Asia*. Aldershot: Ashgate.

Ong, A. and Nonini, D. (eds), 1997, *Underground Empires: The Cultural Politics of Modern Chinese Transnationalism*. New York: Routledge.

Pan, L. (ed.), 1998, *The Encyclopedia of the Chinese Overseas*. Singapore: Archipelago Press.

Sinn, E. (ed.), 1998, *The Last Half Century of the Overseas Chinese*. Hong Kong: Hong Kong University Press.

Sun, W., 2002, *Leaving China: Media, Migration and Transnational Imagination*. Lanham, MD: Rowman & Littlefield.

Tan, C.B. (ed.), 2013, *Routledge Handbook of the Chinese Diaspora*. London: Routledge.

Wang, G., 2000, *The Chinese Overseas*. Cambridge, MA: Harvard University Press.

Zweig, D., 2002, *Internationalizing China: Domestic Interests and Global Linkages*. London: Cornell University Press.

5.1 Chinese diaspora: North America

Bieler, S., 2004, *'Patriots' or 'Traitors'? A History of American-Educated Chinese Students*. New York: M.E. Sharpe.

Charney, M.W., Yeoh, B.S.A., Kiong, T.C. (eds), 2003, *Chinese Migrants Abroad: Cultural, Educational and Social Dimensions of the Chinese Diaspora*. Singapore: Singapore University Press.

Lien, P.-T., 2008, Homeland origins and political identities among Chinese in southern California, *Ethnic and Racial Studies* 31(8): 1381–1403.

Louie, V.S., 2004, *Compelled to Excel: Immigration, Education, and Opportunity among Chinese Americans*. Stanford, CA: Stanford University Press.

Salaff, J., Greve, A. and Wong, S.-L., 2001, Professionals from China: entrepreneurship and social resources in a strange land, *Asian and Pacific Migration Journal* 10(1): 9–34.

Sinn, E. (ed.), *The Last Half Century of the Overseas Chinese*. Hong Kong: Hong Kong University Press.

Wang, S. and Lo, L., 2005, Chinese immigrants to Canada: their changing composition and economic performance, *International Migration* 43(3): 35–72.

Waters, J.L., 2009, Immigration, transnationalism and 'flexible citizenship' in Canada: an examination of Ong's thesis ten years on, *Tijdschrift voor Economische en Sociale Geografie* 100(5): 635–645.

Yung, J., Chang, G.H. and Lai, H.M. (eds), 2006, *Chinese American Voices: From the Gold Rush to the Present*. Berkeley: University of California Press.

5.2 Chinese diaspora: Western Europe

Benton, G. and Pieke, F.N. (eds), 1998, *The Chinese in Europe*. London: Macmillan.

Chang, F.B. and Rucker-Chang, S. (eds), 2012, *Chinese Migrants in Russia, Central Asia and Eastern Europe*. London: Routledge.

Giese, K., 2003, New Chinese migration to Germany: historical consistencies and new patterns of diversification within a globalized migration regime, *International Migration* 41(3): 155–183.

Nieto, G., 2003, The Chinese in Spain, *International Migration* 41(3): 215–234.

Nyiri, P., 2007, *Chinese in Eastern Europe and Russia: A Middleman Minority in a Transnational Era*. London: Routledge.

Pieke, F.N., Nyiri, P., Thund, M. and Ceccagno, A., 2004, *Transnational Chinese: Fujianese Migrants in Europe*. Stanford, CA: Stanford University Press.

Spaan, E., Hillmann, F. and Van Naerssen, T. (eds), 2005, *Asian Migrants and European Labour Markets: Patterns and Processes of Immigrant Labour Market Insertion in Europe*. London: Routledge.

Thuno, M. (ed.), 2007, *Beyond Chinatown: New Chinese Migration and the Global Expansion of China*. Copenhagen: Nordic Institute for Asian Studies Press.

Zhang, G., 2003, Migration of highly skilled Chinese to Europe: trends and perspective, *International Migration* 41(3): 73–95.

5.3 Chinese diaspora: other countries

Frechette, A., 2002, *Tibetans in Nepal: The Dynamics of International Assistance Among a Community in Exile*. New York: Berghahn Books.

Gao, J., 2009, Lobbying to stay: the Chinese students' campaign to stay in Australia, *International Migration* 47(2): 127–154.

Hu-DeHart, E., 2005, On coolies and shopkeepers: the Chinese as huagong (laborers) and huashang (merchants) in Latin America/Caribbean, in Anderson, W.W. and Lee, R.G. (eds), *Displacements and Diasporas: Asians in the Americas*. New Brunswick, NJ: Rutgers University Press, 78–111.

Hugo, G., 2008, In and out of Australia: rethinking Chinese and Indian skilled migration to Australia, *Asian Population Studies* 4(3): 267–291.

Lai, W.L. and Tan, C.-B. (eds), 2010, *The Chinese in Latin America and the Caribbean*. Leiden: Brill.

Oxfield, E., 2007, Still guest people: the reproduction of Hakka identity in Kolkata, India, *China Report* 43(4): 411–435.

Reid, A. (ed.), 2008, *The Chinese Diaspora in the Pacific*. Aldershot: Ashgate.

5.4 Contemporary emigration from the PRC

Alden, C., 2007, *China in Africa*. London: Zed Books.

Brautigam, D., 2009, *The Dragon's Gift: The Real Story of China in Africa*. London: Oxford University Press.

French, H.W., 2014, *China's Second Continent: How a Million Migrants Are Building a New Empire in Africa*. New York: Alfred A. Knopf.

Guo, F., 2010, Demographic structure and international student mobility: an investigation of Chinese students in Australia, *Asian and Pacific Migration Journal* 19(1): 143–156.

Huang, S. and Yeoh, B.S.A., 2005, Transnational families and their children's education: China's 'study mothers' in Singapore, *Global Networks* 5(3): 379–400.

Huynh, T.T., Park, Y.J. and Chen, A.Y., 2010, Faces of China: new Chinese migrants in South Africa, 1980s to present, *African and Asian Studies* 9(3): 286–306.

Ip, M. (ed.), 2011, *Transmigration and the New Chinese: Theories and Practices from the New Zealand Experience*. Hong Kong: HK Institute for the Humanities and the Social Sciences.

Lee, C.K., 2009, Raw encounters: Chinese managers, African workers and the politics of casualization in Africa's Chinese enclaves, *The China Quarterly* 199: 647–666.

Liang, Z. and Morooka, H., 2004, Recent trends of emigration from China: 1982–2000, *International Migration* 42(3): 145–163.

Poston, D.L. and Luo, H., 2007, Chinese student and labor migration to the United States: trends and policies since the 1980s, *Asian and Pacific Migration Journal* 16(3): 323–355.

5.5 Illegal migration from China: trafficking

Chin, K-L., 1999, *Smuggled Chinese: Clandestine Immigration to the US*. Philadelphia: Temple University Press.

Kwong, P., 1997, *Forbidden Workers: Illegal Chinese Immigrants and American Labour*. New York: New Press.

Lin, S. and Bax, T., 2012, Changes in irregular migration: a field report from Fuzhou, *International Migration* 50(2): 99–112.

Skeldon, R., 2000, *Myths and Realities of Chinese Irregular Migration*. Geneva: International Organization for Migration.

Xiang, B., 2012, Predatory princes and princely peddlers: the state and international labour migration intermediaries in China, *Pacific Affairs* 85(1): 47–68.

Zhang, S.X., 2008, *Chinese Human Smuggling Organizations, Families, Social Networks and Cultural Imperatives*. Stanford, CA: Stanford University Press.

5.6 Chinese immigration: return migration

Bodomo, A., 2012, *Africans in China*. New York: Cambria Press.

Brady, A.-M., 2003, *Making the Foreign Serve China: Managing Foreigners in the People's Republic*. Lanham, MD: Rowman & Littlefield.

Cao, C., 2008, China's brain drain at the high end: why government policies have failed to attract first-rate academics to return, *Asian Population Studies* 4(3): 331–345.

Farrer, J., 2010, 'New Shanghailanders' or 'new Shanghainese': Western expatriates' narratives of emplacement in Shanghai, *Journal of Ethnic and Migration Studies* 36(8): 1212–1228.

Haugen, H.O., 2012, Nigerians in China: a second state of immobility, *International Migration* 50(2): 65–80.

Hsing, Y.-T., 1998, *Making Capitalism in China: the Taiwan Connection*. London: Oxford University Press.

Kuah, K.E., 2000, *Rebuilding the Ancestral Village: Singaporeans in China*. Aldershot: Ashgate.

Lankov, A., 2004, North Korean refugees in northeast China, *Asian Survey* 44(6): 856–873.

Lin, P., 2011, Chinese diaspora 'at home': mainlander Taiwanese in Dongguan and Shanghai, *The China Review* 11(2): 43–64.

Lyons, M., Brown, A. and Li, Z., 2012, In the Dragon's Den: African traders in Guangzhou, *Journal of Ethnic and Migration Studies* 38(5): 869–888.

Peterson, G., 2011, *Overseas Chinese in the People's Republic of China*. London: Routledge.

Pieke, F.N., 2012, Immigrant China, *Modern China* 38(1): 40–77.

Teo, S.Y., 2011, 'The moon back home is brighter'? Return migration and the cultural politics of belonging, *Journal of Ethnic and Migration Studies* 37(5): 805–820.

Tseng, Y.-F., 2012, Brave new migrants: Taiwanese skilled workers in Shanghai, in Fell, D. (ed.), *Migration to and from Taiwan*. London: Routledge.

Wang, H., Zweig, D. and Lin, X., 2011, Returnee entrepreneurs: impact on China's globalization process, *Journal of Contemporary China* 20(70): 413–431.

Zweig, D., Chen, C. and Rosen, S., 2004, Globalization and transnational human capital: overseas and returnee scholars to China, *The China Quarterly* 179: 735–757.

5.7 Hong Kong/Macao: immigration and emigration

Chan, Y.-W. (ed.), 2011, *The Chinese-Vietnamese Diaspora: Revisiting the Boat People in Hong Kong*. London: Routledge.

Cheung, C.-K. and Leung, K.-K., 2015, Chinese migrants' class mobility in Hong Kong, *International Migration* 53(2): 219–235.

Chiu, S. and Lui, T.-L., 2009, *Hong Kong: Becoming a Chinese Global City*. London: Routledge.

Constable, N., 1997, *Maid to Order in Hong Kong: Stories of Filipina Workers*. Ithaca, NY: Cornell University Press.

Findlay, A.M. and Li, F.L.N., 1998, A migration channels approach to the study of professionals moving to and from Hong Kong, *International Migration Review* 32(3): 682–703.

Ho, E.S., 2002, Multi-local residence, transnational networks: Chinese 'astronaut' families in New Zealand, *Asian and Pacific Migration Journal* 11(1): 145–164.

Knowles, C. and Harper, D., 2009, *Hong Kong: Migrant Lives, Landscapes and Journeys*. Chicago, IL: University of Chicago Press.

Ku, A. and Pun, N. (eds), 2004, *Remaking Citizenship in Hong Kong: Community, Nation and the Global City*. London: RoutledgeCurzon.

Ley, D. and Kobayashi, A., 2005, Back to Hong Kong: return migration or transnational sojourn? *Global Networks* 5(2): 111–127.

Li, F.L.N., Findlay, A.M., Jowett, A.J. and Skeldon, R., 1996, Migrating to learn and learning to migrate: a study of the experiences and intentions of international student migrants (Hong Kong), *International Journal of Population Geography* 2: 51–67.

McDonogh, G. and Wong, C., 2004, *Global Hong Kong*. London: Routledge.

Newendorp, N.D., 2008, *Uneasy Reunions: Immigration, Citizenship, and Family Life in Post-1997 Hong Kong*. Stanford, CA: Stanford University Press.

Salaff, J., Wong, S.L. and Greve, A., 2010, *Hong Kong Movers and Stayers: Narratives of Family Migration*. Urbana and Chicago: University of Illinois Press.

Siu, H.F. and Ku, A.S.M. (eds), 2009, *Hong Kong Mobile*. Hong Kong: Hong Kong University Press.

Skeldon, R. (ed.), 1994, *Reluctant Exiles? Migration from Hong Kong and the New Overseas Chinese*. New York: Sharpe.

Skeldon, R. (ed.), 1995, *Emigration from Hong Kong*. Hong Kong: Chinese University Press.

Zhang, Z. and Wu, X., 2011, Social change, cohort quality and economic adaptation of Chinese immigrants in Hong Kong, 1991–2006, *Asian and Pacific Migration Journal* 20 (1): 1–29.

On Macao:

Clayton, C.H., 2010, *Sovereignty at the Edge: Macau and the Question of Chineseness*. Cambridge, MA: Harvard University Asian Center.

5.8 Taiwan: emigration and immigration

On emigration and immigration:

Chiu, K.-F., Fell, D. and Lin, P. (eds), 2014, *Migration to and from Taiwan*. London: Routledge.

On immigration:

Cheng, I., 2013, Making foreign women the mother of our nation: the exclusion and assimilation of immigrant women in Taiwan, *Asian Ethnicity* 14(2): 157–179.

Fan, J., 2010, *China's Homeless Generation*. London: Routledge (on migration to Taiwan from the mainland).

Lan, P.-C., 2006, *Global Cinderellas: Migrant Domestics and Newly-Rich Employers in Taiwan*. Durham, NC: Duke University Press.

Tseng, Y.-F. and Wang, H.-Z., 2011, Governing migrant workers at a distance: managing the temporary status of guestworkers in Taiwan, *International Migration* 51(4): 1–19.

Wang, H.-Z., 2007, Hidden spaces of resistance of the subordinated: case studies from Vietnamese female migrant partners in Taiwan, *International Migration Review* 41(3): 706–727.

5.9 Mongolia: emigration and immigration

Batbayar, T., 2005, Foreign migration issues in Mongolia, in Akaha, T. and Vassilieva, A., *Crossing National Borders: Human Migration Issues in Northeast Asia*. Tokyo: United Nations University Press, 215–235.

6 Turbulent transitions
China plus's internal migration flows

6.0 Introduction

This is the big one! This is the chapter in which we try to describe and explain the greatest migration on Earth: internal migration in the People's Republic of China (PRC). There is some dispute about the numbers, but if we were to say that around 120 million people living in the major cities of China (population about 500 million) were born in the countryside, we would give some idea of the scale of this migration. The two main forces producing this migration are: (i) the almost revolutionary capitalist modernization of a largely agricultural society; and (ii) prolonged rapid economic growth resulting from an urban-based manufacturing industrial success.

Three broad stages of post-war development of internal migration can be identified: (i) the period of modest urbanization from 1949 to the mid-1960s; (ii) the Cultural Revolution, when Maoist practice provoked a mass movement of urban youth into the countryside; and (iii) the Reform period since 1978, when the transition to a market economy unleashed the phenomenal rural–urban and interregional migration flows of recent years.

6.1 Urban and regional development in China

In a rural society when modernization arrives, it arrives in the city first. This alone would encourage rural–urban migration, but in China the large and growing income inequalities between the city and the countryside and between the high-income coastal provinces and the low-income inland ones were crucial as the underlying causes of internal migration. So this is where we shall start.

China's provinces (which, with average populations of around 40 million people, would in other parts of the world such as Europe be seen as equivalent to whole countries) are conventionally grouped into three macro-regions: (i) the eastern, largely urban coastal region; (ii) the central, largely rural inland region; and (iii) the western 'frontier' region. The eastern region has relatively high per capita incomes, especially in the three main metropolitan areas – Beijing-Tianjin in the north, Shanghai in the centre, and Guangzhou-Hong Kong in the south. Even outside these metropolitan regions incomes tend to be well above the national average, especially in Liaoning and Shandong near to Beijing-Tianjin, in Zhejiang and Jiangsu near to Shanghai, and in Fujian near to Guangzhou-Hong Kong. The central region has low or very low per capita incomes; it is predominantly a region of wet rice farming, and is the main region of origin for the massive migration flows to the eastern region. The western region is mostly fairly or very sparsely populated. Its income levels are low and it too is a region of out-migration, except that in some cases (notably Xinjiang), state-promoted development encourages in-migration from the east (see Figure 6.1).

While this is the macro picture, spatial income inequalities are also very significant within the provinces. The provincial capital city is typically the place where per capita incomes are highest, where the job market is most diverse, and where upward social mobility is most likely. Lower-level cities have intermediate income levels, and the countryside tends almost universally to have low or very low incomes, especially those areas that are more mountainous and more remote. The infrequent exceptions to this latter generalization arise when an area has special resource endowments (for example, minerals) or has rather special historical or scenic qualities that make it attractive to domestic and/or foreign tourists (for example, the Guilin karst scenery area of Guangxi province). Income inequalities are also very marked within the city, with new, sometimes gated, suburbs for the rich, and old, high-density quarters (often in the form of brick, clay or wooden courtyard housing or *hutongs*) for the poor and for in-migrants.

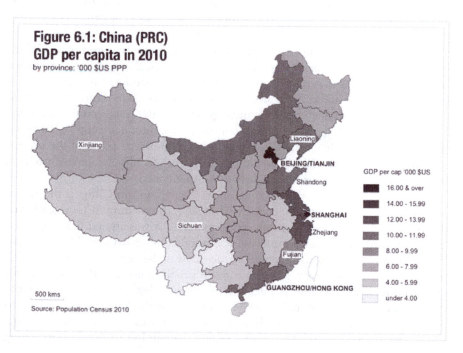

Figure 6.1: China (PRC) GDP per capita in 2010
by province: '000 $US PPP

GDP per cap '000 $US

- 16.00 & over
- 14.00 - 15.99
- 12.00 - 13.99
- 10.00 - 11.99
- 8.00 - 9.99
- 6.00 - 7.99
- 4.00 - 5.99
- under 4.00

500 kms

Source: Population Census 2010

6.2 Ethnic, social and demographic diversity in China

As will be shown in the next section, the main differentiation of the Chinese population is between those who have urban household registrations and those who have rural agricultural ones. Chinese internal migration cannot be understood solely in these terms, however. China's 1.3 billion people are far from being ethnically homogeneous. So strong are the ethnic differences between the Chinese that a Uyghur Muslim migrant from Xinjiang living in Beijing, or a member of the Xiang minority from Western Hunan living in Shanghai, would experience these destinations as if they were foreign countries. Similarly, the migration of Han Chinese into minority-dominated regions such as those found in many areas of western and southwestern China (for example, in Tibet, Xinjiang, Qinghai and Yunnan), is often experienced in the destination regions almost as a type of colonization of the traditional and the powerless by the modern and the powerful. Discrimination, accompanied occasionally by violent hostility against migrant minorities, occurs in both cases.

The victory of the communists in 1949 heralded a period in which traditional class relations in China were turned upside down. Those who had previously owned significant assets in the form, for example, of land and property or businesses and equity, found themselves labelled as 'class enemies' and became marginalized. Strategic economic decisions were taken centrally by the Communist Party, and the local management of assets such as farms and factories, which were now of course owned collectively, was in the hands of groups of workers operating in work units (*danwei*). Some of the strategic decisions taken by the Party had disastrous effects, notably, the 'Great Leap Forward' which exacerbated famine in parts of rural China and led to the migration of destitute individuals and families to more favoured areas. When the Party tried to reinvigorate political activism through what became known as the Cultural Revolution, one of the effects was to send vast numbers (16–18 million) of young adults from urban areas, many of them from what would have previously been considered middle-class family backgrounds, into the countryside to work alongside the peasant farmers and rural activists. Class-based activism was indeed having some strange migration effects! Some of the present and recent leaders in China, including President Xi Jinping, have first-hand experience of what being a 'sent-down' youth entailed.

Finally, a significant factor in contemporary migration in China is the recent demographic history of the country. Initially, the communists argued that overpopulation was a problem of capitalism. Then it was argued that improved living standards would only come about if population growth could be brought under control. The means adopted to do so was the 'one-child' policy. The one-child policy was for a long time fairly strictly enforced (though only for the majority Han Chinese population, and much less so now). One of the long-lasting effects of this policy is the tendency for the 'left-behind' elderly to have nobody to care for them when, as happens in many rural areas, their one child migrates to the city. The central region, having lost so many of its young adults through migration to the eastern coastal region, has many areas within it where the population consists very largely of the elderly and children, where the latter are being cared for by their grandparents on behalf of their out-migrant parents.

6.3 Internal migration in China: the household registration (*hukou*) system

Most of the more advanced countries of East Asia have, over much of their history, had a household registration system. Only in the cases of the PRC and Vietnam, however, have these registration systems had an influence on contemporary migration, and only in China has this influence been really important. The reason why the household registration (*hukou*) system has been so important in China is that it created what one commentator called an 'apartheid' system. What is meant by this is that, inheriting from your mother, you were born with either an urban or an agricultural *hukou*. If it was the former, you were fortunate because you were entitled to live in the city with all its extra job opportunity and quality of life advantages. If it was the latter, you were doomed to live in the rural district in which you were born and brought up, because it was only there that you could claim your social rights – notably, access to health, housing, social welfare and education services. So, rather as the pass laws in South Africa kept the black population in their rural 'Bantustans' and away from the large cities, the *hukou* system kept those with agricultural *hukou* trapped in the countryside, where they produced the food surpluses needed to support the relatively privileged factory workers and bureaucrats who lived in the city.

Except, of course, those with agricultural *hukou* did not stay in the countryside. They migrated to the cities in their millions, especially so following the opening up of the economy to foreign investment after 1978. In many ways this was not a great disaster, at least initially. The young men and women who migrated to the city were at the age when their need for medical care was low, and being mostly single and living in dormitories provided by the employer, they were not concerned about the lack of access to housing or schooling. After all, they were inheritors of the sojourner tradition; they lived away from their hometown, to which, of course, they frequently returned, only as long as was necessary to earn good money and save it to improve living conditions back home. They were the 'floating population' of China's major cities. It was inevitable, however, that as these migrants became increasingly embedded in the city, their lack of social rights came to matter more and more. They became *de facto*, if not *de jure*, urban residents. Soon they wanted their children to live with them in the city, not in the rural backwater where their educational and employment prospects were so poor. Over time they rented housing, changed jobs to improve their wages, sent their children to migrants' fee-paying schools, and generally became a permanent part, albeit a disadvantaged and vulnerable one, of the rapidly growing urban population.

Bureaucrats and Party officials knew that the *hukou* system was unfair and inefficient, yet they did not dare to abolish it for fear that such a step would open the floodgates of rural–urban migration leading to social unrest in the cities. So, perhaps predictably, what has happened instead is a kind of piecemeal breakdown of the system. In certain cities, notably Shanghai, some migrants have already been allowed to transfer to an urban *hukou*, and plans are now in place to end all discrimination against in-migrants in the near future. In other provinces little has changed, and in some cities, notably Beijing, spontaneous initiatives to make life bearable for the 'floating population', such as the building of informal settlements and the setting up of migrants' schools, have been being thwarted by the officials, sometimes with the use of force.

6.4 Urbanization and rural depopulation

The rate of urbanization in China in the recent period is truly remarkable. Great cities were, of course, a legacy of China's illustrious past, and industrial development during the Republican Era had added urban working-class populations to some of these historic cities as well as to certain major ports. In 1950, though, China was still a largely rural agricultural country, and over the next 30 years until 1980, despite village industrialization schemes and the massive investments in heavy industry, for example in the northeastern provinces, this did not fundamentally change. The real burst in urbanization has accompanied the recent transition to a (capitalist) market economy and has occurred during the last 35 years, that is, from around 1980 to today.

Why has this urbanization been so rapid in the recent period? Two major reasons have already been mentioned: (i) because incomes are, on average, much higher in urban areas than in rural ones; and (ii) because the cities are the centres of modern consumption, both utilitarian such as washing machines and refrigerators, and fashionable such as 'cool' clothes, Internet cafés, and clubbing venues.

However, there is more to it than this. The political economy of the transition to capitalism contains several mechanisms that promote rapid urban growth. First, the achievement of economies of scale in the production of goods for domestic and export markets, which calls for large workforces, which in turn generates house building and urban services. Second, the achievement of economies of agglomeration: as cities grow, they pass through threshold sizes that make possible forms of production and association that were previously difficult or impossible. Third, the building of new transport infrastructure (expressways, high-speed rail, airports) which has the effect of generating higher orders of centrality in the space-economy. Fourth, the establishment of pro-growth coalitions of business, Party, and local bureaucratic interests to maximize the gains from land development, specifically the transfer of land from rural (agricultural and forestry) uses to urban ones (industrial estates, commercial strips, new housing developments, etc.). These mechanisms, singly and in association with one another, often contain processes that are self-reinforcing, meaning that once urban growth is underway, it tends to trigger 'positive feedback' loops. These lead to further in-migration and further population and employment growth.

So who, then, are these rural–urban migrants? They include a small number of educationally gifted young men and women who have been successful in their school-leaving exams (the dreaded *gaokao*) and who migrate to the city to attend university. Very few will ever return to live permanently in the village of their birth or upbringing. The flow will also include a small number of parents, spouses and children who come to the city to join a migrant worker who has been particularly successful (perhaps as an entrepreneur or white-collar worker). An overwhelming majority of the migrants from the rural area to the city, however, will be young, single, relatively uneducated men and women who are desperately seeking work. The work that they do varies enormously. The largest group of migrants will work in factories. In the case of Guangdong Province many of the jobs in factories are for young women. They make relatively cheap goods such as toys, garments, shoes, etc. Both men and women are employed in other factories, including those that have been built more recently to supply the parts for, and assembly of, consumer electronics products. Factory jobs are not the only ones that attract migrants, either. There are many jobs in the construction industry for men, and in domestic service for women, and a whole range of service-sector jobs (for example, in commerce and catering) for both men and women. Whatever the sector in which the migrants work, the main feature of their jobs is that they are at the bottom of the pile; they are the jobs that call for relatively little training, the pay levels are low, the working conditions are often poor, job security is low, and they tend to be jobs that are extremely routine and repetitive.

To illustrate the broad features of these rural–urban migration flows I shall focus on the inland, largely rural south-central province of Hunan (see Figure 6.2). Previously relatively inaccessible, Hunan now lies on the main north–south transport axis (consisting of both motorway and high-speed railway), linking Beijing to Guangzhou via Wuhan (Hubei). Since the 1980s, and long before these major infrastructure projects were completed, Hunan has acted as one of the main source regions for migration to the Pearl River Delta region – a region of incredibly rapid urban industrial development located to the south, 'just over the mountain' in Guangdong Province. Figure 6.2 shows through 'migration velocities' (see Box 6.1) that the main destination for recent out-migrants has been Guangdong, followed by Shanghai and Zhejiang. This inter-provincial migration has been predominantly rural–urban, but so too have the migration patterns within Hunan.

Box 6.1 Migration velocities

A 'migration velocity' (MV) is a means of measuring and depicting the rate of flow of migrants (M) between an origin *i* and a destination *j*. It is calculated by dividing the number of migrants between *i* and *j* by the product of the populations (P) at *i* and *j*. Since the outcome of this calculation is inevitably a very small number, it is scaled up by multiplying it by a constant (k). The result is a measurement that allows one to compare migration flows over

time and space – just what we need when studying the spatial patterns and
trends over time of internal migration flows in China.

$$MV = (Mi–j*k) / (Pi*Pj)$$

The rural–urban redistribution of population within Hunan can be seen in
Figure 6.3, which shows inter-censal population change by county for the
period 2000–10. Three main features stand out: (i) the rapid rate of growth of
the provincial capital (Changsha) with its high concentration of manufacturing
and service employment, and of the industrial region around and to the south
of it; (ii) the tendency for population growth (largely, of course, the product of
intra-provincial migration) to occur along the north–south transportation axis
stretching from Yueyang, through Changsha and Hengyang, to Chenzhou in
the south; and (iii) the tendency for the prefectural capitals to have higher rates
of growth than their rural hinterlands. The exceptions to this rule are interesting: they include Shaoyang City where income levels are very low, and
mountainous counties such as Guidong in the southeast and Huayuan in the
northwest which have population growth rates that, due to major infrastructure
investments or the growth of tourism, are higher than those of their prefectural
capitals (Chenzhou and Jishou, respectively).

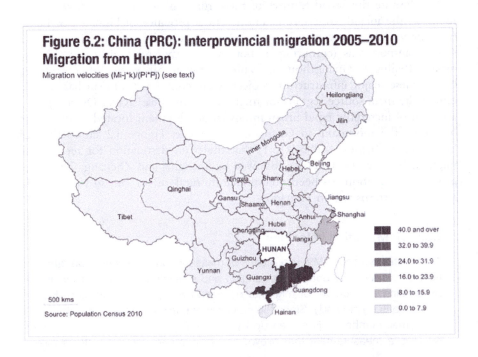

Figure 6.2: China (PRC): Interprovincial migration 2005–2010 Migration from Hunan

Migration velocities (Mi-j*k)/(Pi*Pj) (see text)

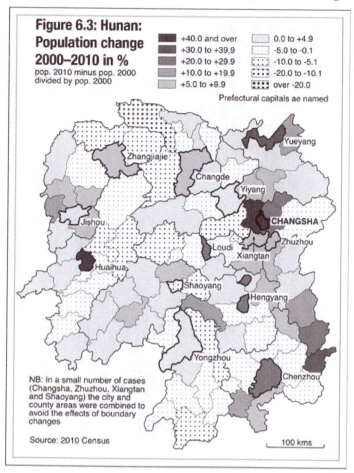

Figure 6.3: Hunan: Population change 2000–2010 in %
pop. 2010 minus pop. 2000 divided by pop. 2000

+40.0 and over
+30.0 to +39,9
+20.0 to +29.9
+10.0 to +19.9
+5.0 to +9.9
0.0 to +4.9
-5.0 to -0.1
-10.0 to -5.1
-20.0 to -10.1
over -20.0

Prefectural capitals ae named

Yueyang

Zhangjiajie

Changde

Yiyang

Jishou

CHANGSHA

Zhuzhou

Loudi

Xiangtan

Huaihua

Shaoyang

Hengyang

Yongzhou

Chenzhou

NB: In a small number of cases (Changsha, Zhuzhou, Xiangtan and Shaoyang) the city and county areas were combined to avoid the effects of boundary changes

Source: 2010 Census

100 kms

To explain these patterns one needs to turn to the distribution of agricultural employment, for it is the hard toil, 'backwardness' of life and poor income prospects of farm work that largely drive rural–urban migration (Figure 6.4). This map pattern is very close to being a mirror image of the map of population change – where agricultural employment dominates, population has either declined or grown very slowly, and vice versa. Agricultural employment is low in the provincial capital and in most of the prefectural capitals (except where they are large in area and thereby include much agricultural land use). Both of the cases where counties are not administrative centres but have location quotients of less than 1.00 are interesting: they lie to the west-southwest of Changsha. The first is Shaoshan, which, as the birthplace of Mao Zedong, attracts many tourists; the second is Lengshuijiang, which is a major mining city (it produces over half the world production of antimony).

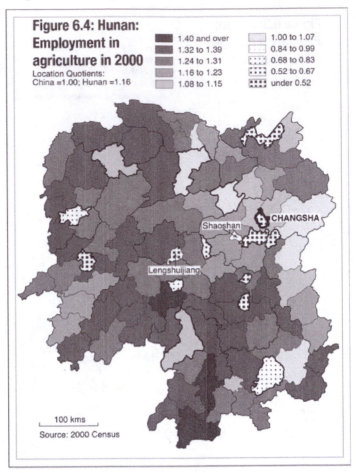

Figure 6.4: Hunan: Employment in agriculture in 2000

Location Quotients: China =1.00; Hunan =1.16

1.40 and over
1.32 to 1.39
1.24 to 1.31
1.16 to 1.23
1.08 to 1.15
1.00 to 1.07
0.84 to 0.99
0.68 to 0.83
0.52 to 0.67
under 0.52

Shaoshan
CHANGSHA
Lengshuijiang

100 kms

Source: 2000 Census

Hunan is predominantly a province of out-migration, but it is also interesting to look at the in-migrants – who they are, where they come from and where they go. Numerically, return migrants form the largest group, most of them coming, of course, from Guangdong. Almost all are factory workers and low-level service-sector workers rejoining their families in Hunan. While some are true 'U-turn' migrants moving back to their villages of origin, others are 'J-turn' migrants settling in the nearby middle-tier towns or in the provincial capital. Long-distance inter-provincial migrants tend to be more middle-class people – professional, technical and managerial employees – who overwhelmingly settle in Changsha. Short-distance inter-provincial migrants, in contrast, are more likely to be rural–rural migrants.

These patterns of in-migration are revealed clearly at the prefectural level in Figure 6.5. The provincial capital, Changsha, has a very distinctive profile: while it has slightly more local migration than the average for Hunan Province,

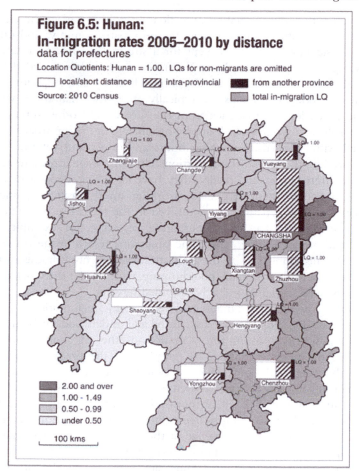

Figure 6.5: Hunan: In-migration rates 2005–2010 by distance
data for prefectures

it has extremely high intermediate-distance in-migration from elsewhere in the province, and it has high long-distance in-migration from other provinces. Major industrial cities close to Changsha (Zhuzhou and Xiangtan) show similar features but at a much lower level, and the transport hubs of Huaihua and Chenzhou have more than average in-migration from other provinces. However, in stark contrast, rural areas have low or very low in-migration at both the intra- and inter-provincial levels (and sometimes even at the local level as well).

6.5 The 'floating population': Beijing, Shanghai and Guangzhou

The insecurity and vulnerability of the migrant workers living in China's largest cities along with their agricultural *hukou* status and therefore their continuing links with the rural areas from which they came, justifies for many commentators their representation as a 'floating population' in the city. These rural–urban migrants, although crucial to the urban economy, and often permanently resident in the city (except for a strong tendency to return to the home village during Chinese New Year), are nevertheless regarded by many city dwellers as outsiders, and thereby attract hostility and suspicion. In addition, their working conditions are typically far worse than those who were born and raised locally. Evidence from the Census and other surveys for the mid-2000s shows that they work disproportionately in the informal sector (65% compared with 30%), their working hours are longer and yet their monthly earnings are less, they suffer disproportionately from wage arrears (especially in the construction sector), and finally, they have far fewer work-related benefits (pensions, unemployment insurance, working injury insurance, and health insurance) – even when they are employed in the formal sector! The combination of low wages and rural upbringing (affecting, for example, dialect), together with negative stereotyping and prejudice, results in the concentration of rural migrant populations in the least attractive neighbourhoods in the city, those areas most likely to contain poor housing, which suffer the worst pollution, and are least well served by publicly provided services.

There are, however, some differences between the major cities in the way in which their 'floating populations' are treated and understood. In Beijing (where non-*hukou* residents account for 8 million of the 21 million population), research on the migrant workers has emphasized the precariousness of their situation. Between 1986 and 1995, for example, five attempts were made to clear Zhejiangcun, the informal settlement built by migrants from Zhejiang Province. In Shanghai (9.5 million non-*hukou* residents in a population of 23 million), the emphasis has mostly been on the accommodations made by the authorities to the permanent presence in the city of millions of migrant workers, and therefore on their integration into urban society. This does not mean, however, that migrants and their families are re-housed by the city authorities when slum clearance occurs – not surprisingly, *hukou* holders have priority over non-*hukou* holders in a situation where the supply of new-build low-cost housing falls vastly short of the need for it. Finally, in Guangzhou, Shenzen and Dongguan, and the Pearl River Delta more generally, although now a smaller part of the picture, the research emphasis has been on the living conditions of young, single women from the countryside (*dagongmei*) working in large factories making inexpensive consumer goods for export markets, and living in dormitory accommodation provided by their employers.

There is some expectation that the *hukou* will eventually be abolished, but that in the meantime, barriers to migration to small and medium-sized cities will disappear (urban registration will be routinely allowed), controls on migration to larger cities will be retained, but will be allowed to vary according to local housing and service-provision conditions, while controls on migration to the very largest cities will remain.

6.6 Interregional migration

In a relatively low-income country undergoing rapid capitalist modernization during a transition from socialism, one would expect four major shifts in interregional migration flows: (i) a tendency for migration distances to increase as overall migration rates went up and as distant parts of the space-economy became increasingly connected; (ii) a tendency for the destinations of the migration flows to reflect the opening up of the economy to international trade and foreign investment, particularly in the early stages of the transition; (iii) as the process matures, a tendency for working-class migrations to be partially replaced by middle-class migrations, especially flows to and from the key urban regions in the system (in this case Beijing-Tianjin, Shanghai, and Guangzhou-Hong Kong); and (iv) a tendency for the flows that were dominant under socialism (often associated with decentralization and the geostrategic integration of the territory) to be replaced by those produced by market relations (often associated with concentration in the core regions which benefit from economies of scale and agglomeration). (For a more detailed account of the logic behind these expectations, see Fielding 2011.)

Do the interregional migration flows in contemporary China match these expectations? This question can be answered with the help of migration velocities (see Box 6.1). Migration velocities standardize the migration flow between origin region and destination region (suitably scaled up), by dividing it by the product of the populations at origin and destination. This allows us to compare the rates of migration flow over time, and over space. The data show: (i) that migration velocities increased for five-year migration flows between 1995–2000 and 2005–10; and (ii) that the rates of increase were particularly strong for origins and destinations that were far apart from one another (see Figure 6.6). So the expectation that a rapid capitalist modernization of the country would lead to a more spatially integrated pattern of migration flows is fully borne out by the facts. People came to migrate more and further.

Second, the data show the enormous attraction of the southeast coastal provinces to interregional migrants. In the late 1990s in particular, the rates of flow of people into Guangdong, Fujian, and Zhejiang Provinces from the inland rural provinces to the west and northwest were quite astounding. This migration is very biased towards young adults, towards women, and towards those with minimal educational qualifications. It is a mass migration associated with the expansion in these provinces of a 'peripheral Fordist' mass production of consumer goods for mass (mostly export) markets. Whatever their family backgrounds (predominantly, of course, farming), this migration turned these young people into proletarian industrial workers. The phenomenal growth of cities in the Pearl River Delta area such as Shenzen and Dongguan, as well as the rapid growth of Guangzhou itself, is a product of these mass migrations (see Figure 6.7).

Third, while most commentators focus only on this mass migration to the coastal provinces of southeast China, plus perhaps migration to Beijing-Tianjin

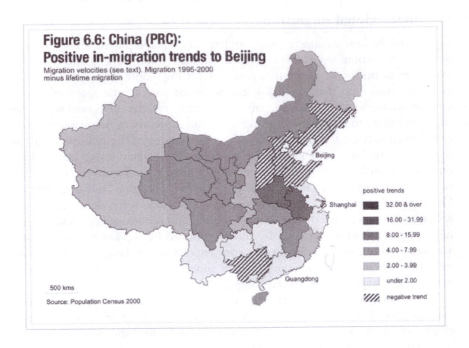

Figure 6.6: China (PRC): Positive in-migration trends to Beijing

Migration velocities (see text). Migration 1995-2000 minus lifetime migration

Beijing

Shanghai

Guangdong

positive trends

32.00 & over

16.00 - 31.99

8.00 - 15.99

4.00 - 7.99

2.00 - 3.99

under 2.00

negative trend

500 kms

Source: Population Census 2000

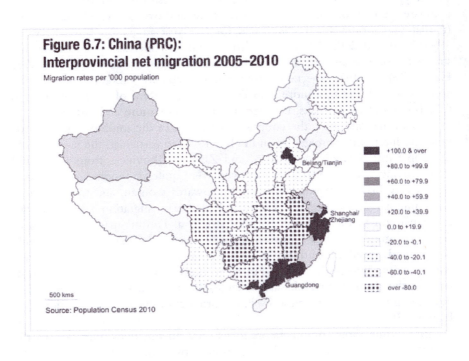

Figure 6.7: China (PRC): Interprovincial net migration 2005–2010

Migration rates per '000 population

Beijing/Tianjin

Shanghai/ Zhejiang

Guangdong

+100.0 & over

+80.0 to +99.9

+60.0 to +79.9

+40.0 to +59.9

+20.0 to +39.9

0.0 to +19.9

-20.0 to -0.1

-40.0 to -20.1

-60.0 to -40.1

over -80.0

500 kms

Source: Population Census 2010

and Shanghai, the truth is that many other kinds of interregional migration exist in China. Mention has already been made of the migration of educationally successful young people to those provinces in which major university cities are located. This channels the 'brightest and the best' towards the largest cities and especially to Beijing-Tianjin and Shanghai. Once there, promotion within managerial careers in both public-sector and private-sector organizations might well involve an intra-organizational transfer to a distant province for a period of time, sometimes with the expectation that such a service will be generously rewarded on the migrant's return (see Figure 6.8). Indeed, an examination of the flows to and from Beijing and Shanghai shows that they are biased towards older adults, those with higher levels of education, and those with professional or managerial occupations. In the case of public-sector employees, the 'law of avoidance' policy has ensured the posting of bureaucrats to counties and townships other than those in which they were brought up.

Finally, the partial and incomplete transition from a centrally planned socialist state to a market economy has, it seems – at least from the evidence of migration flows – diminished the capacity of population redistribution policy to bring about intended development outcomes. If one compares the patterns of flows for the late 1990s with those for the late 2000s, instead of seeing a trend towards migration gains in the regions marked out for growth such as central rural provinces, northeastern provinces, and frontier provinces in the west and southwest, the trend has been unequivocally towards the metropolitan regions of Beijing-Tianjin and Shanghai (especially the latter) becoming even stronger magnets for interregional migrants than they were before (see Figure 6.9). The 2010 Census results show that Shanghai even gained migrants from Beijing, and that the greater Shanghai region (Shanghai, Zhejiang and Jiangsu) was exceptional in that it was the one major area that sent fewer migrants to Beijing in the 2005–10 period than in the 1995–2000 period (presumably due to its own economic dynamism). The big change, however, is in the migration situation of Guangdong Province. Much of its attractiveness, especially to migrants from nearby provinces such as Hunan and Jiangxi, has disappeared, and in 2005–10 Guangdong was a net loser to both the Beijing-Tianjin and Shanghai metropolitan regions. A contributory factor in this might well be the greater cost and difficulty in employing labour in the Pearl River Delta, which along with a shift in the policy emphasis towards the domestic market, is leading to some decentralization of industrial investment away from the coastal provinces and towards those in the interior. This acts as a stern warning to the many commentators who imagine that the patterns of urban and regional migration typical of the recent past will continue unchanged in the future.

6.7 Forced migration and resettlement

As we saw in Chapter 2, China has a long history of forced migration. This was continued under the communist regime since 1949. For the first 30 years, Maoist economic and cultural policies dictated state intervention in the space-economy

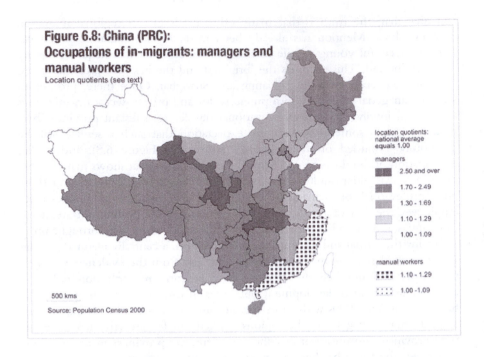

Figure 6.8: China (PRC): Occupations of in-migrants: managers and manual workers
Location quotients (see text)

location quotients:
national average
equals 1.00

managers

2.50 and over

1.70 - 2.49

1.30 - 1.69

1.10 - 1.29

1.00 - 1.09

manual workers

1.10 - 1.29

1.00 - 1.09

500 kms

Source: Population Census 2000

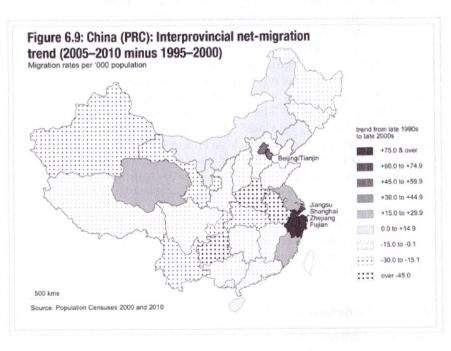

Figure 6.9: China (PRC): Interprovincial net-migration trend (2005–2010 minus 1995–2000)
Migration rates per '000 population

Beijing/Tianjin

Jiangsu
Shanghai
Zhejiang
Fujian

trend from late 1990s
to late 2000s

+75.0 & over

+60.0 to +74.9

+45.0 to +59.9

+30.0 to +44.9

+15.0 to +29.9

0.0 to +14.9

-15.0 to -0.1

-30.0 to -15.1

over -45.0

500 kms

Source: Population Censuses 2000 and 2010

and thereby the redistribution of the population. Three forced migration patterns can be identified for this period: (i) those associated with investments in heavy industry (a good example would be labour that was directed to new locations for the building and operation of new steel mills); (ii) those associated with the opening up of new territories, often with economic, political and strategic objectives (a good example would be migrant workers brought to Xinjiang to work, under almost military conditions, on the cotton farms); and (iii) forced migration in the form of prison settlements – located mostly in the frontier regions of western and southwestern China. The Cultural Revolution in the late 1960s and early 1970s produced its own special form of forced, or at least highly directed, labour. This was associated with the 're-education' of urban youths through 'sending them down' to the countryside where they were expected to learn socialist practice from the peasants through joining them in hard physical labour.

The economic reforms brought in after 1978 by Deng Xiaoping shifted China towards a market economy, and in such an economy there was much less direction of labour by Party officials or the bureaucracy. However, this did not mean an end of forced migration. In particular, major infrastructure investments and agricultural development schemes implied the relocation of populations. The largest of these projects is rightly famous for the scale of population relocation that it caused: the flooding of the Yangtze River consequent upon the building of the high dam at the end of the Yangtze Gorge. This resulted in the displacement of over 1 million people and their resettlement in new villages and towns away from the river.

6.8 Gender and ethnic aspects of migration

Internal migration flows in China are gender specific in many ways. Much depends on the nature of the jobs that migrants take. In the case of migrations to the Pearl River Delta, most of the factory jobs are relatively undemanding in terms of manual strength but very demanding in terms of patience, concentration and dexterity. When combined with gender stereotyping the result is that it is young women from inland rural areas who are sought after. Elsewhere, recruitment for heavy manual factory work and work on construction sites attracts mostly men.

This is the simple part of the picture. Things get more complicated when it comes to the changes in gender relations brought about by migration. Initially, most of the migrants are young and single, but as the migration streams build up and as the migrants themselves form new relationships in both the origin and destination regions, complex patterns of long-distance family relationships develop. In particular, three kinds of rupture to traditional family co-residence occur. First, separation, often for most of the year, of husbands and wives, with either one or the other working in a city that is distant from the village. The left-behind spouse will probably continue the farming of the family's land or other family business during the spouse's absence. Second is the separation between migrant mother or father, or sometimes both migrant parents, and their child or children. The children typically remain in the village in the care of the remaining spouse or with their grandparent(s). Third is the separation between the migrant young adult child or children, single or married, with or without their own children, from their parents and grandparents who usually remain in the village, but who sometimes later join their offspring in the city.

Alluded to at the beginning of this chapter, China is so large and diverse that processes which would usually be associated with international migration are found here to be operating at the level of internal migration. One such process is marriage migration. Men who do low-level jobs (such as farming) in high-income, high-growth coastal provinces often have difficulty in finding wives. Women who face poverty and backwardness in interior provinces are recruited by brokers to migrate to the coastal provinces to marry them. This can have the effect of leaving many men in interior provinces, especially in the remote rural areas of these provinces, as bachelors. Brokers are also involved in the trafficking of rural women into prostitution.

Western media coverage of ethnic relations in China tends to focus on conflicts in western regions that arise, allegedly, from the arrival there of Han migrants from the east. What is usually unreported is the much larger migration of ethnic minority populations, often but by no means always from rural, remote and mountainous regions, to the major cities of central and eastern China. In the major cities of northern China, including Beijing, these minorities consist mainly of ethnic Korean and *Hui* (Muslim) migrants, while in southern China they are largely drawn from the many minority populations living in the southwestern provinces (notably Yunnan, but also Guangxi and Guizhou). Their living conditions in these cities vary greatly. Sometimes the ethnic minority migrants are relatively well educated and form part of the professional/technical middle class (as is often the case with Koreans), but elsewhere, and much more frequently, they suffer prejudice and exclusion. It is important to recognize that the majority ethnic category 'Han' does not refer to a wholly uniform group of people. Significant diversity within the Han population of language (for example, between those speaking Mandarin and those speaking Cantonese) and of culture (for example, between Hakka and other groups in southern China) continues to exist. When migration to another area takes place, such differences can suddenly matter.

6.9 Internal migrations in Taiwan and Mongolia

Internal migration in Taiwan has certain similarities with that of mainland China except that the whole process began much earlier. By 1978, when rural–urban migrations associated with the move towards a market economy was just beginning in the PRC, rural–urban migration, as the dominant feature of Taiwanese migration, was coming to an end. During the previous 30 years, Taiwan had urbanized as it industrialized. It had witnessed the massive growth of the Taipei metropolitan area, rapid growth in other major cities, notably

Kaohsiung, and the development of a zone of high-technology industrial and related urban development to the southwest of the capital, notably around and to the south of Hsinchu City. Today, the rates of population redistribution through internal migration are much lower, but some of the social problems remain. This is especially so for the migration of Taiwan's indigenous population who tend to live in the poorer (for example, river bank) districts of Taiwanese cities.

Mongolia is, of course, totally different. Vast in area and with very low population density, the main migration feature of Mongolia until the very recent past has been nomadism. Pastoral herders move with their sheep, goats, cattle, camels and horses to those areas where grass is to be found in landscapes that are subject to the combined hazards of fiercely cold winters and long periods of drought. Often, and especially in western Mongolia, the general pattern of nomadism is combined with elements of transhumance, where pastoralists will take the livestock to higher, well-watered pastures in the summer months, and bring them down to lower pastures in the winter. The livelihoods of nomadic herdsmen and their families have been adversely affected in recent years by both natural environmental (for example, severe winters in the early 2000s) and socio-political changes. This has led to many of them gravitating towards the capital city, Ulan Bator, where informal settlements on the outskirts of the city have grown up. There is now, however, a new factor: a national economic boom consequent upon the massive foreign investments in mineral extraction. This has resulted in a further development of the capital city, and to the sudden emergence of new settlements at the sites of these new investments, notably at Oyu Tolgoi (copper and gold – 10,000 employees) and Tavan Tolgoi (coal). Meanwhile, migration to illegal mining settlements has also occurred.

6.10 Conclusion

To summarize, the internal migrations of China 'plus' are numerically dominated by labour migration, and especially by the movement of young adults leaving small towns and rural areas to become industrial workers in the major cities. However, the migration of the highly educated and of the professional, technical and managerial middle classes to which they belong – a migration that is often poorly represented in the literature – has been significant throughout the period, and is now becoming increasingly important as the economy matures.

Spatial displacements of population are significant in the PRC. Forced resettlement is most common in areas that are at the margin of cultivation or livestock rearing, but it also results from state-sponsored infrastructure investments. As incomes increase, however, a growing proportion of people can exercise choice about where they live. This is particularly important in the lives of young adults, many of whom are attracted to the main cities not just for employment and career development reasons, but because that is where they can achieve personal independence and enjoy the 'modern' lifestyles that they frequently so passionately seek.

Amongst the many young people who migrate, an increasing proportion are students. Achieving academic success is essential for entry into most middle-class professional, technical and managerial occupations. However, a university education is not just about gaining qualifications. At its best it is also a 'rite of passage' into a wider, more cosmopolitan, power-saturated world. It affects where you settle down (with enormous benefits accruing to those who successfully settle in those cities such as Shanghai and Beijing where upward social mobility is most likely to occur), as well as whom you marry (men gaining educational success and possessing good prospects are likely to be regarded as excellent partner potential). So the subsequent life course migrations of many people will be set in motion by their migration experiences and the social skills that they acquire as students.

The big question is this: Can the political structures of the People's Republic of China, built to secure social stability and the continued rule of the Chinese Communist Party, accommodate, cope with, even perhaps survive, the 'turbulent transitions' set in motion by the sharp shift towards a modern market economy – a shift that could not have happened without the vast migration of people from the villages to the cities and from one region to another, and a shift which, in turn, has been the principal cause of such migrations?

Box 6.2 Migration and employment: circular and cumulative causation

At a general level the relationship between migration and regional develop-ment is fairly straightforward: a region with high wages experiencing rapid growth is likely to attract migrants from regions that have low wages and are in decline. However, dig deeper, and one finds many unexpected outcomes – these relationships are often paradoxical and not as simple as they seem.

Circular and cumulative causation

Absolutely central to an analysis of the relationship between population migration and regional development is the appreciation that the direction of causality can be, and typically is, in both directions: that is, rapid growth of a region's economy will usually result in net in-migration, high net migration gains will usually lead to rapid growth in a region's economy. This creates the strong possibility that there will be positive feedback loops linking, for example, migration and employment, and that processes of circular and cumulative causation will be at work. A representation of this approach, when applied to migration, is provided in Figure 6.10. (The material in this discussion box draws heavily upon Fielding 2016.)

Starting in the lower left-hand corner, regional economic growth will be largely determined by national forces such as technological change and changes in consumer behaviour, mediated by both regional productivity change (investment and innovation) and the inherited regional employment structure. This employment structure, together with the volume and direction of employment change (new jobs created/jobs lost), will largely determine the region's in- and out-migration flows. Interregional migration will affect population growth, not only directly through the net migration balance, but also indirectly through the age composition (and other characteristics) of the migrants. As regional population growth (or decline) occurs, the region gains (or loses) critical mass for its selection as a suitable location for market or labour pool size-related investments. Finally, interregional migration greatly influences regional economic growth through the selectivity of migration. Since migration is generally positively selective of people who have ambition and courage, have qualifications and skills, possess social and cultural capital, tend to be flexible and adaptive, and are in the young adult age groups when their economic potential is at its height, a net migration gain can bestow enormous advantage upon a region's economy. Conversely, a net migration loss can have all the opposite effects – brain drain, ageing population, and a loss of commitment to adjust or change. Interregional migration can also affect regional employment change. Migrants may well only take up those jobs that are attractive – jobs that have good pay, are secure, and offer good prospects. By rejecting the other jobs, either employment growth will be stemmed, or the jobs will, instead, be filled by

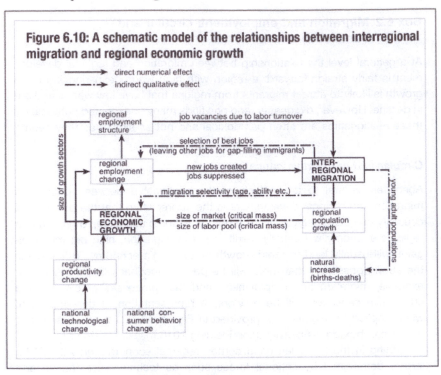

Figure 6.10: A schematic model of the relationships between interregional migration and regional economic growth

foreign workers. This interdependence between domestic interregional migration and international migration has become of great significance in high-income countries around the world (including those in East Asia).

To emphasize in this way the bi-directional flow of causality between population migration and regional development and its potential to result in patterns of cumulative growth and decline, is not to deny, however, the strong logic of neo-classical economic approaches to these same relationships. Regional income convergence in the USA, for example, has been explained as resulting from the combination of the migration of labour from low-income, high-unemployment regions to high-income, low-unemployment ones (thereby raising the scarcity of labour and therefore wages in the former and reducing labour scarcity and wages in the latter), and of the flow of capital in the reverse direction (to take advantage, of course, of the lower costs of labour in the low-income region).

The problem is that many of the expectations about interregional migration based upon this neo-classical economic approach are simply not borne out by the facts: paradoxically, the unemployed are, on average, rather immobile, while home owners, on the other hand, are surprisingly mobile; high-income cities often lose interregional migrants, on balance, rather than gain them, while low-income rural areas often gain migrants rather than lose them. More generally, those who have the highest need to migrate (because they have the lowest incomes and live in the places with the worst economic prospects) tend to migrate the least, while those who have the lowest need to migrate (because they are in secure, well-paid employment and live in the places with the best prospects) tend to migrate the most.

Much of the remainder of this box (and Box 8.1) is concerned with providing explanations for these anomalies while focusing on just a small part of the diagram in Figure 6.10: the one-way causal link between regional economic growth and regional employment change on the one hand and inter-regional migration on the other. Before doing this, though, a note of caution is appropriate. In the past, say 50 years ago, the link between migration and employment was exceedingly close – very few could afford to live away from where jobs were located. Today, two things have changed, especially in high-income capitalist economies, to weaken this link. The first is the decline in the returns to labour relative to the returns to capital. This means that a significant proportion of people – those living off their investments – can choose to live in places that are geographically distant from the places where the economic activities on which their wealth depends are located. Within countries, this can result in the presence in environmentally favoured regions having wealthy in-migrants and net migration gains when those regions are renowned for their low wages and high unemployment. Internationally, the benefits of this separation favour Caribbean island countries, and cities like Dubai and London. This latter migration of wealthy foreigners (viz. Chinese and Hong Kong property owners in London) can have knock-on effects on internal migration. By raising housing and other prices in the main city, it makes it more difficult for ordinary families (such as those of teachers and nurses) to migrate to those cities, and at the same time encourages others to cash in their city properties to enjoy a high standard of living elsewhere.

The second change that has weakened the link between migration and employment is communications technology. It has become possible to work physically apart from your work colleagues while remaining as much in contact with them as if they were in the office next door. As part of this tendency, web conferencing and online meetings have become a part of many people's working lives. This facilitation of physical separation of home and workplace is of great importance to professional men and women in dual-career households. It has the effect of injecting flexibility into situations that might otherwise threaten career development and/or relationship commitments.

Migration and labour markets in China

With migration touching so many political sensitivities, affecting directly and indirectly so many people's lives, and having such significant broader economic and social outcomes, it matters greatly how knowledge about it is collected, organized and conveyed. We can usefully speak about 'narratives' of migration that compete with one another in the arenas of both elite debate and public discourse. The successful narratives then enter our 'taken-for-granted worlds' and thereby become part of our culture. The massively dominant and almost only narrative about contemporary internal migration in the PRC is that it consists of young adult men and women migrating from the interior rural provinces of central and southern China to take up employment in the rapidly expanding industrial cities of the southeastern coastal provinces. These migrants lack urban *hukou* (and therefore social rights in the destination city), and for this reason join the problematic 'floating populations' of these cities. It is not that this narrative is incorrect, of course – only that it is seriously, almost outrageously, incomplete.

An analysis of the statistical correlations between province of origin and the labour market characteristics of the destination areas within Heilongjiang Province in China's far northeast (Fielding 2015) shows that, far from there being only one kind of migration flow (that of peasant youths to cities with manufacturing employment growth), there were, in this instance, four! The first was the very distinctive tendency for migrants from large cities like Beijing and Shanghai to go to those places (especially, of course, the provincial capital, Harbin) that had many jobs in modern sectors such as IT, financial services and real estate. Second, there was uniquely no bias towards urban areas for migrants from the traditional source regions for agricultural migration to Heilongjiang (notably Shandong Province), which indicates a continuation of long-established socio-familial, cultural and economic links between these provinces. Third, yes, there were migrations from rural provinces into the industrial cities in Heilongjiang (such as migrants from Anhui to its mining settlements). This is similar to the mass migrations to the southeast provinces, except for one important thing: Heilongjiang is very decidedly not a province of net in-migration but one of net out-migration! Finally, and intriguingly, in-migrants to Heilongjiang from the southeastern provinces such as Zhejiang and Fujian, although small in number, went overwhelmingly to those places within the province that specialized in trade and commerce (especially towns located on or close to the frontier with Russia). Once again, it seems that both economic and cultural forces are at work: people who come from a region with a well-developed trading culture are responding to new trading opportunities.

All this proves the complexity of interprovincial migration in China and that migration is far from being the one-dimensional process that it is customarily, politically and academically made out to be. However, these findings also demonstrate that, despite this complexity, Chinese interprovincial migration flows have interpretable underlying economic and cultural logics.

References

Fielding, T., 2015, Migration: the economic drivers of contemporary labour mobility in East Asia, in *Globalization in Eurasia and the Pacific Rim*, Vol. 4. Singapore: World Scientific, 51–64.

Fielding, T., 2016 (forthcoming), Population mobility and regional development, in Richardson, D. (ed.), *The International Encyclopedia of Geography*. Oxford: John Wiley and Sons, Ltd.

Selected references

6.0 General

Bakken, B. (ed.), 1998, *Migration in China*. Copenhagen: Nordic Institute of Asian Studies.

Bonnin, M., 2004, *Génération Perdue: Le Mouvement d'Envoi des Jeunes Instruits à la Campagne en Chine, 1968–1980*. Paris: EHESS.

Cai, F. and Wu, Y., 2009, *Migration and Labor Mobility in China*. UNDP: Human Development Research Paper 2009/09.

Chan, K.W., 2010, The global financial crisis and migrant workers in China: 'there is no future as a labourer; returning to the village has no meaning', *International Journal of Urban and Regional Research* 34(3): 659–677.

Davin, D., 1999, *Internal Migration in Contemporary China*. Basingstoke: Macmillan.

Fan, C.C., 2007, *China on the Move: Migration, the State, and the Household*. London: Routledge.

Fei, H.-T. and Chang, C.-I., 1945, *Earthbound China: A Study of Rural Economy in Yunnan*. Chicago, IL: University of Chicago Press.

Murphy, R., 2002, *How Migrant Labour is Changing Rural China*. Cambridge: Cambridge University Press.

Murphy, R. (ed.), 2009, *Labour Migration and Social Development in Contemporary China*. London: Routledge.

Nielsen, I., Smyth, R. and Vicziany, M. (eds), 2007, *Globalisation and Labour Mobility in China*. Melbourne: Monash University Press.

Nyiri, P., 2010, *Mobility and Cultural Authority in Contemporary China*. Seattle: University of Washington Press.

Pai, H.-H., 2012, *Scattered Sand: The Story of China's Rural Migrants*. London: Verso.

Pieke, F.N. and Mallee, H. (eds), 1999, *Internal and International Migration: Chinese Perspectives*. Richmond: Curzon.

Scharping, T. (ed.), 1997, *Floating Population and Migration in China*. Hamburg: Institut für Asienkunde.

Solinger, D.J., 1999, *Contesting Citizenship in Urban China: Peasant Migrants, the State and the Logic of the Market*. Berkeley: University of California Press.

For a fascinating insight into the experiences of migrants and the circumstances of their lives, see:

Dutton, M., 1998, *Streetlife China*. Cambridge: Cambridge University Press (especially Part 2).

6.1 Urban and regional development in China

Bramall, C., 2007, *The Industrialization of Rural China*. London: Oxford University Press.

Chen, A., Liu, G.G. and Zhang, K.H. (eds), 2004, *Urbanization and Social Welfare in China*. Farnham: Ashgate.

Fan, C.C. and Sun, M., 2008, Regional inequality in China, 1978–2006, *Eurasian Geography and Economics* 49(1): 1–18.

Golley, J., 2007, *The Dynamics of Chinese Regional Development*. Cheltenham: Edward Elgar.

Goodman, D.S.G., 2004, The campaign to 'open up the west': national, provincial-level and local perspectives, *The China Quarterly* 178: 317–334.

Groenewold, N., Chen, A. and Lee, G., 2008, *Linkages between China's Regions: Measurement and Policy*. Cheltenham: Edward Elgar.

Huang, Y. and Luo, X., 2009, Reshaping economic geography in China, in *Reshaping Economic Geography in East Asia*. Washington, DC: The World Bank, 196–217.

Kanbur, R. and Zhang, X., 2001, *Fifty Years of Regional Inequality in China: A Journey through Revolution, Reform and Openness*. Ithaca, NY: Cornell University, Department of Applied Economics and Management WP4.

Knight, J. and Song, L., 1999, *The Rural-Urban Divide: Economic Disparities and Interactions in China*. London: Oxford University Press.

Lai, K., 2012, Differentiated markets: Shanghai, Beijing and Hong Kong in China's financial centre network, *Urban Studies* 49(6): 1275–1296.

Li, Y. and Wei, Y.H.D., 2010, The spatial-temporal hierarchy of regional inequality of China, *Applied Geography* 30: 303–316.

Lin, G.C.S., 1999, State policy and spatial restructuring in post-reform China, *International Journal of Urban and Regional Research* 23: 670–696.

Logan, J.R. (ed.), 2008, *Urban China in Transition*. Oxford: Blackwell.

Ma, L.J.C. and Wu, F. (eds), 2004, *Restructuring the Chinese City: Changing Society, Economy and Space*. London: Routledge.

Marton, A.M., 2000, *China's Spatial Economic Development*. London: Routledge.

Renard, M.-F. (ed.), 2002, *China and its Regions: Economic Growth and Reform in Chinese Provinces*. Cheltenham: Edward Elgar.

Saw, S.-H. and Wong, J. (eds), 2009, *Regional Economic Development in China*. Singapore: Institute of South East Asian Studies.

Skeldon, R., 1997, Hong Kong: colonial city to global city to provincial city? *Cities* 14 (5): 265–271.

Wei, Y.D., 2000, *Regional Development in China*. London: Routledge.

Yao, Y., 2009, The political economy of government policies toward regional inequality in China, in *Reshaping Economic Geography in East Asia*. Washington, DC: The World Bank, 218–240.

Ye, Y. and LeGates, R., 2013, *Coordinating Urban and Regional Development in China: Learning from Chengdu*. Cheltenham: Edward Elgar.

Yeung, Y.-M. and Shen, J., 2004, *Developing China's West*. Hong Kong: Chinese University Press.

Yeung, Y.M. and Shen, J. (eds), 2008, *The Pan-Pearl River Delta: An Emerging Regional Economy in a Globalizing China*. Hong Kong: Chinese University Press.

Zheng, J., 2011, 'Creative industry clusters' and the 'entrepreneurial city' of Shanghai, *Urban Studies* 48(16): 3561–3582.

Zhou, Y., 2008, *The Inside Story of China's High-Tech Industry: Making 'Silicon Valley' in Beijing*. Lanham, MD: Rowman & Littlefield.

6.2 Ethnic, social and demographic diversity in China

On social stratification:

Chen, M. and Goodman, D.S.G., 2013, *Middle Class China: Identity and Behaviour*. Cheltenham: Edward Elgar.

Li, C. (ed.), 2010, *China's Emerging Middle Class: Beyond Economic Transformation*. Washington, DC: Brookings Institution.

Zhou, X., 2010, *The State and Life Chances in Urban China: Redistribution and Stratification 1949–1994*. Cambridge: Cambridge University Press.

On ethnicity, gender, inequality:

Gladney, D.C., 1998, *Dislocating China: Muslims, Minorities and Other Subaltern Subjects*. London: Hurst.

Kapstein, M., 2006, *The Tibetans*. Hoboken, NJ: Wiley-Blackwell.

Mackerras, C., 1995, *China's Minority Cultures: Identities and Integration since 1912*. Basingstoke: Macmillan.

Rossabi, M., 2004, *Governing China's Multiethnic Frontiers*. Seattle: University of Washington Press.

Sneath, D., 2000, *Changing Inner Mongolia: Pastoral Mongolian Society and the Chinese States*. London: Oxford University Press.

Zang, X., 2007, *Ethnicity and Urban Life in China: A Comparative Study of Hui Muslims and Han Chinese*. London: Routledge.

On demography of China:

Banister, J., 1987, *China's Changing Population*. Stanford, CA: Stanford University Press.

Cai, F., 2012, Demographic transition and economic and social development, in Li, P. (ed.), *Chinese Society: Change and Transformation*. London: Routledge, 126–147.

Goldstein, A. and Feng, W. (eds), 1996, *China: The Many Facets of Demographic Change*. Boulder, CO: Westview Press.

Peng, X. and Guo, Z. (eds), 2000, *The Changing Population of China*. Oxford: Blackwell.

Zhao, Z. and Guo, F. (eds), 2007, *Transition and Change: China's Population at the Beginning of the 21st Century*. London: Oxford University Press.

6.3 Internal migration in China: the household registration (hukou) system

Bernstein, T.P., 1977, *Up to the Mountains and Down to the Villages*. New Haven, CT: Yale University Press.

Chan, K.W., 2004, Internal migration, in Hsieh, C.-M. and Lu, M. (eds), *Changing China: A Geographic Appraisal*. Boulder, CO: Westview Press, 229–242.

Fan, C.C., 1999, Migration in a socialist transitional economy: heterogeneity, socio-economic and spatial characteristics of migrants in China and Guangdong Province, *International Migration Review* 33(4): 954–987.

Li, P. and Roulleau-Berger, L. (eds), 2013, *China's Internal and International Migration*. London: Routledge.

Li, Z., 2004, *China's Limited Urbanization: Under Socialism and Beyond*. New York: Nova Science.

Liang, Z., 2001, The age of migration in China, *Population and Development Review* 27 (3): 499–524.

Lu, D. (ed.), 2011, *The Great Urbanization of China*. Singapore: World Scientific.

Sit, V.F.S., 2010, *Chinese City and Urbanism: Evolution and Development*. Singapore: World Scientific.

Wang, D. and Cai, F., 2007, *Migration and Policy Alleviation in China*. Geneva: International Organization for Migration, Migration Research Series 27.

On the *hukou* system:

Alexander, P. and Chan, A., 2004, Does China have an apartheid pass system? *Journal of Ethnic and Migration Studies* 30(4): 609–630.

Bao, S., Bodvarsson, O.B., Hou, J.W. and Zhao, Y., 2011, The regulation of migration in a transition economy: China's hukou system, *Contemporary Economic Policy* 29(4): 564–579.

Chan, K.W., 2009, The Chinese hukou system at 50, *Eurasian Geography and Economics* 50(2): 197–221.

Cheng, T. and Selden, M., 1994, The origins and social consequences of China's hukou system, *China Quarterly* 139: 644–648.

Fan, C.C., 2008, Migration, hukou and the city, in Yusuf, S. and Saich, T. (eds), *China Urbanizes: Consequences, Strategies, and Policies*. Washington, DC: The World Bank, 65–91.

Fan, L., 2011, *Social Policy and Migration in China*. London: Routledge.

Fu, Q. and Ren, Q., 2010, Educational inequality under China's rural-urban divide: the hukou system and returns to education, *Environment and Planning A* 42: 592–610.

Mallee, H., 1995, China's household registration system under reform, *Development and Change* 26(1): 1–29.

Shen, J., 2011, Migrant labour under the shadow of the hukou system: the case of Guangdong, in Wong, T.-C. and Rigg, J. (eds), *Asian Cities, Migrant Labour and Contested Spaces*. London: Routledge, 223–245.

Wang, F.-L., 2005, *Organizing Through Division and Exclusion: China's Hukou System*. Stanford, CA: Stanford University Press.

Wu, X. and Trieman, D.J., 2007, Inequality and equality under Chinese socialism: the hukou system and intergenerational mobility, *American Journal of Sociology* 113: 415–445.

6.4 Urbanization and rural depopulation

Chan, A., Madsen, R. and Unger, J., 2009, *Chen Village: Revolution and Globalization*. Berkeley: University of California Press.

Chan, K.W., 2010, A China paradox: migrant labor shortage amidst rural labor supply abundance, *Eurasian Geography and Economics* 51(4): 513–530.

Chen, A., Haute, T., Liu, G.G., Zhang, K.H. (eds), 2004, *Urban Transformation in China*. Farnham: Ashgate.

Chen, A., Liu, G.G. and Zhang, K.H. (eds), 2004, *Urbanization and Social Welfare in China*. Farnham: Ashgate.

Faure, D. and Siu, H.F. (eds), 1995, *Down to Earth: The Territorial Bond in South China*. Stanford, CA: Stanford University Press.

Guang, L., 2005, The state connection in China's rural-urban migration, *International Migration Review* 39(2): 354–380.

Guldin, G.E. (ed.), 1992, *Urbanizing China*. New York: Greenwood Press.

Huang, P. and Pieke, F.N., 2003, *China Migration Country Study*. Paper presented at the Regional Conference on Migration, Development and Pro-Poor Policy Choices in Asia, Dhaka.

Ma, X. and Wang, W. (eds), 1993, *Migration and Urbanization in China*. Beijing: New World Press.

Meng, X., Manning, C., Li, S. and Effendi, T.N. (eds), 2010, *The Great Migration: Rural-Urban Migration in China and Indonesia*. Cheltenham: Edward Elgar.

Taylor, J.E., Rozelle, S. and De Brauw, A., 2002, Migration and incomes in source communities: a new economics of migration perspective from China, *Economic Development and Cultural Change* 52(1): 75–101.

Wu, W. and Gaubatz, P., 2013, *The Chinese City*. London: Routledge.

Yusuf, S. and Saich, T. (eds), 2008, *China Urbanizes: Consequences, Strategies, and Policies*. Washington, DC: The World Bank.

6.5 The 'floating population': Beijing, Shanghai and Guangzhou

On Beijing, Shanghai, Guangzhou:

Cartier, C., 2001, *Globalizing South China*. Oxford: Blackwells.

Fleischer, F., 2011, *Suburban Beijing: Housing and Consumption in Contemporary China*. Minneapolis: University of Minnesota Press.

Gamble, J., 2001, *Shanghai in Transition*. London: Routledge.

He, S., 2010, New-build gentrification in Central Shanghai: demographic changes and socioeconomic implications, *Population, Space and Place* 16: 345–361.

Huang, Y., 2005, From work-unit compounds to gated communities: housing inequality and residential segregation in traditional Beijing, in Ma, L.J.C. and Wu, F. (eds), *Restructuring the Chinese City: Changing Society, Economy and Space*. London: Routledge, 192–221.

Li, L.W., Dray-Novey, A.J. and Kong, H., 2007, *Beijing: From Imperial Capital to Olympic City*. Basingstoke: Palgrave.

Liang, Z., Messner, S., Chen, C. and Huang, Y. (eds), 2011, *The Emergence of a New Urban China: Insiders' Perspectives*. Lanham, MD: Lexington Books.

Lin, Y., De Muelder, B. and Wang, S., 2011, Understanding the 'village in the city' in Guangzhou: economic integration and development issue and their implications for the urban migrant, *Urban Studies* 48(16): 3583–3598.

Ma, L.J.C. and Wu, F. (eds), 2005, *Restructuring the Chinese City: Changing Society, Economy and Space*. London: Routledge.

Pow, C.-P., 2009, *Gated Communities in China: Class, Privilege and the Moral Politics of the Good Life (Shanghai)*. London: Routledge.

Sit, V.F.S., 1995, *Beijing: The Nature and Planning of a Chinese Capital City*. World Cities Series. Chichester: John Wiley.

Wasserstrom, J.N., 2004, *Shanghai: Global City*. London: RoutledgeCurzon.

Wu, F. and Webster, C. (eds), 2010, *Marginalization in Urban China: Comparative Perspectives*. Basingstoke: Palgrave Macmillan.

Xiang, B., 2003, *A Community beyond Borders: A History of Life in Beijing's 'Zhejiang Village'*. Leiden: Brill

On urban migrants: the 'floating populations' of other Chinese cities:

Bray, D., 2005, *Social Space and Governance in Urban China: The Danwei System from Origins to Reform*. Stanford, CA: Stanford University Press.

Chan, C.K.-C., 2010, *The Challenge of Labour in China (Shenzen)*. London: Routledge.

Chen, Y. and Hoy, C., 2011, Explaining migrants' economic vulnerability in urban China: institutional discrimination and market imperatives, *Asian Population Studies* 7(2): 123–136.

Cockain, A., 2012, *Young Chinese in Urban China*. London: Routledge.

Fan, C.C., 2002, The elite, the natives, and the outsiders: migration and labour market segmentation in urban China, *Annals of the Association of American Geographers* 92(1): 103–124.

Howell, A. and Fan, C.C., 2011, Migration and inequality in Xinjiang: a survey of Han and Uyghur migrants in Urumqi, *Eurasian Geography and Economics* 52(1): 119–139.

Li, C., 2012, Migrant workers and social mobility, in Li, P. (ed.), *Chinese Society: Change and Transformation*. London: Routledge, 217–241.

Li, Z., 2010, *In Search of Paradise: Middle-Class Living in a Chinese Metropolis (Kunming)*. Ithaca, NY: Cornell University Press.

Loyalka, M.D., 2012, *Eating Bitterness: Stories from the Front Lines of China's Great Urban Migration*. Berkeley: University of California Press.

Nielsen, I. and Smyth, R. (eds), 2008, *Migration and Social Protection in China*. Singapore: World Scientific Publishing.

Solinger, D.J., 2002, The floating population in the cities: markets, migration, and the prospects for citizenship, in Blum, S.D. and Jensen, L.M. (eds), *China Off Center: Mapping the Margins of the Middle Kingdom*. Honolulu: University of Hawai'i Press, 273–290.

Van Luyn, F.-J., 2008 (2004), *A Floating City of Peasants: The Great Migration in Contemporary China*. New York: The New Press.

Wang, Y.P., 2004, *Urban Poverty, Housing and Social Change in China*. London: RoutledgeCurzon.

Wu, F. (ed.), 2007, *China's New Urbanism*. London: Routledge.

Wu, F., Xu, J. and Yeh, A.G.-O., 2006, *Urban Development in Post-Reform China*. London: Routledge.

Wu, F. et al., 2010, *Urban Poverty in China*. Cheltenham: Edward Elgar.

Zang, X., 2011, *Ethnicity and Urban Life in China*. London: Routledge.

Zhang, L., 2001, *Strangers in the City: Reconfiguration of Space, Power, and Social Networks within China's Floating Population*. Stanford, CA: Stanford University Press.

Zhu, Y. and Chen, W., 2010, The settlement intention of China's floating population in the cities: recent changes and multifaceted individual-level determinants, *Population, Space and Place* 16: 253–267.

6.6 Interregional migration

Bao, S. et al, 2006, Migration and regional development in China, in Bao, S., Lin, S. and Zhao, C. (eds), *The Chinese Economy after WTO Entry*. Basingstoke: Ashgate.

Fan, C.C., 2005, Modeling interprovincial migration in China 1985–2000, *Eurasian Geography and Economics* 46(3): 165–184.

Fielding, T., 2011, Inter-provincial migration in a transition economy: the case of China, *Ritsumeikan Economic Review* 59(6): 3–24.

Lin, J.-Y., Wang, G. and Zhao, Y., 2004, Regional inequality and labour transfers in China, *Economic Development and Cultural Change* 52(3): 587–603.

Liu, Y. and Shen, J., 2014, Jobs or amenities? Location choices of interprovincial skilled migrants in China, 2000–2005, *Population Space and Place* 20(7): 592–605.

Ma, R., 2011, *Population and Society in Tibet*. Hong Kong: Hong Kong University Press.

Seymour, J.D., 2000, Xinjiang's Production and Construction Corps, and the Sinification of eastern Turkestan, *Inner Asia* 2: 171–193.

Shen, J., 2012, Changing patterns and determinants of interprovincial migration in China 1985–2000, *Population, Space and Place* 18: 384–402.

Sun, W., 2006, The leaving of Anhui: the southward journey toward the knowledge class, in Oakes, T. and Schein, L. (eds), *Translocal China: Linkages, Identities and the Reimagining of Space*. London: Routledge, 238–262.

6.7 Forced migration and resettlement

Heggelund, G., 2004, *Environment and Resettlement Politics in China: The Three Gorges Project*. Aldershot: Ashgate.

Jim, C.Y., Yang, F.Y. and Wang, L., 2010, Socio-ecological impacts of concurrent reservoir inundation and reforestation in the Three Gorges region of China, *Annals of the Association of American Geographers* 100(2): 243–268.

Li, H., Waley, P. and Rees, P., 2001, Reservoir resettlement in China: past experience and the Three Gorges Dam, *Geographical Journal* 167(3): 195–212.

McDonald, B., Webber, M. and Duan, Y.-F., 2008, Involuntary resettlement as an opportunity for development: the case of urban resettlers of the Three Gorges Project, China, *Journal of Refugee Studies* 21(1): 82–102.

Padovani, F., 2006, Involuntary resettlement in the Three Gorges Dam area in the perspective of forced migration due to hydraulic planning in China, in Crepeau, F. et al. (eds), *Forced Migration and Global Processes*. Lanham, MD: Lexington Books,

Seymour, J.D. and Anderson, R., 1997, *New Ghosts, Old Ghosts: Prisons and Labor Reform Camps in China*. New York: M.E. Sharpe.

Shi, G. and Chen, S., 2004, China resettlement policies and practices, in Dang, N.A. and Chantavanich, S. (eds), *Uprooting People for their own Good? Human Displacement, Resettlement and Trafficking in the Greater Mekong Sub-Region*. Hanoi: Social Sciences Publishing House, 23–39.

Tan, Y., 2008, *Resettlement in the Three Gorges Project*. Hong Kong: Hong Kong University Press.

Wilmsen, B., Webber, M. and Duan, Y., 2011, Development for whom? Rural to urban resettlement at the Three Gorges Dam, China, *Asian Studies Review* 35: 21–42.

6.8 Gender and ethnic aspects of migration

On gender, ageing and sexuality:

Bodvarsson, O.V. and Hou, J.W., 2010, *The Effects of Aging on Migration in a Transition Economy: The Case of China*. Bonn: IZA DP 5070.

Bossen, L., 2007, Village to distant village: the opportunities and risks of long-distance marriage migration in rural China, *Journal of Contemporary China* 16(50): 97–116.

Fan, C.C., 2003, Rural-urban migration and gender division of labor in transitional China, *International Journal of Urban and Regional Research* 27(1): 24–47.

Gaetano, A.M. and Jacka, T. (eds), 2004, *On the Move: Women and Rural-to-Urban Migration in Contemporary China*. Ithaca, NY: Columbia University Press.

Goldstein, S., Liang, Z. and Goldstein, A., 2000, Migration, gender, and labour force in Hubei 1985–1990, in Entwisle, B. and Henderson, G. (eds), *Re-Drawing Boundaries: Work, Households, and Gender in China*. Berkeley: University of California Press, 197–213.

Guo, M., Chow, N.W.S. and Palinkas, L.A., 2011, Circular migration and life course of female domestic workers in Beijing, *Asian Population Studies* 7(1): 51–67.

He, C. and Gober, P., 2003, Gendering inter-provincial migration in China, *International Migration Review* 37(4): 1220–1251.

Jacka, T., 2005, *Rural Women in Urban China: Gender, Migration and Social Change*. Armonk, NY: M.E. Sharpe.

Liang, Z. and Chen, Y.P., 2004, Migration and gender in China: an origin-destination linked approach, *Economic Development and Cultural Change* 52(2): 423–443.

Pun, N., 2005, *Made in China: Women Factory Workers in a Global Workplace*. Durham, NC: Duke University Press.

Roberts, K., 2002, Female labour migrants to Shanghai: temporary floaters or potential settlers? *International Migration Review* 36(2): 492–519.

Sun, W., 2009, *Maid in China: Media, Morality, and the Cultural Politics of Boundaries*. London: Routledge.

Xu, F., 2000, *Women Migrant Workers in China's Economic Reform*. London: Macmillan.

Yan, H., 2008, *New Masters, New Servants: Migration, Development, and Women Workers in China*. Durham, NC: Duke University Press.

Zheng, T., 2009, *Red Lights: The Lives of Sex Workers in Postsocialist China*. Minneapolis: University of Minnesota Press.

On ethnic aspects of internal migration:

Dillon, M., 1999, *China's Muslim Hui Community: Migration, Settlement and Sects*. Richmond: Curzon.

Hansen, M.H., 2005, *Frontier People: Han Settlers in Minority Areas of China*. Vancouver: University of British Columbia Press.

Honig, E., 1992, *Creating Chinese Ethnicity: Subei People in Shanghai 1850–1980*. New Haven, CT: Yale University Press.

Iredale, R., Bilik, N., Su, W., Guo, F. and Hoy, C., 2001, *Contemporary Minority Migration, Education and Ethnicity in China*. Cheltenham: Edward Elgar.

Iredale, R., Bilik, N. and Fei, G. (eds), 2003, *China's Minorities on the Move: Selected Case Studies*. Armonk, NY: M.E. Sharpe.

Paik, W. and Ham, M., 2012, From autonomous areas to non-autonomous areas: the politics of Korean minority migration in contemporary China, *Modern China* 38(1): 110–133.

Zang, X., 2007, *Ethnicity and Urban Life in China: A Comparative Study of Hui Muslims and Han Chinese*. London: Routledge.

6.9 Internal migrations in Taiwan and Mongolia

On Taiwan:

Lin, J.-P. and Tsay, C.-L., 2000, Labour migration and allocation of human resources in Taiwan: return and onward cases, *Asian and Pacific Migration Journal* 9(1): 1–34.

Mullan, B.P., Li, C.-H., Gallin, R.S. and Gallin, B., 1998, Family and internal migration in Taiwan, *Asian and Pacific Migration Journal* 7(1): 43–66.

Selya, R.M., 2004, *Development and Demographic Change in Taiwan*. Singapore: World Scientific.

Speare, A., Liu, P.K.C. and Tsay, C.L., 1988, *Urbanization and Development: The Rural-Urban Transition in Taiwan*. Boulder, CO: Westview Press.

On Mongolia:

Bruun, O. and Narangoa, L. (eds), 2006, *Mongols from Country to City: Floating Boundaries, Pastoralism and City Life in the Mongol Lands*. Honolulu: University of Hawai'i Press.

Humphries, C. and Sneath, D., 1999, *The End of Nomadism? Society, State and the Environment in Inner Asia*. Durham, NC: Duke University Press.

UNDP/Government of Mongolia, 2003, *Human Development Report: Mongolia 2003: Urban-Rural Disparities in Mongolia*. Ulaanbaatar: UNDP.

7 Capitalism's global warriors

Japanese and Korean international migration flows

7.0 Introduction

Northeast Asia (especially Japan and South Korea) is a key part of the East Asian migration system. Not only do Japan and South Korea supply many of the well-educated foreigners now found in most of the largest cities in Southeast Asia and China plus, but they are the origin of many of the foreign students and highly skilled workers in the high-income countries of North America, Europe and Australasia. Above all, the global reach of Japanese and South Korean professional, technical and managerial employees reflects the global scale of those countries' companies – the Toyotas, Hyundais, Hitachis, Sonys and Samsungs of this world.

Yet at the same time, Japan and South Korea are two of the most important destinations for migrants from other East Asian countries. The People's Republic of China (PRC) and the countries of Southeast Asia (plus Korea in the case of Japan) represent the main source countries of foreign permanent residents. This is so despite the fact that both countries' governments have, over the whole post-war period and despite very low birth rates, set themselves firmly against large-scale immigration.

The other two countries in Northeast Asia could hardly be more different. North Korea remains a country of essentially zero immigration, and of escapees rather than emigrants (since permission to leave is not normally given). The Soviet Union between 1945 and 1990 was almost equally closed to migration in and out, but since its collapse and the end of the Cold War, migration across the borders of Russia has returned, and some of these movements have become highly politically controversial.

7.1 Japanese emigration

After World War II the Japanese government negotiated for a resumption of emigration to Latin American countries (see Chapter 2, section 2.3), and about 65,000 left Japan under these schemes in the period before 1965. Poverty in Japan was severe in the early post-war period, and it was widely agreed that the country was overpopulated. It was also argued that the country faced an extra burden from the forced resettlement back in Japan of many former emigrants to Korea, China and Taiwan.

By the mid-1960s, however, things were changing quickly. Japan had entered its 'high-growth' period. Emigration of Japan's poor fizzled out. Japan's cities were booming and there were lots of jobs for working-class youngsters in construction, manufacturing industry and the service sector. Now there was no need for them to leave the country. However, almost as soon as the working classes ceased to leave, the middle classes began to take their place. Professional, technical and managerial workers were posted by large Japanese companies to the far-flung places that became, initially, just markets for their products, but subsequently became their off-shore sites for production. Alongside this internationalization of Japanese manufacturing, Japanese banks also set up offices in the capital cities and main commercial centres of high-income countries around the world, most notably in London and New York, but also in smaller financial cities such as Dusseldorf. This posting abroad of Japanese men, sometimes alone, but often with their families, resulted in the sudden emergence of Japanese enclave communities around the world, both in the major cities and in towns close to the centres of manufacturing production. Japanese schools, letting agencies, travel agencies, logistics companies, karaoke bars, food shops and restaurants became part of the urban landscapes of both Western cities and cities in developing countries. Gender role segregation – men earn the money, women raise the children – ensured that hardly any women were posted abroad in this way. When the women did migrate (and often they did not), they were 'trailing spouses'; they set up home, looked after their children's education, and formed the core of the social life of the tightly knit, but hierarchically structured, Japanese community.

Sometime around 1990 a strange thing happened: the emigrant Japanese communities that were located in the largest cities quietly transformed themselves from patriarchal, business-oriented, 'salaryman'-centred expat enclave communities into diverse 'communities' of lifestyle and career development migrants, consisting of students, women young and old (many of them 'cultural refugees' – see Chapter 1), artists and performers, and many others who had no connections at all with corporate Japan. These new migrants, mostly highly educated people, of Japanese descent but sometimes no longer of Japanese nationality (for example, if they married locals), now form an active and often socially progressive part of the *de facto* multicultural global cities (for example, Los Angeles) in which they now live.

So what this means is that while economic migrants (for example, transferees within large corporations) continue to be a significant part of Japanese emigration, they have been joined more recently by cultural refugees from Japan (often in the creative industries), by students (especially postgraduates – many of them women), and by marriage migrants (again, many of them women). Finally, a small number of emigrants from Japan are retirement migrants seeking pleasant social and scenic environments in countries where the cost of living is lower than in Japan. Malaysia has been a significant destination for these retirement migrations.

7.2 Korean emigration (South and North)

Some of the points made above about Japanese emigration apply also to emigration from South Korea. Korean corporate enclave communities are found around the world in those cities and countries where large-scale foreign investments have occurred. Also, in South Korea, as in Japan, many local women became the brides of US servicemen posted to their country, and returned with their husbands to the USA at the end of their tour of duty.

Yet there are several features of post-war Korean emigration that are truly unique. The first is related to one of the legacies of the ferocious Korean War in the early 1950s. South Korea became the leading country for the adoption of babies. Westerners, notably from North America and Northern Europe, adopted 148,000 of Korean babies and brought them up as their own children. In many ways this was a merciful release for these children; life for poor families in South Korea in the 1950s and 1960s was very hard, and the children generally went to affluent professional households in high-income countries. However, it could hardly be otherwise than that complex issues of ethnic and social identity have accompanied, and continue to accompany, the journeys through childhood, into adulthood, and now sometimes into old age of these adoptees.

Second, South Korean construction companies and their workforces played a particularly significant role in the economic boom that accompanied the shift of wealth to Saudi Arabia and the Persian Gulf countries following the sharp increases in the price of oil in the mid- and late 1970s. The outflow of male contract workers to the Middle East peaked at around 150,000 in 1982. Emigration to the Persian Gulf was the dominant feature of Korean international migration at that time. It brought significant remittance income to South Korea, thereby reducing the balance of payments constraint on economic growth.

Third, Korean emigration to the USA had some distinctly specific features. These were rather poignantly revealed at the time of the Los Angeles riots in 1992 when ethnic Koreans and their businesses, mostly small convenience stores, were the main target for the anger and violence of the black population of south-central Los Angeles following the beating up of Rodney King by white police officers. Korean immigrants were strongly represented in the small business community, and, operating in areas that insurers avoided, they suffered not only the hatred and threatening behaviour of the black residents (towards whom, it should be said, some had racially prejudiced attitudes), but also the full financial loss when the businesses were trashed or burnt down.

Finally, in the last 20 years or so, a more middle- or even upper middle-class form of emigration has evolved. Like the education systems in neighbouring countries such as Japan and the PRC, the South Korean system puts enormous pressure on the child to succeed, especially at the university entrance exam stage. However, success in South Korea in a global world is constrained by the limited international status of the Korean language, so, even more than is the case elsewhere, international success requires fluency in English. Families will go to extreme lengths to ensure that their children not only learn in a supportive, high-quality but 'laid-back' environment, but in an environment where the teaching medium is English. To achieve this they sometimes choose to split up, with the mother and child, or children, living in an English-speaking country (the USA, Canada, Australia, New Zealand or the UK), while the father continues to work in South Korea or in a non-English-speaking country. Such families are called *kirogi gasok*, meaning 'wild geese families' – the metaphor referring not only to their remarkable spatial mobility but also to the dependable commitment of a mating pair of geese towards each other, and towards their offspring.

Emigration from North Korea is a world apart. First, North Korea is one of the few remaining countries in the world where permission to leave has to be obtained (and would normally not be granted). Emigration is tantamount to treason because it implies a rejection of the socialist project (*Juche*) begun by the country's founder and 'Dear Leader', Kim Il Sung. So, when people emigrate they very predominantly do so as criminals, as escapees (the small exception to this are the 65,000 – and growing – North Koreans who work in state-run work programmes in Russia, and in the Persian Gulf countries, notably Qatar). The fear of these 'illegal' emigrants being returned to North Korea to face social stigma and the wrath of the regime places them in an extraordinarily vulnerable position in the country to which they escape – the PRC. Thus, especially during the famine period when surveillance of the borders was weak, many desperate migrants left North Korea for China, where they typically led an underground life, some of them as semi-slave labour, others as the bought wives of Chinese farmers. A small number travel across China, enter, under high-risk conditions, a Southeast Asian country (usually Thailand), and then, through the South Korean Embassy, achieve passage to South Korea. About 25,000 North Koreans now live in South Korea. Despite the assistance they receive, both through official and NGO channels, they find it extraordinarily difficult to adjust to South Korean workplace and home life cultures.

Emigration from the Russian Far East into East Asia is insignificant compared with the out-migration westwards to the rest of Russia. There is a small Russian community in Japan (centred on Niigata) and young Russian women are sometimes recruited for East Asia's fashion and hospitality industries.

7.3 'Oldcomer' immigrants in Japan

The big story of post-war immigration to Japan is undoubtedly the arrival of the 'newcomers' – that is, the arrival, mostly since the 1980s, of migrants from East and Southeast Asia and Latin America. However, the picture of Japan as a country of immigration would be incomplete without considering what happened after 1950 to those who had migrated there earlier, during the three or four decades before 1950. They came from Korea (mostly from its southern regions, and especially from Cheju Island) and from Taiwan, and they arrived as Japanese citizens, albeit as colonial subjects. By 1952, however, their status had been altered – they were now foreigners. This meant that they had limited political and social rights, their pathways to social promotion were hampered (for example, through barriers to access higher education), they were banned from certain occupations (notably in the public sector), and they had difficulty travelling outside Japan. It is not surprising, then, that upward social mobility was sought through the small independent business sector (a well-known but nevertheless atypical example being the ownership of 'one-armed bandit' (*pachinko*) gambling parlours). Over time, these permanent resident foreigners saw their social rights improved, travel restrictions lifted, and barriers to employment lowered, but it remains remarkable to almost everyone except those within the Japanese establishment (and perhaps the xenophobic right wing), that most of the second-, third- and fourth-generation descendants of early–mid 20th-century migrants are still not Japanese citizens today. Naturalization has occurred, of course, but it is usually associated with inter-marriage – that is, the increasingly common marriage of a 'Korean' to a Japanese national. Not even Germany has held on to the *jus sanguinis* (right to citizenship through blood line) principle as determinedly as this!

People of Korean descent became divided between those who identified with South Korea (members of *Mindan*) and those who, usually because of their anti-imperialist and pro-socialist principles, identified with North Korea (members of *Chongryun*). This latter group, although physically located in Japan, educated their children in (old-fashioned) Korean in North Korean schools (under pictures of Kim Il Sung) and in a North Korean university, all paid for by the North Korean government – amazing! The Japanese government offered them a chance to migrate to North Korea in the 1960s and many of them took it. What resulted was one of the most bizarre migrations in modern history: a return migration that took people whose origins were in South Korea, though many had been born in Japan, and 'returned' them to North Korea. Rejoicing as they left Japan, they thought that they were going to a socialist paradise. How courageous they were. How cruelly sad was the outcome.

7.4 'Newcomer' immigrants in Japan: 'multicultural coexistence'

For a long time after 1950, the 'oldcomer' migrants and their descendants, numbering about 600,000, dominated the foreign resident population of Japan. Despite rapid economic growth through the 1960s, 1970s and 1980s, Japan remained closed to immigration, at least, that is, on paper. In practice, small communities of foreign migrant populations established themselves: Iranian, Nepalese and Pakistani male factory and workshop workers in and around Tokyo, Filipino and Thai hostesses and sex workers working in city-centre clubs and in places such as the *onsen* (hot spring bathing) resorts scattered around the extended capital region, and Chinese male factory and agricultural workers located in both the cities and the countryside. Many migrants at this time were illegal, or to be more precise, were legal entrants to Japan, but became illegal through overstaying their visas. Despite language problems and the difficulties of adjusting to Japanese culture, people were desperate to work in Japan because jobs were plentiful, wages were high, and the Japanese currency (especially after 1985) was strong.

By 1990 the increase in the number of people (including returnee migrants) coming to live in Japan was so great that it outpaced the growth of Japanese people emigrating from Japan: Japan became a country of net immigration. That this turning point coincided with the end of the high-growth period (the bursting of the so-called 'bubble economy') and the start of Japan's 'lost decade' of zero growth, definitely calls for explanation: how could a country that was switching from high growth to no growth be switching at the same time from net emigration to net immigration (see Box 5.1)? Part, but only part, of the answer lies in the arrival of a new migration stream, the *Nikkeijin* – that is, people of Japanese descent coming from Latin America. They, and many new arrivals from East, South and Southeast Asia brought the total number of foreign residents to over 1.6 million by the time of the 2010 Census (but note that this is still less than 2% of the population of Japan).

Data from the 1990, 2000 and 2010 Censuses can be used to provide an overview of Japan's immigrant populations (Figures 7.1 and 7.2). Koreans no longer constitute the largest group of foreign nationals living in Japan. At 423,000 in 2010 they have a spatial distribution that reflects their original role as factory workers, construction workers and miners when they, or their parents or grandparents, came, or were brought, to Japan in the 1910–45 colonial period. They are thus heavily concentrated in the Kansai region (Osaka, Hyogo and Kyoto Prefectures), with outliers in Tokyo, Aichi and Yamaguchi Prefectures. Perhaps, then, it is surprising that their occupational structure now differs only slightly from that of the host population. They are over-represented in the personal services and manager/owner categories and under-represented in public-sector employment, but no longer are they heavily concentrated in the blue-collar working class. One would be correct to speculate that the newcomers amongst the Korean nationals would be differently distributed from the oldcomers, with many more being located in the Tokyo metropolitan region and very few in Kansai. In fact, 16.3% of Tokyo's Koreans arrived in the five years before the 2010 Census, compared with only 6.1% in Japan as a whole.

The Chinese, at 460,000 in 2010, now form the largest group of foreign nationals, their numbers having grown rapidly over the last 20 years. They are distributed throughout central main island Japan (Honshu), but with a heavy concentration in Tokyo Prefecture. Once again, personal services are over-represented, but so too are blue-collar occupations (including, especially recently, farm work), and, unlike other immigrant groups from Asia, there are many Chinese nationals employed in professional and technical jobs (note that

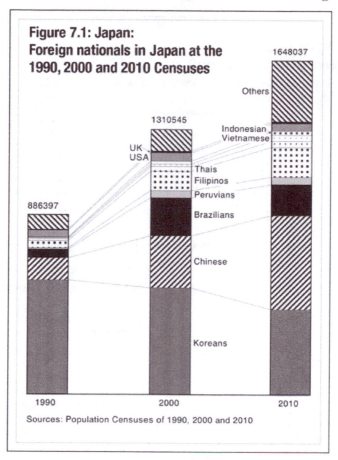

Figure 7.1: Japan: Foreign nationals in Japan at the 1990, 2000 and 2010 Censuses

Sources: Population Censuses of 1990, 2000 and 2010

the figures include migrants from Hong Kong). The nationals from the four main Southeast Asian countries numbered 224,000 in 2010. Those from the Philippines (146,000) and Thailand (30,000) are predominantly female and live in the outer city-regions of Tokyo (especially the Thais) and Nagoya (especially the Filipinos). They are very heavily concentrated in the personal services and blue-collar worker categories; however, the number of male Filipino factory workers has also recently increased substantially. Other Southeast Asians, Vietnamese (30,000) and Indonesians (19,000) are more widely distributed, are mostly male, and are heavily concentrated in blue-collar employment. The 'others' category in Figure 7.1 includes South Asians, whose numbers have greatly increased in the recent period.

This leaves two main groups, both very different from the ones we have discussed so far. The first are the Latin American *Nikkeijin*, the migrants of Japanese descent coming mostly from Brazil and Peru, but also from Bolivia, Colombia and Paraguay (note that there are also a small number of *Nikkeijin*

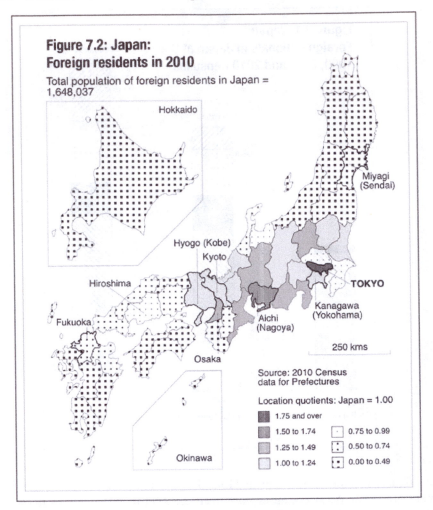

Figure 7.2: Japan:
Foreign residents in 2010

Total population of foreign residents in Japan =
1,648,037

Source: 2010 Census
data for Prefectures

Location quotients: Japan = 1.00

- 1.75 and over
- 1.50 to 1.74
- 1.25 to 1.49
- 1.00 to 1.24
- 0.75 to 0.99
- 0.50 to 0.74
- 0.00 to 0.49

returnees from the Philippines). There were 190,000 nationals from Brazil and
Peru living in Japan in 2010 (but many others who retained their Japanese
citizenship). Their spatial distribution is very distinctive: they are most decidedly not to be found in Tokyo itself; rather, they are living in the small and
medium-sized cities around and to the west of Tokyo (especially near to
Nagoya), precisely where the companies that supply parts to the vehicle, electrical goods and electronic equipment industries are located. They are almost
totally employed in blue-collar jobs (around three times the national average in
2000), and, perhaps partly due to the fact that they are recent migrants to
Japan, they are highly segregated at the local level from both the Japanese
population and from other immigrant groups.

Finally, nationals from Western countries (48,000, for example, from the USA and the UK) live overwhelmingly in Tokyo (with very minor concentrations in the prefectures containing the cities of Yokohama, Kyoto and Kobe). They are predominantly male, and they are, to a quite remarkable extent, concentrated in professional, technical and managerial occupations. There are, in addition, about 48,000 US military personnel based in Japan, half of whom are located in Okinawa.

To generalize, the migrants from Southeast Asia and Latin America tend to be manual working class; the migrants from Northeast Asia (South Korea and China) are more mixed and include many students and professionals; the migrants from Western countries tend to be managers and professionals working in international business, but some of them are English-language teachers (such as the young graduates who teach for a year or two on the JET programme). Japanese nationals returning to Japan tend to be professionals and managers, many of them as intra-organizational transferees, others having completed postgraduate education abroad.

In their very different ways all these migrants add diversity to a population that tends to see itself as mono-ethnic – as uniquely uniform in race, language and culture. Herein lies a problem, because despite the rhetoric of first the 'internationalization' (*kokusaika*) of Japanese society, and more recently of 'multicultural coexistence' (*tabunka kyousei*), the reality is that many, perhaps most, Japanese find it difficult, if not impossible, to accept that people born and brought up outside Japan could ever become part of 'their' society. Being polite to foreigners? No problem, it comes naturally. Being friends with foreigners abroad and good hosts if they visit Japan? No problem, it is good to compare the way that things are done in other cultures with what 'we Japanese' do in our country. Sharing your hot spring (*onsen*) break with foreigners? That is another matter. 'They' (the foreigners) do not (indeed cannot) understand the many rituals and emotions surrounding taking a bath in a hot spring – only Japanese people share that (tacit) understanding! I exaggerate, of course, but the gap between the enthusiasm among elites for Japan to sign up to international agreements on human rights, racial and sexual equality, etc., and the putting into practice of non-discrimination and openness to difference in daily life is real enough.

There are two arenas in which this gap is rather embarrassingly exposed. The first is refugee policy. Japan is fully signed up to international conventions on refugee protection and support. Japan's contribution, however, to 'sharing the burden' of refugee support is miniscule, and this is so despite the fact that the head of the UNHCR from 1991–2001 was a Japanese national, Sadako Ogata! Japan does have a small number of Vietnamese, Kurdish and Burmese refugees, but the success rate for asylum seekers in Japan is extremely low, and provision for their settlement is minimal. The second arena is immigration policy implementation. The Japanese government, the right-of-centre Liberal Democrat Party, in the context of an overall policy of not permitting labour immigration, meets the needs of its friends, the employers, by allowing several 'side-door' mechanisms for them to recruit foreign blue-collar manual workers. The main one has been the 1990 Act that allowed the immigration and settlement of people of Japanese descent from Latin America, but another mechanism that has been very significant has been the trainee programmes that have allowed firms to recruit mostly Chinese labourers, ostensibly to provide them with training, but actually, in almost all cases, to use them as cheap foreign labour. The point is that central government, having signed up to agreements about the treatment of non-nationals, then leaves it to firms and local authorities to provide for the daily needs of these workers (such as housing, education, and health) – a provision that is very patchy in coverage and often falls way short of international standards (revealed, for example, in the low school attendance rates of *Nikkeijin* children).

It is thought that about 5% of the immigrant foreigners in Japan are 'irregular', most of them having entered the country legally as tourists or visitors but having overstayed their visas. The size of the irregular immigrant population probably peaked around 1994 when it was thought that nearly 300,000 people had overstayed. They mostly work in the urban informal economy, 'under the radar' of the authorities, often sharing overcrowded accommodation with co-ethnic immigrants. For much of the time they are of no interest to the police, but periodically, the salacious reporting in the media of crimes (allegedly) committed by foreigners, provokes a crackdown on 'illegals', leading to their arrest and deportation. Unfortunately, the Japanese judicial process is not flawless when it comes to the conviction of foreigners; courts, for example, have attracted criticism for the poor quality of their interpretation services.

Despite the many differences in language and culture, most international migrants to Japan, being lively young adults, settle down fairly quickly, become socially embedded in their neighbourhoods, and adjust well to the institutions of the host society. This is partially revealed by the degree of socio-spatial segregation of different immigrant populations. Broadly speaking, the Koreans and the Filipinos show the lowest levels of segregation from the Japanese population (with indices of dissimilarity of 24%). This is hardly surprising, (i) because the Koreans are now second-, third- and fourth-generation immigrants and have lost much of their cultural and linguistic distinctiveness, and (ii) because many of the Filipinos are women who are now married to, or in a relationship with, Japanese men. Next come the Chinese (at 32%), then those from the USA (35%), both with middle levels of segregation, while the Brazilians (37%) and Peruvians (44%) have the highest levels. Again, this can be explained, especially in the case of the Latin Americans, by their relatively recent arrival, and in the case of the Americans, by their relative affluence (and thus their confinement to the more expensive districts of the city).

7.5 Female migration to Japan from Southeast Asia

The migration of women to Japan from Southeast Asia, initially largely from Thailand and the Philippines, now also from Vietnam and Indonesia, deserves special attention. Much to the annoyance of female students, highly educated wives and independent professional women from these countries, most Southeast Asian women living in Japan are assumed to be either 'entertainers' or 'marriage migrants'. Both are looked down upon by a majority of Japanese people, the former (the *japayuki*) because they are regarded as 'living off immoral earnings' as sex workers or club hostesses, the latter because they are regarded as being so poor and desperate that they were forced by their circumstances to marry those Japanese men (such as farmers) who could not find Japanese wives. Needless to say, the reality is more complicated than this. Take, for example, the Filipino brides of Touhoku farmers. Despite extensive coverage in the media, their numbers are very small, frequently the marriages are, to the surprise of many, successful, and most Filipino (and now Chinese) women married to Japanese men live in any case not in the northern countryside, but in the urban areas of central Japan. Stereotypes typically contain some truth, but they also usually misrepresent the wider picture. Whatever the circumstances that brought them to Japan or their degree of agency in that process, Southeast Asian female migrants now occupy many different work and family roles, ranging from successful entrepreneurs to destitute unemployed, and from family linchpin with much-loved bi-racial (*haafu*) children to abandoned mother with stateless children. Most are, of course, situated well away from these extremes, but unfortunately with a bias towards the less fortunate end of the range.

Much of the debate about immigration policy in Japan today focuses on the fact that Japan's falling population is ageing fast due to high longevity (life expectation at birth is the highest in the world) and low fertility (Japan's total fertility rate has been well below replacement level (2.1) for 40 years, and now stands at about 1.4). The argument goes that this ageing population needs to be looked after, and, since Japanese women are now in the labour force developing their own working lives, this caring will have to be done by foreign women brought to Japan from Southeast Asia.

Leaving aside the many weaknesses and omissions in this argument (relating, for example, to Japan's high wage costs, cramped housing conditions, changing gender relations, and weakening family system), the logic behind it has propelled the government into bilateral agreements with the Philippines and Indonesia to bring young women to Japan to train them to become *herupaa* – nurses and health-care workers. Unfortunately, the bar has been set so high (especially with respect to language proficiency), that of the few candidates for this programme who gain access to it, even fewer pass the exam to gain permanent residency in Japan. In addition, however, there is now a policy to trial the migration of foreign domestic workers to the Kansai region (Osaka). It is based on the argument that this would release the highly educated Japanese female workforce from domestic duties and would thereby result in the full realization of their economic potential. Maybe, but many would argue that the poor promotion of women in the Japanese labour market has little to do with their work-life balance, and that, knowing what has happened in Singapore and Hong Kong, one might be forgiven for asking what the cost of this development would be to the migrant women and their families in South and Southeast Asia?

Finally, the global reach of Japanese business and the frequency of Japanese international student migrations have resulted in many bi-cultural/bi-racial relationships and marriages. While most of these marriages result in Japanese women living outside Japan, a significant number of foreign partners and spouses, both male and female, now live (semi-)permanently in Japan. Since Japan does not permit dual citizenship, many of these partners retain the nationality of their country of birth.

7.6 Youth migration to Japan

Many young adults come to Japan to study. Those from Asian countries often take courses in scientific and technical subjects. They return with knowhow and skills (for example in structural engineering) that are useful both to them in their careers and to the economic development of their home countries. Others from Asian countries, however, came to Japan on student visas, but enter the workforce not as part-time workers (which they are allowed to do) but as full-time workers (which they are definitely not allowed to do). Students from Western countries often focus more on Japanese language and culture, some-times, of course, to advance a business career, but often simply because they want to meet the challenge of understanding a history and a culture that is very different from their own. In many cases they will teach English as a means of paying for their fees and living expenses.

Large numbers of young adult male immigrants, however, come to Japan on trainee visas organized by their Japan-based company employers. The condi-tions in which these young men work and live vary, but at its worst, this is nothing more than a 'scam' or ruse by which companies that are having trouble recruiting labour in Japan obtain a cheap, easily manageable and dependent labour force.

7.7 *Nikkeijin* migrants to Japan from Latin America

Of all the recent migrations to Japan, those of people of Japanese descent coming from Latin America (*Nikkeijin*) raise some of the most interesting issues. They were invited to migrate to Japan: (i) because they were desperately needed by Japanese manufacturers supplying the major 'big-brand' companies in the vehicle, electrical goods and electronic equipment industries; and (ii) because, as Japanese people, they represented no threat to the celebrated mono-cultural character of Japanese society (in contrast, it was thought, to migrants to the multicultural, conflict-ridden societies of North America and Western Europe).

There is no argument that the *Nikkeijin* performed their intended economic function to the letter. Many companies with contracts to supply parts to the big-brand producers quickly came to rely on workers from Brazil, Peru, Argentina, Bolivia, Dominican Republic, etc. (not all of whom were as descended from Japanese emigrants as they claimed), but their ethnicity came as a shock – they were truly 'strangers in the ethnic homeland' (Tsuda 2003). Few were fluent in Japanese, many were Catholic, most had no real connection with their origins in Japan, and all were culturally, socially, politically and emotionally Latin American. The paradox is that the *Nikkeijin* were encouraged to migrate to Japan because of their supposed Japaneseness (when, in fact, as soon became obvious, they were very unlike their Japanese hosts), while it is the Koreans who are still institutionally treated as foreigners (when in occupations, behaviours, and values they are, in fact, very Japanese). This 'un-Japanese' character of the *Nikkeijin* is partially represented by Figure 7.3 in Box 7.1. Distances 2 and 3 are particularly significant: the first represents the great identity distance between the 'returnees' and their 'hosts' in Japan; the second represents the even greater identity distance between the 'returnees' and the memories of Japan retained by their parents, grandparents and sometimes even great-grandparents who remain in Latin America. The twist to the *Nikkeijin* story is that as a result of the poor performance of the Japanese economy in recent years, and especially since 2008, there has been some return migration of *Nikkeijin* 'returnees' to Latin America.

Box 7.1 Migration, culture, emotion and identity

There is something strange about the way we study migration. (These first few paragraphs draw heavily upon Fielding 1992.) We know, often from personal experience, but also from family talk, that moving home from one place to another is nearly always a major event – one of those around which an individual's biography is built. The feelings associated with migration are usually complicated; the decision to migrate is typically difficult to make, and the outcome usually involves mixed emotions. An anticipatory excitement about life in the new place often coexists with anxieties about the move; pleasure about leaving the old place is often disturbed by the feeling that one has almost betrayed those who remain behind. Migration tends to expose one's personality. It expresses one's loyalties and reveals one's values and attachments (often previously hidden). It is not just about material gain (the focus of most migration research), it is a statement of a person's worldview, and is, therefore, an extremely cultural event.

What then, in the context of migration, is 'culture'? Culture can be viewed as a property of individuals and groups; it arises historically through the sharing of practices and the inter-subjective negotiation of meanings, and it refers both to deeply felt values and to all those things that are taken for granted in our relations to others as we live out our daily lives. Furthermore, although far from being ephemeral, cultures change over time (as is shown below, this is important for migration studies), and in any particular country (even in Japan), there is not one culture but many, and this plurality of cultures has a structure of its own, with some cultures dominant and others subordinate.

So migration is a cultural event and it stirs strong emotions. Some of these emotions are very positive. Migration can be experienced as a kind of 'stairway to heaven' – full of excitement and challenge. Examples are when migration is experienced as freedom – freedom from the familiar, the routines of family life, the restrictions that arise when one's position in society is known and fixed; freedom from obligations to family, friends and neighbours, to take risks away from the solicitous gaze of those who love you; freedom from the moral order of the society in which one is embedded, to decide which moral code one is going to live by; freedom to present oneself as a different sort of person, indeed, to become a different sort of person. Migration can also be experienced as a new beginning. It allows us to 'wipe the slate clean' on past failures and to start afresh. It also facilitates changes in our social lives; one can avoid the anguish of rural loneliness, for example, by migrating to the city as one 'joins in', or avoid the stress of modern corporate working lives by migrating to a beautiful rural or coastal place as one 'opts out'. Finally, migration can be experienced as 'going places'; the excitement and challenge comes from being active, making tough decisions, grasping opportunities, moving up in the world. Since the status and style of a place rubs off on the person who lives there, migration can be partly interpreted as the lifetime search for the 'right' place – the emotional 'home'.

However, 'going places' can subtly morph into 'moving on', so that migration becomes habitual – a kind of drug to which the hyper-mobile are addicted.

Other emotions associated with migration are far more negative. It can be experienced as being 'crippled inside' – full of sadness and the confusion that arises from losing one's roots. Examples are when migration is experienced as rupture – as when raw hurt and jangled emotions accompany the breakup of a close personal relationship, or, more generally, when the migrant is rejected by those around him or her. Migration is often accompanied by a deeply felt loss of contentment; one aches to be back in those landscapes and meeting places where one was so happy in the past; to lose the familiar, the trusted, the permanent can be highly unsettling, unnerving, disorienting. Migration can also be experienced as 'facing the inevitable' – confronting the fact that one has reached a dead end and that migration is the only way out. Sometimes this situation is associated with the conviction that one has been born and brought up in the wrong place at the wrong time – that one is simply ill-fated – and that absolutely nothing can be done about it. The feelings attached to migration can just as easily be those of frustration and failure as anticipation and celebration.

So emotionally charged is migration that it is often difficult, or even impossible, for an individual to admit that his or her migration project has failed. To return without success (that is, without money, goods, useful contacts, new skills, amazing experiences) is to admit stupidity, gullibility, lack of cunning, lack of drive or ambition, possibly even lack of courage – you are a loser, 'big time'. What do you say to those who had such high hopes for your success, and who often paid a heavy price, frequently both emotionally and monetarily, to help you migrate? So powerful are these emotions that the migrant will sometimes stay away far longer than intended in the desperate hope that his or her fortunes will change and that the project will eventually be counted as a success.

Culture and emotion come together in the feelings that people have towards the places and people, and, by extension, the countries that they have left behind, and in which they now live. Where is your home? Where do your loyalties lie? Are you Brazilian or Japanese (or both), Chinese or Indonesian, Vietnamese or Korean? The trouble with posing the question in this way is that it tends to 'buy into' (or conform to) an 'essentialist' view of culture and ethnicity – a view that exaggerates the stability and coherence of the values and beliefs that we hold. In reality, cultures and ethnicities are malleable and fluid, fuzzy and opaque.

It has been shown already in this book that ethnic differences, and the conflicts that have sometimes focused on those differences, have encouraged the migration of ethnic minorities. What has not yet received attention is the way that these ethnic differences can be, and indeed almost always are, altered by the experience of migration. Despite a determination, sometimes explicitly expressed, to defend minority ethnic and national origin distinctiveness, one's values and behaviours, assumptions and aspirations, tend to adjust quietly – typically towards the norms and expectations, the 'taken-for-granted' worlds – of those amongst whom you now live.

This line of argument can be explored using the case of the Latin American *Nikkeijin* – that is, people of Japanese descent living in Brazil, Peru, Bolivia, Paraguay, Dominican Republic, etc., some of whom have 'returned' to Japan in the recent period (especially after 1990). The situations of Korean ethnic 'returnees' from northeast China (the *Josenjok*) and the Kuomintang- descended 'returnees' to the PRC from Taiwan (the *Waishengren*) are, in many respects, parallel cases. As the lives of *Nikkeijin* unfolded in South America, and each new generation lost the 'burden' of a directly experienced Japanese past, their Japaneseness tended to become something that was 'performed' by them, especially on special occasions, rather than lived out in daily practice (although this was more the case, perhaps, in cosmopolitan São Paulo than in a remote *colonia* in Bolivia). While most remained 'emotionally' Japanese, they increasingly spoke Portuguese or Spanish, embraced Catholicism, adopted Latin American forms of sociability, and in many cases took citizenship of their South American country of residence (which of course, according to the rules, meant giving up their Japanese citizenship). It should come as no surprise, therefore, that distance 2 in Figure 7.3 (feeling 'South American' in Japan) should matter so much to the 'returnee' migrants – and also to their Japanese hosts. Over time, and as a result of subtle cultural transformations, they truly had become 'strangers in their ethnic homeland'. This helps to explain, alongside the low levels of occupational mobility and lack of niches in small and medium-sized firms, the very low degree of upward social mobility of the *Nikkeijin* in Japan (often despite their middle-class backgrounds and formal education assets). So little social promotion has there been that they have come to be seen as an instance of 'negative assimilation'.

References

Fielding, T., 1992, Migration and culture, in Champion, T. and Fielding, T. (eds), *Migration Processes and Patterns Vol. 1: Research Progress and Prospects*. London: Belhaven Press, 201–214.

Fielding, T., 2010, The occupational and geographical locations of transnational immigrant minorities in Japan, in Kee, P. and Yoshimatsu, H. (eds), *Global Movements in the Asia Pacific*. Singapore: World Scientific, 93–121.

Sasaki, K., 2013, To return or not to return: the changing meaning of mobility among Japanese Brazilians, 1908–2010, in Xiang, B., Yeoh, B.S.A. and Toyota, M. (eds), *Return: Nationalizing Transnational Mobility in Asia*. Durham, NC: Duke University Press, 21–38.

Figure 7.3: Schematic (and necessarily simplistic) representation of the changing national and ethic identities of Latin American Nikkeijin

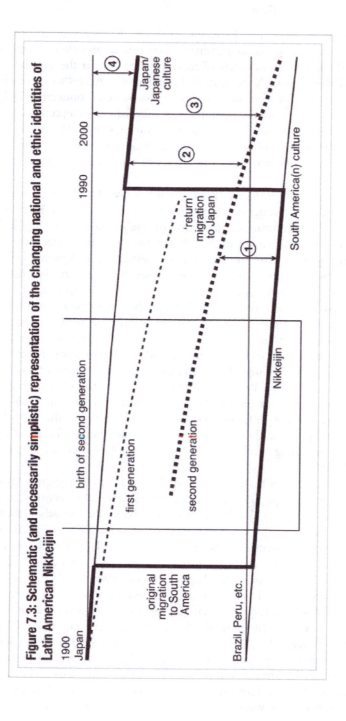

7.8 Korean immigration

There are numerous similarities between the South Korean immigration story and that for Japan. A longstanding antipathy towards large-scale immigration is combined with significant numbers of foreign migrants 'on the ground'. Like Japan, South Korea is now 'a country of immigration'. Access to citizenship is predominantly on the basis of *jus sanguinis* or blood-line connection. Priority for entry is given to 'co-ethnic' migrants and, like Japan, exceptions are made for migrants who belong to business or professional elites. However, South Korea is also interestingly different from Japan, mostly because of recent changes in policy resulting in part from the efforts of a strong and effective NGO sector.

Over most of the last 100 years Korea/South Korea has been a country of net emigration. This net emigration continued after the end of the Korean War in 1953. As a poor, war-torn country ruled by the military, there was little to attract migrants to South Korea in this early post-war period. US forces were stationed in many regions of the country, but despite many liaisons with local women, very few servicemen stayed on after their tour of duty. Furthermore, during the early days when South Korea became a newly industrialized country and experienced rapid economic growth from the 1970s onwards, there was little impact on immigration. This was largely because of the large reserves of indigenous labour located in rural areas and more remote regions (notably the southwest quarter of the country) which could be drawn upon to meet this new demand for labour. Then things changed. As industrialization and urbanization continued into the 1980s and 1990s, labour shortages began to appear, and the need for immigrant blue-collar workers materialized. The build-up of immigration began in the 1990s but became especially rapid in the early 2000s. Most of these migrants settled in the Seoul metropolitan region, and in the industrial zone stretching south from Seoul towards Daejeon (see Figures 7.4 and 7.5, and Table 7.1).

The source countries of these migrant workers fall into two groups: (i) those with co-ethnic Korean populations resulting from early 20th-century emigrations, notably the PRC, but also the Central Asian Republics (mostly Uzbekistan and Kazakhstan, and Russia – the *Koryo-saram*); and (ii) those without co-ethnic populations – mostly countries in Southeast Asia. The largest numbers in the first group come from the northeast provinces of China, and especially from the Yanbian Korean Autonomous Region in Jilin Province. These Chinese of Korean ancestry (*Joseonjok*) bear a similar relationship to contemporary South Korea as the *Nikkeijin* do to Japan; that is, they are welcomed because of their Koreanness, only to be subsequently found to be very culturally Chinese. Another similarity with the *Nikkeijin* is that many of these migrations involve 'brain waste' because often the well-paid low-level jobs that the immigrants do in South Korea call for lower levels of skill, formal qualifications and education than the migrants possess. The *Joseonjok* are heavily concentrated in the Seoul capital region where they work in both the manufacturing and service sectors.

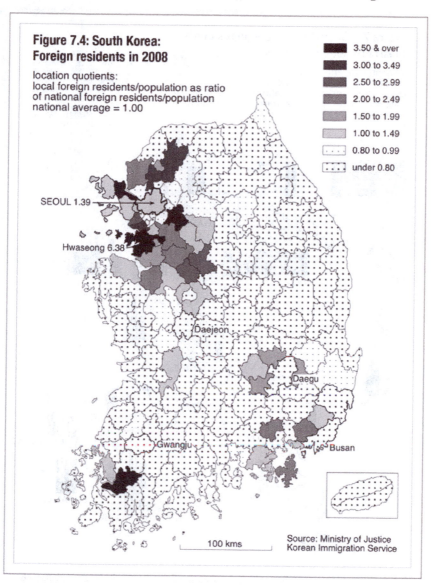

Figure 7.4: South Korea:
Foreign residents in 2008

location quotients:
local foreign residents/population as ratio
of national foreign residents/population
national average = 1.00

3.50 & over
3.00 to 3.49
2.50 to 2.99
2.00 to 2.49
1.50 to 1.99
1.00 to 1.49
0.80 to 0.99
under 0.80

SEOUL 1.39

Hwaseong 6.38

Daejeon

Daegu

Gwangju

Busan

100 kms

Source: Ministry of Justice
Korean Immigration Service

Immigrants from Uzbekistan and Kazakhstan perform a similar economic role as those from the PRC (as 'gap fillers', doing the dirty, difficult and dangerous jobs that are avoided by the indigenous population), but they are sometimes also (as are some of the *Joseonjok*) marriage migrants – women who are recruited to become the marriage partners of hard-to-marry South Korean men (again biased towards rural small-business owners such as farmers).

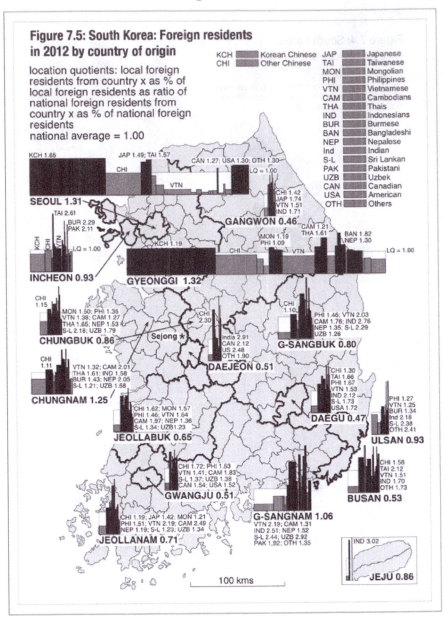

Figure 7.5: South Korea: Foreign residents in 2012 by country of origin

Immigrants from Southeast Asia (but also from Mongolia) fall in turn into two main groups: the first are those, both men and women, who are employed as manual workers in factories and on building sites especially in the industrial zones around and to the south of the capital region; second, many women from Southeast Asia come to South Korea to marry Korean men. Vietnamese nationals, for example, show a spatial distribution that reflects this process. They

Table 7.1 South Korea: regional distribution of foreign residents in 2012 (LQs)

	SE	BU	DG	IN	GJ	DJ	UL	SJ	GG	GW	CB	CN	JB	JN	SB	SN	JJ
Korean Chinese	1.65	0.28	0.31	0.81	0.32	0.28	0.90	0.47	1.19	0.38	0.60	0.69	0.32	0.38	0.30	0.31	0.19
Other Chinese	0.97	1.58	1.30	0.99	1.72	2.30	0.53	0.97	0.78	1.42	1.15	1.11	1.62	1.19	1.10	0.66	1.80
Japanese	1.49	1.30	0.82	0.64	0.89	1.14	0.55	0.53	0.69	1.74	0.81	0.94	1.20	1.42	0.84	0.66	0.89
Taiwanese	1.57	2.12	1.66	2.61	0.98	1.44	0.61	0.33	0.38	1.85	0.93	0.57	1.08	0.38	0.45	0.26	1.51
Mongolian	0.86	0.44	0.53	1.26	0.81	1.16	1.14	1.47	1.19	1.23	1.50	0.84	1.57	1.21	0.82	0.63	1.00
Filipino	0.44	1.18	1.67	1.14	1.53	1.06	1.27	1.30	1.09	1.40	1.35	1.00	1.46	1.51	1.46	1.16	1.34
Vietnamese	0.23	1.51	1.53	1.06	1.41	1.02	1.25	1.98	0.82	1.51	1.38	1.32	1.64	2.19	2.03	2.19	1.60
Cambodian	0.10	0.75	1.05	0.70	1.83	0.71	0.87	1.60	1.21	1.93	1.27	2.01	1.97	2.49	1.76	1.31	1.66
Thai	0.21	0.58	0.57	1.42	0.99	0.44	0.45	2.09	1.61	0.98	1.65	1.61	1.00	1.09	1.00	0.95	0.58
Indonesian	0.10	1.70	2.12	1.23	1.23	0.46	0.95	1.71	0.80	1.71	1.06	1.58	0.91	1.11	2.76	2.51	3.02
Burmese	0.15	2.07	1.10	2.29	1.23	0.29	1.34	2.18	1.29	0.18	0.87	1.43	1.00	0.62	1.33	1.26	0.28
Bangladeshi	0.18	0.63	1.28	1.79	0.54	0.64	0.64	1.23	1.82	0.50	0.93	0.69	0.92	0.53	1.10	0.95	0.12
Nepalese	0.18	0.75	1.19	1.15	1.01	0.43	0.81	0.99	1.30	1.19	1.53	2.05	1.36	1.19	1.35	1.52	0.96
Indian	1.18	0.95	0.77	0.35	1.15	2.91	2.18	1.03	0.94	0.69	0.33	0.22	1.07	0.38	0.88	1.56	0.47
Sri Lankan	0.05	0.93	1.73	0.79	1.37	0.27	2.38	1.66	1.07	0.55	2.18	1.21	1.34	1.23	2.29	2.44	0.76
Pakistani	0.47	1.12	3.69	2.11	1.26	1.46	0.69	0.52	1.04	0.18	0.82	0.42	0.83	0.36	1.16	1.92	0.99
Uzbek	0.21	1.18	1.12	0.98	1.38	0.63	1.06	1.29	1.02	0.61	1.79	1.58	1.23	1.34	1.26	2.92	0.22
Canadian	1.27	2.06	2.04	0.83	1.54	2.12	1.09	0.79	0.66	1.79	0.83	0.49	0.87	1.02	0.73	0.64	2.05
US	1.30	1.51	1.72	0.73	1.52	2.48	1.18	0.88	0.69	1.45	0.72	0.67	0.81	0.68	0.93	0.80	1.67
Other	1.30	1.73	1.02	0.92	0.83	1.90	2.41	0.65	0.64	1.10	0.66	0.70	0.67	0.61	0.62	1.35	1.23

Source: Korean Immigration Service.
Notes: The figures are location quotients (local % in foreign residents from country x divided by national % from country x)
Country codes are the same as on Figure 7.5. Regional codes as follows: SE = Seoul; BU = Busan; DG = Daegu; IN = Incheon; GJ = Gwangju; DJ = Daejeon; UL = Ulsan; SJ = Sejong; GG = Gyeonggi; GW = Gangwon; CB = Chungcheongbuk; CN = Chungcheongnam; JB = Jeollabuk; JN = Jeollanam; SB = Geongsangbuk; SN = Geongsangnam; JJ = Jeju.

are especially concentrated in rural areas – their correlation at the county level with employment in agriculture, forestry and fishing is +0.75 – when most other immigrant groups are found in areas with urban functions such as trade and services (notably those from China and Taiwan, Russia and the USA). In the cases of migrants from the Philippines and Indonesia there is no urban or rural bias suggesting that the roles played by these migrants as both workers and marriage partners are multiple and complex (to take a specific example, many Filipino female sex workers live close to the bars and clubs located outside the US military bases).

Foreign nationals from countries having average incomes per capita that are higher than that of South Korea, tend through their strong links with the major corporations (the *chaebol*) and the government, to be heavily concentrated in the Seoul metropolitan region. The Japanese are an interesting exception, being located in rural areas and in areas with employment in hotels and catering, and in the culture and media industries, but marriage-related migration is also important, with a number of Japanese women marrying Korean men through religious connections.

Many of the generalizations made above are supported by the evidence presented in Figure 7.6 and Table 7.2. These show the visa categories for immigrant residents in 2012. Those coming from Southeast Asia and from the poorer countries of South Asia arrive very largely on E9 (guest worker) visas (which comprise 24.9% of the 219,000 entries during that year). Notice, however, the importance of F2 and F6 (marriage) migrants in the case of Vietnam and the Philippines, E6 (entertainers) in the case of the Philippines and Russia, and A1–3 visas (official/waiver) in the case of Thailand. This latter flow reflects the role of Thailand in channelling North Korean escapees to South Korea. In contrast, business (D7–9), university and language tutor (E2) visas dominate for those coming from high-income countries (plus India and Southwest Asia), and co-ethnic migrations (F4 visas) (which comprise 27.8% of all entries) dominate the flows from the PRC (85,800) and Uzbekistan.

7.9 Emigration from and immigration to the Russian Far East

The collapse of the Soviet system had devastating effects on the Russian Far East (RFE). Before 1989, the region had been essentially closed to international migration, but had figured importantly in interregional migration within the Soviet Union. Migrant workers and their families had been attracted to the RFE by high living standards underpinned by significant wage subsidies. By Soviet standards ordinary workers could earn a lot of money by working in this most inhospitable region. Yes, its winters were long and extraordinarily harsh, and yes, you were in the 'back of beyond', cut off for long periods from well-stocked shops, social gatherings, and decent medical and educational facilities; but you had status, you were the well-rewarded intrepid frontier heroes of a socialist society.

After 1991 everything changed. With freedom from communism came lower wages and higher unemployment, breakdowns in essential services (including electricity supply), fatalism towards the future (with crisis levels of

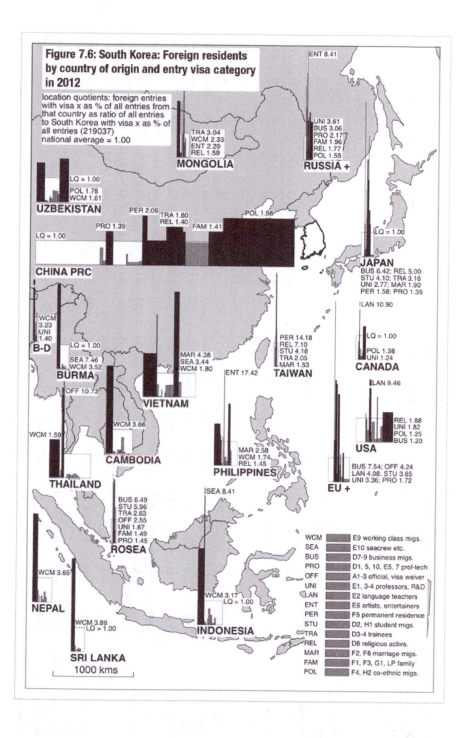

Figure 7.6: South Korea: Foreign residents by country of origin and entry visa category in 2012

location quotients: foreign entries with visa x as % of all entries from that country as ratio of all entries to South Korea with visa x as % of all entries (219037)
national average = 1.00

MONGOLIA
TRA 3.04
WCM 2.33
ENT 2.29
REL 1.59

ENT 8.41

RUSSIA +
UNI 3.61
BUS 3.06
PRO 2.17
FAM 1.96
REL 1.77
POL 1.55

UZBEKISTAN
LQ = 1.00
POL 1.78
WCM 1.61

CHINA PRC
LQ = 1.00
PRO 1.39
PER 2.06
TRA 1.60
REL 1.40
FAM 1.41
POL 1.98

JAPAN
LQ = 1.00
BUS 6.42; REL 5.00
STU 4.10; TRA 3.16
UNI 2.77; MAR 1.90
PER 1.58; PRO 1.35

B-D
WCM 3.23
UNI 1.40

BURMA
LQ = 1.00
SEA 7.46
WCM 3.52
OFF 10.73

VIETNAM
MAR 4.38
SEA 3.44
WCM 1.80

ENT 17.42

TAIWAN
PER 14.18
REL 7.10
STU 4.18
TRA 2.05
MAR 1.53

ILAN 10.90

CANADA
LQ = 1.00
POL 1.38
UNI 1.24

ILAN 9.46

CAMBODIA
WCM 3.66

THAILAND
WCM 1.59

PHILIPPINES
MAR 2.58
WCM 1.74
REL 1.45

USA
REL 1.88
UNI 1.82
POL 1.25
BUS 1.20

EU +
BUS 7.54; OFF 4.24
LAN 4.08; STU 3.65
UNI 3.36; PRO 1.72

ROSEA
BUS 6.49
STU 5.96
TRA 2.63
OFF 2.55
UNI 1.67
FAM 1.49
PRO 1.45

ISEA 8.41

NEPAL
WCM 3.65

INDONESIA
WCM 3.17
LQ = 1.00

SRI LANKA
WCM 3.86
LQ = 1.00

1000 kms

WCM — E9 working class migs.
SEA — E10 seacrew etc.
BUS — D7-9 business migs.
PRO — D1, 5, 10, E5, 7 prof-tech
OFF — A1-3 official, visa waiver
UNI — E1, 3-4 professors, R&D
LAN — E2 language teachers
ENT — E6 artists, entertainers
PER — F5 permanent residence
STU — D2, H1 student migs.
TRA — D3-4 trainees
REL — D6 religious activs.
MAR — F2, F6 marriage migs.
FAM — F1, F3, G1, LP family
POL — F4, H2 co-ethnic migs.

Table 7.2 South Korea: foreign residents by country of origin and entry visa category in 2012 (LQs)

FROM	WCM	SEA	BUS	PRO	OFF	UNI	LAN	ENT	PER	STU	TRA	REL	MAR	FAM	POL	Total
People's Republic of China	0.01	0.72	0.17	1.39	0.01	0.46	0.13	0.18	2.06	1.02	1.60	1.40	0.96	1.41	1.98	1.00
Japan	0.00	0.00	6.42	1.35	0.28	2.77	0.28	0.48	1.58	4.10	3.16	5.00	1.90	1.32	0.07	1.00
Taiwan	0.00	0.00	1.26	0.83	0.04	0.80	0.02	0.12	14.18	4.18	2.05	7.10	1.53	0.89	0.02	1.00
Mongolia	2.33	0.00	0.25	0.14	0.17	0.19	0.00	2.29	0.21	0.96	3.04	1.59	0.58	0.79	0.00	1.00
Philippines	1.74	0.00	1.28	1.04	0.09	1.18	0.00	17.42	0.17	0.35	0.17	1.45	2.58	0.61	0.00	1.00
Vietnam	1.80	3.44	0.05	0.51	0.02	0.28	0.00	0.00	0.14	0.48	0.50	0.08	4.38	0.62	0.00	1.00
Cambodia	3.66	0.00	0.00	0.10	0.08	0.00	0.00	0.00	0.02	0.15	0.12	0.17	0.67	0.05	0.00	1.00
Thailand	1.59	0.00	0.09	0.33	10.73	0.18	0.00	0.01	0.04	0.14	0.10	0.01	0.16	0.08	0.00	1.00
Indonesia	3.17	8.41	0.09	0.14	0.03	0.12	0.00	0.25	0.04	0.67	0.40	0.03	0.07	0.28	0.00	1.00
Myanmar	3.52	7.46	0.02	0.05	0.02	0.00	0.00	0.00	0.00	0.19	0.09	0.10	0.02	0.12	0.00	1.00
Bangladesh	3.23	0.05	0.77	0.57	0.12	1.40	0.00	0.00	0.16	0.79	0.15	0.06	0.23	1.19	0.00	1.00
Nepal	3.65	0.00	0.08	0.49	0.00	0.28	0.00	0.00	0.02	0.24	0.11	0.13	0.42	0.20	0.00	1.00
India	0.00	0.00	10.96	5.47	0.35	28.65	0.00	0.08	0.10	1.13	0.57	0.55	0.12	7.46	0.00	1.00
Sri Lanka	3.86	0.00	0.02	0.25	0.03	0.22	0.00	0.00	0.01	0.09	0.12	0.16	0.07	0.11	0.00	1.00
Pakistan	2.00	0.00	4.41	0.71	0.14	2.05	0.00	0.00	0.20	2.23	0.36	0.12	0.68	3.00	0.00	1.00
Uzbekistan	1.61	0.00	0.06	0.07	0.02	0.05	0.00	0.14	0.23	0.15	0.47	0.01	0.44	0.30	1.78	1.00
Canada	0.00	0.00	0.52	0.76	0.19	1.24	10.90	0.19	0.12	0.44	0.11	0.43	0.15	0.28	1.38	1.00
USA	0.00	0.00	1.20	0.94	0.49	1.82	9.46	0.45	0.14	0.86	0.12	1.88	0.14	0.65	1.25	1.00
Rest of Southeast Asia	0.00	0.00	6.49	1.45	2.55	1.67	0.00	0.27	0.09	5.96	2.63	0.37	0.50	1.49	0.01	1.00
Rest of Central Asia	0.60	0.00	0.36	1.54	0.11	0.19	0.00	0.31	0.22	2.31	1.20	0.00	1.02	0.52	1.52	1.00
Southwest Asia	0.00	0.00	10.02	1.61	2.69	3.43	0.00	0.00	0.05	2.94	2.85	0.58	0.20	4.76	0.02	1.00
Russia plus	0.00	0.00	3.06	2.17	0.34	3.61	0.02	8.41	0.67	1.61	0.82	1.77	0.40	1.96	1.55	1.00

FROM	WCM	SEA	BUS	PRO	OFF	UNI	LAN	ENT	PER	STU	TRA	REL	MAR	FAM	POL	Total
EU plus	0.00	0.00	7.54	1.72	4.24	3.36	4.08	0.32	0.15	3.65	0.67	1.13	0.19	1.20	0.11	1.00
Oceania	0.00	0.00	3.75	1.74	4.05	1.01	4.32	4.06	0.13	0.77	0.12	0.58	0.32	1.18	1.04	1.00
Rest of world	0.47	0.00	4.08	1.51	2.90	1.35	4.11	3.00	0.08	2.27	2.23	0.62	0.21	1.25	0.05	1.00

Source: Korean Immigration Servic

Notes: The visa categories are defined in Figure 7.6. Russia plus = Russia and former Soviet Union countries and communist Eastern European countries other than those now in the EU; EU plus = EU countries plus Norway, Switzerland and Iceland; Oceania = Australia, New Zealand, and the Pacific Islands.

alcoholism), and criminality at the highest levels (especially in the regional capital city, Vladivostok). One of the main results was flight. This overwhelmingly took the form of migration to other regions within Russia rather than emigration. Much of the emigration to nearby East Asian countries that did take place was associated with new legal trading opportunities (such as cross-border trade with China, businesses in Vietnam, and the import of second-hand cars from Japan), but some of it was linked to smuggling (including drugs) and, above all, prostitution. Russian sex workers, some of them the victims of trafficking, operate in many of the major cities and tourist resorts of East and Southeast Asia (such as Shanghai, Macao and Bangkok).

It is not, however, the emigration from the RFE that has attracted the most media attention and political controversy, but the immigration to the RFE of Chinese nationals. It is difficult in this instance to separate fact from polemic, but what is certain is that the opening up of the RFE after 1991 resulted in the arrival in that region of many short-stay traders from China, and also of longer-term migrant workers employed by Russian construction companies and factory owners. In a small number of cases, much to the annoyance of Russian xenophobes, ethnic Chinese have become the owners of businesses themselves and have employed Russians as well as co-ethnic Chinese.

The political sensitivity of this migration is partially explained by the fears harboured by many Russians that the Chinese want to 'take over' (or even worse, 'take back') the RFE. This fear is based upon three undisputed facts about the region: (i) that it is very sparsely populated by ethnic Russians and that the Russian population is declining further through out-migration; (ii) that the region is extraordinarily rich in precisely those resources (minerals, hydrocarbons, timber) that are required for the booming Chinese economy; and (iii) that the RFE borders a region of China that has high population density and, as a result of undergoing economic restructuring due to the decline of state-owned enterprises in the heavy industry sectors, has a large 'surplus' population available for migration.

The migration is real, the fears about that migration are real, but 'on the ground' the Chinese are not taking over the RFE. They are minor, but significant, players in the RFE economy, their sojourns in the RFE are typically short term, and, from a Chinese point of view, one is tempted to ask why they would risk political or even military conflict when they can obtain everything they need through their power as wealthy customers of the region's resources?

7.10 Conclusion

Northeast Asia is a key part of the East Asian migration picture. It is the preferred destination for many of East Asia's aspiring working-class migrants, and recruits also from Latin America and South Asia. It is the origin of many of East Asia's foreign students, at both undergraduate and postgraduate levels, studying in universities in the USA, Canada, Australia, New Zealand, the UK and the EU. In return, as a place to immerse oneself in another culture and to earn money teaching English, Northeast Asia figures in the imaginations and place preferences of many of the young educated people of those same Western countries. It is both a destination and a source for marriage migrants, mostly Southeast Asian and Chinese women in, and Japanese women out. It provides two of the most intriguing instances of potential political problems caused by migration (the expected mass movement of North Koreans southwards consequent upon reunification of the Korean peninsula, and the Chinese presence in the RFE). Finally, it is the origin of two of the world's largest diaspora business communities brought about by the spectacular successes of the Japanese and South Korean capitalist economies in the last 50 years – to a considerable degree, scattered around the world in rich countries and in poor ones, the members of these business communities, with their competence in English, fierce loyalty to their multinational corporations, and aggressive enthusiasm for technical innovation, are 'capitalism's global warriors'.

Selected references

7.0 General

Akaha, T., 2004, Cross-border migration as a new element of international relations in northeastern Asia: a boon to regionalism or a new source of friction? *Asian Perspective* 28(2): 101–133.

Hur, J.-J., 2008, Demographic change and international labour mobility in Northeast Asia – issues, policies and implications for cooperation, in Hugo, G. and Young, S. (eds), *Labour Mobility in the Asia-Pacific Region: Dynamics, Issues and a New APEC Agenda*. Singapore: Institute of South East Asian Studies, 63–92.

Van Ardsol, M.D. et al., 2005, Population trends and migration patterns in Northeast Asia, in Akaha, T. and Vassilieva, A., *Crossing National Borders: Human Migration Issues in Northeast Asia*. Tokyo: United Nations University Press, 11–44.

Yamanaka, K., 2011, Policies, civil society and social movements for immigrant rights in Japan and South Korea: convergence and divergence, in Vogt, G. and Roberts, G.S. (eds), *Migration and Integration: Japan in Comparative Perspective*. Munich: Iudicium, 89–109.

7.1 Japanese emigration

Azuma, E., 2002, Historical overview of Japanese emigration 1868–2000, in Kikumura-Yano, A. (ed.), *Encyclopedia of Japanese Descendants in the Americas*. Lanham, MD: Rowman & Littlefield, 32–48.

Befu, H. and Guichard-Anguis, S. (eds), 2001, *Globalizing Japan: Ethnography of the Japanese Presence in Asia, Europe, and America*. London: Routledge.

On Japanese emigration to North America:

Azuma, E., 2002, Japanese American historical overview 1868–2001, in Kikumura-Yano, A. (ed.), *Encyclopedia of Japanese Descendants in the Americas*. Lanham, MD: Rowman & Littlefield, 276–292.

Crawford, M., Hayashi, K. and Suenaga, S., 2009, *Japanese War Brides in America: An Oral History*. New York: Palgrave.

Takenaka, A., 2009, How diasporic ties emerge: pan-American Nikkei communities and the Japanese state, *Ethnic and Racial Studies* 32(8): 1325–1345.
On Japanese emigration to South America:
Adachi, N. (ed.), 2010, *Japanese and Nikkei at Home and Abroad: Negotiating Identities in a Global World*. Amherst, NY: Cambria Press.
Endoh, T., 2009, *Exporting Japan: Politics of Emigration to Latin America*. Urbana: University of Illinois Press.
On Japanese emigration to Asia:
Chan, Y., 2011, *Abandoned Japanese in Postwar Manchuria*. London: Routledge.
Itoh, M., 2010, *Japanese War Orphans in Manchuria: Forgotten Victims of World War II*. Basingstoke: Palgrave.
Watt, L., 2009, *When Empire Comes Home: Repatriation and Reintegration in Postwar Japan*. Cambridge, MA: Harvard University Press.
On Japanese contemporary emigration for work purposes:
Eades, J.S., Gill, T. and Befu, H. (eds), 2000, *Globalization and Social Change in Contemporary Japan*. Melbourne: Trans Pacific Press.
Goodman, R., Peach, C., Takenaka, A. and White, P. (eds), 2003, *Global Japan: The Experience of Japan's New Immigrant and Overseas Communities*. London: RoutledgeCurzon.
Hook, G.D. and Weiner, M.A. (eds), 1992, *The Internationalization of Japan*. London: Routledge.
Mizukami, T., 2007, *The Sojourner Community: Japanese Migration and Residency in Australia*. Leiden: Brill.
Sakai, J., 2000, *Japanese Bankers in the City of London: Language, Culture and Identity in the Japanese Diaspora*. London: Routledge.
Yamada-Yamamoto, A. and Richards, B.J., 1998, *Japanese Children Abroad: Cultural, Educational and Language Issues*. Clevedon: Multilingual Matters.
On Japanese contemporary emigration for cultural/lifestyle reasons:
Fujita, Y., 2009, *Cultural Migrants from Japan: Youth, Media, and Migration in New York and London*. Lanham, MD: Lexington Books.
Kelsky, K., 2001, *Women on the Verge: Japanese Women, Western Dreams*. Durham, NC: Duke University Press.
Sato, M., 2001, *Farewell to Nippon: Japanese Lifestyle Migrants in Australia*. Melbourne: Trans Pacific Press.
Yamashita, S., 2012, Here, there, and in-between: lifestyle migrants from Japan, in Haines, D.W., Yamanaka, K. and Yamashita, S. (eds), *Wind over Water: Migration in an East Asian Context*. Oxford: Berghahn Books.
On Japanese contemporary emigration of students:
Ono, H. and Piper, N., 2004, Japanese women studying abroad: the case of the United States, *Women's Studies International Forum* 27: 101–118.
On Japanese contemporary emigration for marriage purposes:
Ma, K., 1996, *The Modern Madame Butterfly: Fantasy and Reality in Japanese Cross-Cultural Relationships*. Rutland, VT: Tuttle.
On Japanese contemporary emigration for retirement:
Toyota, M., 2006, Ageing and transnational householding: Japanese retirees in Southeast Asia, *International Development Planning Review* 28(4): 515–531.

7.2 Korean emigration (South and North)

Abelmann, N., Newendorp, N. and Sangsook, L.-C., 2014, East Asia's astronaut and geese families: Hong Kong and South Korean cosmopolitanisms, *Critical Asian Studies* 46(2): 259–286.

Collins, F.L. and Pak, S., 2008, Language and skilled migration: the outcomes of overseas language study for South Korean students in New Zealand, *Asian Population Studies* 4(3): 347–362.

Dhinga, P., 2007, *Managing Multicultural Lives: Asian American Professionals and the Challenges of Multiple Identities*. Stanford, CA: Stanford University Press.

Finch, J. and Kim, S.-K., 2012, Kirogi families in the US: transnational migration and education, *Journal of Ethnic and Migration Studies* 38(3): 485–506.

Gap Min, P., 1996, *Caught in the Middle: Korean Communities in New York and Los Angeles*. Berkeley: University of California Press.

Hubinette, T., 2007, Asian bodies out of control: examining the adopted Korean existence, in Parrenas, R.S. and Siu, L.C.D. (eds), *Asian Diasporas*. Stanford, CA: Stanford University Press, 177–200.

Kim, Y.J., 2010, The gendered desire to become cosmopolitan: South Korean women's motivations for migration to the UK, *Women's Studies International Forum* 33: 433–442.

Lankov, A., 2013, Ethnic Koreans in Yanbian, *Korea Times*, 13 October.

Noh, S., Kim, A.H. and Noh, M.S. (eds), 2012, *Korean Immigrants in Canada: Perspectives on Migration, Integration and the Family*. Toronto: University of Toronto Press.

Pak, J., 2012, *Korean American Women: Stories of Acculturation and Changing Selves*. London: Routledge.

Schwekendiek, D., 2012, *Korean Migration to the Wealthy West*. New York: Nova.

Yoon, I.-J., 2012, Migration and the Korean diaspora: a comparative description of five cases, *Journal of Ethnic and Migration Studies* 38(3): 413–435.

7.3 'Oldcomer' immigrants in Japan

Chung, E.A., 2010, *Immigration and Citizenship in Japan*. Cambridge: Cambridge University Press.

Denoon, D., Hudson, M., McCormack, G. and Morris-Suzuki, T. (eds), 1996, *Multicultural Japan: Paleolithic to Postmodern*. Cambridge: Cambridge University Press.

Komai, H., 2001, *Foreign Migrants in Contemporary Japan*. Melbourne: Trans Pacific Press.

Lie, J., 2001, *Multiethnic Japan*. Cambridge, MA: Harvard University Press.

Morris-Suzuki, T., 2002, Immigration and citizenship in contemporary Japan, in Maswood, J., Graham, J. and Miyajima, H. (eds), *Japan: Change and Continuity*. London: RoutledgeCurzon, 163–178.

Morris-Suzuki, T., 2010, *Borderline Japan: Foreigners and Frontier Controls in the Postwar Era*. Cambridge: Cambridge University Press.

Yamanaka, K., 2004, Japan: government policy, immigrant reality, in Cornelius, W.A. et al. (eds), *Controlling Immigration: A Global Perspective*, 2nd edn. Stanford, CA: Stanford University Press, 439–480.

Yamawaki, K., 2000, Foreign workers in Japan: a historical perspective, in Douglass, M. and Roberts, G.S. (eds), *Japan and Global Migration: Foreign Workers and the Advent of a Multicultural Society*. London: Routledge, 38–51.

On Korean 'oldcomers':
For an excellent and absorbing treatment of the situation of the 'North Koreans' in Japan, see:

Ryang, S., 1997, *North Koreans in Japan: Language, Ideology and Identity*. Boulder, CO: Westview Press.
And her edited collection:
Ryang, S. (ed.), 2000, *Koreans in Japan: Critical Voices from the Margin*. London: Routledge.

See also:
Chapman, D., 2008, *Zainichi Korean Identity and Ethnicity*. London: Routledge.
De Vos, G.A., 1992, *Social Cohesion and Alienation: Minorities in the US and Japan*. Boulder, CO: Westview Press (especially Chapter 5: Ethnic persistence and role degradation: Koreans in Japan, 176–205).
Fukuoka, Y., 2000, *Lives of Young Koreans in Japan*. Melbourne: Trans Pacific Press.
Gap Min, P., 1992, A comparison of Korean minorities in China and Japan, *International Migration Review* 26(1): 4–21.
Hayes, C., 2000, Cultural identity in the work of Yi Yang-ji, in Ryang, S. (ed.), *Koreans in Japan: Critical Voices from the Margin*. London: Routledge, 119–139.
Hicks, G., 1997, *Japan's Hidden Apartheid: The Korean Minority and the Japanese*. London: Ashgate.
Kim, B., 2011, Changes in the socio-economic position of ziainichi Koreans: a historical overview, *Social Science Japan Journal* 14(2): 233–245.
Kim, J.J., 2005, *Hidden Treasures: Lives of First-Generation Korean Women in Japan*. Lanham, MD: Rowman & Littlefield.
Lie, J., 2008, *Zainichi (Koreans in Japan): Diasporic Nationalism and Postcolonial Identity*. Berkeley: University of California Press.
Ryang, S. and Lie, J. (eds), 2008, *Diaspora Without Homeland: Being Korean in Japan*. Berkeley: University of California Press.
Wender, M.L., 2005, *Lamentations as History: Narratives by Koreans in Japan 1965–2000*. Stanford, CA: Stanford University Press.

On Chinese and other 'oldcomers':
Han, P., 2008, Hidden 'in-betweenness': an exploration of Taiwanese transnational identity in contemporary Japan, *Asian Ethnicity* 9(2): 121–132.
Vasishth, A., 1997, A model minority: the Chinese community in Japan, in Weiner, M. (ed.), *Japan's Minorities: The Illusion of Homogeneity*. London: Routledge, 108–139.

On Korean returnees:
Morris-Suzuki, T., 2005, A dream betrayed: Cold War politics and the repatriation of Koreans from Japan to North Korea, *Asian Studies Review* 29: 357–381.

7.4 'Newcomer' immigrants in Japan: 'multicultural coexistence'

Cornelius, W.A., 1994, Japan: the illusion of immigration control, in Cornelius, W.A., Martin, P.L. and Hollifield, J.F. (eds), *Controlling Immigration: A Global Perspective*. Stanford, CA: Stanford University Press, 375–410.
Douglass, M. and Roberts, G.S. (eds), 2000, *Japan and Global Migration: Foreign Workers and the Advent of a Multicultural Society*. London: Routledge.
Komai, H., 1995, *Migrant Workers in Japan*. London: Kegan Paul International.

Roberts, G., 2007, Labor migration to Japan: comparative perspectives on demography and the sense of crisis. *Japan Focus*, japanfocus.org/products/topdf/2519 (accessed 19 September 2007).

Sassen, S., 1991, *The Global City: New York, London, Tokyo*. Princeton, NJ: Princeton University Press.

Sellek, Y., 2001, *Migrant Labour in Japan*. Basingstoke: Palgrave.

Shimada, H., 1994, *Japan's 'Guest Workers': Issues and Public Policies*. Tokyo: University of Tokyo Press.

Vogt, G. and Roberts, G.S. (eds), 2011, *Migration and Integration: Japan in Comparative Perspective*. Munich: Iudicium Verlag.

On Northeast Asian 'newcomers':

Liu-Farrer, G., 2011, *Labor Migration from China to Japan: International Students, Transnational Migrants*. London: Routledge.

On Southeast Asian 'newcomers':

Haines, D.W., Minami, M. and Yamashita, S., 2007, Transnational migration in East Asia: Japan in comparative focus, *International Migration Review* 41(4): 963–967.

Iguchi, Y., 2002, Foreign Workers and labour migration policy in Japan, in Debrah, Y. A. (ed.), *Migrant Workers in Pacific Asia*. London: Frank Cass, 119–140.

Shipper, A.W., 2002, The political construction of foreign workers in Japan, *Critical Asian Studies* 34(1): 41–68.

Tajima, J., 2000, A study of Asian immigrants in global city Tokyo, *Asian and Pacific Migration Journal* 9(3): 349–364.

Weiner, M. (ed.), 1997, *Japan's Minorities: The Illusion of Homogeneity*. London: Routledge.

Willis, D.B. and Murphy-Shigematsu, S. (eds), 2008, *Transcultural Japan: At the Borderlands of Race, Gender and Identity*. London: Routledge.

Yamanaka, K., 2011, Increasing gaps between immigration policies and outcomes in Japan: the responsibility of researchers in international migration studies, *Social Science Japan Journal* 14(2): 247–252.

On high-status/skill 'newcomers':

Chiavacci, D., 2012, Japan in the 'global war' for 'talent': changing concepts of valuable foreign workers and their consequences, *Asien* 124: 27–47.

On the low social standing of returnee women, and the (supposed) special educational problems of returnee children:

Goodman, R., 1990, *Japan's International Youth*. London: Oxford University Press.

Macdonald, G. and Kowatari, A., 1995, A non-Japanese Japanese: On being a returnee, in Maher, J.C. and Macdonald, G. (eds), *Diversity in Japanese Culture and Language*. London: Kegan Paul International, 249–269.

Pang, C.L., 2004, *Negotiating Identity in Contemporary Japan: The Case of the Kikokushijo*. New York: Columbia University Press.

On Japanese multiculturalism and its opponents:

Dale, P.N., 1986, *The Myth of Japanese Uniqueness*. London: Routledge.

Flowers, P.R., 2012, From *kokusaika* to *tabunka kyousei*: global norms, discourses of difference, and multiculturalism in Japan, *Critical Asian Studies* 44(4): 515–542.

Graburn, N., Ertl, J. and Tierney, R.K. (eds), 2007, *Multiculturalism in the New Japan: Crossing the Boundaries Within*. Oxford: Berghahn.

Ishiwata, E., 2011, 'Probably impossible': multiculturalism and pluralisation in present-day Japan, *Journal of Ethnic and Migration Studies* 37(10): 1605–1626.

Kajita, T., 1998, The challenge of incorporating foreign workers in Japan: 'ethnic Japanese' and 'sociological Japanese', in Weiner, M. and Hanami, T. (eds), *Temporary Workers or Future Citizens? Japanese and US Migration Policies*. Basingstoke: Macmillan, 120–148.

Sugimoto, Y., 1999, Making sense of nihonjinron, *Thesis Eleven*, 57: 81–96.

Weiner, M. (ed.), 2002, *Japan, Race and Identity*, 3 vols. London: Routledge.

Yoshino, K., 2001, Globalization as 'internationalization': perspectives on nationalism in Japan, in Starrs, R. (ed.), *Asian Nationalism in an Age of Globalization*. Richmond: Japan Library, 19–33.

On refugees and refugee policy:

Akashi, J., 2006, Challenging Japan's refugee policies, *Asian and Pacific Migration Journal* 15(2): 219–238.

Dean, M. and Nagashima, M., 2007, Sharing the burden: the role of government and NGOs in protecting and providing for asylum seekers and refugees in Japan, *Journal of Refugee Studies* 20(3): 481–508.

Iwasaki, A., 2006, Open the door – Japan's policy of exclusion of refugees (Parts 1 and 2), *Japan Focus*, japanfocus.org/article.asp?id=527 (accessed 23 February 2006).

On immigration policy (human rights, etc.):

Bartram, D., 2005, *International Labour Migration: Foreign Workers and Public Policy*. Basingstoke: Palgrave.

Befu, H., 2001, *Hegemony of Homogeneity: An Anthropological Analysis of Nihonjinron*. Melbourne: Trans Pacific Press.

Chapman, D. and Krogness, K.J. (eds), 2012, *The State and Social Control: Citizenship and Japan's Household Registration System*. London: Routledge.

D'Costa, A.P., 2008, The barbarians are here: how Japanese institutional barriers and immigration policies keep Asian talent away, *Asian Population Studies* 4(3): 311–329.

Hatsuse, R., 2010, Foreign residents: Japanese immigration policy and its problems, in Takeda, H. and Hook, G.D. (eds), *Ending the Postwar in Japan*. London: Routledge.

Kondo, A. (ed.), 2008, *Migration and Globalization: Comparing Immigration Policy in Developed Countries*. Tokyo: Akashi Shoten.

Mori, H., 1997, *Immigration Policy and Foreign Workers in Japan*. Basingstoke: Macmillan.

Shipper, A.W., 2008, *Fighting for Foreigners: Immigration and its Impact on Japanese Democracy*. Ithaca, NY: Cornell University Press.

Surak, K., 2008, Convergence in foreigners' rights and citizenship policies? A look at Japan, *International Migration Review* 42(3): 550–575.

Tsuda, T. (ed.), 2006, *Local Citizenship in Recent Countries of Immigration: Japan in Comparative Perspective*. Lanham, MD: Rowman & Littlefield.

Weiner, M. and Hanami, T. (eds), 1998, *Temporary Workers or Future Citizens? Japanese and US Migration Policies*. Basingstoke: Macmillan.

Yoshino, K., 1992, *Cultural Nationalism in Contemporary Japan*. London: Routledge.

On illegal immigration/overstayers (crime, etc.), regulation and policy implementation:

Friman, H.R., 2001, Informal economies, immigrant entrepreneurship and drug crime in Japan, *Journal of Migration and Ethnic Studies* 27(2): 313–333.

Morita, K. and Sassen, S., 1994, The new illegal immigration in Japan 1980–1992, *International Migration Review* 28(1): 153–163.

Ventura, R., 1992, *Underground in Japan*. London: Jonathan Cape.

On settlement in Japan (e.g. social and spatial segregation):

Arudou, D., 2006, *Japanese Only: The Otaru Hot Springs Case and Racial Discrimination in Japan*. Tokyo: Akashi Shoten.

Tsuneyoshi, K., Okano, H.H. and Boocock, S. (eds), 2010, *Minorities and Education in Multicultural Japan*. London: Routledge.

7.5 Female migration to Japan from Southeast Asia

Ball, R. and Piper, N., 2002, Globalisation and regulation of citizenship: Filipino migrant workers in Japan, *Political Geography* 21: 1013–1034.

Caouette, T. and Saito, Y., 1999, *To Japan and Back: Thai Women Recount their Experiences*. Geneva: International Organization for Migration.

Faier, L., 2009, *Intimate Encounters: Filipina Women and the Remaking of Rural Japan*. Berkeley: University of California Press.

Mackie, V., 1998, Japayuki Cinderella girl: containing the immigrant other, *Japanese Studies* 18(1): 45–63.

Matsui, Y., 1995, The plight of Asian migrant women working in Japan's sex industry, in Fujimura-Fanselow, K. and Kameda, A. (eds), *Japanese Women: New Feminist Perspectives on the Past, Present, and Future*. New York: The Feminist Press, 309–319.

Parrenas, R.S., 2011, *Illicit Flirtations: Labor, Migration, and Sex Trafficking in Tokyo*. Stanford, CA: Stanford University Press.

Piper, N., 2002, Global labour market and national responses: legal regimes governing female migrant workers in Japan, in Gills, D.S. and Piper, N. (eds), *Women and Work in Globalizing Asia*. London: Routledge, 188–208.

Suzuki, N., 2007, Marrying a Marilyn of the tropics: manhood and nationhood in Filipina-Japanese marriages, *Anthropological Quarterly* 80(2): 427–454.

Watanabe, S., 1998, From Thailand to Japan: migrant sex workers as autonomous subjects, in Kempadoo, K. and Doezema, J. (eds), *Global Sex Workers: Rights, Resistance and Redefinition*. New York and London: Routledge.

7.6 Youth migration to Japan

Belanger, D., Ueno, K., Hong, K.T. and Ochiai, E., 2011, From foreign trainees to unauthorized workers: Vietnamese migrant workers in Japan, *Asian and Pacific Migration Journal* 20(1): 31–53.

Oishi, N., 1995, Training or employment? Japanese immigration policy in dilemma, *Asian and Pacific Migration Journal* 4: 2–3, 367–385.

7.7 Nikkeijin migrants to Japan from Latin America

Adachi, N. (ed.), 2010, *Japanese and Nikkei at Home and Abroad: Negotiating Identities in a Global World*. Amherst, NY: Cambria Press.

De Carvalho, D., 2003, *Migrants and Identity in Japan and Brazil: The Nikeijin*. London: RoutledgeCurzon.

Hirabayashi, L.R., Kikumura-Yano, A. and Hirabayashi, J.A. (eds), 2002, *New Worlds, New Lives: Globalization and People of Japanese Descent in the Americas and from Latin America in Japan*. Stanford, CA: Stanford University Press.

Linger, D.T., 2001, *No One Home: Brazilian Selves Remade in Japan*. Stanford, CA: Stanford University Press.

Roth, J.H., 2002, *Brokered Homeland: Japanese Brazilian Migrants in Japan*. Ithaca, NY: Cornell University Press.

Suzuki, T., 2010, *Embodying Belonging: Racializing Okinawan Diaspora in Bolivia and Japan*. Honolulu: University of Hawai'i Press.

Takenaka, A., 2000, Transitional community and its ethnic consequences: the return migration and the transformation of ethnicity of Japanese Peruvians, in Foner, N., Rumbaut, R.G. and Gold, S.J. (eds), *Immigration Research for a New Century: Multi-disciplinary Perspectives*. New York: Russell Sage Foundation, 442–458.

Tsuda, T., 2003, *Strangers in the Ethnic Homeland: Japanese Brazilian Return Migration in Transnational Perspective*. New York: Columbia University Press.

Tsuda, T. (ed.), 2009, *Diasporic Homecomings: Ethnic Return Migration in Comparative Perspective*. Stanford, CA: Stanford University Press.

7.8 Korean immigration

Abelmann, N. and Kim, H., 2005, A failed attempt at transnational marriage: maternal citizenship in a globalizing South Korea, in Constable, N. (ed.), *Cross-Border Marriages: Gender and Mobility in Transnational Asia*. Philadelphia: University of Pennsylvania Press, 101–123.

Ahn, J.-H., 2012, Transforming Korea into a multicultural society: reception of multiculturalism discourse and its discursive disposition in Korea, *Asian Ethnicity* 13(1): 97–109.

Cheng, S., 2010, *On the Move for Love: Migrant Entertainers and the U.S. Military in South Korea*. Philadelphia: University of Pennsylvania Press.

Freeman, C., 2005, Marrying up and marrying down: the paradoxes of marital mobility for Chosunjok brides in South Korea, in Constable, N. (ed.), *Cross-Border Marriages: Gender and Mobility in Transnational Asia*. Philadelphia: University of Pennsylvania Press, 80–100.

Gray, K., 2006, Migrant labour and civil society relations in South Korea, *Asian and Pacific Migration Journal* 15(3): 381–390.

Jeong, Y.-J., You, H.-K. and Kwon, Y.-I., 2014, One family in two countries: mothers in Korean transnational families, *Ethnic and Racial Studies* 37(9): 1546–1564.

Kim, C.S., 2011, *Voices of Foreign Brides: The Roots and Development of Multiculturalism in Korea*. Lanham, MD: Rowman & Littlefield.

Kim, E., 2007, Our adoptees, our alien: transnational adoptees as specters of foreignness and family in South Korea, *Anthropological Quarterly* 80(2): 497–531.

Kim, J.K., 2011, The politics of culture in multicultural Korea, *Journal of Ethnic and Migration Studies* 37(10): 1583–1604.

Kim, N.-K., 2014, Multicultural challenges in Korea: the current stage and a prospect, *International Migration* 52(2): 100–121.

Lee, J.J. and Kim, D., 2010, Brain gain or brain circulation? US doctoral recipients returning to South Korea, *Higher Education* 59: 627–643.

Lee, Y., 2009, Migration, migrants, and contested ethno-nationalism in Korea, *Critical Asian Studies* 41(3): 363–380.

Lim, T.C., 2012, South Korea as an 'ordinary' country: a comparative enquiry into the prospects for 'permanent' immigration to Korea, *Journal of Ethnic and Migration Studies* 38(3): 507–528.

Seol, D.H., 2011, Ethnic enclaves in Korean cities: formation, residential patterns and communal features, in Wong, T.-C. and Rigg, J. (eds), *Asian Cities, Migrant Labour and Contested Spaces*. London: Routledge, 133–155.

Seol, D.-H. and Skrentny, J.D., 2004, South Korea: importing undocumented workers, in Cornelius, W.A. et al. (eds), *Controlling Immigration: A Global Perspective*, 2nd edn. Stanford, CA: Stanford University Press, 481–516.

Yea, S., 2004, Runaway brides: anxieties of identity among trafficked Filipina entertainers in South Korea, *Singapore Journal of Tropical Geography* 25(2): 180–197.

On immigration to North Korea:

Morris-Suzuki, T., 2007, *Exodus to North Korea: Shadows from Japan's Cold War*. Lanham, MD: Rowman & Littlefield.

7.9 Emigration from and immigration to the Russian Far East

Abazov, R., 2009, *Current Trends in Migration in the Common Wealth of Independent States*. UNDP: Human Development Research Paper 2009/36.

Akaha, T. and Vassilieva, A., 2005, *Crossing National Borders: Migration and Human Security Implications in Northeast Asia*. Tokyo: United Nations University Press.

Alexseev, M.A., 2006, *Immigration Phobia and the Security Dilemma: Russia, Europe and the United States*. Cambridge: Cambridge University Press.

Chang, F. and Rucker-Chang, S.T. (eds), 2010, *Chinese Migrants in Russia, Central Asia and Eastern Europe*. London: Routledge.

Ioffe, G. and Zayonchkovskaya, Z., 2010, Immigration to Russia: inevitability and prospective inflows, *Eurasian Geography and Economics* 51(1): 104–125.

Ivakhnyuk, I., 2009, *The Russian Migration Policy and its Impact on Human Development: The Historical Perspective*. UNDP: Human Development Research Paper 2009/14.

Larin, A.G., 2013, The Chinese in Russia, in Tan, C.-B. (ed.), *Routledge Handbook of the Chinese Diaspora*. London: Routledge, 191–204.

Saveliev, I., 2002, Chinese migration to Russia in space and time, in Nyiri, P. and Saveliev, I. (eds), *Globalizing Chinese Migration: Trends in Europe and Asia*. Aldershot: Ashgate, 35–73.

Wishnick, E., 2008, The securitisation of Chinese migration to the Russian Far East: rhetoric and reality, in Curley, M.G. and Wong, S.-L. (eds), *Migration and Securitisation in Southeast Asia*. London: Routledge, 83–99.

8 Confucian capitalism's hyper-urbanization

Japanese and Korean internal migration flows

8.0 Introduction

Looking back, it is quite staggering how rapid the urbanization of Northeast Asia has been since World War II. In 1945, affected by the special circumstances of wartime bombing, only 27.0% of Japan's population lived in the eight prefectures that make up the extended metropolitan regions of the three largest cities – Tokyo, Osaka and Nagoya. The rapid return to the cities resulted in this figure jumping to 30.6% by 1950. Then, instead of slowing down, urbanization really took off, and the proportion continued to increase at about the same rate, so that by 1975 the figure had reached 43.5%. Thirty years later, in 2005, however, the figure was only just slightly higher at 46.0%.

What was happening at the macro regional scale was being repeated at the micro local scale: villages in the remoter, rural and mountainous areas were dramatically losing their populations through out-migration over that 30-year period 1945–75 to the nearby towns, the prefectural cities and, above all, to the regional capitals such as Fukuoka, Sendai and Hiroshima. It should be clear from those figures, however, that equally remarkable as the rapid urbanization of the first 30 years, was the sudden slowing down, indeed almost cessation, of urbanization in the next 30. Somehow we need to explain both. With a time lag, starting after the Korean War, comparable figures could be provided for urbanization in South Korea.

8.1 Urban and regional development in Japan

The key to the very rapid urbanization in Japan was the remarkable growth in the Japanese economy over the four decades after 1950. This growth was based on: (i) export performance – eye-watering success in selling modern consumer goods into the North American and Western European markets; (ii) a very high savings ratio – this facilitated the implementation of technological upgrading, the long-term financing of manufacturing investment, high levels of auto-financing by corporations, and high levels of expenditure by the public sector on transport, communications and utilities infrastructures, and on urban built form; and (iii) the widespread distribution of the benefits of this growth to the public at large through a rapid and sustained increase in the wages of ordinary workers – this was 'Fordist' growth in the sense that it was based on the mass production of standardized goods for mass markets. A virtuous circle was established between efficient production and high levels of consumption.

How did these characteristics of economic growth impact on the geography of Japan? The export success led to the massive expansion of manufacturing and service employment in the major port cities such as Tokyo, Yokohama, Osaka, Kobe, Fukuoka, Hiroshima, Niigata and Nagoya, and to the growth of the shipbuilding industry in several of these ports. The high savings ratio led to the transformation of the Japanese landscape – a boom in the construction of high-speed railways (*shinkansen*), expressways, tunnels and bridges, science cities (such as Tsukuba), new ports and airports (such as Narita Airport outside Tokyo), but above all, a landscape of factories and newly built houses partially to replace a landscape of paddy fields and villages.

It was the Fordist nature of this growth that was crucial. Mass production required very large workforces working and living in very large cities; mass consumption likewise. Furthermore, each large assembly plant needed, preferably nearby for 'just-in-time' production, a host of suppliers – factories producing the parts that went into the cars, TVs, and 'white goods' (washing machines, cookers and refrigerators), on the production of which the economy had come to depend. So the largest cities expanded fastest, and, as the intervening spaces became urbanized, an almost continuous belt of urban built form and land use was created. This extended from the Kanto (Tokyo and Yokohama) metropolitan region in the east, through the Nagoya industrial region in the centre, to the Kansai (Osaka, Kobe, Kyoto) metropolitan region in the west. This urban industrial belt then extended in a less continuous form westwards along the north shore of the inland sea (*Seto*) between the islands of Honshu and Shikoku, to the northern corner of the island of Kyushu.

8.2 Rural depopulation and urbanization in Japan

This urbanization and industrialization was accompanied by a revolution in values and behaviour – the arrival of post-war modernity. So the exodus from the countryside to the city was not just about getting work and improving one's economic prospects; it was about joining the modern world, a world of fashionable clothes, popular music, department stores, cinemas, expensive restaurants, clubs and bars. The city was where important people lived, and big events happened, it was full of 'cool', bright, ambitious, independent people – in short, of 'winners' – it was Western, secular and modern. In contrast, the countryside was full of 'losers' – old people, unmarried men, men and women burdened by the hard labour of paddy farming, women burdened by the raising of large families and ruled over by their mothers-in-law – and above all, it was the source and repository of Japanese tradition (with all the constraints, both secular and religious, on behaviour that this implied). I exaggerate, of course, but the perceptions at this time of rural Japan were almost unanimously negative, and those of the city almost as unanimously positive.

With economy and culture lined up in this way, it was inevitable that urbanization and rural depopulation would dominate population redistribution in Japan in the period 1945–75. The highest rates of net out-migration were from the most rural regions, notably Tohoku (Northern Honshu), from the most rural prefectures, and from the most rural areas within the prefectures, notably those furthest away from the major towns (often inland mountainous areas). So rapid was this rural depopulation of working-age adults that these areas suddenly shifted, despite higher fertility rates, towards being dominated by the elderly – a situation that has persisted right up to the present day.

8.3 The population 'turnaround' in Japan

Then something rather strange and unexpected happened. Starting in the early 1970s, before the economic crisis brought about by the massive increases in the price of oil, the flows of migrants towards the major cities began to be matched by those in the opposite direction, and for a time the net migration gains were experienced in the provinces rather than in the Kanto or Kansai regions. This quite sudden reversal in net migration trends, which has a number of names in Japan – 'turnaround', 'U-turn' (that is, return migration to the origin village or district), and 'J-turn' (that is, return migration, but not to the rural area but to the main town in the prefecture of origin) – is not by any means unique to Japan. It was identified also in other advanced capitalist countries at about the same time, where it was generally called 'counter-urbanization'. In the USA the most popular explanation for counter-urbanization was a shift in migration preferences. People were expressing their 'love of the new', their 'frontier spirit' and, above all, their search for a 'rural idyll' by migrating away from the big city and towards the countryside. However, this explanation carries little or no weight in Japan. Here, the rural areas remained tainted by poverty, dull thankless hard work, and backwardness; nobody in their right minds would want to live there! In particular, unlike Western Europe and North America, there had been no tradition in Japan of spending your great wealth gained from trade or manufacturing on fine mansion houses set in landscaped parkland away from the city. Wealth and prestige stayed in the city – and especially in Tokyo.

So, if place preference shift was not the cause of this remarkable population turnaround, what was? The answer lies largely in the workings of the space-economy. So successful had export-led manufacturing growth been, that labour shortages began to be felt in the main metropolitan regions by the late 1960s and early 1970s. (Something rather similar, perhaps, is occurring today in the Pearl River Delta area in China.) The result was that firms began to locate their new plants in those places where land and congestion costs were lower and where labour reserves could be found – a case of the work going to the workers rather than workers going to the work. These tended to be provincial towns and rural districts, often, as in the case of Tohoku, located a long way away from the major metropolitan regions.

This decentralized investment had a double effect on population mobility: (i) it kept a number of working-age adults in the regions when otherwise they would have migrated to the city, allowing them often to combine factory employment with maintaining the family farm or small business; and (ii) it provided jobs for those who wanted to return to their region of birth and upbringing, sometimes because by doing so they could combine employment in the modern sector with their traditional (and often deeply felt) obligations towards their families. Combined with much public-sector infrastructure investment in the peripheral regions during this period (by a centre-right government with strong links to the construction industry), it is not surprising, perhaps, that this period (1970–85) was dubbed by some the 'era of the regions'.

8.4 Migration to and from the Tokyo metropolitan region

Using annual resident registration data, we can follow the migration fortunes of the three main metropolitan regions over the period 1954–2012 (Tokyo: composed of Tokyo, Kanagawa, Chiba and Saitama prefectures; Nagoya: composed of Aichi, Gifu and Mie prefectures; and Osaka: composed of Osaka, Hyogo, Kyoto and Nara prefectures) (see Figure 8.4 in the discussion box). The picture that emerges is remarkable in three respects. First, for the very great gains by internal migration of all three metropolitan regions up until the early–mid-1970s. At its peak period in the early 1960s, over 500,000 more people each year were moving to these three metropolitan areas than were moving away from them. Second, for the very low gains (by Tokyo) and losses (by Nagoya and Osaka) in the following ten years. Third, for the way that Tokyo went its own way in attracting many migrants in the late 1980s and then again in the 2000s (until the recent crisis), while Nagoya and Osaka either gained very slightly (Nagoya) or lost considerably (Osaka). Clearly, after the turn-around, new forces came into play that differentiated Tokyo from the other main metropolitan regions.

The solution to this puzzle lies, of course, in the increasing importance of financial and business services in the national economy, employment in which is overwhelmingly concentrated in the Tokyo city-region (but for a fuller explanation see Box 8.1). This can be seen very clearly in Figure 8.1. Apart from small net gains by migration in a few provincial capitals (notably Fukuoka and Kobe), the spread of Kansai urban development into Shiga Prefecture, and the continued attractiveness of Nagoya, the picture is entirely dominated by the Tokyo metropolitan region – the highest rates of net gain being in the suburban prefectures, but the highest absolute gain being in Tokyo itself. In the recent period (2007–12), however, Tokyo has witnessed a sharp drop in its net migration gains (from 155,000 to 67,000), while Osaka has gone from being a net loser (which it had been for every year since 1974) to rough balance (-16,000 to +1,000). Economic crisis can also, it seems, have significant migration effects.

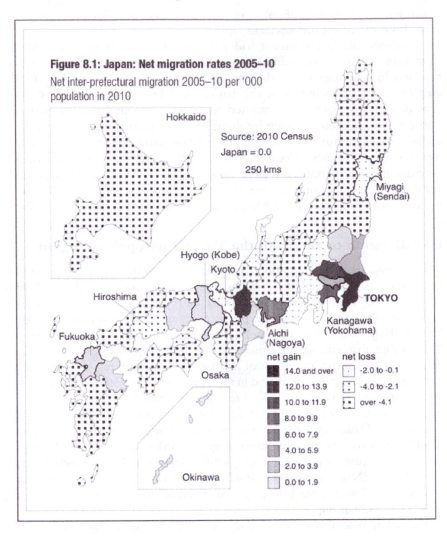

Figure 8.1: Japan: Net migration rates 2005–10

Net inter-prefectural migration 2005–10 per '000 population in 2010

Source: 2010 Census

Japan = 0.0

250 kms

Hokkaido

Miyagi (Sendai)

Hyogo (Kobe)

Kyoto

Hiroshima

Fukuoka

Aichi (Nagoya)

TOKYO

Kanagawa (Yokohama)

Osaka

Okinawa

net gain	net loss
14.0 and over	-2.0 to -0.1
12.0 to 13.9	-4.0 to -2.1
10.0 to 11.9	over -4.1
8.0 to 9.9	
6.0 to 7.9	
4.0 to 5.9	
2.0 to 3.9	
0.0 to 1.9	

More detail about the geography of migration flows to the Tokyo metropolitan region is provided by Figure 8.2. Two features stand out: the first is the tendency for the highest values, representing high rates of flow, to be from the prefectures located to the north of the Tokyo region. This reflects not just current economic conditions but the continuation of a long historical tradition of migration from the Touhoku region to the capital. The second is the tendency for values from the prefectures containing the main provincial university cities (Miyagi, Aichi, Kyoto, Osaka, Hyogo, Hiroshima, and Fukuoka) to show higher rates of flow to the Tokyo region than surrounding areas. In 2013, the only prefecture to which the Tokyo region lost migrants was Okinawa.

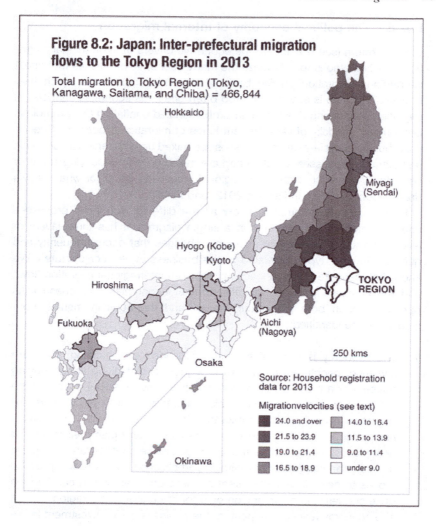

Figure 8.2: Japan: Inter-prefectural migration flows to the Tokyo Region in 2013

Total migration to Tokyo Region (Tokyo, Kanagawa, Saitama, and Chiba) = 466,844

Hokkaido

Miyagi (Sendai)

Hyogo (Kobe)

Kyoto

Hiroshima

TOKYO REGION

Fukuoka

Aichi (Nagoya)

250 kms

Osaka

Source: Household registration data for 2013

Migrationvelocities (see text)

24.0 and over	14.0 to 16.4
21.5 to 23.9	11.5 to 13.9
19.0 to 21.4	9.0 to 11.4
16.5 to 18.9	under 9.0

Okinawa

Box 8.1 The political economy of internal migration

We now return (see Box 6.1) to the economic drivers of interregional migration. The first step is to categorize the many economic processes that affect interregional migration on the basis of the time spans over which they operate. This step is essential: far too often one finds economic analyses of migration floundering due to the un-problematized conflation (for example in econometric models) of very different kinds of migration processes. Specifically, business cycle-related processes are mixed up with regional economic restructuring processes, which in turn are mixed up with underlying and only very slowly changing patterns of regional inequality. (Much of what follows draws upon chapter 4 in Fielding 2012, and Fielding 2016.)

Figure 8.3 is an attempt to show all the different economic processes affecting interregional migration in a single diagram. It has three layers or levels. The top layer refers to economic changes that occur frequently and quickly. They are typically related to the business cycle ('conjuncture'). We know that there are close connections between interregional migration flows and the business cycle in capitalist market economies, and these links operate through both the labour market and the housing market. Four stages can be identified:

1   The economy is in its 'rise' phase. Confidence is growing, firms are investing, people are moving to new jobs, and thinking about moving house. For a high-income region within a national space-economy the typical migration responses to this stage in the business cycle are: in-migration low but rising; out-migration high but falling; with house prices rising, people put their houses on the market and plan their moves to new places; with unemployment falling, people contemplate taking the risk of changing job, often with the implication that this will provoke moves to new places. The effect of these changes, which can happen quite suddenly, is net migration gain for the high-income region.

2   The economy reaches the peak of the business cycle. Investment levels and job opportunities remain high, there is a lot of construction both of dwellings and of commercial property, and unemployment is low. Turnover in both the labour and housing markets is high. In-migration peaks high, out-migration bottoms out low, so high net migration gain is the result.

3   The economy is in its 'fall' phase. Confidence is declining, firms are cutting back, people are reluctant to move to new jobs or to move house. House prices begin to fall and unemployment begins to rise. The migration responses in a high-income region are: in-migration is high but falling; out-migration is low but rising; and net migration shifts from net gain to net loss.

4   Finally, we reach the trough in the cycle – recession. Unemployment goes up sharply, house building comes almost to a halt, and confidence

Figure 8.3: Population migration and regional development: (the Fielding '3-layer model')

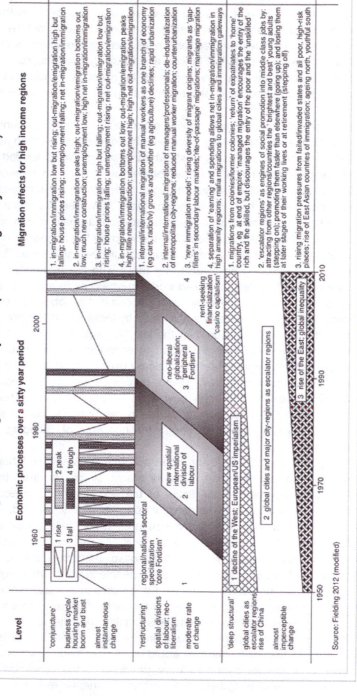

Level	Economic processes over a sixty year period	Migration effects for high income regions
'conjuncture' business cycle/ housing market boom and bust almost instantaneous change	1 rise 2 peak 3 fall 4 trough	1. in-migration/immigration low but rising; out-migration/emigration high but falling; house prices rising; unemployment falling; net in-migration/immigration 2. in-migration/immigration peaks high; out-migration/emigration bottoms out low; much new construction; unemployment low; high net in-migration/immigration 3. in-migration/immigration high but falling; out-migration/emigration low but rising; house prices falling; unemployment rising; net out-migration/emigration 4. in-migration/immigration bottoms out low; out-migration/emigration peaks high; little new construction; unemployment high; high net out-migration/emigration
'restructuring' spatial divisions of labour; neo-liberalism moderate rate of change	regional/national sectoral specialization 'core Fordism' new spatial/ international division of labour neo-liberal globalization; 'peripheral Fordism' rent-seeking financialization 'casino capitalism'	1. internal/international migration of manual workers as one branch of economy (eg cars, radio/tv) grows and another (eg agriculture) declines; rapid urbanization 2. internal/international migration of managers/professionals; de-industrialization of metropolitan city-regions; reduced manual worker migration; counterurbanization 3. 'new immigration model': rising diversity of migrant origins; migrants as 'gap-fillers' in secondary labour markets; 'rite-of-passage' migrations; marriage migration 4. separation of 'earning' and spending allows net in-migration/immigration in high amenity regions; mafia migrations to global cities and immigration gateways
'deep structural' global cities as escalator regions; rise of China almost imperceptible change	1 decline of the West; European/US imperialism 2 global cities and major city-regions as escalator regions 3 rise of the East; global inequality	1. migrations from colonies/former colonies; 'return' of expatriates to 'home' country, eg at end of empire; 'managed migration' encourages the entry of the rich and the skilled, but discourages the entry of the poor and the 'unskilled' 2. 'escalator regions' as engines of social promotion into middle class jobs by: attracting from other regions/countries the 'brightest and best' young adults (stepping on); promoting them faster than elsewhere (going up); and losing them at later stages of their working lives or at retirement (stepping off) 3. rising migration pressures from failed/invaded states and all poor, high-risk places; rise of East Asian countries of immigration; ageing north, youthful south

Source: Fielding 2012 (modified)

in the economy plummets. People and firms tend in these circum-stances to 'bunker down' – that is, to reduce their activities, expendi-tures, overheads and commitments, so that they can weather the economic storm and be in a suitable position to benefit from the upturn when it comes. The migration responses to recession tend to reflect the low turnovers in both the labour and housing markets, so rates of migration flow are at a very low level: in-migration bottoms out low; out-migration peaks high; and net migration loss is to be expected.

The reader will probably have noticed a contradiction in the account given above. During recession mobility rates tend to be low, and yet high net out-migration is expected. In times past, when business cycles tended to be more local, perhaps even differing from one region of a country to another, it would have been possible for the out-migrants from a region in recession to have gone to a region that was booming. Today, however, in general that is not what happens. Globalization tends to ensure that there is a synchroni-zation of business cycles, so recession tends to be the condition across a whole country, indeed across many countries, at the same time. There is, therefore, nowhere booming to go to for those who are adversely affected by recession. Furthermore, in the real world, business cycle migration effects tend to be modified or even overlain by migrations that are obeying a different economic logic. This point can be illustrated by looking at the migrations to and from the Tokyo city region over the last 60 years (see below).

The second layer in Figure 8.3 refers to economic processes that take place over a much longer time span, typically over a period long enough for three or four business cycles. These processes are called 'economic restructuring' because they imply new ways of organizing what, how and where goods and services are produced. In this author's judgement, the best way to envisage them is through the concepts of changing spatial divisions of labour.

In the period from 1950–70 the dominant spatial division of labour was regional sectoral specialization. What is meant by this is, first, that the nation-state largely defined the limits of the economy – most economic transactions were internal to the national space-economy. Second, regions specialized in those branches of production for which their special endow-ments of physical and social resources (local climates, mineral resources, labour skills, work cultures, etc.) were best suited. Third, the incomes earned by the sale of these goods and services to people living in other regions of the country would be used to purchase the goods and services produced in those other regions. Finally, the agency for the exchange of these goods and services would be the market. This implies that the spatial or geo-graphical division of labour would coincide with the social division of labour – that is, the distribution that would result from market exchange. The implications of this for migration were profound. If the specialization on which a region's economy depended suffered decline, for example, through changing consumer preferences, technological change, or a low-income elasticity of demand, then businesses would fail, jobs would disappear and out-migration would follow.

In the 1950s and 1960s, most high-income countries experienced rapid rural depopulation. This came about because technological change was revolutionizing food production, leading to much lower labour inputs, food and agricultural products had a low-income elasticity of demand (demand increased very little as incomes went up), and rural businesses in all three macro-sectors (agriculture, etc., manufacturing, and services) tended to be small, technically backward, labour intensive, and uncompetitive. In contrast, large factory industrialization and services-based urbanization were making the cities rich in employment opportunities. The result was a mass movement from the countryside to the city.

However, rural depopulation was not the only migration pattern for this period. Old industrial areas built upon coal and steel, shipbuilding and textiles, were also losing out economically to the centres of Fordist production (the mass production of standardized goods for mass markets – products such as automobiles, white goods and electrical goods – which were very much in demand during this period). Fordist forms of production called for very large workforces and very large markets. These were to be found only in the largest and wealthiest of cities – the metropolitan conurbations and national capitals.

Connecting with and, for a time, coexisting with regional sectoral specialization, we witness during the 1970s the emergence of a different spatial division of labour coinciding with a rapid growth in the size of both private-sector firms and public-sector organizations – the new spatial division of labour. Instead of a region being defined by the sector of the economy that dominates its labour force, it becomes defined by the role that its labour force plays in the production process – as headquarters staff managing the affairs of the whole company (located in the capital city region and/or main financial centre), as research and development staff bringing new products to market or evaluating new production technologies (located in urbanized countryside close to the metropolis or in a major university city), as skilled workers needed to produce those goods and services calling for particular knowledge or experience (located in provincial cities and in new industrial areas), and as raw labour engaged in routine unskilled production (located in regions with large labour surpluses such as agricultural regions and old industrial areas).

Now the spatial division of labour coincides with the technical division of labour – that is, a planned separation of tasks designed to maximize the efficiency and/or profit performance of the whole organization. Once again, the migration implications were profound. Since the new spatial division of labour brought the work to the workers (at the same time, incidentally, as welfare payments helped unemployed people to survive in situ), working-class migration became much less important, and indeed, in most high-income countries total interregional migration rates began to fall during this period.

However, below the surface, two important new trends were developing. The first was the growth of intra-organizational transfers – as organizations managed their large and widely distributed workforces to achieve efficiency, they deployed their managerial, professional and technical staffs to their various operations located in different regions of the country. So middle-class mobility was being boosted just at the time when working-class mobility was being suppressed. The occupational class compositions of interregional migration flows were being transformed. Second, the labour and other costs incurred by companies in the metropolitan cities were too high to sustain the more routine parts of their production processes. As a result, there was a major decentralization of industrial and routine service-sector employment away from the metropolitan city regions towards small town and rural areas where labour was cheap and plentiful. With this change in the geography of investment we see the migration 'turnaround' – a shift from urbanization towards counter-urbanization. This counter-urban migration trend of the 1970s and early 1980s was found in all high-income countries. In some, notably the USA, it was largely interpreted as a response to the changing place preferences of populations (favouring the rural over the urban), but in most cases, it was seen as being the result of shifts in the political economy of production, often combined with demographic factors (Ishikawa 2001).

From the late 1970s, building up over the next 20–30 years, a further change in the spatial division of labour occurs. This time the driving force is not organizational change affecting firms operating within the national space-economy, but the strong development of links that are external to the national territory – in short, globalization. The effect of this at the level of regions within a country is to produce regional functional disconnection. This means that regions are increasingly neither linked to each other through market mechanisms (exchanges of goods and services), nor through the planned separation of tasks (as in the new spatial division of labour), but are instead disconnected from each other – each one linked independently through global connections of ownership, management, and the flows of goods, money, information and people *to places outside the national terri-tory*, to other parts of the world. The London city region represents, perhaps, an extreme version of this process. So seemingly cut off from the rest of the UK has it become as its global city character has displaced its national and regional economic roles, that it is sometimes spoken of as if it were a 'different country'.

Globalization also weakens labour in its relations with capital allowing forms of flexible specialization to emerge along with new industrial districts and industrial clusters. As a result of these changes, regional functional disconnection has two major implications for migration. The first is that it further reduces those many economic connections between regions that previously acted as conduits for migration (for example, intra-organizational transfers). The second is that by forging relationships at the global scale, it promotes international migration and thereby helps to bring about the new 'super-diversity' of metropolitan cities in high-income countries. The social significance of these international migrations lies in the fact that they add populations at both ends of the social spectrum – both at the top in the form of business owners, highly paid professionals and managers, and at the bottom in the form of gap-filler migrants where the immigrants do the jobs that the locals, including interregional migrants, cannot, or will not, do.

From about the mid-1990s onwards we have witnessed another change in the political economy of advanced capitalist countries – a change that has tended to focus net migration gains in the major metropolitan city regions once more. This change does not involve the end of globalization, but rather its transformation from being primarily about the integration of markets for the production and distribution of material goods to the establishment of global networks for the trading of immaterial goods and services – a shift to what is sometimes referred to as the 'knowledge-based economy' or 'cognitive capitalism'. This trend towards the financialization and commoditization of key social relationships and the partial replacement of wealth creation by wealth capture favours those regions that are the linchpins of the global economy – places where rent-seeking behaviours are most likely to be rewarded: New York, London and Tokyo, of course, but also globally significant cities like Hong Kong, Singapore, Shanghai and Mumbai.

The third layer in Figure 8.3 refers to economic processes that work themselves out extremely slowly, say over a person's lifespan or over three or four economic restructurings, and are therefore called 'deep structural' processes. This change is so slow that it is almost imperceptible. The underlying macro geography of wealth and poverty, both within and between countries, is the kind of thing to which this label refers. At the global level, the deep structural processes include those that help to maintain the inequalities between developing and developed countries, and the slow but steady shift of wealth and power since the 1950s towards East Asia. At the regional (that is, sub-national) scale, certain metropolitan city regions seem to dominate the space-economy in wealth and power from one generation to the next – Paris does so for France, Beijing and Shanghai do so for the People's Republic of China (PRC). One of the principal reasons for this stability of wealth concentration is interregional migration. These metropolitan city regions attract 'the brightest and the best' from all over the country; they socially promote them at rates that are much higher than other regions; and they lose them to other regions at later stages in their careers, or at, or close to, retirement from the labour market. The metaphor of the escalator has been used to describe this process – hence these regions become 'escalator regions' (see Box 4.1).

It is sensible to draw some of these ideas together through the use of an empirical example: Japan. The focus will be upon the net migration gains and losses of the three major metropolitan regions – Tokyo, comprising the four prefectures of the Southern Kanto region; Osaka, comprising the four core prefectures of the Kansai region; and Nagoya, comprising the three core prefectures of the Chubu region (see Figure 8.4).

The first thing to notice is the variability of the net migration curves, and the tendency for the peaks to coincide with periods of business confidence and the troughs with periods of economic difficulty or recession.

Second, the early 1970s – that is, before the oil crisis of 1974–75 – marks a turning point in the migration flows to Japanese cities. Before this point, all three metropolitan regions are the beneficiaries of net migration from the rest of Japan, and the order is simple: the largest gain the most. The 1950s and 1960s were the peak years for rural depopulation in Japan, and hundreds of thousands of people, mostly young men and women from farming and small-business backgrounds, were migrating each year to the major industrial cities as regional sectoral specialization favoured these centres of Fordist production over traditional provincial Japan. After the turning point, however, something very interesting happens: Tokyo takes off *on its own* as a major destination for internal migration. This is largely explained by the transition to the new spatial division of labour. Tokyo is the corporate headquarters location for Japanese domestic and international business. The 1980s was the period when these major corporations were achieving astounding success both in Japan and elsewhere, and Tokyo, not Osaka or Nagoya, was the major beneficiary of that success. Tokyo's global city success, however, suffered a severe blow during the Japanese financial crisis of the early 1990s: net migration gain momentarily became net migration loss, as asset values tumbled and business confidence plummeted. Since that time, significant net migration gains have returned, and held up until the recent crisis starting in 2008.

However, stand back from the detail and Figure 8.4 also shows us something else: the enduring attractiveness throughout business cycles and restructuring periods of the Tokyo metropolitan region to internal migrants. Tokyo is the 'one-point concentration' of the Japanese space-economy. If you are able, active and ambitious, where do you go? You go to the centre of bureaucratic power and corporate wealth, of luxury consumption, artistic creativity and celebrity success: you go to Tokyo. It is, itself, a major hub for university education (Tokyo University being the most prestigious in the country), but it is also the destination for many students graduating from other university cities around the country. These other university cities, especially Kyoto, but also major provincial cities such as Osaka, Nagoya, Fukuoka, Sendai and Hiroshima, act as 'siphon cities', recruiting bright students from nearby regions and from further afield, then channelling them on to Tokyo after graduation. When they get there, they benefit from the massive opportunities for upward social mobility that Tokyo offers them relative to other places in Japan (especially so, incidentally, for women).

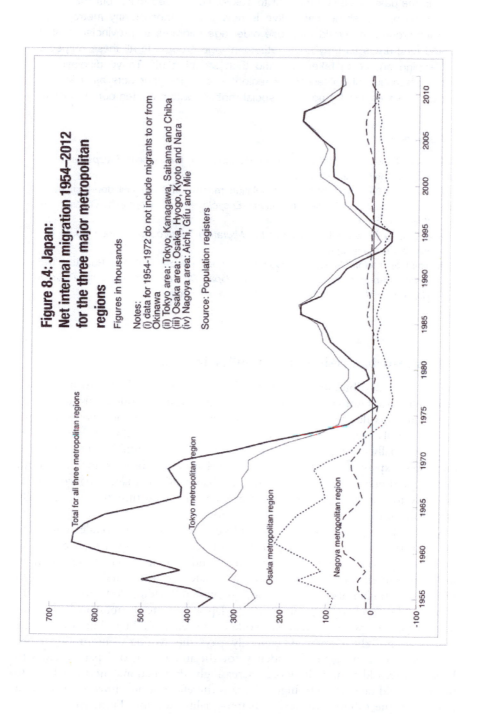

Figure 8.4: Japan:
Net internal migration 1954–2012
for the three major metropolitan
regions

Figures in thousands

Notes:
(i) data for 1954-1972 do not include migrants to or from Okinawa
(ii) Tokyo area: Tokyo, Kanagawa, Saitama and Chiba
(iii) Osaka area: Osaka, Hyogo, Kyoto and Nara
(iv) Nagoya area: Aichi, Gifu and Mie

Source: Population registers

Total for all three metropolitan regions

Tokyo metropolitan region

Osaka metropolitan region

Nagoya metropolitan region

In the past, once you made it to Tokyo, you stayed there, but the recent Census results show that Tokyo is now joining those many metropolitan cities around the world that lose older-age migrants to provincial, coastal and rural areas as they enter retirement age groups. In all these respects, stepping on, being taken up, and then stepping off, Tokyo displays the characteristics of an 'escalator region' – a region that acts as a kind of permanent engine for upwards social mobility within contemporary society.

References

Fielding, T., 2012, *Migration in Britain: Paradoxes of the Present, Prospects for the Future*. Cheltenham: Edward Elgar.

Fielding, T., 2016 (forthcoming), Population mobility and regional development, in Richardson, D. (ed.), *The International Encyclopedia of Geography*. Oxford: John Wiley and Sons, Ltd.

Ishikawa, Y. (ed.), 2001, *Studies in the Migration Turnarounds*. Kyoto: Kyoto University Press (in Japanese).

Ministry of Internal Affairs and Communications (Japan) Statistics Bureau, 2013, *Annual Report on Internal Migration in Japan Derived from the Basic Resident Registers 2012*. Tokyo: Statistics Bureau (in Japanese).

8.5 Intra-urban residential mobility in Japan

Population redistribution at the micro (intra-regional) level has also undergone major changes. During the period of rapid urbanization, roughly from 1950 to 1970, migrants flooded into the already built-up areas of the city which thus became highly congested mixed residential and industrial districts. As incomes grew, especially during the period from 1970–90, house building increased and the cities expanded outwards. This suburbanization process included both housing and employment, but many suburban residents made long commuter journeys to and from the city centre each day, a feature that is especially significant in the Tokyo metropolitan region.

What is perhaps surprising is that, unlike other advanced capitalist countries, this expansion of the city in Japan was not accompanied by a high degree of social segregation. There are neither the rundown 'inner cities' so common in North America nor the suburban 'sink estates' or 'banlieues' so common in Europe. A number of reasons have been suggested (Fielding 2004) to explain this anomaly. First, relatively poor people in Japan can afford suburban living, not just because the wages of manual workers are relatively high, but because the employer, not the employee, generally pays the worker's commuting costs. Second, there is no general tendency for the inner areas of Japanese cities to have poorer, older, and therefore increasingly dysfunctional housing because in situ rebuild rates are very high. There is therefore no incentive for people to migrate to the suburbs for newer, better-quality housing. Furthermore, while some social housing projects exist (*danchi*), they are generally fairly small in scale and are not occupied by the poorest households. Third, houses in Japan do not express a person's standing in the community to the degree that they do in other high-income countries. The social reputations of men and women, for example, are based much more on position in the organization (for men) and the respectability of the family and educational success of the children (for women). This means that there is no point in migrating to a high-status suburb – particularly since, because the home is a very private space, nobody you might want to impress will see it anyway. Fourth, as was hinted above, another reason why social segregation is low is the complexity of both land ownership and land use within the city, largely due to historic factors and to the low salience of land-use planning. Fifth, residential mobility associated with the social and physical upgrading of older, inner-city neighbourhoods (gentrification) and their replacement by new middle-class districts in inner-city locations is virtually absent in Japanese cities. This is related in part to the lack of a reason (such as immigrant populations, ethnic conflict or high crime rates) to leave the inner city in the first place, so migration to suburban or ex-urban locations to avoid social risk ('white flight' in the USA) is unnecessary in Japanese cities (the important exception to this generalization is the stigma attached to living in a *buraku* (outcast) district, but these are scattered around the city and are not concentrated, for example, in inner-city areas). Finally, one would expect the level of social segregation to be lower in a society in which income inequality is relatively low (such as Japan) than in a society in which that inequality was much higher (such as the USA).

So the product of the high-growth period ending around 1990 was a spatially dispersed but relatively socially mixed city. Then what happened? Well, the decline in housing and land values meant that much of the dynamism of the urban development process was lost. Japanese cities entered a period of relative stability – in fact a degree of stability not seen since the first 'opening up' of Japan in 1868. Since many of the young adults who previously would have entered jobs that were well paid and offered lifetime employment now remained outside the formal labour market, they tended also not to become home owners and not to marry and start a family. Indeed, many returned to their parental homes and became 'parasite singles'.

So suburbanization and peri-urbanization (the spread of new housing development to small towns and villages around the metropolitan areas) largely stalled. Only in Tokyo was this lack of urban development clearly not the case. As we saw above, the Tokyo metropolitan region gained by net internal migration (as it did also, of course, from international migration), as its financial services and capital city functions expanded. Many of these migrants went to the inner parts of the metropolitan region, and the wealthier amongst them joined the boom in 'new-build gentrification'. What this means in the Tokyo context is the building of high-rise apartment complexes on land in, or accessible to, the city centre which had typically been vacated by non-residential land uses (such as old railway yards or factory sites). This new-build gentrification, coinciding with new levels of income inequality, has helped to alter significantly the demography and the skyline of Tokyo. It has reflected and facilitated a shift in the age structure of the population towards young adults, it has reinforced the *embourgeoisement* of Tokyo as the professional and managerial middle classes displace (sometimes literally) the manual and low-level white-collar working classes, and it has introduced residential high rise in a city largely dominated before by low-rise housing (sometimes, as in the case of Roppongi Hills, to spectacular effect).

8.6 Gender, ethnicity and the life course in Japan: relations to migration

Urban socio-spatial segregation may be low, but adult gender role segregation, despite some recent changes in attitudes towards work and family life, remains very strong in Japan. The husband (marriage is the norm) is regarded as having one responsibility above all else: to earn enough money to provide a good quality of life for his family. The wife should raise the children well, run the household financially, and keep house for the whole family (which may include her husband's parents). What this means in practice is that men are often tied to the needs of their employer; if the company or public corporation says that the employee should move to a new location, he moves. This creates problems. Whereas intra-organizational transfers in Western countries are problematic largely because of the difficulty of maintaining two careers (it puts pressure on the other partner – typically the woman – to give up her job and risk a break in her career), in Japan the problem is more frequently the educational needs of the children. With enormous pressure to succeed in their university entrance exams (in what is often called a 'one-chance society'), parents are extremely reluctant to risk their children's performance by removing them from their current school or schools (many children go to 'cram' schools in the evenings and at weekends). Add to this the responsibilities that the family often has towards elderly parents, their multiple embeddedness in the local community, and their duty to protect family property, and the resistance to a migration brought on by the father's posting is complete. The solution is very often to allow the husband to migrate on his own to the new job location while leaving the wife, children and elderly to remain in their current place of residence. This *tanshinfunin* (moving away alone to a new posting) has been a significant feature of Japanese internal migration for many generations (indeed, of course, it has origins in obligations towards your lord or emperor in feudal Japan). These days women are often asked by the employer on recruitment whether or not they want to join the career path taken by their male colleagues; most of them, realizing the impossibility of leaving the region for family reasons, opt for the non-career path, and by doing so, accept that they will achieve no significant promotion within the organization.

For those who are not married and are ambitious for career advancement, the path to occupational promotion almost always lies in migrating to the

Tokyo metropolitan region. Here, the immense range and density of job opportunities makes upward social mobility for both men and women much easier than in the rest of Japan, and the greater acceptance of gender equality means that such opportunities are especially strong for women. Tokyo, like Shanghai (discussed in Chapter 6), is an 'escalator region', and as such it plays a very formative role in the production of Japanese elites, and of its professional and managerial middle classes.

In the early modern (but post-1868) period there had been quite significant ethnic aspects to internal migration in Japan. Okinawans experienced discrimination in the Kansai region, and the Tohoku (Northern Honshu) region had a distinctively separate migration system involving long-distance, but often seasonal, migration to the Tokyo area. Some aspects of these older migration patterns continued after 1945, notably the traditional family-based Tohoku migration system, but the second opening of Japan after 1945 with its enthusiastic embrace of Western, and especially American, cultural values, largely eradicated these ethnic-specific migration processes.

What that modernization failed to do, however, was to alter the distinctively Japanese character of the link between migration and the life course. In Western countries there is a strong tendency for people to migrate to those places where people like them (that is, in the same age group and at the same stage in the life course) are located (18-year-old students go to university cities where other 18-year-olds congregate; 40-year-old married people with children go to big city suburbs and peri-urban areas where others like them live; well-off retired go to rural and coastal areas where other retired have already settled). In Japan it is different. Partly because mobility rates are lower, thus reducing the impact of age-specific migration rates on the age structure of the population, but mostly due to family obligations and city-living preference, there is a strong tendency for Japanese migrants to move to the most dynamic urban places in the space-economy whatever their age or stage in the life course. In particular, older migrants tend to move to the cities where their offspring live. These are largely the same places that are the typical destinations for working-age adults and students (the exception for students is their high concentration in the city of Kyoto). Apart from young adult returnees and excluding those places located at the edges of large cities, hardly anyone in Japan migrates to a rural area (this has changed a little in the recent period).

Before leaving Japan, it is important to stress that in addition to the mass migrations brought about by regional and urban-rural inequalities operating over long periods of time, there are also the very sudden demographic effects of natural disasters. Twice in the last 20 years Japan has suffered major earthquakes: the first in the Kansai region centring on Kobe in 1995 which killed 6,400 residents and displaced about 100,000 people; the second in the Touhoku region around and to the north of Sendai in 2011 which, largely as a result of the ensuing tsunami, killed 18,500 residents and displaced 340,000 people. Some of these displacements resulting from natural disasters are temporary – people stay with family members in other places and return as soon as repairs or rebuilding are under way – but permanent displacement also occurs. It is unlikely that the inner part of Kobe (especially Nagata ward, which was the location of many small businesses as well as high-density low-rise housing) will ever again regain its pre-earthquake level of population, and a zone around the Fukushima Dai-Ichi nuclear power station (which experienced reactor meltdowns) will be uninhabitable for decades.

8.7 Internal migration in South (and North) Korea

It is often said that Japan's economic space is characterized by 'one-point concentration' (the concentration of wealth and power in the Tokyo metropolitan area), but this is even more the case for South Korea, where the proportion of the country's population concentrated in the Seoul metropolitan area (the three provinces of Seoul, Incheon and Geonggi-do) is even higher (at 49%) than that of Tokyo in Japan (27%). Exacerbated by the upheavals and dislocations brought about by the Korean War, rural depopulation after 1952 was extremely rapid and spatially widespread. Many migrants settled in the large regional cities: Pusan in the southeast, Gwangju in the southwest, Daegu in the centre southeast, and Daejeon in the centre west of the peninsula. However, the overwhelming net migration gains were experienced by Seoul itself and its immediate surroundings, plus the built-up area stretching west to the port city of Incheon, and southwards, where an extended zone of urban industrial development came into being.

Absolutely key to this urbanization was the growth of the industrial conglomerates (the *chaebol*). In close association with the authoritarian state, these major companies, Hyundai, Samsung, LG, etc. invested heavily in, or close to, the main urban areas during the 1960s, 1970s and 1980s as they expanded to meet export demand for their consumer goods products such as cars, radios and TVs, and household electrical goods. Eventually, as in Japan, the momentum of industrial growth led to the exhaustion of the reserves of mobile labour in the cities, and a process of more dispersed industrialization ensued. By this time, however, the population of South Korea had become very largely urban, and has remained so since.

The industrial success of South Korea continued into the 1990s and 2000s but was momentarily checked by the East Asian financial crisis in 1997. The big companies developed new lines of consumer products, notably computers and mobile phones, and increasingly operated not only in South Korea but also in the PRC and Southeast Asia. Meanwhile, after a long struggle, the country adopted a pluralistic form of democratic politics with a strong civil society (NGO) sector. This means that South Korea's urban populations, many of them first- or second-generation migrants from the rural regions, not only enjoy good wages and high levels of consumption, but also a bundle of social and political rights from which they had never benefited before.

The results of this rapid economic growth are South Korean cities that are physically and socially very distinctive. They are planned landscapes, dominated by large high-rise housing projects, often with skylines punctured by the spires of Christian churches. In all of these respects they differ from the landscapes of Japanese cities.

We can obtain a picture of contemporary patterns of internal migration at the provincial level from the household registration data for 2012 from the Korea Statistical Office, which show, first, that the level of inter-provincial migration (at 5.0% of the population) was significantly lower in 2012 than it had been in 2007 (5.9%), and much lower than it had been in 1975 (at 8.1%). This represents both the maturing of the Korean economy and the recent downturn in its performance, but, more generally, the substitution of older spatial divisions of labour (notably regional sectoral specialization) by newer ones – ones that no longer require the mass movement of workers to the high-growth regions. Second, the data show that the extended Seoul (three-province) region was still a slight net gainer by internal migration, but with the distinctive feature, so common in so-called 'escalator regions', of major migration gains in the capital city itself of those aged 20–24 and 25–29. This is not a feature of South Korea's other major cities. Third, the cities and regions to the south of Seoul were net migration gainers. This is where major invest-ments, such as the building of the new 'information' city of Sejong, are occurring. Finally, the regions of southern South Korea, specifically Gwangju and the surrounding Jeolla provinces in the southwest, and Pusan and the Gyongsang provinces in the southeast, were significant net losers by internal migration.

We can know very little indeed about internal migration in North Korea, but we do know that permission is required for a move to Pyongyang. Indeed, permission is required for any internal migration, so those selected for employment at the South Korean factories located in the Kaesong Industrial District were not spontaneous migrants.

8.8 Migration from North Korea to South Korea

Migration between the two Koreas is almost entirely one-way – from North to South. It is, of course, an international migration, but so anachronistic is the division of the Korean peninsula (as one of the last vestiges of the Cold War), that it seems sensible to include it in this chapter. The migration is not only one-way but the numbers are minute. Over the 60 years since the end of the Korean War just 25,000 migrants have 'escaped' through migration to South Korea. They are given: (i) special financial assistance (after being intensively interviewed to ensure that they are not North Korean spies); (ii) help with jobs and housing; and (iii) instruction on how to live in South Korea at the special centre set up for that purpose (Hanawon). In truth, the story of North Koreans living in South Korea is not a totally happy one; adjustment is difficult and many of the escapees have sought to move on to third countries. Some, but very few, have returned to North Korea.

8.9 Internal migration to, from, and within the Russian Far East

In almost every respect the internal migration situation in the Russian Far East (RFE) contrasts with the rest of Northeast Asia. First, the vast territory of the RFE is extremely sparsely populated, with much of that population arriving during the Soviet period. Second, its recent migration history since the collapse of the Soviet Union has been one of out-migration not just from the countryside but also from the cities. That migration has very largely been of ethnic Russians, so the RFE joins much of the rest of the former periphery of the Soviet Union (which includes the countries of the Caucasus and of Central Asia) in experiencing net out-migration of both ethnic Russians and others to the core regions of European Russia.

A key reason for this net migration loss was the withdrawal of the special benefits in terms of wages and infrastructure investment that the populations of the RFE had enjoyed under the Soviet system. Wages, for example, were routinely 20% higher in the RFE than in the rest of the Soviet Union. The Far East was crucial to the Soviet Union for all sorts of reasons. It was a major source of key resources, especially minerals and timber, it was strategically important in the superpower contest with the USA with naval bases, missile defences, and other military establishments, and it was one of the main regions for the banishment and punishment of political prisoners in work camps (*gulags*).

When, after 1990, the RFE was 'abandoned' by the central government, there were several results: (i) incomes went down, often quite precipitously; (ii) key utilities failed – in such a harsh environment (winter temperatures regularly fall to below -20°C) it was potentially life threatening when, for example, electricity outages occurred or communications repair work was not carried out; (iii) unemployment rose, and prospects for young people coming onto the labour market suddenly worsened; (iv) criminal gangs and corruption filled the power vacuum left by the disappearance of Soviet discipline – Vladivostok, in particular, gained the reputation of being a city run by the Russian mafia; and (v) not surprisingly, there appeared all the social ills associated with fatalism and despair – alcohol and drug abuse, and risks to personal safety through theft and violence.

The outcome was amazing. The population declined sharply during the 1990s, mostly due to out-migration but also because fertility rates were low. School leavers and graduates alike sought futures outside the region, so that the population structure became biased towards the elderly. This depopulation, which continued, albeit at lower rates, through the 2000s, was most severe in the northern and most remote parts of the region. Only in Khabarovsk and Vladivostok, and along the border with China were populations able, to some degree, to maintain their pre-1990 levels. New resources came along, such as the oil and gas fields of Sakhalin, but the population and migration effects of these developments were minimal.

We can obtain a reasonably up-to-date picture of these internal migration flows by using the one-year migration flow data from the Russia Statistical Office from the 2010 Census. This shows that the RFE as a whole lost over

35,000 people (or about 0.6% of the population) through internal migration in just one year. All of the sub-regions (oblasts/krais) of the RFE experienced net migration loss except the Jewish Autonomous Region, and the rates of loss were especially high in Magadan, Khabarovsk and Kamchatka. Even Primorski krai, containing the largest city in the RFE – Vladivostok – lost by net migration at a rate of 5.5 per thousand population in 2009/10. These losses were partially offset by the arrival in the RFE of 15,000 migrants from the Commonwealth of Independent States countries (mostly former Soviet Union countries in Central Asia), and of 12,000 migrants from other countries (presumably mostly from China and North Korea). This data source cannot tell us, of course, how many people emigrated abroad from the RFE during that year, or what their destinations might have been.

8.10 Conclusion

Despite the rich mineral resources in North Korea and the even richer mineral, hydrocarbon and timber resources of the Russian Far East, the economic giants of Northeast Asia are Japan and South Korea. They have both enjoyed rapid economic growth in the post-1950 period, first Japan, then South Korea. This growth set in motion vast redistributions of their populations, so that today a large part of their populations are not just urban, they are metropolitan. Seoul and Tokyo are massive, complex metropolitan city-regions inhabited largely by relatively affluent people who are South Korean and Japanese by nationality and identity, pro-capitalist and democratic in political persuasion, and Confucian in values and behaviour. These are the capital cities of societies that have experienced an extraordinary transformation in the post-1950 period – a hyper-urbanization.

Selected references

8.1 *Urban and regional development in Japan*

Fujita, M. and Tabuchi, T., 1997, Regional growth in postwar Japan, *Regional Science and Urban Economics* 27: 643–670.

Kawashima, T., 1980, The regional pattern of the Japanese economy: its characteristics and trends, in Association of Japanese Geographers (ed.), *Geography of Japan*. Tokyo: Teikoku-Shoin, 390–414.

Murayama, Y., 2010, *Japanese Urban System*. Berlin: Springer.

Yamamoto, K., 1987, Regional disparity and its development in postwar Japan, *Journal of International Economic Studies* 2: 131–170.

On relations between the country and the city:

Kelly, W.W., 1990, Regional Japan: the price of prosperity and the benefits of dependency, *Daedalus* 119: 209–228.

On effects of natural disasters on migration/displacement:

Edgington, D.W., 2011, *Reconstructing Kobe: The Geography of Crisis and Opportunity*. Vancouver: University of British Columbia Press.

Matanle, P., 2013, Post–disaster recovery in ageing and declining communities: the great East Japan disaster of 11 March 2011, *Geography* 98(2): 68–76.

8.2 Rural depopulation and urbanization in Japan

Knight, J., 2003, Repopulating the village? in Traphagan, J.W. and Knight, J. (eds), *Demographic Change and the Family in Japan's Aging Society*. Albany, NY: State University of New York Press, 107–124.

Kuroda, T., 1976, Urbanization and population redistribution in Japan, in Goldstein, S. and Sly, D.F. (eds), *Patterns of Urbanization: Volume 2*. Liège: International Union for the Scientific Study of Population, 433–464.

Liaw, K.-L., 1992, Interprefectural migration and its effects on prefectural populations in Japan: an analysis based on the 1980 census, *Canadian Geographer* 36(4): 320–335.

Otomo, A., 1990, Japan, in Nam, C. et al. (eds), *International Handbook on Internal Migration*. New York: Greenwood Press, 257–274.

Rabson, S., 2011, *The Okinawan Diaspora in Japan: Crossing the Border Within*. Honolulu: University of Hawai'i Press.

Sorensen, A., 2002, *The Making of Urban Japan: Cities and Planning from Edo to the Twenty-First Century*. London: Routledge.

8.3 The population 'turnaround' in Japan

Glickman, N.J., 1979, *The Growth and Management of the Japanese Urban System*. New York: Academic Press.

For other discussions on the U-turn and on internal migration patterns more generally:

Ishikawa, Y. (ed.), 2001, *Studies in the Migration Turnaround*. Kyoto: Kyoto University Press (in Japanese).

Tsuya, N.O. and Kuroda, T., 1989, Japan: the slowing of urbanization and metropolitan concentration, in Champion, A.G. (ed.), *Counterurbanization*. London: Edward Arnold, 207–229.

On intra-organizational transfers:

Wiltshire, R., 1990, Employee movement in large Japanese organizations, in Johnson, J. H. and Salt, J. (eds), *Labour Migration*. London: David Fulton, 32–52.

For interesting work on the migration of the elderly:

Otomo, A., 1993, Elderly migration and population redistribution in Japan, in Rogers, A. (ed.), *Elderly Migration and Population Redistribution*. London: Belhaven Press, 185–202.

On economic restructuring and population redistribution:

Child Hill, R. and Fujita, K., 1993, Japanese cities in the world economy, in Fujita, K. and Hill, R.C. (eds), *Japanese Cities in the World Economy*. Philadelphia: Temple University Press, 3–25.

Edgington, D., 1997, The rise of the yen, hollowing out and Japan's troubled industries, in Watters, R.F. and McGee, T.G. (eds), *Asia-Pacific: New Geographies of the Pacific Rim*. London: Hurst, 170–189.

McDonald, M.G., 1996, Farmers and workers in Japan's regional economic restructuring, 1965–1985, *Economic Geography* 72(1): 49–72.

Shapira, P., Masser, I. and Edgington, D.W. (eds), 1994, *Planning for Cities and Regions in Japan*. Liverpool: Liverpool University Press.

Uriu, R.M., 1996, *Troubled Industries: Confronting Economic Change in Japan*. Ithaca, NY: Cornell University Press.

For social changes in rural areas:

Waswo, A. and Nishida, Y. (eds), *Farmers and Village Life in Twentieth Century Japan*. London: Routledge.

8.4 Migration to and from the Tokyo metropolitan region

For migration to and from the Tokyo region:

Ishikawa, Y. and Fielding, A.J., 1998, Explaining the recent migration trends of the Tokyo metropolitan area, *Environment and Planning A* 30: 1797–1814.

On 'one-point concentration' (in Tokyo):

Fujita, K., 1991, A world city and flexible specialisation: restructuring and the Tokyo metropolis, *International Journal of Urban and Regional Research* 15(2): 269–284.

Machimura, T., 1992, The urban restructuring process in Tokyo in the 1980s: transforming Tokyo into a world city, *International Journal of Urban and Regional Research* 16: 114–128.

Waley, P., 1998, Tokyo: patterns of familiarity and partitions of difference, in Marcuse, P. and Van Kempen, R. (eds), *The Partitioned City*. Oxford: Blackwell, 128–156.

However, living in Tokyo is not without its problems:

Bestor, T.C., 1989, *Neighbourhood Tokyo*. Stanford, CA: Stanford University Press.

Cybriwsky, R., 1998, *Tokyo: The Changing Profile of an Urban Giant*. London: Belhaven.

Lutzeler, R., 2008, Population increase and 'new-build gentrification' in central Tokyo, *Erdkunde* 62(4): 287–299.

Seidensticker, E., 1991, *Tokyo Rising: The City since the Great Earthquake*. Cambridge, MA: Harvard University Press.

8.5 Intra-urban residential mobility in Japan

Fielding, A.J., 2004, Class and space: social segregation in Japanese cities, *Transactions of the Institute of British Geographers* NS29: 64–84.

Ronald, R. and Alexy, A. (eds), 2011, *Home and Family in Japan: Continuity and Transformation*. London: Routledge.

8.6 Gender, ethnicity and the life course in Japan: relations to migration

Gill, T.P., 2001, *Men of Uncertainty: The Social Organization of Day Labourers in Contemporary Japan*. Albany, NY: State University of New York Press.

Kitaguchi, S., 1999, *An Introduction to the Buraku Issue*. Folkstone: Japan Library.

Valentine, J., 1990, On the borderlines: the significance of marginality in Japanese society, in Ben-Ari, E., Moeran, B. and Valentine, J. (eds), *Unwrapping Japan: Society and Culture in Anthropological Perspective*. Manchester: Manchester University Press, 36–57.

Wagatsuma, H. and De Vos, G.A., 1967, The outcast tradition in modern Japan: a problem in social self-identity, in Dore, R.P. (ed.), *Aspects of Social Change in Modern Japan*. Princeton, NJ: Princeton University Press, 373–409.

On migration and the life course:

Fielding, A.J. and Ishikawa, Y., 2003, Migration and the life course in contemporary Japan, *Geographical Review of Japan* 76(12): 882–893.

8.7 Internal migration in South (and North) Korea

Bae, C.-H.C. and Richardson, H.W. (eds), 2011, *Regional and Urban Policy and Planning on the Korean Peninsula*. Cheltenham: Edward Elgar.

Choi, J.H., 2009, *The Causes and Selectivity of Internal Migration in Korea*, International Union for the Scientific Study of Population, Marrakesh conference presentation.

Mobrand, E., 2012, Reverse remittances: internal migration and rural-to-urban remittances in industrializing South Korea, *Journal of Ethnic and Migration Studies* 38(3): 389–411.

Park, S.O., 2009, A history of the Republic of Korea's industrial structural transformation and spatial development, in *Reshaping Economic Geography in East Asia*. Washington, DC: World Bank, 320–337.

8.8 Migration from North Korea to South Korea

On internal migration in North Korea:

Spoorenberg, T. and Schwekendiek, D., 2012, Demographic changes in North Korea: 1993–2008, *Population and Development Review* 38(1): 133–158.

On migration from North Korea to South Korea (via China):

Chung, B.-H., 2009, Between defector and migrant: identities and strategies of North Koreans in South Korea, *Korean Studies* 32: 1–27.

Foley, R., 2003, *Korea's Divided Families: Fifty Years of Separation*. London: Routledge.

Haggard, S. and Noland, M. (eds), 2006, *The North Korean Refugee Crisis: Human Rights and International Response*. Washington, DC: US Committee for Human Rights in North Korea.

Kim, S.K., 2012, 'Defector', 'refugee', or 'migrant'? North Korean settlers in South Korea's changing social discourse, *North Korean Review* 8(2): 94–110.

Lankov, A., 2004, North Korean refugees in northeast China, *Asian Survey* 44(6): 856–873.

Smith, H., 2005, North Koreans in China: sorting fact from fiction, in Akaha, T. and Vassilieva, A., *Crossing National Borders: Human Migration Issues in Northeast Asia*. Tokyo: United Nations University Press, 165–190.

Song, J., 2013, 'Smuggled refugees': the social construction of North Korean migration, *International Migration* 51(4): 158–173.

8.9 Internal migration to, from, and within the Russian Far East

Bradshaw, M.J. and Vartapetov, K., 2003, A new perspective on regional inequalities in Russia, *Eurasian Geography and Economics* 44(6): 403–429.

Gerber, T.P., 2006, Regional economic performance and net migration rates in Russia 1993–2002, *International Migration Review* 40(3): 661–697.

Grandstaff, P.J., 1980, *Interregional Migration in the USSR: Economic Aspects 1959–1970*. Durham, NC: Duke University Press.

Heleniak, T., 1999, Out-migration and depopulation of the Russian north during the 1990s, *Post-Soviet Geography and Economics* 40(3): 155–205.

Lewis, R.A. and Rowland, R.H., 1979, *Population Redistribution in the USSR: Its Impact on Society, 1897–1977*. New York: Praeger.

Thornton, J. and Zeigler, C.E., 2002, *Russia's Far East: A Region at Risk*. Seattle, WA: National Bureau of Asian Research.

9 Migration and globalization

East Asian migrations now and in the future

9.0 Introduction

This final chapter has two main functions – to pull together the topics so ruthlessly separated by the classification of materials adopted in this book, notably, first, the harsh distinction between Southeast Asia, 'China', and Northeast Asia. This chapter will focus especially on those issues that cross the geographical frontiers of these three macro regions. Second, the strict separation of international migration from internal migration. Some of the most exciting analyses of East Asian migration purposely bring these migrations together and treat them as part of larger multi-scale processes. In addition, the chapter takes a glance, albeit a highly speculative one, into the future. How are the trends already in play, and those likely to emerge in the near future, going to alter the picture of migrations presented here?

9.1 Trade, investment and migration in East Asia: the effects of the global economic crisis

In the 60 plus years since 1950, East Asia has changed from being many, mostly national, economic spaces with strong external links, to become, to a significant degree, a single economic space with strong internal links. During roughly the first half of this period, the steps towards the creation of a single economic space were timid, local and limited; in the second half, due very largely to the opening up of China, the steps were bold, East Asia-wide and far reaching. In the earlier period, increases in trade, notably growth in exports, were key to economic development, but it was trade that was largely directed to external, especially North American, markets. By the end of the period, most of the largest trading partners for East Asian countries were other East Asian countries. However, it was not just a matter of flows of goods; flows of capital also became diverted – to such a degree that significant slices of the industrial and service economies of most East Asian countries are now commanded by firms based in other East Asian countries.

Do these changes in trade and capital flows affect migration? Yes, they do – both directly and, in some ways more importantly, indirectly. Trade in commodities (and later services) called for the setting up of offices and commercial outlets in key 'gateway' cities (many of them capital cities) in the country of the trading partner. In this way, the Japanese general trading companies (*sougou shousha*), Korean conglomerates (*chaebol*), Hong Kong banks and Singapore shipping companies spread throughout the main cities and ports of East and Southeast Asia. Foreign direct investment went further: it not only required company staff to oversee such investments from big city company offices, but also called for managers and technicians 'on the ground', located at the factory, mining or construction sites wherever these might be. By this means, Taiwanese and Singaporeans came to live and work in the provinces of the People's Republic of China (PRC), and Japanese and Koreans came to live and work in the countries of Southeast Asia. Was this all? No, because the firms not only brought capital, technology and employees to the country in which they invested, but took back nationals from those countries as both promotion-track staff and as industrial trainees to their home base – typically to the industrial or commercial cities from which they had originally expanded their operations.

Yet it is, perhaps, through the indirect effects of trade and investment that we witness the greatest migration outcomes. When a foreign company builds a factory in low labour-cost agrarian country it tends to trigger a string of interconnected migration events. First at the local level, and then at an interregional level, it uproots (deracinates) people from their village lives, peasant mentalities and agricultural economies, and moves them to the dormitories of the 'special economic/enterprise zone' or industrial estate where the factory is located. They must quickly learn the time and work disciplines of the factory, and to become an employee at the bottom of a hierarchy of authority. They are proletarianized. Their wages are, of course, very low, and yet the near absence of money previously means that they now possess new power and status. When they return to the village, for example, this is expressed not only in the ability to give to those, such as family members, from whom they previously received, but to express success through the clothes they wear, the gadgets they use, and the new confidence they show in relationships to others (including those who previously ranked above them in local society). Not surprisingly, this demonstrates to others the obvious good sense of migrating to the city or the industrial zone to get employment in the same foreign-owned business or factory. In this way, a growing wave of migration from the rural areas to the city occurs … which, in turn, encourages further foreign investment.

At this point something else happens. It is as if there is the sudden realization that the country from which this firm comes is a land of long life, a high material standard of living, greater personal freedom, and modern culture. The products being made in the factory are amazing: they are technologically sophisticated, well designed, reliable and resistant to damage. Why not migrate to the country where the ownership of these products is a commonplace? Having glimpsed that the 'grass is indeed greener on the other side of the fence', what is there to keep you here – where life is short, poverty is the norm, and you are tied down by obligation and tradition? I simplify and exaggerate, of course, but trade and investment can help to break down the barriers, both informational and aspirational, to what kind of future one can imagine for oneself. They thus become one of the mechanisms by which a migration stream from the low-income country to the high-income one becomes established.

9.2 Migration and labour market integration in East Asia

Until now, the nation-state has acted as the framework for analysis. It has provided the bounded space within which internal migration flows have been studied, and it has been treated as either an origin or a destination for international migrations. The problem with this approach is that it tends to miss features of the wider (that is, East Asian) migration system. Labour market integration has occurred within countries, most importantly within China, and it has also occurred at the level of the wider region as a whole. Almost all pairs of countries now have complex migration interdependencies. Take, for example, China and Japan. Chinese migrants now form the largest immigrant minority in Japan (despite the frosty political relations between their governments and populations): they are there as temporary residents (for example, students) and workers (for example, trainees), but also as permanent workers, wives and long-term residents (especially in the Tokyo metropolitan area). At the same time, increasing numbers of Japanese people are living, sometimes temporarily (for example as students), often more permanently (as employees of major companies or as independent workers), in the PRC (especially in Shanghai). Young Koreans (such as English-language students), adult Koreans (such as company employees and their families) and older Koreans (such as the retired) are living in the Philippines. At the same time, many thousands of young adult Filipinos are working hard in the factories and workshops, offices and shops of Korea's major cities (but especially in and around Seoul).

The product of these many labour market intersections in East Asia is a growing ethnic diversity of national workforces. Apart, perhaps, from the case of Singapore, and maybe also individual gateway cities such as Bangkok, Hong Kong, Shanghai, and Tokyo, this is not yet the 'superdiversity' that is such a talking point in the EU, but it does represent a sharp turn towards East Asian countries becoming multicultural societies, even in cases such as Japan, Thailand and South Korea where mono-ethnicity is still widely celebrated.

Maybe so, but it certainly does not follow that this ethnic diversity is being built on the basis of mutual respect for one another's cultures, or of equal power and status in the labour market. Coincident with the spatial mixing of populations through migration is the emergence of ethnic divisions of labour in national workforces. To varying degrees in time and over space, immigrant workers are filling specific employment niches – capitalist entrepreneurs or construction workers here, sex workers or doctors there. This tendency to separation tends to underline their 'otherness', and to make them the victims of either envy or stigmatization (and sometimes both).

9.3   East Asia's 'new migrations': the highly skilled moving to and from North America and Australasia

The emphasis so far in this chapter has been on the tendency for the parts of East Asia to become increasingly interconnected through their migration flows, but there is one part of the changing reality that does not conform to this picture. Very many young adult East Asians pursue their undergraduate or postgraduate careers in countries where the language of instruction is English (USA, Canada, Australia, New Zealand, UK and certain other EU countries). For the most part they come from wealthy or middle-class backgrounds, and are supported emotionally and financially by their parents. Some of these students settle well and stay on to form their professional or managerial careers in the country in which they studied. There, they are joined by other well-educated adults from East Asia who, for career-development, cultural-political and family-related reasons migrate to the same countries. The result is the emergence of significant 'Asian' communities, consisting of business owners, academics, medical workers, accountants, information technologists, artists, etc., in major North American, Australasian, and European cities (for example, Koreans in Auckland, Japanese in Los Angeles and Vancouver, Malaysians in Sydney). Yes, they are different, and are sometimes made to feel different, from their host populations, but as they become socially and culturally embedded in societies where to be different is usually okay, and sometimes even 'cool', and where human rights and equality before the law are more than just rhetoric, many choose to take the path to citizenship and become permanent members of their adopted countries.

9.4   Gender and family: demography and the environment

In the early years of the emergence of an 'East Asian migration system' most of the migrants, both within the region and to outside destinations such as the Middle East, were young adult male employees. Since then, an increasing diversity of types of migration and types of migrant has developed. Part of this trend is encompassed by the notion of a 'feminization of migration' as female migrants have caught up, and frequently surpassed, the number of male migrants. Since many of these women are mothers who migrate alone, leaving their children in the care of their partners and parents, there is a significant increase in 'transnational households' – that is, households in which key practical and emotional relationships are now being played out at the international level. Part of this diversity is also accounted for by the expanding list of reasons for migration. It is no longer the case, if it ever was, that people are leaving their home country or region exclusively for economic reasons – they go for study, relationship/marriage, lifestyle, politico-cultural, and retirement reasons as well.

Having said this, the evidence from all over East Asia is that earning a living and improving one's economic prospects are at the centre of most migration decisions. Where incomes are low and job prospects are poor, men and women will leave to find work that is better paid and more secure. These origin countries and regions tend to be characterized by high fertility and large completed family size; the destination countries and regions tend to be characterized by low fertility and small completed family size. However, the migration between them is no simple demographic balancing act. Poverty tends to result in both large families and out-migration; wealth does the opposite – the labour market of an affluent country usually has few local entrants because of past low fertility, and it also has big gaps where locals are reluctant to do the jobs that are routine, risky or wretched … which then leads to in-migration.

Poor or rich, most countries and regions in East Asia are subject to environmental shocks. They vary enormously from one place to another (drought in western China, floods in southern China and Thailand, earthquakes and tsunamis in the Pacific and Indian Ocean rim countries – especially Japan, Taiwan, Philippines, and Indonesia – typhoons in countries bordering the Pacific, volcanic eruptions, etc.), but through their destructive effects, they induce population movements, sometimes temporary (as along the Aceh coast after the 2004 tsunami), sometimes close to permanent (as around Fukushima after the meltdown at the nuclear energy plant following the tsunami in 2011). The big issue in East Asia, however, is not the known risks of periodic environmental disasters for which each society is, to some extent, prepared, but the poorly known and almost completely unanticipated effects of global environmental change (see below).

9.5 Migration policies, ethnicity and citizenship

It was emphasized in Chapter 2 that for much of its history, East Asia was a space dominated by one centre of wealth and power: China. The parts of East Asia typically had multiple allegiances – to the local lord, to the king of the wider territory, and to the emperor of China. The region's late 19th- and 20th-century history was marked by a very different formation: the emergence of 'Westphalian' nation-states – that is to say, ethnically defined land-based sovereign states occupying non-overlapping territories. Membership of such states was achieved through descent; you 'belonged' to that country to which your parents (and through them, your ancestors) belonged. So, the legal principle of membership was *jus sanguinis* or blood-line connection. You could not claim citizenship through the principle of *jus soli* or place-of-birth connection (East Asia has no country with unrestricted *jus soli* – *jus sanguinis* dominates across the region; weak elements of *jus soli*, however, are found in Hong Kong [see Section 5.7], Cambodia, Thailand and Malaysia).

This is of enormous significance when it comes to contemporary (that is, post-1950) migration policies of the countries of East Asia, and the treatment by them of their immigrant minorities. Without, of course, being aware of it, the governments of East Asian countries tend to subscribe to a Michael Walzer 'communitarian' view of the nation-state (see Figure 9.1 in Box 9.1). What this means is that, for a well-ordered society in which members are prepared to forego their own narrow interests for the sake of the wider community, you need a strong sense of 'us' – a sense of everyone belonging to the same group, a group that is usually defined on the basis of ethnicity (racial origin, often backed up by a common religious affiliation, a shared history, and a common cultural, linguistic, and artistic heritage). The problem with a strong sense of 'us' is that it results in an equally strong sense of 'them'.

A communitarian approach to issues of migration and citizenship tends, therefore, to produce the following outcomes: (i) an extreme reluctance to allow people who are not co-ethnics to enter or reside in the country or, above all, to become accepted as members; (ii) conversely, a predilection to allow co-ethnics living outside the territory of the state to enter without too much difficulty; and finally, (iii) a tolerance of the suffering of immigrant minorities which is often distinctly at odds with what are usually the dominant practices of the host society – politeness towards strangers, and empathy for the down-trodden. Communitarian-based policies thus tend to be socially conservative, nationalistic (sometimes even racist), inward-looking, and somewhat authoritarian.

The problem is that whatever their suitability for a Westphalian system of nation-states, these policies and attitudes are increasingly poorly suited to the emerging multicultural world that is East Asia today. As immigrant minorities grow in size and diversity, an alternative model of membership is called for – one that emphasizes mutuality, celebrates difference and, above all, allows the individual to pass from being an 'alien', through 'denizenship' (the status of being allowed to live and work in the country but not to participate in its politics or to have those jobs, such as many public-sector jobs, that are reserved for citizens), to full citizenship. The sad fact is that there is, at the moment, in my judgement, no country in East Asia (and, to be fair, only a few outside it) that even aspires to these goals, let alone attains them.

Box 9.1 Migration policies – a politico-philosophical overview: East Asia in context

Figure 9.1 (the modified version of a diagram in Fielding 2010) is an attempt to represent in a simple schematic way the essential differences between a Western (EU) approach to immigration policy and an East Asian (mostly Japanese and South Korean) approach. The two axes represent fundamental variables: the horizontal one stands for the left–right divergence in views on society and politics – that is, the division between those who support a strong state and socialist government on the left and those who support a weak state and neo-liberal capitalist regulation by the market on the right; the vertical axis stands for the short-term vs long-term divergence in views about policy formulation for the future – that is, the division between those who are concerned with the practical problems of today and of the

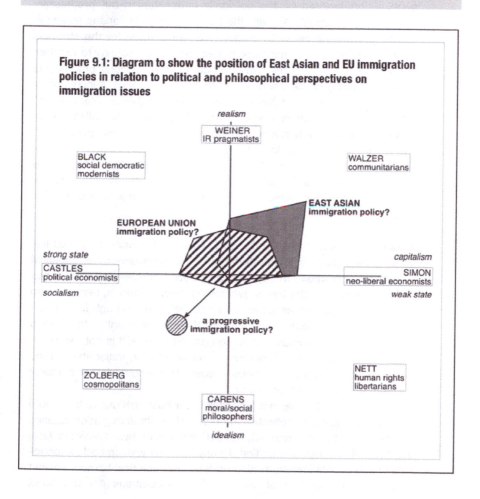

Figure 9.1: Diagram to show the position of East Asian and EU immigration policies in relation to political and philosophical perspectives on immigration issues

immediate future higher up and those who support a broader, more principled and future-oriented perspective lower down.

This allows us to identify eight positions, each with a label and an identifying author. These eight positions can be seen as four pairs of opposites:

1   The left-right (W–E) pair contrasts the pro-regulation political economists with their deeply pessimistic concerns about the suffering of working-class populations (both indigenous and immigrant) under contemporary migration regimes (exemplified by the early Marxist writings of Stephen Castles), with the anti-regulation laissez-faire 'everyone benefits in the end' optimism of neo-liberal economists (exemplified by the writings of Julian Simon).

2   The NW–SE pair contrasts the social democratic modernists (decision makers who do not reject capitalism but want it to work better for ordinary people – represented by the politically unthreatening but progressive writings of Richard Black), with the human rights libertarians (exemplified by the brilliant essay by Roger Nett), who argue for the stripping away of all barriers to the migration of people from one country to another.

3   The N–S pair contrasts the extreme international relations pragmatists who blame many of the world's problems (ethnic conflict, security risks) on the failure of nation-states to control migration (Myron Weiner), with moral/social philosophers who try to puzzle out the moral dilemmas of population mobility within a highly normative, even idealistic perspective (viz. the early writings of Joseph Carens).

4   The NE–SW pair contrasts the communitarian position (exemplified by Michael Walzer – see discussion in main text), with those who embrace ethnic diversity – the cosmopolitans (exemplified by the work of Aristide Zolberg).

The location (indicative only) of the EU in Figure 9.1 reflects the Janus-like character of the institution: it is both the builder of a framework for capitalist accumulation (for example, through its competition policies and its defence of the 'four freedoms' – the free movement of people, goods, services and capital within the EU), and an agent for social cohesion through its support for poverty-alleviation programmes, and for the enhancement of the human and social rights of indigenous and foreign residents alike. It is not, however, renowned for its anticipation of, or long-term planning for, major shifts in the economy and demography of Europe – shifts that would almost certainly imply alterations to immigration policy.

East Asia is different. It has not (yet) built the robust institutions that could represent and act upon its collective interests. Thus, its immigration policies tend to be nationally and narrowly based, often with two overriding (and partially contradictory) concerns: first, to appease the widespread xenophobia of its voting populations by setting up legal and practical barriers against the large-scale immigration of working-class populations (by the 'front door'); and second, to match the needs of employers for unskilled labour by setting up effective 'side door' entry mechanisms through trainee and student recruitment schemes and through rotating 'guest worker' policies, which allow migrant workers to come to these countries in sufficient numbers to unblock serious labour shortage 'bottlenecks'.

If you would allow me a small indulgence (after all, we are nearing the end of the book), neither EU nor East Asian immigration policies get close to where, in the opinion of this author, a progressive immigration policy would be located in Figure 9.1.

References

Black, R., 1996, Immigration and social justice: towards a progressive European immigration policy, *Transactions of the Institute of British Geographers* 21(1): 64–75.

Castles, S., 1998, New migrations in the Asia-Pacific region: a force for social and political change, *International Social Science Journal* 156: 215–227.

Fielding, T., 2010, The occupational and geographical locations of transnational immigrant minorities in Japan, in Kee, P. and Yoshimatsu, H. (eds), *Global Movements in the Asia Pacific*. Singapore: World Scientific, 93–121.

Nett, R., 1971, The civil right we are not ready for: the right to free movement of people on the face of the Earth, *Ethics* 81(3): 212–227.

Simon, J., 1990, *The Economic Consequences of Immigration*. London: Blackwell.

Walzer, M., 1983, *Spheres of Justice*. New York: Basic Books.

Weiner, M., 1995, *The Global Migration Crisis*. New York: Harper.

Zolberg, A., 1992, Labor migration and international economic regimes, in Kritz, M. M., Lim, L.L. and Zlotnik, H. (eds), *International Migration Systems*. Oxford: Oxford University Press, 315–334.

9.6 Migration and political, economic, and environmental instability

It is arguably the case that more progressive behaviours and practices towards immigration and immigrant minorities flourish when the host country is experiencing political stability, economic prosperity and confidence in the future. For many countries in East Asia, however, this is not the reality of their current situation, or recent past. Almost every country has experienced political instability in the post-1950 period, and many face seemingly intractable conflicts today. Inter-ethnic conflicts bedevil several Southeast Asian countries (Indonesia, Thailand, Myanmar, and the Philippines), and parts of China (notably where Han Chinese live in areas with large Tibetan and Uyghur populations). Class-based conflicts continue in Thailand ('reds', who are largely rural and working class, versus 'yellows' who are largely urban and middle class and support the monarchy), and in the Philippines. A crisis of political identity (pitting the 'greens', who are pro-independence from the PRC, versus the 'blues' who are more concessionary towards the PRC) has been a lasting feature of Taiwan's politics.

These political conflicts (i) affect migration policies, and (ii) tend to spill over international borders to produce problems for neighbouring countries. A good example of the former is the suspicion surrounding female migration from the PRC to Taiwan, making it an exception to the rule about the welcome that co-ethnics tend to receive in East Asian countries. A good example of the latter is the way that conflicts in other parts of Southeast Asia tend to result in migration to Thailand (notably, of course, from Myanmar).

Economic instability has also plagued much of East Asia in the recent period, despite the region's overall record of GNP growth and poverty reduction. The economic crises of 1997 and 2008 had very significant migration effects: the former especially in Southeast Asia where the mass deportation of illegal migrants was practised; the latter in China (where internal migration flows were affected), and in Japan and South Korea (where trends in international migration were partially reversed).

Yet perhaps it is confidence in the future that, if eroded, is most damaging to the openness of a society towards its strangers outside and its 'others' within. The 2011 earthquake and tsunami in Japan, for example, heightened by the nuclear disaster at Fukushima, added further fuel to an already existing widespread negativity towards the government (both politicians and bureaucrats), big business, and the wider social system – this in a country experiencing prolonged economic stagnation, 'super-ageing', and now, for the first time in its modern history, population decline. The danger is that this negativity will be harnessed by those political forces (pro-nationalist, anti-human rights) that are least likely to support either integrationist (*tabunka kyousei*) or pro-immigration agendas.

Finally, East Asia faces the likelihood that there will be further outbreaks of infectious or contagious diseases such as those that are sexually transmitted, and influenza epidemics, but also those that produced major, if temporary, population displacements in the recent past – notably SARS (severe acute respiratory syndrome). It will also face the certainty of major 'natural' disasters, such as earthquakes, volcanic eruptions, and typhoons, which will result in mostly temporary, but sometimes permanent, movements of population.

9.7 Illegal migration and trafficking in East Asia

Nothing provides more strength to those authoritarian, nationalist voices (discussed above) than the widespread perception that many foreigners do not have the legal right to live and work in the country. Undocumented migrants do indeed exist in almost all of the countries of East Asia, but popular perceptions as to their number (typically exaggerated) and composition (expected to be desperately poor) do not necessarily bear much relation to reality. It becomes possible, therefore, for men and women who have a legal right to live and work in the country to be assumed by members of the host population to be illegal immigrants, and for perfectly law-abiding people to be suspected, due to their 'strange' behaviour, unusual appearance or different language, of having criminal intentions.

There is only one border in East Asia that is essentially impenetrable – that between South and North Korea. All the others are crossed, sometimes almost unchecked, by commuters, seasonal workers, traders, family members and labour migrants. The border crossings are so frequent, routine and unregulated that it is relatively easy, if it is necessary to do so (border officials can sometimes, of course, be bribed), to hide the presence of trafficked persons – women being trafficked for sexual exploitation, children for prostitution and domestic labour, men for heavy labour on the plantations, fish farms, or construction sites. Trafficking is not confined, of course, to the crossing of international borders; the forced migration of persons for labour and sexual exploitation is also a significant problem in internal migration flows – notably in the PRC, but also in several countries of Southeast Asia.

9.8 Relationships between internal and international migration

Earlier, in Box 5.1, the 'new immigration model' was set out. It explains many of the migration and demographic changes in East Asia through analysing internal and international migrations within a single framework. Is this the only way in which internal migration and international migration connect with one another? By no means. As has been pointed out in several chapters of this book, East Asia is witnessing something that migration theorists have been far too slow to recognize – that processes which were previously largely confined to the spaces within national territories have broken their bounds and are now to be found operating at an international scale or even at a global level. Many examples of these processes (such as migrations for study and training, love and marriage, employment and career development, lifestyle improvement and retirement) have been found to be operating at the scale of the whole East Asian region in the recent period.

9.9 Migration and East Asian development: prospects for the future

What will happen to East Asian migrations over the next 50 years? It is very difficult to answer this question. Given the complexity of the processes involved and the power of modern computing to encompass such complexity, we might be tempted to turn to a multi-regional demographic forecasting model. Such a model would take the existing populations of countries and regions, add new births using current age of mother-specific fertility rates, age populations already born, calculating survivorship using current age-specific mortality rates, and migrate populations from one region/country to another using current age-specific and distance-dependent migration rates. This would produce data – 'hard facts'; except, unfortunately, they would not be hard (in the sense of certain), or facts! They would in truth tell us more about what is happening now (albeit in a novel way) than what will happen in the future.

All right then, perhaps each of these rates could be projected into the future on the basis of past trends. Then the model results would be less tied to present conditions. Yes, but it would take very little for certain trends (such as the decline in fertility) to be reversed by new migrations (such as those that would produce a higher proportion of foreign-born mothers). Such migrations are notoriously difficult to predict.

So do we give up? Is there no point in even considering what future population distributions and migration patterns might look like?

Put bluntly, we collectively cannot afford not to consider future migration patterns. Many of the public-sector and corporate policy decisions taken today (and I am not just thinking here of major public infrastructure investment decisions) will have effects well beyond the middle of the 21st century. They will need to be made on the basis of judgements about where people will be living (cities or countryside, coast or inland, 'north' or 'south'), what kinds of lives they will be leading (materially rich or poor, work dominated or leisure oriented), and what sort of society they will be living in (at peace or at war, capitalist or communist, ecologically sustainable or experiencing environmental crisis).

To whom does one turn to provide guidance for the making of these judgements? Why, one turns to geographers, demographers, and other social scientists, of course. No pressure then!

Let us proceed from the least uncertain to the most uncertain. In the absence of major wars or pandemic diseases, according to UN Economic and Social Commission for Asia and the Pacific (ESCAP) 2012 projections, the population of East Asia in 2030 is expected to be 2.31 billion. By then, its growth rate will be very low so that the figure for 2060 will be not much greater. It will, however, be an older population than the one we see today. Indeed, population ageing is regarded as one of the few near-certainties about the future.

Will this affect migration flows? Other things being equal, elderly people and older adults would be expected to migrate less, thus reducing the size of migration flows. The very elderly, however, also need care services, which might give rise to migration from countries with youthful populations to those with aged ones. The small beginnings of this are observable in the agreement between Japan on the one hand and the Philippines and Indonesia on the other, which brings young female nurses and care workers from Southeast Asia to work in Japan. Improved governance in these sending countries might also see them become destinations for a far larger number of retirement migrants from Japan and South Korea (to be joined later by China?) than occurs at present.

Another near certainty is climate change. East Asia will have about half of the world's largest cities, and many of these are now, and will continue to be, located on coastal plains or on the floodplains of major rivers. These will be liable to flooding from higher sea levels and from more extreme weather conditions, sometimes from a combination of the two. The effects of this will be largely felt on internal migration flows, when parts of cities may have to be evacuated or even abandoned. Particular concern on this matter has been expressed for Ho Chi Minh City and parts of the Mekong Basin in Vietnam and Cambodia, Bangkok and the lower reaches of the Chao Phraya in Thailand, and Shanghai and the Lower Yangtze/Taihu Basin in the PRC.

Much less certain are what the levels of GNP per capita will be in 2060. It seems likely, on the basis of the current economic dynamism of the region, that they will be significantly higher than they are at present, and that therefore, assuming some redistribution, poverty levels will be lower. Does this mean that all the countries and regions of East Asia will be past the 'migration hump' – that is, past the point of peak migration when the mass of the population has sufficient wealth to fund a migration flow, but not yet enough to be satisfied with their lives at their current place of residence? The answer is probably yes, in which case we might expect: (i) smaller flows overall; and (ii) a significant shift in the social class composition of both internal and international migration flows – a decline in the proportion of 'blue-collar' working-class migrants and an increase in professional and managerial middle-class migrants.

Very closely related to living standards is the issue of what the dominant form of economic organization will be in 2060. Will it be further neo-liberal capitalist globalization? The answer for all sorts of reasons, but many of them connected to the declining influence of the USA, is probably not. So, what might it be? It could well be an outgrowth of the emerging compromise between state and capital, whereby market economies are permitted, even encouraged, and yet are strictly contained and constrained within fairly authoritarian bureaucratic state systems (as pertains today in the PRC and Vietnam, but arguably also in Japan, South Korea, Thailand and Malaysia). What this means for migration is: (i) a continuing policy concern and intervention in the distribution of population and economic activity within countries – we should not expect East Asian governments to totally abandon these to market forces; and (ii) a check on the development of ethnic diversity – such diversity might be expected to increase but not to reach the 'superdiversity' of the kind found in London, New York, or Los Angeles. East Asian countries seem likely to remain among the least multi-ethnic societies in the world (despite their often striking internal cultural complexity).

Finally, least certain of all is the political make-up of East Asia in 2060. Will China be a single country? Will the Korean peninsula be politically united? Will the steps taken towards economic cooperation in Southeast Asia lead also to forms of political association? Indeed, more generally, will the world of 2060 still be composed of 'Westphalian' nation-states? For all the economic and social progress of the last 30 years, East Asia might yet become an arena for major clashes between nations (Japan and China), economic ideologies (communism and capitalism), and cultural identities (Buddhist, Christian, Muslim, and secular). Attempting to predict the migration outcomes, which could be massive, of such inherently unpredictable conflicts is not practical or sensible.

So much for the effects of demography, environment, and political economy on migration, but what about the reverse causality – the effects of migration on

East Asia's peoples and places? Living together in places that are being rapidly transformed by migration, people from different backgrounds are making new lives, forming new friendships, and forging new identities. So there is one thing about which we can be certain: migration is shaping, and will continue to shape, in quite fundamental ways, the paths down which East Asian peoples, along with the countries and regions, cities and countrysides that they inhabit, are travelling.

Selected references

9.0 General

Ahsan Ulla, A.K.M., 2010, *Rationalizing Migration Decisions: Labour Migrants in East and South-East Asia*. Farnham: Ashgate.

Asis, M.M.B., 2005, Migration trends in international migration in Asia and the Pacific, *Asia-Pacific Population Journal* 20(3): 15–38.

Chan, Y.-W., Haines, D. and Lee, J. (eds), 2014, *The Age of Asian Migration*, 2 vols. Newcastle upon Tyne: Cambridge Scholars Publishing.

Haines, D.W., Yamanaka, K. and Yamashita, S. (eds), 2012, *Wind over Water: Migration in an East Asian Context*. Oxford: Berghahn Books.

Huguet, J.W., 2003, Can migration avert population decline and ageing in East and Southeast Asia? *Journal of Population Research* 20(1): 107–124.

International Organization for Migration et al., 2008, *Situation Report on International Migration in East and South-East Asia*. Bangkok: IOM.

Lai, A.E., Collins, F.L. and Yeoh, B.S.A. (eds), 2013, *Migration and Diversity in Asian Contexts*. Singapore: Institute of South East Asian Studies.

Leong, C.-H.L. and Berry, J. (eds), 2009, *Intercultural Relations in Asia: Migration and Work Effectiveness*. Singapore: World Scientific.

Martin, P., 2009, *Migration in the Asia-Pacific Region: Trends, Factors, Impacts*. UNDP: Human Development Research Paper 2009/32.

Ong, J.H., Chan, K.B. and Chew, S.B. (eds), 1995, *Crossing Borders: Transmigration in the Asia-Pacific*. Upper Saddle River, NJ: Prentice-Hall.

Skeldon, R., 2013, Migration and Asia: reflections on continuities and change, *Asia-Pacific Population Journal* 27(1): 103–118.

Wong, T.-C. and Rigg, J. (eds), 2010, *Asian Cities, Migrant Labor and Contested Spaces*. London: Routledge.

Xiang, B., Yeoh, B.S.A. and Toyota, M. (eds), 2013, *Return: Nationalizing Transnational Mobility in Asia*. Durham, NC: Duke University Press.

Yoshihara, N. (ed.), 2012, *Global Migration and Ethnic Communities: Asia and Latin America*. Balwyn North: Trans Pacific Press.

9.1 Trade, investment and migration in East Asia: the effects of the global economic crisis

Aoki, M. and Hayami, Y. (eds), 2009, Reshaping Economic Geography in East Asia, in *Reshaping Economic Geography*. Washington, DC: World Bank Report.

Castles, S., 2009, Development and migration or migration and development: what comes first? *Asian and Pacific Migration Journal* 18(4): 441–471.

Hugo, G. and Stahl, C., 2004, Labor export strategies in Asia, in Massey, D.S. and Taylor, J.E. (eds), *International Migration: Prospects and Policies in a Global Market*. London: Oxford University Press, 174–200.

Ito, S. and Iguchi, Y., 1994, Japanese direct investment and its impact on migration in the ASEAN 4, *Asian and Pacific Migration Journal* 3(2–3): 265–294.

Kim, W.B., 1996, Economic interdependence and migration dynamics in Asia, *Asian and Pacific Migration Journal* 5(2–3): 303–317.

Lloyd, P.J. and Williams, S. (eds), 1996, *International Trade and Migration in the APEC Region*. Melbourne: Oxford University Press.

Martin, P., 2002, The role played by labor migration in the Asian economic miracle, in Mason, A. (ed.), *Population Change and Economic Development in East Asia: Challenges Met, Opportunities Seized*. London: Stanford University Press, 332–358.

Tsai, P.-L. and Tsay, C.-L., 2004, Foreign direct investment and international labour migration in economic development: Indonesia, Malaysia, Philippines and Thailand, in Ananta, A. and Arifin, E.N. (eds), *International Migration in Southeast Asia*. Singapore: Institute of South East Asian Studies, 94–136.

Wong, T.-C., 2011, International and intra-national migrations: human mobility in Pacific Asian cities in the globalization age, in Wong, T.-C. and Rigg, J. (eds), *Asian Cities, Migrant Labour and Contested Spaces*. London: Routledge, 27–44.

World Bank/International Organization for Migration, 2004, *Trade and Migration: Building Bridges for Global Labour Mobility*. Paris: Organisation for Economic Co-operation and Development.

9.2 Migration and labour market integration in East Asia

Arnold, F. and Shah, N.M. (eds), 1986, *Asian Labor Migration: Pipeline to the Middle East*. Boulder, CO: Westview.

Asian Development Bank Institute, 2014, *Labor Migration, Skills and Student Mobility in Asia*. Tokyo: ADBI.

Athukorala, P., Manning, C. and Wickaramasekara, P., 2000, *Growth, Employment and Migration in Southeast Asia: Structural Change in the Greater Mekong Countries*. Cheltenham: Edward Elgar.

D'Costa, A.P., 2010, *International Mobility and the Transformation of Global Capitalism*. London: Routledge.

Debrah, Y.A. (ed.), 2002, *Migrant Workers in Pacific Asia*. London: Frank Cass.

Hewison, K. and Young, K. (eds), 2006, *Transnational Migration and Work in Asia*. London: Routledge.

Hugo, G. and Young, S. (eds), 2008, *Labour Mobility in the Asia-Pacific Region: Dynamics, Issues and a New APEC Agenda*. Singapore: Institute of South East Asian Studies.

Kaur, A. and Metcalfe, I. (eds), 2006, *Mobility, Labour Migration and Border Controls in Asia*. Basingstoke: Palgrave.

Kim, W.B., 1995, Regional interdependence and migration in Asia, *Asian and Pacific Migration Journal* 4(2–3): 347–366.

Organisation for Economic Co-operation and Development, 2001, *Migration and the Labour Market in Asia: Recent Trends and Policies*. Paris: OECD.

Piper, N., 2005, Transnational politics and organization of migrant labour in South-East Asia: NGO and trade union perspectives, *Asia-Pacific Population Journal* 20(3): 87–110.

Skeldon, R., 2006, Recent trends in migration in East and Southeast Asia, *Asian and Pacific Migration Journal* 15(2): 277–294.

Stahl, C., 2001, The impacts of structural change on APEC labour markets and their implication for international migration, *Asian and Pacific Migration Journal* 10(3–4): 349–378.

9.3 East Asia's 'new migrations': the highly skilled moving to and from North America and Australasia

Boeri, T. et al. (eds), 2012, *Brain Drain and Brain Gain: The Global Competition to Attract High-skilled Migrants*. London: Oxford University Press.

Butcher, A., 2004, Departures and arrivals: international students returning to the countries of origin, *Asian and Pacific Migration Journal* 13(3): 275–303.

Chalamwong, Y., 2005, The migration of highly-skilled Asia workers to OECD member countries and its effects on economic development in East Asia, in Fukasaku, K. et al. (eds), *Policy Coherence Towards East Asia*. Paris: Organisation for Economic Co-operation and Development.

Charney, M.W., Yeoh, B.S.A. and Kiong, T.C., 2003, *Asian Migrants and Education*. Dordrecht: Kluwer.

Colic-Peisker, V., 2011, A new era in Australian multiculturalism? From working-class 'ethnics' to a 'multicultural middle-class', *International Migration Review* 45(3): 562–587.

Ho, E. and Bedford, R., 2008, Asian transnational families in New Zealand: dynamics and changes, *International Migration* 46(4): 41–62.

Hugo, G., 2008, In and out of Australia: rethinking Chinese and Indian skilled migration to Australia, *Asian Population Studies* 4(3): 267–291.

Iredale, R., 2000, Migration policies for the highly skilled in the Asia-Pacific region, *International Migration Review* 34(3): 882–906.

Iredale, R., Guo, F. and Rozario, S. (eds), 2003, *Return Migration in the Asia Pacific*. Cheltenham: Edward Elgar.

Khoo, S.-E., Hugo, G. and McDonald, P., 2008, Which skilled temporary migrants become permanent residents and why? *International Migration Review* 42(1): 193–226.

Ley, D., 2010, *Millionaire Migrants: Trans-Pacific Life Lines*. New York: John Wiley.

Li, W. (ed.), 2006, *From Urban Enclave to Ethnic Suburb: New Asian Communities in Pacific Rim Countries*. Honolulu: University of Hawai'i Press.

Neubauer, D.E. and Kuroda, K. (eds), 2012, *Mobility and Migration in Asian Pacific Higher Education*. Basingstoke: Macmillan.

Park, H., 2010, The stranger that is welcomed: female foreign students from Asia, the English language industry, and the ambivalence of 'Asia rising' in British Columbia, Canada, *Gender, Place and Culture* 17(3): 337–355.

Robertson, S., 2011, Cash cows, backdoor migrants, or activist citizens? International students, citizenship, and rights in Australia, *Ethnic and Racial Studies* 34(12): 2192–2211.

Spaan, E., Hillmann, F. and Van Naerssen, T. (eds), 2005, *Asian Migrants and European Labour Markets*. London: Routledge.

Yeoh, B.S.A. and Huang, S. (eds), 2013, *The Cultural Politics of Talent Migration in East Asia*. London: Routledge.

9.4 Gender and family: demography and the environment

Battistella, G. and Paganoni, A. (eds), 1996, *Asian Women in Migration*. Quezon City: Scalabrini Migration Center.

Constable, N., 2010, *Migrant Workers in Asia: Distant Divides, Intimate Connections*. London: Routledge.

Devasahayam, T.W. and Yeoh, B.S.A. (eds), 2007, *Working and Mothering in Asia: Images, Ideologies and Identities*. Singapore: National University of Singapore Press/ University of Hawai'i Press.

Douglass, M., 2006, Global householding in Pacific Asia, *International Development Planning Review* 28(4): 421–446.

Esim, S. and Smith, M., 2004, *Gender and Migration in Arab States: The Case of Domestic Workers*. Geneva: International Labour Organization.

Fawcett, J.T., Khoo, S.-E. and Smith, P.C. (eds), 1984, *Women in the Cities of Asia: Migration and Urban Adaptation*. Boulder, CO: Westview Press.

Ford, M. and Lyons, L. (eds), 2010, *Masculinities in Southeast Asia*. London: Routledge.

Haseen, F. and Sureeporn, P., 2010, Impact of ageing on migration in Asia, in Hofmeister, W. (ed.), *Ageing and Politics: Consequences for Asia and Europe*. Singapore: Konrad-Adenauer-Stiftung, 15–35.

Huang, S. et al., 2005, *Asian Women as Transnational Domestic Workers*. Singapore: Marshall Cavendish.

Hugo, G., 1996, Environmental concerns and international migration, *International Migration Review* 30(1): 105–131.

Hugo, G., 1998, The demographic underpinnings of current and future international migration in Asia, *Asian and Pacific Migration Journal* 7(1): 1–26.

Hugo, G., 2006, Women, work and international migration in southeast Asia, in Kaur, A. and Metcalfe, I. (eds), *Mobility, Labour Migration and Border Controls in Asia*. Basingstoke: Palgrave, 73–114.

Human Rights Watch, 2008, *'As If I Am Not Human': Abuses Against Asian Domestic Workers in Saudi Arabia*. New York: HRW.

International Organization for Migration, 2009, *Gender and Labour Migration in Asia*. Geneva: IOM.

Jones, G. and Shen, H.-H., 2008, International marriage in East and Southeast Asia: trends and research emphases, *Citizenship Studies* 12(1): 9–25.

Kaur, A. (ed.), 2006, *Women Workers in Industrializing Asia: Costed, Not Valued*. Basingstoke: Palgrave.

Kim, Y., 2011, *Transnational Migration, Media and Identity of Asian Women*. London: Routledge.

Knodel, J., 1999, The demography of Asian ageing: past accomplishments and future challenges, *Asia-Pacific Population Journal* 14(4): 39–56.

Lee, S.-H. and Mason, A., 2010, International migration, population age structure, and economic growth in Asia, *Asian and Pacific Migration Journal* 20(2): 195–213.

Lim, L.L. and Oishi, N., 1996, International labour migration of Asian women: distinctive characteristics and policy concerns, *Asian and Pacific Migration Journal* 5(1): 85–116.

Mason, A., 2002, *Population Change and Economic Development in East Asia: Challenges Met, Opportunities Seized*. London: Stanford University Press.

Ochiai, E. and Aoyama, K. (eds), 2013, *Asian Women and Intimate Work*. Leiden: Brill.

Oishi, N., 2005, *Women in Motion: Globalization, State Policies, and Labour Migration in Asia*. Stanford, CA: Stanford University Press.

Parrenas, R.S. and Siu, L.C.D. (eds), 2007, *Asian Diasporas: New Formations, New Conceptions*. Stanford, CA: Stanford University Press.

Piper, N. and Roces, M. (eds), 2003, *Wife or Worker? Asian Women and Migration*. Lanham, MD: Rowman & Littlefield.

Rahman, M.M. and Lian, K.F., 2009, Gender and the remittance process: Indonesian domestic workers in Hong Kong, Singapore and Malaysia, *Asian Population Studies* 5 (2): 103–125.

Werbner, P. and Johnson, M., 2011, *Diasporic Journeys, Ritual, and Normativity among Asian Migrant Women*. London: Routledge.

Yang, W.-S. and Lu, M. (eds), 2008, *Asian Cross-Border Marriage Migration: Demographic Patterns and Social Issues*. Amsterdam: Amsterdam University Press.

Yeoh, B.S.A., 2009, Making sense of 'Asian' families in the age of migration, *Asian Population Studies* 5(1): 1–3.

Yeoh, B., Graham, E. and Boyle, P., 2002, Migrations and family relations in the Asia Pacific region, *Asian and Pacific Migration Journal* 11(1): 1–12.

9.5 Migration policies, ethnicity and citizenship

Aguilar, F.V., 1999, The triumph of instrumental citizenship? Migrations, identities, and the nation-state in Southeast Asia, *Asian Studies Review* 23(3): 307–336.

Asis, M.M.B. and Batistella, G., 2013, Multicultural realities and membership: states, migrations and citizenship in Asia, in Lai, A.E., Collins, F.L. and Yeoh, B.S.A. (eds), *Migration and Diversity in Asian Contexts*. Singapore: Institute of South East Asian Studies, 31–55.

Carens, J., 1996, Realistic and idealistic approaches to the ethics of migration, *International Migration Review* 30(1): 156–170.

Castles, S. and Kosack, G., 1975, *Immigrant Workers and Class Structure in Western Europe*. Oxford: Oxford University Press.

Christiansen, F. and Hedetoft, U. (eds), 2004, *The Politics of Multiple Belonging: Ethnicity and Nationalism in Europe and East Asia*. Aldershot: Ashgate.

Davidson, A. and Weekley, K. (eds), 1999, *Globalization and Citizenship in the Asia Pacific*. London: Macmillan.

Ford, M., 2006, Migrant labour NGOs and trade unions: a partnership in progress?, *Asian and Pacific Migration Journal* 15(3): 299–312.

He, B. and Kymlicka, W., 2005, Introduction, in Kymlicka, W. and He, B. (eds), *Multiculturalism in Asia*. London: Oxford University Press, 1–21.

Hugo, G., 2009, Best practice in temporary labour migration for development: a perspective from Asia and the Pacific, *International Migration* 47(5): 23–74.

Iredale, R., Hawksley, C. and Castles, S. (eds), 2003, *Migration in the Asia Pacific: Population, Settlement and Citizenship Issues*. Cheltenham: Edward Elgar.

Kalir, B. and Sur, M. (eds), 2012, *Transnational Flows and Permissive Polities: Ethnographies of Human Mobilities in Asia*. Amsterdam: Amsterdam University Press.

Lee, Y.-J., 2011, Overview of trends and policies on international migration to East Asia: comparing Japan, Taiwan and South Korea, *Asian and Pacific Migration Journal* 20 (2): 117–131.

Lorente, B.P. et al. (eds), 2005, *Asian Migrations: Sojourning, Displacement, Homecoming and Other Travels*. Honolulu: University of Hawai'i Press.

Piper, N., 2004, Rights of foreign workers and the politics of migration in South-East and East Asia, *International Migration* 42(5): 71–95.

Seol, D.-H. and Skrentny, J.D., 2009, Why is there so little migrant settlement in East Asia? *International Migration Review* 43(3): 578–620.

Tsuda, T., 2009, *Diasporic Homecomings: Ethnic Return Migration in Comparative Perspective*. Stanford, CA: Stanford University Press.

Ullah, A. and Rahman, M., 2012, *Asian Migration Policy*. Hauppauge: Nova Science.

Yeoh, B. and Willis, B. (eds), 2004, *State/Nation/Transnation: Perspectives on Transnationalism in the Asia-Pacific*. London: Routledge.

9.6 Migration and political, economic, and environmental instability

Abella, M. and Ducanes, G., 2009, *The Effect of the Global Economic Crisis on Asian Migrant Workers and Governments' Responses*. Bangkok: International Labour Office Regional Office.

Asian Development Bank, 2009, *Climate Change and Migration in the Asia and the Pacific*. Bangkok: ADB.

Battistella, G. and Asis, M.M.B., 1999, *The Crisis and Migration in Asia*. Manila: Scalabrini Migration Center.

Hedman, E.-L.E., 2006, Forced migration in Southeast Asia: international politics and the reordering of state power, *Asian and Pacific Migration Journal* 15(1): 29–52.

Herdt, G. (ed.), 1997, *Sexual Cultures and Migration in the Era of AIDS: Anthropological and Demographic Perspectives*. London: Oxford University Press.

Jatrana, S., Toyota, M. and Yeoh, B.S.A. (eds), 2005, *Migration and Health in Asia*. London: Routledge.

Jayasariya, S. and McCawley, P., 2010, *The Asian Tsunami: Aid and Reconstruction after a Disaster*. Cheltenham: Edward Elgar.

Kiernan, B., 2003, The demography of genocide in Southeast Asia: the death tolls in Cambodia 1975–1979, and East Timor 1975–1980, *Critical Asian Studies* 35(4): 585–597.

Manning, C., 2002, Structural change, economic crisis and international labour migration in East Asia, *World Economy* 25(3): 359–385.

Naik, A., Stigter, E. and Laczko, F., 2007, *Migration, Development and Natural Disasters: Insights from the Indian Ocean Tsunami*. Geneva: International Organization for Migration.

Skeldon, R., 1999, Migration in Asia after the economic crisis: patterns and issues, *Asia-Pacific Population Journal* 14(3): 3–24.

Tyner, J., 2009, *War, Violence, and Population*. New York: Guilford Press.

Vachani, S. and Usmani, J. (eds), 2014, *Adaptation to Climate Change in Asia*. Cheltenham: Edward Elgar.

9.7 Illegal migration and trafficking in East Asia

Asis, M.M.B., 2004, Borders, globalization and irregular migration in Southeast Asia, in Ananta, A. and Arifin, E.N. (eds), *International Migration in Southeast Asia*. Singapore: Institute of South East Asian Studies, 199–227.

Asis, M.M.B., 2008, Human trafficking in East and Southeast Asia, in Cameron, S. and Newman, E. (eds), *Trafficking in Humans*. Tokyo: UN Press, 181–205.

Battistella, G. and Asis, M.M.B. (eds), 2003, *Unauthorized Migration in Southeast Asia*. Quezon City: Scalabrini Migration Center.

Brown, L., 2000, *Sex Slaves: The Trafficking of Women in Asia*. London: Virago.

Constable, N., 2012, International marriage brokers, cross-border marriages and the US anti-trafficking campaign, *Journal of Ethnic and Migration Studies* 38(7): 1137–1154.

Curley, M.G. and Wong, S.-L. (eds), 2007, *Migration and Securitisation in Southeast Asia*. London: Routledge.

Ford, M., Lyons, L. and Van Schendel, W. (eds), 2012, *Labour Migration and Human Trafficking in Southeast Asia: Critical Perspectives*. London: Routledge.

Lee, J.J.H., 2005, Human trafficking in East Asia: current trends, data collection, and knowledge gaps, *International Migration* 43(1/2): 165–201.

Lindquist, J., Xiang, B. and Yeoh, B.S.A., 2012, Opening the black box of migration: the organization of transnational mobility and the changing political economy of Asia, *Pacific Affairs* 85(1): 7–19.

Rajaram, P.K. and Grundy-Warr, C., 2004, The irregular migrant as homo sacer: migration and detention in Australia, Malaysia and Thailand, *International Migration* 42(1): 33–63.

Samarasinghe, V., 2007, *Female Sex Trafficking in Asia*. London: Routledge.

Skeldon, R., 2000, Trafficking: a perspective from Asia, *International Migration* 38(3): 7–30.

Surak, K., 2013, The migration industry and developmental states in East Asia, in Gammeltoft-Hansen, T. and Sorensen, N. (eds), *The Migration Industry and the Commercialization of International Migration*. London: Routledge.

Vlieger, A., 2012, Domestic workers in Saudi Arabia and the Emirates: trafficking victims? *International Migration* 50(6): 180–194.

9.8 Relationships between internal and international migration

Skeldon, R., 2006, Interlinkages between internal and international migration and development in the Asian region, *Population, Space and Place* 12: 15–30.

9.9 Migration and East Asian development: prospects for the future

Attane, I. and Barbieri, M., 2009, Demography of the world's regions: situation and trends: East and Southeast Asia, *Population-E* 64(1): 7–146.

Hugo, G., 2004, International migration in the Asia-Pacific region: emerging trends and issues, in Massey, D.S. and Taylor, J.E. (eds), *International Migration: Prospects and Policies in a Global Market*. London: Oxford University Press, 77–103.

Index

eBooks
from Taylor & Francis

Helping you to choose the right eBooks for your Library

Add to your library's digital collection today with Taylor & Francis eBooks. We have over 50,000 eBooks in the Humanities, Social Sciences, Behavioural Sciences, Built Environment and Law, from leading imprints, including Routledge, Focal Press and Psychology Press.

Free Trials Available

We offer free trials to qualifying academic, corporate and government customers.

Choose from a range of subject packages or create your own!

Benefits for you
- Free MARC records
- COUNTER-compliant usage statistics
- Flexible purchase and pricing options
- 70% approx of our eBooks are now DRM-free.

Benefits for your user
- Off-site, anytime access via Athens or referring URL
- Print or copy pages or chapters
- Full content search
- Bookmark, highlight and annotate text
- Access to thousands of pages of quality research at the click of a button.

eCollections
Choose from 20 different subject eCollections, including:

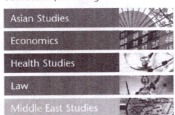

- Asian Studies
- Economics
- Health Studies
- Law
- Middle East Studies

eFocus
We have 16 cutting-edge interdisciplinary collections, including:

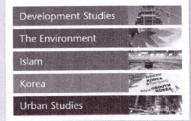

- Development Studies
- The Environment
- Islam
- Korea
- Urban Studies

For more information, pricing enquiries or to order a free trial, please contact your local sales team:

UK/Rest of World: **online.sales@tandf.co.uk**
USA/Canada/Latin America: **e-reference@taylorandfrancis.com**
East/Southeast Asia: **martin.jack@tandf.com.sg**
India: **journalsales@tandfindia.com**

www.tandfebooks.com